HOW TO PUBLISH

YOUR NOVEL

KEN ATCHITY

WITH ANDREA McKEOWN, JULIE MOONEY, AND MARGARET O'CONNOR

SQUAREONE
WRITERS GUIDES

Cover Designer: Phaedra Mastrocola
In-House Editor: Joanne Abrams
Typesetter: Gary A. Rosenberg

Square One Publishers
115 Herricks Road
Garden City Park, NY 11040
(516) 535-2010 • (877) 900-BOOK
www.squareonepublishers.com

Library of Congress Cataloging-in-Publication Data

Atchity, Kenneth John.
    How to publish your novel : a complete guide to making the right
publisher say yes / Ken Atchity, with Julie Mooney, Andrea McKeown,
and Margaret O'Connor.
        p. cm. — (SquareOne writers guides)
    Includes index.
    ISBN 0-7570-0049-5 (pbk.)
    1. Fiction—Marketing. I. Mooney, Julie. II. McKeown, Andrea. III. O'Connor,
Margaret. IV. Title. V. Series.
PN3365.A83 2005
070.5'2—dc22

                                                                    2005018499

Printed in the United States of America

10   9   8   7   6   5   4   3   2   1

CONTENTS

A Note on Gender, iv
Acknowledgments, v

Part One: The Basics

1. An Introduction, 3

2. Where Does Your Novel Fit In?, 7

3. The Business of Publishing Novels, 45

Part Two: Getting a Novel Published

4. Finding the Right Representative, 63

5. Finding the Right Publisher, 77

6. Preparing the Package, 107

7. Using the Square One System, 139

8. The Deal, 157

9. When It Doesn't Happen, 183

Part Three: Building a Writing Career

10. From Signing to Publication, 213

11. Perfecting Your Craft, 225

12. Promoting Your Novel, 251

Conclusion, 277

Glossary, 279
Resource List, 293
About the Authors, 303
Index, 305

A NOTE ON GENDER

To avoid long and awkward phrasing within sentences, the publisher has chosen to alternate the use of male and female pronouns according to chapter. Therefore, when referring to the third-person writer, editor, or reader, odd-numbered chapters use male pronouns, while even-numbered chapters employ female pronouns, to give acknowledgment to writers, editors, and readers of both genders.

$\mathcal{A}$CKNOWLEDGMENTS

It's truly impossible, in the whirlwind of my last decade of story merchandising, to thank everyone by name whose wisdom and knowledge have contributed to what you read in these pages.

In the Resource List, we attempt to give acknowledgement and credit to the many how-to books we've raided to verify the information you'll find here. In the preparation of the manuscript, I'm especially grateful for the nuts-and-bolts *sang-froid* of Atchity Entertainment International's (AEI's) executive VP Brenna Lui; as well as for the story wisdom of my partner Chi-Li Wong, President of AEI—who one of our novelists refers to in *his* acknowledgements as "Dragon Bitch Reader from Hell . . . the most precise, diligent, merciless, insightful reader/editor/developer who ever reduced me to a quivery mass."

The numerous clients, editors, novelists, agents, and attorneys who are my extended creative family—and who enrich every moment of my life—are credited within their sidebars offered throughout the book.

When I consider how many people it takes to make a publishing village, I realize, once again, the power of stories and the importance of storytelling.

Given the crush of everyday events in the mad, mad, mad world of entertainment and publishing, this book would never have seen the bookstore shelf without the dedication, precision, and hard work of my coauthors Julie Mooney, Andrea McKeown, and Margaret O'Connor. Thank you for your research and writing assistance. But all of our work on condensing the vast scope of publishing a novel in today's complicated world into a handbook for writers would still have been inadequate without the intervention and hands-on contributions of our Square One editor Joanne Abrams and publisher Rudy Shur.

And to my wife, Kayoko Mitsumatsu, whose support is my private eternal flame, I promise: I'll never write another book—at least not for a few months.

Ken Atchity
Los Angeles and New York

$\mathcal{T}$HE BASICS

Every writer—whether he dreams of getting a single novel into print or of launching a full-time writing career—has to know certain basics or he'll waste his time channeling his efforts in the wrong direction. First, he has to understand the various categories of novels, and what they mean to both an editor and the marketplace. Then, he has to attain a grasp of the publishing world and how it works. That's what Part One is all about. After the introduction provided in Chapter 1, Chapter 2 will break down the different categories—from mainstream and literary novels to mysteries and Westerns—and help you determine the group into which your novel falls. It will also look at the marketplaces through which different categories are made available to their readers. Then Chapter 3 will familiarize you with the publishing industry and describe the different types of publishing houses to which a novel may be submitted.

In the following pages, you will:

■ Learn about the different categories of novels, with an eye to pinpointing the one in which your book belongs.

■ Discover the elements that are important in each novel genre.

■ Learn the types of publishing houses that produce each category of novels.

■ Examine the importance of meeting your reader's expectations.

■ Gain an understanding of the standard marketplaces that serve the novel-reading public.

■ Examine the different types of commercial publishing houses, including the primary strengths and weaknesses of each one.

■ Learn about those noncommercial houses that can serve as a stepping-stone to commercial publication.

Whatever your dreams, whatever your goals—and whether you've written a sophisticated literary work, a formula romance, or a high fantasy novel—Part One will help you lay the necessary groundwork for success in the publishing world.

CHAPTER 1

An Introduction

How to Publish Your Novel provides the comprehensive, practical information critical to fiction writers who want to break into the world of publication. The information and advice presented in this book are the result of years of experience—writing, editing, teaching, publishing, and managing—as well as extensive research into current industry trends.

There is no denying that publishing a first novel is probably the most difficult challenge a writer can face—especially in a world where every third adult seems to believe he or she is a novelist. If you find this reality discouraging, consider the words of coach Jimmy Dugan in the movie *A League of Their Own*. When a team member complains that baseball is just too hard, Jimmy replies that it's the "hard" that makes it so good, because if it wasn't difficult, everyone would be able to play. Seeing your words take shape beneath your pen, or on your computer screen, is an exciting process. But when you see those same words between the covers of a book, that thrill will be compounded. And part of that thrill will come from knowing that you have succeeded where so many others have failed.

My aim is to coach you through the difficulties to *your* goal of success. You've already moved closer to being published because you've armed yourself with invaluable information by picking up this book, which presents a proven system of submissions that will (1) allow you to avoid the common mistakes that turn editors off, (2) allow you to find those houses best suited to your novel, (3) save you valuable time and money, and (4) increase your odds of having your novel accepted. Let's look at each of these points in turn.

AVOIDING MISTAKES THAT TURN EDITORS OFF

It's vital to remember that editors are busy people who can devote very little time to each proposal they receive. That's why it's so important to create an effective but concise submission package that avoids taxing the editor's patience.

Editors are busy people whose desks are generally piled with manuscript submissions, and whose days are filled with competing tasks. If they see something in your manuscript or query letter that triggers doubt or tries their patience, they'll instantly reject your novel. I'll show you how to rid your submission package of the words, phrases, and other submission *faux pas* that can cause an editor to slam the door on your book.

FINDING HOUSES SUITED TO YOUR NOVEL

Most writers in search of a publisher focus so much energy on finding a publishing house—*any* publishing house—willing to produce their book, that they pay little attention to choosing a company that will truly serve their needs. I'll show you how to determine and locate the type of company that is right for both you and your novel.

SAVING TIME AND MONEY

It takes time to print, check, and assemble a submission package, and it costs serious money to mail a bulky stack of pages. You owe it to yourself to make your time and money count. I'll show you how to streamline the process of assembling your package, and I'll offer ways to save money on postage.

INCREASING YOUR ODDS OF ACCEPTANCE

Just as there are many ways to kill an editor's interest in your novel, there are numerous ways to turn an editor on to your project. I'll explain proven techniques for capturing an editor's attention.

WHAT'S IN THIS BOOK

How to Publish Your Novel is divided into three parts, each of which addresses the needs of writers at various stages of their publishing career, as well as the needs of people who are *not* working toward a writing career, but would simply like to get their story into print.

Part One first provides a basic introduction to the business of writing novels. Following this introductory chapter, Chapter 2 discusses the different novel categories, explains what they mean to an editor and the marketplace, and helps you determine the category into which your book falls. Then Chapter 3 walks you through the business aspects of novel publishing and explains the differences between large, mid-sized, and smaller publishing houses, including the benefits each size house has to offer. By the end of Part One, you should have a clearer idea of where you want to go and how you can best get there.

When you have a full understanding of what your novel is and what audience it addresses, you'll want to turn to Part Two, which is a detailed guide to getting your book into publication. First, Chapter 4 introduces you to the world of agents, managers, and attorneys—the middlemen who can be invaluable in getting your novel through the door of a publishing house. One thing you'll learn, though, is that first-time novelists often find it difficult to secure representation. If this is your experience, or if you simply prefer to approach publishers directly, you'll want to read Chapter 5, which helps you use the many available resources to home in on those publishers that are the best match for your novel.

Once you've put together a list of potential publishers or agents, Chapter 6 walks you through the creation of an effective submission package, including a strong cover letter, an intriguing synopsis, and flawless sample chapters. Chapter 7 then guides you in using the Square One System, a step-by-step strategy for sending your letter-perfect package out in a way that will maximize your chance of success while minimizing your effort, time, and costs.

Every novelist dreams of the day when the mailbox yields a letter of acceptance. With this in mind, Chapter 8 prepares you for striking a deal with a publisher once an offer has been made. What if no publisher expresses an interest in your creation? Then you'll want to turn to Chapter 9, which provides constructive advice about other avenues that may be open to your work, including self-publishing, e-publishing, and selling your novel to Hollywood.

Part Three provides invaluable guidance that you'll want to examine once your book has been accepted by a publisher. Chapter

10 shows you the physical stages your book will go through between signing and publication. What will happen to your book during the editorial process? Will you have the opportunity to review galleys before the book is printed? Chapter 10 details this and much more, including your own responsibilities during this important phase of your book's production.

Although some writers produce only one book in a lifetime, others want to pursue a career in novel writing. If you fall into the second category, Chapter 11 presents insights into perfecting your craft and becoming the best writer you can be. Finally, Chapter 12 offers advice on building your career with tips on marketing your book; networking through workshops, conferences, and the Internet; getting your novel reviewed; and more.

Throughout the book, you'll find sample query letters and synopses, lists of do's and don'ts, pet peeves, and advice gleaned from years of experience—both mine and those of fellow agents, editors, and writers.

Whether you are a first-time novelist who is serious about building a full-time career, or you simply want to get your one book into print, *How to Publish Your Novel* will guide you every step of the way. Most important, it will arm you with the knowledge you need to get your name on a publishing contract—and on the cover of a novel.

CHAPTER 2

WHERE DOES YOUR NOVEL FIT IN?

You're on a plane, pretending you speak only Latvian to avoid engaging the person in the next seat in conversation because it's crystal clear that she's eyeing the manuscript you're reading with pen in hand—and dying to pitch you her story. But the fatal moment comes when your flight attendant asks your meal choice and you answer in perfect English, "I'll take the lasagna." You're doomed. The aspiring novelist next to you says, "Are you an editor?" and proceeds to describe her story.

"Is this a novel?" you interrupt, "or is it nonfiction?"

"Oh, it's definitely a fiction novel," she replies.

"What type of novel is it?"

"What do you mean? It's a novel!"

"Well, there are different types of fiction. You know how bookstores are arranged in sections? What section would your book be sold in?"

"That's the beauty of it," the writer exults. "It can fit in anywhere. It has everything in it—science fiction, horror, religion, the true story of my husband's physical handicap, and it's a thriller, too."

This imaginary anecdote is too painful to continue, but suffice it to say that when someone describes their manuscript in this way, I know that it will be nearly impossible to place their book with an established publisher.

If you met me on a plane—or anywhere else—would you be able to tell me what type of book you're writing? Could you tell me the audience for which your book is geared? How about its marketplace?

At this point, you might be thinking, "Well, I think I can answer those questions. I definitely know what kind of book I'm writing. And I'm pretty sure who my readers are going to be and where my book will sell." If you are like most writers, though, you have only a general notion of where your book fits in—and you probably think that this general idea is adequate. After all, you're a writer, not an editor, and any editor should be able to figure out your book's category, audience, and marketplace. But the fact is that if you send a proposal to an editor and rely on that editor to fill in the details of where your book belongs, you will definitely decrease your chance of getting your work reviewed and accepted. As an author, it is vital that you understand your book in terms of its category, audience, and marketplace. And it is equally important to communicate this information to the publisher if you want to get your book into print.

This chapter discusses the major categories of adult novels. It also offers some thoughts on understanding the expectations of your book's audience, and explores each major marketplace that can make your novel available to the audience you've targeted. By identifying these three elements, you will be better able not only to find a publisher who produces books in the appropriate area, but also to convince that publishing house that your book does, indeed, have an existing audience that can be readily reached.

WHAT ARE BOOK CATEGORIES?

Book categories were created to help people organize and locate books. It's important to recognize that there are several different book classification systems in use. First, are the systems used by libraries. Based on either the Library of Congress or Dewey decimal system, these methods of classification allow libraries to keep track of thousands of volumes. Next, are the categories used by bookstores. These are designed as a promotional tool that enables consumers to find the books they want. Last, are the categories created by publishers to identify the types of titles in which they specialize and—in some cases—to indicate the outlets through which their books will be sold.

Clearly, many of the book categories created by these systems overlap. They have many of the same names and, to a degree, use the same criteria to arrange titles. But—and this is an important "but"—many have created book categories that are unique to their own needs. For example, bookstores often have classifications such as *New York Times* Best Sellers." So what's the problem? If you're simply browsing the shelves of a bookstore, there is none. But if you were trying to describe your book in a proposal to a publisher, would you ever describe it as a future *New York Times* Best Seller? If you did, you can imagine how she might react. Just as important, if you did describe your book using that label, it would fail to tell the publisher anything she needs to know about the book.

Where does that leave you? It leaves you in search of a classification system that meets your specific needs. Fortunately, there is one—the Square One Book Classification System.

THE SQUARE ONE BOOK CLASSIFICATION SYSTEM

The Square One Book Classification System was specifically designed to help authors explain their projects to publishers. It presents novel categories that editors can understand because it tells them exactly what they want to know. Just as important, the system avoids all those categories that will only confuse and bewilder editors—and make you look as though you don't have a clue about your own book.

Before we list the individual categories, it's important to note that in general, commercial fiction is divided into "category" fiction, "mainstream" fiction, and "literary" fiction. Each type of category fiction has its own loyal cadre of readers, while mainstream and literary fiction typically—though not always—have broader appeal. Another name for "category fiction" is "formula fiction." In other words, these novels deliver their stories according to an expected formula. (See the inset on page 11 for more information on formula fiction.) On the next page, you'll find a category for mainstream fiction, a category for literary fiction, and a number of different ones for formula novels. Altogether, the Square One system for adult novels is composed of twenty-two categories, which include:

Knowing the category into which your novel falls will help you:

❑ Create a list of publishing houses that are best suited to accept and market your work.

❑ Send your manuscript to the appropriate editor within the company.

❑ Identify and analyze competing books in the marketplace.

As you read about the twenty-two categories of the Square One Book Classification System, you will notice a certain fluidity between categories. While some books clearly belong in a specific grouping, others are a blending of two or more categories. For instance, a historical fantasy novel includes fantasy elements in a story set in a specific historical period. And some published books cross over from one category to another during their "lives," moving from romance to mainstream fiction, for instance. This is important to keep in mind as you identify the category in which your own book belongs.

1. Mainstream Novels

2. Literary Novels

3. Adventure Novels

4. Erotica

5. Ethnic Novels

6. Fantasy Novels

7. Feminist Novels

8. Gay, Lesbian, Bisexual, and Transgender (GLBT) Novels

9. Gothic Novels

10. Historical Novels

11. Horror Novels

12. Humor Novels

13. Military/War Novels

14. Mysteries

15. Occult Novels

16. Religious Novels

17. Romance Novels

18. Science Fiction Novels

19. Spiritual/New Age Novels

20. Sports Novels

21. Suspense Novels

22. Westerns

1. Mainstream Novels

Mainstream novels are works of fiction that do not follow a formula, such as a romance or mystery formula. A mainstream novel may borrow elements from category fiction—for instance, it may involve a mystery or draw on the structure of a romance. But much of its

Formula Novels

As explained on page 9, adult fiction can be loosely grouped into three divisions. *Mainstream novels* and *literary novels* aim for a general audience, while *category* or *formula novels* target a niche market—although in some cases, that niche is quite large. In fact, probably 70 percent of all novels sold are category novels, and reports state that over a third of all fiction sold falls into the single category of romance novels. Other popular categories include mysteries, historical fiction, and science fiction. These different categories are often referred to as *genres*.

As the name implies, a formula novel tells its story according to an expected formula. In a typical romance novel, for instance, the protagonist is a woman in need—whether that need is emotional, financial, physical, or spiritual—who at some point meets a man who can fill that need. At first, she is either in conflict with him or in conflict within herself over being involved with him. A novel set in the Civil War, for instance, may place the heroine in the North, but make the hero a member of the Confederate Army. But eventually, the heroine and hero declare their love for each other, and the heroine's problem is solved.

A good category or formula novel manages to conceal the formula while remaining true to it. Readers judge writers by their ability to take the same old familiar story and make it interesting and unique through the creation of appealing characters and plot twists. No matter how "different" a category book is, though, it is comforting because of its predictability. Readers know, for instance, that Agatha Christie's amateur sleuth Miss Marple will always learn "whodunit" by the end of the tale. And writers keep their contract with their readers by always delivering what's expected. Those who do this with creativity and who consistently produce good formula books—Christie wrote *seventy-nine* novels and short story collections—have large readerships and enormous fan clubs.

If you choose to write a category novel, it is vital to learn everything you can about the books in that category and the formulas they use. As a start, read, read, read, choosing the best books you can find—leaders in the field. Whenever possible, also track down publications that focus on that particular category. The *Romantic Times Book Club Magazine,* for example, reviews new romance titles every month and points to what publishers are buying. When you are thoroughly familiar with the category, write, write, write, honing your craft until your books don't merely follow the formula, but offer the reader something new and interesting that will hold her attention from the first page to the last.

strength comes from ignoring and departing from category formulas as a means of appealing to a wide audience rather than a niche market. Moreover, mainstream novels are generally better written than category novels. Perhaps this is why mainstream novels are far more likely than category novels to become bestsellers and, ultimately, motion pictures.

Robert James Waller's *The Bridges of Madison County*, which is viewed as a mainstream novel, borrowed much of its structure from the romance category, but departed somewhat from that structure, and thus appealed to a broader audience.

Mainstream novels can usually be found under the heading "New Fiction" in major chain bookstores such as Barnes & Noble and Borders. You may consider some of these mainstream books to be category books—thrillers, mysteries, or romances, for instance. In fact, sometimes formula books do transcend their categories and cross over to the mainstream. Examples of this include Nicholas Sparks' bestseller *The Notebook,* which crossed over from the romance category; Larry McMurtry's *Lonesome Dove,* which rose out of the Western category; J.R.R. Tolkien's *The Hobbit,* which crossed over from fantasy; and Kurt Vonnegut's *Slaughterhouse Five,* which travelled to the mainstream by way of science fiction. If you have read any of these books, you probably understand why they became crossover titles. While they have much in common with other books in their category, they rose above "formula" by exploring more complex, universal themes.

Most mainstream novels are published by major publishing houses, who are able to afford the advances commanded by these novelists, and—once the book is out—have access to suitable marketplaces such as major bookstore chains.

Of the twenty-two categories, is this the most appropriate for your title?

Tom Clancy's *The Hunt for Red October* was originally published by the Naval Institute Press—an academic publisher that could reach only a small readership. When the book proved popular, it was purchased by a major publishing house, Berkley Books, and became a mainstream novel. Eventually, the tech-thriller rose to the *The New York Times* Best Sellers list and was also produced as a blockbuster film.

To Learn More About Mainstream Novels . . .

To learn more about mainstream novels, look for these great titles on the shelves of your local library or bookstore. Note that all of the following books became major motion pictures.

☐ Fannie Flagg's *Fried Green Tomatoes at the Whistle Stop Café* (Vintage) features a tale of friendship that endures a lifetime.

☐ John Irving's *The World According to Garp* (Modern Library) is the story of the tragic life of a quirky author.

☐ Tom Wolfe's *The Bonfire of the Vanities* (Farrar, Straus & Giroux) is the story of investment banker Sherman McCoy, who, after a car accident, gets entangled in a web of lies and deceit.

2. Literary Novels

Literary novels are much like mainstream novels in that they do not follow a formula. Like mainstream fiction, they may borrow elements from category novels, but they are likely to be relatively unique in structure simply because they are written without any overt attempt to appeal to a commercial readership. Instead, the author of a literary novel generally follows her own personal vision, conforms to her own esthetics, or focuses on delivering a specific message.

A literary novel can also be discriminated from other novels by its quality and its richness of detail. In category books, such as romance novels and works of science fiction, main characters are often developed just enough to advance the plot and keep the reader interested. In mainstream novels, characters are likely to be more fully developed. In literary novels, however, characters are usually described in rich detail. In fact, while genre novels are event-driven, literary novels are nearly always character-driven. Yes, a literary novel can involve some action, but generally the focus is on character and style—not plot.

The same attention to detail shown in character depiction is also shown in the description of the literary novel's setting. While the setting of a category novel or even a mainstream novel is likely to be drawn in broad strokes, the background of a literary work is rendered in minute detail, and often seems like another character in the story.

Because literary novels do not cater to the demands of the broad book-buying public, they are generally produced by small to mid-sized publishing companies, or by highly selective imprints within larger companies. These publishers are willing to gamble on high-quality writing that may not have commercial appeal. They know that 95 percent of all literary novels don't reach a significant readership, and that they'll be fortunate if they sell a thousand hardback copies. Occasionally, literary novels do cross over to become mainstream fiction. Examples of such books include Laura Esquivel's *Like Water for Chocolate*, Umberto Eco's *The Name of the Rose*, and Gabriel García Márquez's *Love in the Time of Cholera*, two of which also became motion pictures.

Of the twenty-two categories, is this the most appropriate for your title?

Because literary novels have much in common with mainstream novels, they are sometimes viewed as a subcategory of mainstream fiction.

To Learn More About Literary Novels . . .

To learn more about literary fiction, look for these classic titles on the shelves of your local library or bookstore.

☐ Albert Camus' *The Stranger* (Vintage) is the story of an ordinary man unwittingly drawn into a senseless murder on an Algerian beach. In this novel, Camus explores what he termed "the nakedness of man faced with the absurd."

☐ Marcel Proust's *Remembrance of Things Past* (Vintage), a sprawling three-volume autobiographical masterpiece, begins with the narrator's earliest childhood perceptions and sorrows.

Then, over several thousand pages, it retraces the course of his adolescence and adulthood, dividing his experiences among the narrator and a sprawling cast of characters.

☐ Ayn Rand's *The Fountainhead* (New American Library) addresses the universal themes of individual strength, the tug between good and evil, and the threat of fascism. Through her main character, Rand presents her philosophy, "Objectivism," a belief in the individual's need to pursue self-interest and his own happiness.

3. Adventure Novels

Most popular category fiction contains a substantial amount of adventure. Western novels certainly do, and some mysteries involve a considerable degree of adventure. The adventure novel can be discriminated from these by the fact that action is the key ingredient in this category of works. The story may pit person against person, person against organization or government, or person against the environment, but whatever the foe may be, the main character, who is always in tremendous jeopardy, cannot triumph by recourse to established institutions and agencies, but must resort to action—and usually, to some degree of violence.

While most category fiction contains a substantial amount of action, in the adventure novel, action is the key ingredient.

The adventure category embraces several subcategories, including *disaster adventure*, which involves some sort of dramatic natural or manmade disaster, such as a tornado or a fire; *espionage adventure*, which involves spies and secret agents; *industrial/financial adventure*, which involves intrigue and spying by large industrial and financial organizations; *male action adventure*, which involves relatively stereotypical characters and considerable action and violence; *military/ naval adventure*, which places members of the armed forces in some sort of war or military conflict; *political intrigue adventure*, which uses

---

To Learn More About Adventure Titles . . .

To learn more about adventure books, look for these great titles on the shelves of your local library or bookstore.

☐ Daniel Defoe's *Robinson Crusoe* (Modern Library) is the classic story of the sole survivor of a shipwreck, who lives on a deserted island for more than twenty-eight years.

☐ Richard Condon's *The Manchurian Candidate* (McGraw-Hill)—a chilling tale of political intrigue—tells the story of an American prisoner of war who is programmed by his captors to kill on command.

☐ Douglas J. Preston's *The Codex* (Forge Books) is a tale of greed, adventure, and betrayal involving brothers who compete for buried treasure left to them by their father.

---

a government setting along with political characters and situations; *survival adventure,* which tells the story of one or several persons' survival in the wilderness or some other threatening or isolated area; and *thriller adventure,* which takes the thriller aspect to maximum intensity by focusing on the hero's survival in an action-filled plot involving narrow escapes, chases, and rescues. Some of the hallmarks of adventure fiction include a strong, action-oriented male main character with extraordinary abilities; a realistic or semi-realistic environment, including detailed descriptions of actual weapons; a plot of almost continuous action; and a variety of life-threatening situations. Avid readers of the adventure novel, who are mostly men—although adventure novels for women are now gaining in popularity—love the fast-paced plot, and also appreciate the fact that these books are relatively easy "reads."

Adventure novels are published by all sizes of commercial publishers, small, medium-sized, and large.

Of the twenty-two categories, is this the most appropriate for your title?

4. Erotica

In novels that are classified as erotica, the story typically revolves around a sexual theme. Stories in other categories can deal with sex rather explicitly and still not be classified as erotica. But in erotic novels, sex pervades the theme, the tone, and the action. The goal of erotic

To Learn More About Erotic Novels . . . .

To learn more about the erotica category, look for these titles in some mainstream and specialty bookstores, as well as on the Internet.

☐ Dominique Aury's *The Story of O* (Ballantine Books), published in 1954 under the pseudonym Pauline Reage, relates the passions of a beautiful Parisian fashion photographer. As part of her intense love, she demands debasement and severe sexual and psychological tests.

☐ Zane's *Sisters of the APF: The Indoctrination of Soror Ride Dick* (Atria Books) follows the APF (Alpha Phi Fuckem), a sorority dedicated to sexual freedom.

☐ Noire's *G-Spot: An Urban Erotic Tale* (One World/ Strivers Row) tells the sizzling story of a young virgin in Harlem who becomes the mistress of the most sexually incompetent nightclub owner in the world, and has to look elsewhere for satisfaction.

☐ Nikki Gemmell's *The Bride Stripped Bare: A Novel* (Fourth Estate) charts the sinuous paths of a nameless thirty-something housewife who searches for sexual happiness outside the marital bed. This tale, presented as a series of journal entries, was inspired by a manuscript written by an anonymous Elizabethan woman.

fiction is to arouse. The works of the Marquis de Sade and Leopold Von Sacher-Masoch—from which we derived the words "sadist" and "masochist"—are prime examples of classic erotic fiction.

The general category of erotica can be loosely divided into erotica for women, and erotica for men. Erotica for women is basically a combination of romance and erotica. Sometimes referred to as *romantica*, these novels emphasize both the sexual and emotional aspects of the relationship.

Male erotica, rather than emphasizing relationships, usually combines erotica with elements of other fiction categories that are popular with men. For instance, subcategories include *erotic adventure*, which fuses elements of an adventure tale with sexual themes; *erotic fantasy*, in which tales of explicit sexuality take place in a world different from our own; *erotic science fiction*, which infuses sex into a scientific premise; and *erotic horror*, which includes elements of both the horror novel and erotica. Still other subcategories include *erotic contemporary*, which uses a contemporary setting; *erotic Gothic and Victorian*, which tends to deal with fetishes such as bondage; *urban erotic fiction*, which uses a city setting and often features African-American characters; and erotica that is geared for gay, lesbian, bisexual, or transgender readers.

Although fewer publishers produce erotica than produce other categories of novels, a number of large and medium-sized houses do handle this type of fiction. Erotic novels are also published by a handful of smaller publishers, some of which specialize in these books.

Of the twenty-two categories, is this the most appropriate for your title?

5. Ethnic Novels

Ethnic novels feature characters from a group of people who share a common and distinctive racial, national, religious, linguistic, or cultural heritage, and who are living outside their country or area of origin. In the United States, the largest subcategory of this genre is the African-American novel, but many other groups are also the focus of these books, including the Chinese, Japanese, Indians, Hispanics, and Jews.

Although many ethnic novels are geared toward readers from the featured group, these books also enlighten other people about that culture. Common themes in ethnic fiction include the immigrant experience, clashes between different cultures, conflicts between recent immigrants and first- and second-generation Americans, distinctive cultural practices and beliefs, prejudice, and assimilation. Although these novels often examine the problems of that group—their difficulty in finding acceptance in a foreign country,

Ethnic novels often explore both the problems and the strengths of people in a particular ethnic group.

To Learn More About Ethnic Novels . . .

To learn more about ethnic novels, look for these great titles on the shelves of your local bookstore or library.

☐ Terry McMillan's *Mama* (Houghton Mifflin)—McMillan's first novel—tells the story of a proud black mother's struggle to overcome poverty and despair in a Detroit slum.

☐ Amy Tan's *The Joy Luck Club* (Putnam) explores the lives of four women who immigrate from

China to America, and the tenacious bonds that bind them to one another and to their daughters.

☐ Jhumpa Lahiri's best-selling novel *The Namesake* (Houghton Mifflin) is a family drama that sensitively explores the Indian immigrant experience, the clash of cultures, the conflicts of assimilation, and the tangled ties between generations.

for instance—they also commonly explore the strengths of that culture, such as strong family bonds that sustain individuals in times of trouble.

Ethnic novels are produced by publishing companies of all sizes—small, medium, and large.

Of the twenty-two categories, is this the most appropriate for your title?

6. Fantasy Novels

Many retail bookstores shelve fantasy and science fiction together, often to the annoyance of fans. Both genres include elements of the fantastic. But while science and technology figure largely in a work of science fiction, fantasy books usually involve magic or the supernatural. The term *speculative fiction* is sometimes used to refer to both science fiction and fantasy.

There is no single definition of a fantasy novel, simply because there are so many types of fantasy. A critical feature of any fantasy, though, is that it takes place in a world that is different in some way from the world we know, and that this difference is not the result of science or technology—as it would be in a science fiction story—but rather, the result of magic or some anomalous phenomenon. Although the particulars of each fantasy world vary from novel to novel, one law prevails: Each world must adhere to its own logic and consistently operate according to its own set of rules. Like some science fiction, some fantasy novels uses the genre to explore an aspect of human society. Marion Zimmer Bradley's *The Mists of Avalon*, for instance, has distinct feminist themes.

The category of fantasy includes several subcategories, including *high fantasy*, which is serious in tone, epic in scope, and includes fan-

---

To Learn More About Fantasy Novels . . .

To learn more about fantasy novels, look for these classic titles on the shelves of your local library or bookstore.

☐ J.R.R. Tolkien's *Lord of the Rings* trilogy (Houghton Mifflin) is the quintessential high fantasy novel. Tolkien's mythic world of Middle Earth is so richly detailed—with highly complex histories, fascinating cultures, and entire languages—that numerous books have been written about its design.

☐ Piers Anthony's *On a Pale Horse* (Ballantine Books) takes us inside the author's highly stylized world of puns and layered meanings, and lets us experience that world through the eyes of a character who is forced to fill in for Death.

☐ Marion Zimmer Bradley's *The Mists of Avalon* (Del Ray Books) retells the Arthurian legend in a classic fantasy style, but from the perspective of Arthur's half-sister.

tastical races such as elves and dwarves; *sword and sorcery*, which features muscular heroes in violent conflict with villains who, unlike the heroes, have supernatural powers; *contemporary fantasy*, which is set in the real world in contemporary times, where, it is revealed, supernatural creatures exist; *comic fantasy*, which is set in imaginary worlds and is primarily humorous in intent and tone; *romantic fantasy*, which deals with the development of a romantic relationship, but includes fantasy elements; *historical fantasy*, which is set in a specific historical period, but includes fantasy elements; and *erotic fantasy*, which uses erotica in a fantasy setting.

Because fantasy is a popular genre, many major houses, medium-sized houses, and small houses publish books in this category.

Of the twenty-two categories, is this the most appropriate for your title?

7. Feminist Novels

As the name suggests, feminist novels use their story lines to explore themes of interest to feminists. While every feminist novel in some way involves feminism's core belief—that men and women should be equal politically, economically, and socially—other themes explored are as varied as the many theories of feminism. For instance, the book may focus on the belief that women are basically

To Learn More About Feminist Novels . . .

To learn more about feminist novels, look for these great titles on the shelves of your local library or bookstore.

☐ Margaret Atwood's *The Handmaid's Tale* (McClelland and Stewart), examines a near-future society in which women are strictly controlled, unable to have jobs or money, and assigned to various classes.

☐ Michael Cunningham's *The Hours* (Farrar, Straus, and Giroux) intertwines the story of novelist Virginia Woolf with that of a modern-day reincarnation of Woolf's character Mrs. Dalloway, and a 1940s housewife who is unable to cope with the constraints of her "perfect" suburban family life.

☐ Nancy Price's *Sleeping With the Enemy* (Simon and Schuster) follows the metamorphosis of Sara Burney, an abused wife who leaves her husband to start a new life. Readers who previously only knew the film version of this story may be surprised to find that portions of the book read like a feminist tract.

different from men, and that this difference should be celebrated, or that women should separate themselves from men in order to see themselves in a different context. Often, feminist novels depict the oppression of women. Sometimes these themes are explored with subtlety, while in other books, there is a more heavy-handed approach.

Publishers of all sizes produce feminist novels. A handful of small publishers specialize in these novels only.

Of the twenty-two categories, is this the most appropriate for your title?

8. Gay, Lesbian, Bisexual, and Transgender (GLBT) Novels

As the name implies, the books in this category—which is often referred to as GLBT literature—focus on themes important to gay, lesbian, bisexual, and transgender readers. The subjects explored in these novels include coming out, gay relationships, and challenges posed by society.

The various subcategories of GLBT literature include GLBT mys-

To Learn More About GLBT Novels . . .

To learn more about gay, lesbian, bisexual, and transgender novels, look for these great titles on the shelves of your local library or bookstore, or find them in Internet bookstores.

- [ ] Radclyffe Hall's 1928 *The Well of Loneliness* (Anchor)—a classic portrayal of lesbian love that was at one time banned for obscenity—tells the thinly disguised story of the author's own life.

- [ ] Oscar Wilde's *Teleny* (Gay Man's Press) is a classic work of fiction about a young stud, who, in seeking voluptuous and forbidden pleasures, finds love and tragedy when he becomes embroiled in a mysterious cult devoted to fulfilling only the very darkest of fantasies.

- [ ] Karin Kallmaker's *Substitute for Love* (Bella Books) chronicles the love life of Holly Markham, who starts the book in an unsatisfying straight relationship and, through a journey of self-discovery, finds greater satisfaction in a lesbian romance.

- [ ] Tom Dolby's debut novel *Trouble Boy: A Novel* (Kensington) is a hip, sexy story about a Yale-educated gay freelance writer who navigates the shark-infested waters of Manhattan hoping to score a screenplay deal and a loyal boyfriend.

tery books, historical novels, erotica, science fiction, fantasy, romance, and more. As you might guess, the books in each of these subgroups includes elements of another category while maintaining a focus on GLBT relationships and issues.

GLBT novels are produced by publishers of all sizes. While larger publishers may produce a line of GLBT books in addition to their other titles, smaller publishers often specialize in this category or in only a segment of this category, such as lesbian feminist literature.

Of the twenty-two categories, is this the most appropriate for your title?

To gain a greater familiarity with GLBT novels, both old and new, log onto www.publishingtriangle.org/100best.asp, and find a list of the "100 Best" books in this category.

9. Gothic Novels

Created in the mid-eighteenth century, the Gothic novel features a number of distinctive elements, including a castle setting that often involves secret passages, hidden staircases, and the like; an atmosphere of brooding, gloom, mystery, and suspense; omens, portents, secrets, and visions; supernatural and otherwise inexplicable events, such as ghosts and vampires; high, even overwrought emotions, including feelings of impending doom; and women in distress, most

To Learn More About Gothic Novels . . .

To learn more about Gothic novels, look for these great titles on the shelves of your local library or bookstore.

- ☐ Emily Bronte's *Wuthering Heights* (Penguin) is the epitome of Old Gothic fiction. Set in the wild, bleak Yorkshire Moors, it depicts the love between the willful Cathy and the dark and brooding Heathcliff—a love that destroys not only the lives of those around them, but their own, and transcends even death.

- ☐ Mary Wollstonecraft Shelley's *Frankenstein, or the Modern Prometheus* (Modern Library), is the classic masterpiece about a man whose hunger to create life drives him to build a

monster, and ultimately results in his own ruin.

- ☐ Daphne Du Maurier's *Rebecca,* often called the quintessential modern Gothic novel, tells the story of an innocent young woman of small means who, after marrying a brooding and mysterious older man, is taken to live at Manderley—a vast estate ruled by a villainous housekeeper.

- ☐ Francesa Stanfill's *Wakefield Hall* (Villard) is a sophisticated contemporary Gothic, in which the heroine moves through real mazes and internal labyrinths to discover her identity and the love of her life.

It is generally agreed that the Gothic novel was invented by Horace Walpole, whose 1764 novel *The Castle of Otranto* contained all the essential elements of the Gothic category. Walpole's novel was widely imitated during his time, and continues to influence prose, poetry, and film.

particularly, a lonely and oppressed heroine who is threatened by a tyrannical passion-driven male.

Many people confuse Gothic novels with the horror genre. While both do include macabre and violent acts, Gothic novels typically show a high sense of morality—a feature generally lacking in works of horror. In Gothic fiction, evil is always destroyed, and morality triumphs.

Publishing houses of all sizes—large, medium, and small—produce works in this category.

Of the twenty-two categories, is this the most appropriate for your title?

10. Historical Novels

While there is great controversy over many particulars of the historical novel, it is generally agreed that to be deemed historical, a book must have been written at least fifty years after the events described, by an author who was not alive at the time of those events. It is important to emphasize that the story must be set before the *author's* lifetime. Even if the author has written of something that occurred well before the reader was born, the book is not considered a historical novel if it took place during the author's lifetime. The author must have learned about the novel's setting through research, rather than actual experience.

Historical novels can generally be grouped into two broad subcategories. In the first type of historical novel, the story includes no historical events or characters—only fictional characters involved in events created by the author. In the second subcategory, both the setting and the supporting characters are factual. For instance, a Revolutionary War novel may include General George Washington as a character, and relate his movements during an actual military campaign. Some historical novels are simply fictional retellings of true -.

Historical fiction is usually detail-oriented, and part of the author's intention is often to enhance the reader's knowledge of past events, lives, and customs. While much of the audience for historic fiction merely want to read a good story, historical or not, a percentage of historic fiction readers are interested in specific historic set-

To Learn More About Historical Novels . . .

To learn more about historical fiction, look for these fine titles on the shelves of your local library or bookstore.

☐ Margaret Mitchell's *Gone With the Wind*, a sweeping romance set in the South during and after the Civil War, has been praised by scholars for its historical accuracy. The film is as famous as the novel.

☐ Patrick O'Brien's *Master and Commander* (W.W. Norton & Company) is a classic example of nautical fiction, and goes into minute detail about early sailing vessels. This David and Goliath story, set aboard a British man-of-war, became a feature film.

☐ Charles Frazier's *Cold Mountain* (Atlantic Monthly Press)—which was based on local history and family stories passed down by the author's great-great-grandfather—tells of a wounded soldier who walks away from the ravages of war and back home to his prewar sweetheart. Frazier's book was made into a star-studded feature film.

tings. For instance, some historical fiction fans read only Civil War-era or World War II-era novels.

The major players in this category of fiction tend to be the large publishers, and are often the houses and imprints that also produce literary fiction. However, several medium-sized and small companies also produce historical novels.

Of the twenty-two categories, is this the most appropriate for your title?

11. Horror Novels

Like many of the categories already discussed, that of horror novels is not easy to define, partly because so many types of horror fiction now exist. At its most basic level, horror fiction is designed to elicit fear and dread on the part of the reader. This can be done through the inclusion of some or all of a number of different elements, including: a plot containing frightening and unexpected incidents; violence that is often graphic in nature, and may be accompanied by explicit sexuality; a mood that is dark, foreboding, menacing, and bleak; an exploration of the dark, malevolent side of humanity; a sequence of events that begins with ordinary situations but eventually involves supernatural elements; and a protagonist who deals with overwhelming dark and evil forces, and must triumph over them if lives are to be saved.

To further explore the horror novel category, visit the website of the Horror Writers Association at www.horror.org, and find writing tips, suggested reading lists, and more.

To Learn More About Horror Novels . . .

To learn more about horror fiction, look for these fine titles on the shelves of your local library or bookstore.

☐ Stephen King's *The Stand* (Doubleday) is one of King's longest works, and has arguably one of the grandest scopes in the contemporary horror category, dealing as it does with a disease-borne apocalypse. You'll never enter another highway tunnel calmly after reading this novel.

☐ Thomas Harris's *Red Dragon* (Dutton Books) is a pulse-pounding novel that examines the thoughts and actions of a killer who, tormented into madness as a child, now maims and murders entire families in hideous ways.

☐ Peter Straub's *Ghost Story* (Coward, McCann, & Geoghagan Inc.) is a chilling classic that tells the story of four men who, in their youth, accidentally kill a woman—and then must live with the ghostly consequences.

As already mentioned, there are many types of horror novels. Some of the subcategories include *ancient evil,* which tells stories of evil, often hidden for centuries, that is awakened and threatens civilization; *black magic,* in which magic is used for evil purposes; *contemporary horror,* which is set in contemporary times in familiar settings; *dark suspense,* which relies on psychological terror; *erotic horror,* which includes explicit sexual activity, usually of a violent nature; *ghost stories,* in which the spirits of the dead intervene in some way; *Gothic horror,* which includes elements of the Gothic novel, such as ruined castles and wild landscapes; *historical horror,* which is set in the past using realistic settings; *horror mysteries,* which include a detective and other elements of mystery novels; *horror sagas,* which follow several generations of doomed or evil families; and more. The categories are limited only by the imagination of the writer, and, as you can see, there is considerable overlap between the horror category and other categories.

For quite a while, this area of fiction has been dominated by well-known horror novelists such as Stephen King, Anne Rice, and Dean Koontz, and by the major publishing houses that produce their books. Although this market is difficult to break into, some large houses—always looking for the next big author—still take an occasional chance on first-time novelists. In addition, several medium-size and small houses publish these books.

Of the twenty-two categories, is this the most appropriate for your title?

12. Humor Novels

Humor novels generally feature comical characters embroiled in outrageous situations, although many examples of this category are subtle. Depending on the novel, the humor may lean more on style and character than on situation to produce a laugh. Humorous novels run the gamut from wry and dry to utterly silly.

Some humor novel subcategories borrow elements from other fiction categories, while some are unique to the humor category. Thus, there are *mystery humor novels*, which feature absurd cases, quirky plot twists, and unlikely detectives and suspects; *science fiction humor novels*, which include science that is questionable, outlandish, or utterly nonsensical; *horror humor novels*, in which the monster may wonder why everyone thinks he's funny instead of frightening; *romantic humor novels*, which are a humorous version of romance novels; *high society humor novels*, in which the writer pokes fun at the eccentricities and excesses of the upper class; and *social satire humor novels*, in which everyday life is presented comically to highlight the absurdities of modern life. Be aware that much of what is referred to as "chick-lit" fits into the romantic humor category.

Humor novels are produced by publishing companies of all sizes—small, medium, and large.

Of the twenty-two categories, is this the most appropriate for your title?

Chick-lit is popular fiction that is written for young women—especially single women in their twenties who work in the business world. *Bridget Jones's Diary* by Helen Fielding is a prime example of humorous chick-lit. Nearly all the major publishers now produce books in this area.

To Learn More About Humor Novels . . .

To learn more about humorous fiction, look for these great titles on the shelves of your local library or bookstore.

☐ Carrie Fisher's *Postcards from the Edge* (Pocket Books) tells a serious story with deliciously absurd humor.

☐ Thorne Smith's *Night Life of the Gods* (Modern Library) focuses on scientist Hunter Hawk, who manages to transform marble statues into living Greek gods and goddesses—and then looses them on 1920s Manhattan.

☐ John Kennedy Toole's *A Confederacy of Dunces* (Grove Press) is a perennial favorite about a perennial underachiever.

☐ P.G. Wodehouse's *Jeeves* series (Penguin Books), the tales of a hapless English blueblood and his canny "gentleman's gentleman," offers a fine example of classic British wit.

13. Military/War Novels

Military/war fiction features characters and situations that have military themes as their defining feature. The action generally takes place in the center of a conflict—such as the Civil War, the Cold War, or World War II—and sometimes incorporates real historical events and people. Common themes involve heroism in battle by an individual or group; doing justice to a cause; moral codes and idealism; courage or lack thereof; "war is hell"; brotherhood; career military personnel versus volunteers; good versus evil; and the strong versus the weak. Not surprisingly, the dominant readership for this category is male, although female readership is growing larger as more women join the armed forces. Like historic fiction readers, military fiction fans are often highly knowledgeable about the subject matter they read, so this is another research-intensive category.

The category of military/war novels includes several subcategories, including *military adventure*, which involves life-threatening situations, details of military operations, and action-packed endings; *military thrillers*, which are often contemporary, include a high degree of technology, and involve unusually high stakes, as well as an

To Learn More About Military/War Fiction . . .

To learn more about military fiction, look for these great titles on the shelves of your local library or bookstore.

- [ ] Dale Brown's *Flight of the Old Dog* (G. P. Putnam's Sons) launched a successful series about the crew of a B-52 bomber. The novel includes much detail on airborne and naval high-tech equipment.

- [ ] Richard Marcinko's *Rogue Warrior* series (Simon & Schuster) turned the author's thirty years of experience in diplomacy, intelligence, counterterrorism, and special operations as a Navy SEAL into high-testosterone adventure.

- [ ] Tom Clancy's *Clear and Present Danger* (G. P. Putnam's Sons) involves a military mission to battle Colombian drug lords, and the CIA's effort to rescue the stranded soldiers, abandoned by the U.S. government after the mission's failure.

- [ ] W.E.B. Griffith's eight-book series *The Corps* (Jove Books) chronicles the feats of a group of Marines during World War II.

enemy who is often a terrorist; *military science fiction*, which generally takes place in the not-too-distant future, and usually includes an enemy who is from another planet or star system and is a threat to mankind; *military historical*, which revisits a war or battle that occurred in the past, and incorporates real-life people; *military mystery*, which often involves spies or espionage, as well as a war crime or unexplained event that must be investigated; *military saga*, which follows either one character or a group of characters through a long conflict or a series of conflicts; and *military lifestyle*, which explores the day-to-day life of a soldier.

Military/war novels are produced by publishing companies of all sizes—small, medium, and large.

Of the twenty-two categories, is this the most appropriate for your title?

14. Mysteries

In its most basic form, a mystery novel involves an unresolved or unexplained event—usually, a murder—that the reader is challenged to solve before it is solved by a professional or amateur detective. Mystery fiction can also be defined by looking at its general characteristics, which include the presence of a dead body or a crime, a puzzle that must be solved to find the guilty party, suspects, clues, a detective, a solution, and—eventually—order restored and justice served.

Despite these unifying features, there are many different types of mysteries and many subcategories, including *caper mysteries*, which involve a light story and generally some bumbling on the part of the good or bad guys; *classic whodunits*, which feature strong puzzle elements, quirky but bright detectives, and little sex or explicit violence; *clever crook mysteries*, which involve elegant criminals, sometimes known as rogues, who steal from the rich; *comic mysteries*, which are humorous in approach; *cozy mysteries*, which are gentle reads that feature amateur detectives, a small town, and detailed character relationships; *crime mysteries*, which involve illegal activities such as drug trafficking; *detective mysteries*, which feature amateur or professional detectives who rely on personal skills and experience to solve the crime; *espionage or spy mysteries*, which include all activities related to finding and sharing secret information; *forensic mysteries*, which

Mystery lends itself well to franchise characters that can come back, novel after novel, to tackle a new criminal conundrum. Note how Sue Grafton built a whole series around the device of letters of the alphabet, and Lillian Jackson Braun defined her own formula by creating a series of books whose titles all begin, "The Cat Who . . ." Such devices keep fans coming back for more as they follow a well-loved sleuth solving crimes in a comfortingly familiar setting.

To Learn More About Mysteries . . .

To learn more about mysteries, look for these fine titles on the shelves of your local library or bookstore.

☐ Agatha Christie's *The Mirror Crack'd* (Signet) features the massively popular amateur detective Miss Marple, who this time must solve the murder of a local woman who was slipped a lethal cocktail at a charity event hosted by an American film star.

☐ Sue Grafton's *M is for Malice* (Henry Holt & Company) sends popular sleuth Kinsey Millhone on a hunt for a wealthy family's black-sheep brother, missing for decades.

☐ Josephine Tey's beautifully written *Daughter of Time* (Touchstone) has Scotland Yard's Inspector Alan Grant delving into history books to solve a centuries-old crime—the murder of Richard III's young nephews. This is a classic.

emphasize scientific crime-solving; *hard-boiled mysteries*, which feature detectives who are rough and physical in their approach; *police procedurals*, which detail the day-to-day realities of police work; *private eye mysteries*, which involve paid professionals working alone; and *thrillers*, which involve a high degree of action and adventure. But there is really no end to mystery subcategories, and most of these subgenres—many of which have given rise to successful and long-lived series—have an army of loyal fans, most of whom are female.

Most of the major publishers that produce mysteries are interested in all types, from the comfortable cozy mystery to the action-packed thriller. Smaller publishers, of course, have smaller lists, and often specialize in only one or two subcategories. But companies of all sizes produce mysteries.

Of the twenty-two categories, is this the most appropriate for your title?

15. Occult Novels

Occult titles feature some aspect of the supernatural as a major element of their story lines. Specifically, they deal with pagan beliefs and practices, such as witchcraft, voodoo, sorcery, demonism, shamanism, ceremonial magic, the evocation of spirits, and clairvoyance, as well as with the more mystical aspects of Christianity, Judaism, and other religions. Common themes include possession by demons or other supernatural forces; people or creatures rising from

To Learn More About Occult Novels . . .

To learn more about occult fiction, look for these fine titles at your local library or bookstore.

☐ Ann Rice's *The Witching Hour* (Ballantine Books) is a tale of the occult that spans four centuries to follow a family of witches haunted by a powerful, dangerous, and seductive being.

☐ Umberto Eco's *Foucault's Pendulum* (Harcourt) follows three book editors who try to invent a history of the occult by feeding random entries into a computer—until the computer starts taking over.

☐ Kelley Armstrong's *Bitten: Meet the Women of the Otherworld, Book I* (Viking) chronicles the only female werewolf in existence, Elena Michaels, as she learns to live within the pack.

---

the dead; psychic abilities; and societies, guilds, or other groups that perform ancient rituals in secret.

You may note some overlap in theme between occult fiction and the horror, fantasy, and Gothic categories. Horror novels can deal with witchcraft, for instance, while fantasy novels can include magic and Gothic novels can feature spirits rising from the dead. However, the primary focus of occult fiction is to identify and explore the power of occult practices, and to enchant the reader with its mystical elements. This is different from the focus of the other categories mentioned.

Publishers of all sizes produce occult novels, and some smaller publishers specialize in this category.

Of the twenty-two categories, is this the most appropriate for your title?

The word *occult* comes from the Latin *occultus*, meaning "hidden" or "secret." Thus, occult novels often deal with the study or use of "hidden" wisdom, such as Cabala or Wicca.

16. Religious Novels

Unlike spiritual/New Age fiction, which might be described as "generic nondenominational" (see page 34), religious fiction deals with a particular religious tradition, such as that of Christianity or of a specific denomination of Christianity. Certainly, the number of Christian novels is larger than any other within this category. But a novel in this category can also deal with other religious traditions, from Judaism to Hinduism.

Within the broad category of religious fiction, you will find several subcategories, including *apocalyptic fiction*, which deals with the end of life as we know it, and often involves elements such as the rise of the Antichrist; *biblical fiction,* which involves stories of characters, both real and imagined, who lived or might have lived in the times of the Old and New Testaments; *contemporary religious fiction,* which deals with religious themes through stories set after World War II; *religious fantasy and science fiction,* which combines religious themes with those of fantasy or science fiction; *religious historical fiction,* which presents religious themes in stories set before World War II; *religious mystery/suspense,* which presents suspenseful stories using religious themes and perspectives, and often involves clergy who are sleuths; and *religious romance,* which involves romantic stories that use religious themes. Some people also include a category called *gentle reads,* which are generally cheerful, positive stories set in a comfortable setting, such as a small town, and offering ordinary characters dealing with ordinary situations.

Publishing houses of all sizes—large, medium, and small—produce works in this category. While larger publishers might produce different novels that focus on different religions—they might, for instance produce both a Christian gentle read and a mystery that features a Jewish detective—some smaller niche publishers specialize in only one religious tradition.

Of the twenty-two categories, is this the most appropriate for your title?

To Learn More About Religious Novels . . .

To learn more about religious novels, look for these great titles on the shelves of your local library or bookstore.

☐ Jan Karon's cozy *At Home in Mitford* (Viking Book)—the first book in a series of best-selling novels—is a "gentle read" about a small-town Episcopalian rector and the people in his parish.

☐ Tim LaHaye and Jerry B. Jenkins' *Left Behind: A Novel of the Earth's Last Days* (Tyndale House)

is the first book of a series that chronicles the last days of Earth, the coming of the Antichrist, and the heroic efforts of the Tribulation Force that opposes Him.

☐ Salman Rushdie's *Satanic Verses* (Viking) tells of two Indian actors who meet when their Air India jet is blown apart by Sikh terrorists. The author calls this a story "about transformation, about religious fate," but when the book came out, faithful Muslims were offended by its content.

WORDS FROM A PRO

Charles Adams

Executive Editor, Algonquin Books

Write for the reader and not for yourself. If you're asking someone to pay money for what you've written, then you've got to direct what you've written to them—and you've got to have respect for them. Many writers make the mistake of feeling superior to both their material and their audience. This is true in particular of "literary" writers lusting after "commercial" success. They'll read a bestselling book by a particularly successful writer (usually a novelist) and say to themselves, "I can write that crap." Then they sit down and do just that: they write absolute "crap." They forget that Danielle Steel and John Grisham and Nora Roberts write from the heart, telling stories that mean something to them, stories that they want to share with their readers. Yes, they make a lot of money doing this, but they didn't start writing because they wanted to get rich; they wrote because they believed in what they had to say. My moral: Write from the heart and believe in what you write. If you have talent, they will find you.

17. Romance Novels

Romance is the reigning champion of category fiction. No other category can match its sales record. Romance readers have voracious appetites. It's not uncommon for romance fans to take more than a dozen titles at a time to a bookstore's cashier, and return for more books the following week.

In order for a novel to be considered a romance, it must meet two criteria. First, it must focus on the romantic love between a man and a woman. Second, it must have a positive, emotionally satisfying ending that leads the reader to believe that the couple's love and relationship will endure forever. Moreover, the story line usually follows a well-known formula. As mentioned earlier in the chapter, in a typical work of romance, the heroine is a woman in some type of need, and the hero is a man who can fill that need. Some type of barrier prevents them from getting together at the start of the novel—in some cases, a barrier erected by the hero or heroine—but by the end of the novel, they have discovered how to overcome this obstacle, and the heroine's problem is solved by their union.

Romance is such a vast, varied, and highly developed category that it contains several clearly defined subcategories. These include

Category fiction is addictive, and its consumers are avid buyers, but no category is more addictive than romance. At one point in recent history, romance novel readers were spending an average of $60 a month on an average of seven novels a month. That kind of consumerism leads to big profits for the publishers, some of whom regard category fiction as their bread and butter.

To Learn More About Romance Novels . . .

If you are interested in learning more about romance novels, look for these titles on the shelves of your local library, bookstore, or mass market outlet.

☐ Kathleen Eagle's *You Never Can Tell* (William Morrow), a contemporary romance, involves a reporter's entanglement with a dashing Native American man who harbors a tragic past.

☐ J.D. Robb's *Purity in Death* (Berkley) is a futuristic suspense romance featuring a deadly computer virus. Robb is the pseudonym of author Nora Roberts, who has written several books under this name.

☐ Mary Stewart's Gothic romance *Nine Coaches Waiting* (HarperTorch) tells of the deadly happenings at an opulent manse.

☐ Jill Barnett's *Sentimental Journey* (Pocket Books), a historical romance, is the story of a young blind woman who is captured by Nazis, and the handsome army officer who comes to her rescue.

☐ Jo Beverley's Regency romance *The Devil's Heiress* (Signet) tells the love story of an heiress in Georgian England and her suitor, Major "Hawk" Hawkinville.

☐ Susan Andersen's *Getting Lucky* (Avon Books), a suspense romance, places a love affair in the midst of a deadly kidnapping plot.

☐ Diana Gabaldon's *Outlander* (Dell), the first in a series of time travel romances, transports a World War II-era nurse back to the 1740s, where she meets a gallant Scots warrior.

According to a recent report, romance books represent 34.6 percent of all popular fiction sales. Mainstream fiction accounts for 24.1 percent of sales, and mysteries constitute 23.1 percent.

contemporary romances, which take place in the present, and can even touch upon serious real-life issues such as alcoholism and spousal abuse; *category romances*—also called *series romances*—which are published in monthly "lines" and for the most part take place in the present, but are shorter than the typical contemporary romance; *fantasy, futuristic, and paranormal romances,* which leave the real world behind and may include characters such as aliens or werewolves; *Gothic romances,* which involve dark emotions, brooding heroes, and other elements of the Gothic novel; *historical romances,* which are set in the past, usually before World War II; *Regency romances,* which are different from historical romances set in the Regency period in that they are shorter and emphasize dialogue over action and sex; *romantic suspense,* which blends romance with danger and often involves drug dealers, smugglers, serial killers, and the like; *time travel romances,* which generally feature a heroine who travels backwards in time and meets her true love; and *inspirational romances,* in which religious faith is a significant element of the story. Some of these subcategories are further broken down into sub-subcategories. Historical romances, for instance, are further subdivided by era, with the American West, Medieval England, and Regency England being the most popular.

Because of the popularity of romance books, publishers of all sizes have gotten in the act, with some companies producing several different subcategories, and others specializing in only one type of romantic novel.

Of the twenty-two categories, is this the most appropriate for your title?

18. Science Fiction

Any book whose story takes place against the backdrop of space may find itself lumped into the science fiction category, but the plots of *true* science fiction novels depend fundamentally upon a scientific premise, without which the story could not be told. The technology of the story may be the plot's driving force, or may merely provide the setting for the story, but almost all science fiction tends to predict or define the future. Moreover, much of the best science fiction uses the genre to explore some aspect of human society.

Since science fiction stories vary widely in theme and plot, there is no general agreement on subcategories. Many people, however, loosely group science fiction works into the two subcategories of hard science fiction and soft science fiction. *Hard science fiction* is characterized by a pronounced focus on natural science and technological developments. Often, the writers have a strong science back-

French novelist Jules Verne and English novelist H.G. Wells are often called the founding fathers of science fiction. Verne's *A Journey to the Center of the Earth* (1864) and Wells' *The Time Machine* (1895) are classics.

To Learn More About Science Fiction Novels . . .

To learn more about science fiction, look for these classic titles on the shelves of your local bookstore or library.

☐ Frank Herbert's *Dune* (Ace Books)—one of the most famous science fiction stories ever written—takes place on a desert planet, and involves a man's struggle to avenge the plot against his family.

☐ Isaac Asimov's *Positronic Man* (Doubleday) tells the tale of an android who gives up immortality to discover what it means to be human.

☐ Robert Heinlein's *Farnham's Freehold* (Putnam) relates the story of Hugh Farnham, whose family is propelled into the far future by the blast of an atomic bomb, and finds itself under a new and oppressive political regime.

ground, are meticulously detailed in their descriptions of science and technology, and avoid the inclusion of implausible scientific possibilities. *Soft science fiction* focuses less on physical laws and technological hardware, and more on philosophy, politics, and sociology—the soft sciences. For instance, a soft science fiction novel may explore the reactions of a society to problems posed by a specific technological development, without going into much detail about the science involved. The technology is merely a means to an end.

Publishing houses of all sizes produce science fiction.

Of the twenty-two categories, is this the most appropriate for your title?

19. Spiritual/New Age Novels

Although it's difficult to pinpoint when it began, in recent years, there has been a significant growth of the spiritual market. While previously these offerings came strictly from religious/spiritual publishers, the novels are now often produced by general "secular" trade publishers, as well.

Unlike religious fiction, which presents the doctrine and traditions of a specific system of beliefs, such as Christianity, spiritual fiction explores the nonmaterial world without association to a particular religion—although these books may certainly borrow concepts from existing religions and philosophies. Some of the themes

To Learn More About Spiritual/New Age Novels . . .

To learn more about spiritual/New Age novels, look for these titles on the shelves of your local library or bookstore.

☐ James Redfield's *The Celestine Prophecy* (Warner Books)—sometimes referred to as a spiritual guide for the New Age—revolves around the discovery of an ancient manuscript containing nine key insights that humans are predicted to grasp as they move towards a completely spiritual culture on Earth.

☐ Richard Bach's *Jonathan Livingston Seagull* (Avon Books), an inspirational favorite, tells the simple, lyrical story of a seagull's search for a higher purpose in life.

☐ Theodore J. Nottingham's *The Final Prophet: The Messiah Chronicles* (Sovereign Publishing) takes place during a time of global turmoil, when a Christlike prophet appears, ready to teach a core of believers to live an enlightened, conscious life.

addressed by spiritual/New Age novels include man's ability to more fully realize and develop his spiritual potential; man's relationship to others, to a higher power, and to the universe; and the existence of spiritual beings. This category also includes books that involve New Age themes such as reincarnation, synchronicity, auras, and energy transfers, as well as inspirational books that have no specific religious orientation.

The themes of spiritual/New Age novels are varied, but all books in this category seem to explore the idea that the material world we know is not the totality of our existence, but is part of something bigger.

The category of spiritual/New Age novels embraces several subcategories, including *spiritual afterlife fiction,* which explores themes of life after death; *spiritual quest* and *spiritual journey fiction,* which deal with the search for spiritual knowledge, including the knowledge of good and evil, of the self, and of the mysteries of life; *spiritual mystery/suspense,* which are mysteries driven by spiritual themes and perspectives; *spiritual fables,* in which the spiritual message is wrapped in metaphor and folk elements; and *spiritual science fiction,* in which sci-fi elements are used to explore spiritual themes.

Because of the increased popularity of this category, publishers of all sizes produce spiritual/New Age fiction.

Of the twenty-two categories, is this the most appropriate for your title?

20. Sports Novels

A sports novel, predictably, focuses on a given sport and its participants. Some focus on the struggles of a specific player; some, on the travails of a specific team. Sports fiction plots involve themes such as

To Learn More About Sports Novels . . .

To learn more about sports fiction, look for these great titles on the shelves of your local library or bookstore.

☐ Mike Lupica's *Full Court Press* (G.P. Putnam's Sons) tells the tale of the NBA's first female player and the many obstacles she faces.

☐ John Grisham's *Bleachers* (Doubleday), a departure from Grisham's usual courtroom fare, revolves around a man who returns home to bury his high school football coach.

☐ Bernard Malamud's *The Natural,* a modern-day classic, chronicles the life of Roy Hobbs, a superbly gifted baseball player whose career is sidetracked by a bizarre incident.

competition, winning, excellence, persistence, sportsmanship, and similar concepts. While many take place in the present, others take the reader back to a bygone era. As you might guess, these novels have a predominately male readership.

Publishers of all sizes produce sports novels. Although some produce books that deal with a range of sports and themes, other houses—especially the smaller ones—may focus on only one sport.

Of the twenty-two categories, is this the most appropriate for your title?

21. Suspense Novels

Not all publishing companies who produce suspense novels actually list "suspense" as an area of interest. So, when putting together a list of potential publishers for your novel of suspense, you'll want to look at companies that produce mystery novels and even mainstream fiction, and see if their lists include books in this category.

While most people recognize a novel of suspense when they read one, this is a difficult category to define. The story centers on a largely external conflict, usually takes place in the present time, and has an exciting plot that features characters in high jeopardy—usually, with life or death stakes. Although the story may involve romance, it doesn't have to. At its most basic level, a novel of suspense simply pits the good guy against the bad guy, all the while keeping the reader on the edge of her seat. An atmosphere of menace is key—as is the reader's emotional involvement in every twist and turn of the plot.

Some people use the term "suspense novel" as a synonym for "mystery," "crime novel," or "thriller." While suspense novels may take the form of a mystery or of one of the two mystery subcategories just mentioned, not all mysteries are works of suspense. Mysteries

To Learn More About Suspense Novels . . .

To learn more about novels of suspense, look for these great titles on the shelves of your local bookstore or library.

☐ Mary Higgins Clark's *All Around the Town* (Simon & Schuster) tells the tale of a college student who is accused of murdering her professor, but has no memory of the crime. This story of a tortured woman features many twists and turns, and is a roller coaster ride of suspense.

☐ James Patterson's *The Big Bad Wolf* (Little, Brown & Co.) chronicles Alex Cross on a case only he can solve: a team of kidnappers snatching successful, upstanding men and women right before their families' eyes on the streets of D.C.

☐ Nelson DeMille's *Up Country* (Warner Books) explores the mystery surrounding the murder of a lieutenant during the Vietnam War.

are more or less puzzles in which the reader must try to solve an unexplained event—usually, a murder—before it is solved by a detective. But in a novel of suspense, the reader often learns who committed the crime quite early in the story, and the tension—the suspense—results not from the solution of the crime, but from the manner in which the story's conclusion is reached. Indeed, suspense fiction does not always involve a crime at all, although it usually does involve some sort of misdeed.

Publishing houses of all sizes produce novels in this popular category.

Of the twenty-two categories, is this the most appropriate for your title?

22. Westerns

A Western novel is set in the American West, usually in the period from 1850 to 1900, when the area was fully open to white settlers. As everyone knows, the setting of the Western features immense plains, sprawling ranches, towering mountain ranges, and dusty frontier towns. Staple figures include cowboys, white pioneers, Native Americans, cattle ranches, farmers, sheriffs, U.S. marshals, and outlaws.

Observers have noted that whenever a new Western film is issued, the popularity of Western novels soars.

In the conventional Western, a frontier environment gives rise to a protagonist who exercises his heroism against an antagonist who is clearly a "bad guy," and who has threatened the peace or stability of the community. The protagonist can be reluctant or bold, but he eventually must face the antagonist in a showdown in front of that community—much as the matador faces a bull in the crowd-filled arena.

The Western novel has changed very little over the years, although it is now somewhat more friendly to both Native Americans and women, and even features some heroines. A few recent Westerns have even been penned by female writers. Still, most writers and readers of the Western are male.

Observers in the industry have noted that the popularity of the Western ebbs and flows with the availability of Western films. When Western films are issued, readership of the Western novel increases. Even when readership of this category is down, though, there is always an audience. For that reason, publishers of all sizes continue to produce the Western novel.

Of the twenty-two categories, is this the most appropriate for your title?

To Learn More About Western Novels . . .

To learn more about Westerns, look for these great titles on the shelves of your local library or bookstore.

☐ Zane Grey's 1912 *Riders of the Purple Sage* (Pocket Books) is the story of a headstrong female rancher who incurs the wrath of the Mormon community when she refuses to marry one of its elders. As consequences turn deadly, she finds help in a heroic stranger with whom she falls in love. This tale of adventure became the prototype for the twentieth century Western novel.

☐ Louis L'Amour's *Jubal Sackett* (Bantam Books), the first in a series featuring the Sackett family, revolves around a medicine man who blazes a trail through the American wilderness.

☐ Elmore Leonard's *Escape From Five Shadows* (Harper Torch) is the story of a man who is framed and put in a brutal frontier prison—and of the scores he is determined to settle.

THE IMPORTANCE OF UNDERSTANDING YOUR NOVEL'S AUDIENCE

A book *can* appeal to more than one type of audience. But you're actually hurting your chances of making a sale by promoting it this way. Publishers see a book that fits very solidly into one established market as a safer risk than one that bends the rules. When books "cross over" from one category to another, they usually do so *after* publication. Novels are seldom designed or sold to cross over.

All too often, prospective authors tell editors, "My book is written for everyone." From a publisher's perspective, a book written "for everyone" will appeal to no one. If you want to interest an editor in your project, you must have a clear understanding of your audience.

Each of the book categories I've just described is designed for a specific type of reader. Certainly there are consumers who read novels in more than one category, but as you've seen from the category descriptions, when a reader goes looking for a Western, she's got a clearly definable set of expectations. If you disappoint her, your career as a Western novelist will be pretty short. In fact, it may never get started.

In the case of certain types of fiction, you will be able to pinpoint the gender of most of your readers. Men make up the readership of most adventure, science fiction, sports, and Western novels, while women constitute the readership of most feminist, romance, and mystery novels. This is important to keep in mind as you write and revise your story. Just as vital, though, is to understand the expectations of the readers for each type of book. Beyond the "formula" itself used in many category novels—boy meets girl, etc.—readers of each category are looking for particular language and tone, a specific pace, a certain level of detail (or lack of it), a certain level of violence or romance (or lack of it), particular kinds of characters, and specific settings. You don't want to startle the reader of a cozy English mystery with the violence and harsh language best suited to a hard-boiled mystery, or with the action-packed pace of an adventure novel. Similarly, you don't want to alienate the reader of a Regency romance with the sophisticated language and detailed character development characteristic of a literary novel.

What's the best way to understand your reader's expectations? Read! Select two or three of the most successful titles in your category or subcategory, and read them from cover to cover. Note the language, the construction of the plot, the relationship between dialogue and action, the way in which sex is handled, the manner in which clues are revealed, etc. It's no coincidence that most successful mystery novelists are avid mystery readers. Their ability to write a good mystery is partly due to the fact that they *know* mysteries. If you are an enthusiastic reader of books in your category or subcategory, you may already have the familiarity you need to write well in that genre. If not, take this reading assignment seriously. After immersing yourself in several good examples of survival adventure books, comic fantasy, contemporary horror, or whatever, you will probably be able to hear the correct language and tone in your head. If so, you're ready to write!

Does this mean that if you are writing a category novel, you must be a slave to a specific formula or a particular style of writing? No. There is certainly room for creativity in terms of plot and for your own unique style of writing—as long as you work within the structure of that category. Remember that formula fiction excels when the author makes the required elements of that category interesting and unexpected, and develops them in ways the reader hasn't yet encountered—not when the author takes it upon herself to leave out the required elements.

Readers have certain expectations when they pick up a book in a specific category. To avoid disappointing them, become as familiar as possible with the best titles in your chosen genre so that you will be sure to use the appropriate language, plot construction, and dialogue when telling your story.

THE IMPORTANCE OF UNDERSTANDING YOUR MARKETPLACE

At this point, you should know what your book's category and/or subcategory is and what your audience expects. Now you need to understand your book's marketplace—the place or system through

WORDS FROM A PRO

April Christofferson
Author of Clinical Trial *(Forge)*

If you want your novel published, study the market; see what's selling. Does that mean you can't write from the heart? Absolutely not. Find a way to blend writing something "marketable" with things you care deeply about: issues, experiences, people, and places.

I write medical thrillers. I set my books in places I love (usually the West) and deal with issues I feel passionate about (corporate greed, the environment, Native American rights). I'd always wanted to set a book on an Indian reservation—not the most likely setting for a medical thriller. But then I remembered the Hantavirus outbreak in the Four Corners region. In *Clinical Trial,* I wrote about a new vaccine for the deadly Hantavirus. I set the book in Montana, on the Blackfoot reservation, and made one of my main characters an Indian activist. Every single day of working on that book was a joy for me. Isn't that what writing's about?

Tap into whatever passions you have, then couple that with doing your homework on what's selling. Not only will the writing process be that much more enjoyable for you, it will make your stories come alive and may reward you with the commercial success that will enable you to focus on what you really love to do: write.

which a book is sold to consumers. Without a clear understanding of where your book is going to sell, you cannot select an appropriate publisher—a publisher who is equipped to promote and distribute your book properly.

A century ago, the marketplace for books was both limited and uncomplicated. The vast reading audience was generally reached through bookstores and libraries. Publishing firms had salesmen who promoted their companies' lines throughout their territories. Books were then directly sold and distributed by the book publishers to bookstores and libraries. But as time went on, and an ever-increasing audience became even more eager to buy books, the number and types of marketplaces increased. Now, any one novel may be sold through a host of different outlets.

Let's look at some of the standard marketplaces that serve the novel-reading public. After reading this section, you will better understand how your particular book can reach its audience.

Traditional Retail Bookstores

When the publishing industry refers to traditional retail bookstores, it is speaking of stores whose stock is primarily composed of books. Of course, in addition to books, many of these bookstores carry sidelines such as paperweights, book ends, pens, bookmarks, calendars, cards, book lights, videos, DVDs, CDs, and other related items. This marketplace includes chain stores like Barnes & Noble and Borders, as well as independent bookstores.

Most of the books sold in these stores are published by trade publishers. Their stock includes hardbacks, paperbacks, and mass market paperbacks. Often, they also carry a selection of audio books.

Trade publishers promote their books through sales calls made by either their own sales force or the sales force of a distributor employed by the publisher. They also advertise in trade journals such as *Publishers Weekly,* and through mailings of brochures and seasonal catalogues. A number of the larger trade houses promote their books in newspapers and popular magazines. The stores purchase their books either directly from the publisher or through a distributor.

Unsold books that are held by bookstores can be returned to the distributor and/or ultimately the publisher for full credit, generally for up to one year. This returns policy—which is so different from that used in many other businesses—creates a very risky situation for the publisher.

Specialized Retail Bookstores

Specialized retail bookstores are stores that primarily sell books which focus on a particular topic or fall within a specific category. Possible areas of interest include feminism, fantasy, gay and lesbian lifestyle, mystery, occult, religion, romance, and spiritualism, to name just a few. Often, a store targets a specific audience within one of these areas. For instance, rather than offering books on religion in general, a store will usually focus on Judaic books, Christian books, or a similar category. In addition, many of these stores carry sidelines related to the store's specialty. A Christian bookstore may offer rosaries, holy medals, scapulars, chalices, and framed pictures of saints; while a fantasy bookstore may also sell a line of role-playing games and figurines. Included in this marketplace are chain specialty bookstores and independent specialty bookstores.

A number of years ago, terms like distributor, jobber, and wholesaler had very specific meanings in the book business. A *distributor* was a company that inventoried and sold books for publishers, usually on an exclusive basis. Based on their agreement, distributors could sell titles to wholesalers, bookstores, libraries, and nontraditional outlets. A *wholesaler* was a company that inventoried and sold books to bookstores on a nonexclusive basis—sometimes within a local vicinity, sometimes within a regional area, and sometimes on a national basis. A *jobber* was a wholesaler who specialized in selling mass market books to bookstores and supermarkets. Today, in spite of the fact that distributors may still have exclusive agreements with certain publishers, the three terms are used interchangeably.

Most of the books sold in these stores are published by trade publishers. Their stock includes hardbacks and paperbacks, as well as audio books, and they generally stock nonfiction books as well as novels. Publishers promote their books in this marketplace just as they do in the traditional trade retail marketplace. The stores purchase books either directly from the publisher or through a distributor, and unsold books can be returned to the distributor and/or ultimately the publisher for full credit for usually up to one year.

Online Retailers

With the emergence of the Internet has come a new way of selling just about anything. E-commerce is composed of Internet stores that allow web browsers to buy products from the comfort of their homes or offices at any time. Large online stores such as Amazon.com and Barnes&Noble.com have found clever ways to duplicate the traditional bookstore experience, such as allowing a customer to click on the cover for a close-up, or to peek inside at a few pages of the text. In addition, there are literally hundreds of other sites that sell thousands of products, including books.

A majority of the books sold on these websites are trade books, and include novels of all types. Some sites, on the other hand, specialize in one category of fiction—mysteries or romance books, for example. Their stock includes hardbacks, paperbacks, mass market paperbacks, and audio books.

To date, few trade publishers have advertised their books through website promotion. Instead, they have relied on the media exposure of a title to result in higher Internet sales. Online retailers purchase their inventory directly from the publisher or through a distributor. Most online retailers keep a limited supply of books on hand. At the moment, sales through websites represent up to 5 percent of a given publisher's sales.

Like traditional bookstore retailers, online retailers can return unsold books to the distributor and/or ultimately the publisher for full credit for up to one year.

Mass Market Outlets

Mass market paperbacks are $4\frac{1}{2}$ x 7-inch softcover editions that sometimes are reprints of hardcover trade books, and sometimes are written specifically for paperback publication. While mass market outlets include traditional bookstores, the term *mass market outlet* really refers to book outlets that can be found in high-traffic areas such as airport stores, urban newsstands, drugstores, discount retailers like Kmart and Wal-Mart, and supermarket chains—outlets that can reach the "mass" audience rather than the general bookstore's trade audience.

Few publishers sell their titles directly to mass market outlets. Most books that reach these outlets are sold through wholesalers known commonly as IDs (independent distributors).

Instead of returning unsold mass market books to publishers for credit, IDs rip the covers off the unsold books. They do this because the freight costs involved in returning these inexpensive books to the publisher cannot be recouped, as the publisher cannot resell these books as they can resell hardbacks. To keep the IDs in business, the mass market publishers have agreed to accept a verification sheet stating that the covers of the unsold books have been stripped off, and that the remaining inventory has been destroyed. In turn, the unsold inventory is deducted from the publisher's bill. Publishers may have up to 70 percent of their books returned.

> Mass market book outlets include supermarket chains, drugstores, discount retailers like Kmart and Wal-Mart, airport stores, and urban newsstands—outlets in high-traffic areas that can reach the "mass" audience rather than the bookstore's trade audience.

Libraries

Books are sold to a wide variety of libraries, including public libraries; state, county, and regional libraries; federally sponsored libraries; educational libraries, such as those found in public schools and colleges; and specialized libraries that serve the needs of specific readers, such as the business community or the music community.

Publishers promote their books to libraries via sales calls, catalogues, brochures, and attendance at library conventions and meetings. Libraries are also reached through trade publications such as *Publishers Weekly, Library Journal, School Library Journal, Choice, Booklist,* and *Kirkus Reviews.* Wholesale distributors also often recommend specific titles to libraries based on the profile of the library's patrons. In fact, the majority of library sales are channeled through these distributors, who give larger discounts than those provided by publishers, and also simplify the ordering process by enabling the library to contact one business rather than a myriad of separate publishing houses.

Book Clubs

Much has changed since the Literary Guild and Book-of-the-Month Club were launched in the 1920s. While general interest clubs still exist, many clubs now cater to special groups of readers, such as those interested in erotica, mysteries, science fiction and fantasy novels, and romances. A wider range of titles is also provided now, enabling the reader to exercise greater freedom of choice.

Book clubs, which advertise in newspapers and magazines, offer their members substantial savings. In return, members must purchase a minimum number of books within a stated period of time. All clubs contract for rights to the titles they offer, and produce lower-priced editions by using the publisher's plates and/or economizing during production.

CONCLUSION

The author who approaches an editor with unrealistic ideas regarding her book's category, audience, and marketplace holds up a red flag, and on this flag is clearly printed the words "Bad Risk." But the author who has a clear knowledge of a book's category, who has properly targeted the book's audience, and who understands how and where the book may be sold is viewed by potential publishers as a valuable asset in the publishing process. If you have read this chapter, you have taken an important and fundamental step towards turning your manuscript into a published book. The next chapter will take you further on your journey by explaining the business of publishing and guiding you towards publishers who can help you meet your goals.

CHAPTER 3

The Business of Publishing Novels

Most new novelists submit their books to publishers on a hit-or-miss basis. They don't make an effort to research the houses to which they're submitting their stories, and, as a result, they waste a great deal of time and money. If you arm yourself with a basic understanding of the publishing industry, and can demonstrate in your query letter that you've taken the time to get to know the individual house you're querying, you will automatically distinguish yourself from the crowd.

This chapter will provide you with a basic understanding of the publishing industry. It describes the different types of commercial houses that publish novels, presents their general editorial structures, and explains the basic criteria they use to review and determine the fate—the acceptance or rejection—of a novel submission. It also points out the advantages and disadvantages of each type of house for prospective authors, and clearly illustrates what happens to a submission once it is in the hands of a particular publishing house.

A BRIEF HISTORY OF PUBLISHING

The practice of making copies of manuscripts began in ancient times. As early as 600 BC, scribes were known to have copied poems and speeches onto papyrus scrolls and to have sold them at high prices. In Rome, trained slaves copied manuscripts, which were then sold by booksellers to the wealthy. Indeed, for hundreds of years, all manuscripts had to be laboriously copied by hand. Then in 1450, Johann Gutenberg invented the first printing press, and it finally became possible to mass-produce books. Soon, the book publishing industry sprang into existence.

The first significant publishing house was founded in 1583 by the Elzevir family in Holland. As the number of readers grew, more European houses came into being, with many being well established by the late 1700s. Edinburgh, Florence, London, Paris, Milan, Zurich, and Vienna all have long traditions of publishing. Gradually, publishing houses were founded in the New World, as well, with the cities of Boston, Philadelphia, and especially New York taking the lead.

Initially, publishers often produced many different printed materials, including not only books, but also maps and music. Over time, however, specialization became an increasingly significant feature of the publishing industry, with music, map, and book publishing each becoming a separate business. During the late 1800s and throughout the 1900s, book publishers further specialized, as certain firms began to produce only children's books, only religious books, or only textbooks, for instance. Those houses that published several types of books often created a separate division for each type—one division for the general trade and another for reference books, for example. Specialization manifested itself in other ways as well, with separate departments being created for the editorial process, the production process, sales, and marketing.

Whether or not the companies were specialized in their focus, for hundreds of years, publishing remained an industry of many small privately owned firms. The owner-publishers who founded these businesses saw publishing as an art, and valued excellence above commercialism. Standards for editors and authors were high, and staff advancements usually came after years of apprenticeship.

The face of publishing began to change in 1959, when Random House went public and attracted Wall Street's attention to the book business. The close attention to the growth of the industry continued throughout the 1960s. Simultaneously, trade publishing exploded with the advent of highly visible author promotions. Wall Street was impressed by the potential.

The 1970s saw a new breed of book publisher as many smaller houses were swallowed up to form such publishing goliaths as McGraw-Hill, Prentice Hall, and Simon & Schuster. The smaller houses engulfed by these new conglomerates often became mere imprints under the aegis of their new owners. In turn, many of the newly created publishing giants were bought by larger corporations in other countries, such as the Pearson Group of England and Germany's Bertelsmann Group. Rather than producing a handful of lovingly crafted masterpieces, these massive, mega-merged houses could pour out a thousand titles a year by streamlining their production process and reducing the time spent shaping each project. With the industry's eye ever on the bottom line, the writer who wanted to see his work in print couldn't afford to merely make his writing *good*; he also had to make it *commercial*. The sizzle had become as important as the steak.

On the plus side, as the commercial book business expanded, the overall market for books—including novels of many types—had grown. Supersized bookstores like Borders and Barnes & Noble began popping up throughout the country, and books also began finding their way into a growing number of nontraditional markets. No longer were libraries and bookstores their main outlets. Now books were sold in drugstores, airports, supermarkets, and wholesale clubs. In essence, more and more books were being sold everywhere.

But not all publishing companies had been swallowed up by mergers. Now, many small and moderate-sized publishing houses like Algonquin, Chronicle, and Capra Press continue to compete with the larger publishers. Although these smaller firms are attentive to the bottom line, many still maintain high standards and devote ample time to the crafting of each title. These smaller firms are also often willing to take a few risks, and so are usually the best places for fledgling novelists to start their careers.

Along with the emergence of the mega-merged publishing houses came significant breakthroughs in publishing. Computer programs designed to create typeset pages not only sped the movement of titles from manuscript to printed book, but also reduced the cost of book production, giving rise to a large and growing number of smaller independent publishing firms.

COMMERCIAL PUBLISHING HOUSES

Commercial publishing houses are those companies that publish books in order to make a profit. Not all book publishers are *commercial* publishers. University presses, for instance, produce books primarily for the purpose of making information available. Their chief interest is in the message, not the money. But such entities rarely deal in fiction. (The occasional exception will be discussed later in the chapter, on page 59.) Therefore, I'll assume for now that you're interested in commercial publication.

Traditional commercial publishers can be categorized as large, moderate-sized, or small. Each has its own internal dynamics based upon the company's history, the company's goals, and the personalities that determine if a book is signed, as well as how the book is produced and marketed. While many publishing firms have their own distinct company cultures, dictated in great part by corporate ownership, the basic principles underlying their day-to-day operations tend to be universal.

Many writers, especially those who are trying to get their work published for the first time, tend to think only in terms of large publishing houses. This is certainly understandable, considering that the larger firms usually dominate the bestsellers lists. When the average individual reads of multimillion-dollar advances given to best-selling authors, it is always the larger publishing houses that are behind these big-money offers. By their very nature—and for the sake of their shareholders—large publicly traded companies must be seen continually as important players in the industry.

There are, however, literally hundreds of excellent small and moderate-sized publishing houses that can provide a wonderful home for a writer's book. Many, in fact, may be more appropriate than larger firms for certain titles. Without a clear understanding of the wide diversity of existing publishers, writers decrease their odds of landing book contracts. Authors also may limit potential book sales by going to press with a company that is not suited to promote their work.

Large Houses

Since I've just emphasized the power of profit in today's publishing world, I'll bet you've already guessed the single most important factor that places a publishing house in the "large" category: profit. A large house makes $50 million or more in annual sales.

The second distinguishing feature of a major house is organization. Large publishers have highly defined organizational structures in which departmental roles as well as individual accountabilities are clearly defined. Through every stage of the creation of a book—from its acquisition and production to its marketing and promotion—everyone involved knows the responsibilities and parameters of his specific job.

Although many writers insist on sending their manuscripts to only large publishing houses, small and mid-sized companies are often more appropriate for certain titles. Moreover, smaller houses are far more likely to consider the works of first-time authors.

Finally, large houses can be distinguished by the number of books they produce—generally over 500 titles a year, and usually well over that number.

Acquiring Manuscripts

In large publishing houses, each acquisitions editor has a specific number of titles he has to sign on each year, and a set of criteria that each title must meet. When analyzing a manuscript for possible approval, an acquisitions editor considers two basic questions. Will the book sell enough copies to make a profit? Is the book a good fit for the publishing house? The following is a look at how these criteria are regarded in a large publishing house.

■ *Will the Novel Sell Enough Copies to Make a Profit?*
In a large commercial publishing house, profitability is the prime criterion for selecting a manuscript. Acquisitions editors—who are often responsible for finding titles in a specific category, as well as pursuing other titles—learn to gauge a book's profitability by studying the market for that book's particular category. That's why, as I stressed in Chapter 2, it's so important for you to know your novel's category. The acquisitions editor has no means of assessing your book's profitability without this information.

Before the editor breathes a word about the project to other editors, he has a firm estimate of the size of the novel's audience and the number of copies the house can expect to sell. He then uses that number to determine the dollar amount the novel is likely to earn. In some houses, the editor's department head, along with the marketing or sales department, prepares a profit-and-loss statement (P & L) to establish if the sales profits will outweigh the losses from advances, royalties, and production and marketing costs. In other houses, the acquisitions editor himself prepares the P & L. His job is on the line when he makes these estimates. If too many of his picks fail to meet these numbers, his days as an editor are likely to be over.

When the acquisitions editor feels that the book would be sufficiently profitable, he needs to secure between one and three other positive reads from his fellow editors. Only with those reads in hand can he take it to an editorial committee for approval. Even if the committee likes a project, the editor's department head often has the final

Most publishers spend an average of $25,000 to $35,000 to turn a manuscript into an edited, printed book—and this cost includes only a modest advance of $5,000 or less. Clearly, this is a considerable investment that must be carefully weighed by the publishing company.

say, and can either approve or "kill" it. It's the job of the committee and department head to weed out all but the most financially promising books. But the vast majority of submissions die before they even reach the committee.

■ *Is the Novel Right for This House?*

Even if the acquisitions editor thinks that a novel will be lucrative, he has to consider another criterion: Is it right for this particular company? In major houses, an acquisitions editor uses specific editorial profiles to determine if a book is a good fit for his company's lists. He looks at how well the novel fits its category as defined by that house. He also considers whether the subject is one of current interest and whether the manuscript is in sufficiently good shape. He may like a novel a lot, but if it needs substantial work, he may not feel he has the luxury of taking it on.

How a Manuscript Reaches an Editor's Desk

In a big publishing house, novels find their way onto the editor's desk in one of two ways. In the vast majority of cases, they're recommended by an author's representative whom the editor knows and trusts. Many literary agents have cultivated working relationships with editors, and pitch only those proposals that are appropriate. The manuscript may come from a new author or from a previously published author—perhaps one whose earlier books were produced by that house.

Very rarely, a manuscript is sent in after the editor responds positively to a great query letter. In most cases, though, a manuscript that shows up unbidden in the mail from someone the editor doesn't know is termed *unsolicited*, and in a major house, with very few exceptions, it gets sent back unread.

Why does a represented novel generally receive preferential treatment? Trade house editors are extremely busy people and count on reps to weed out the bad manuscripts that would otherwise waste too much of their time. Unagented manuscripts, on the other hand, get added to the "slush pile" to be read when the editor gets around to it—which may be never. The odds of finding a gem in slush piles are so small that most editors spend little time on them. That's why your chance of selling your novel to a major house is much better when you have a good literary agent on your side. It's not absolutely necessary to have a representative, but it helps—a lot.

Things to Consider When Working With a Large House

The big-name publishing houses are the ones most likely to offer hefty advances and arrange for high-profile publicity. They have the greatest resources, the most competitive sales forces, and the strongest connections to distributors. But just because a giant publishing house has these resources to offer doesn't mean that a first-time author will benefit from them. Publishing houses are happy to marshal their resources to promote a proven author—one who's brought in a string of bestsellers. But these companies are not likely to give the star treatment to a rookie. When you consider that the vast majority of new novels fail, you can see that it simply doesn't make good business sense to commit resources to an unknown commodity. Publishers expect the author to prove himself first.

You may be thinking that more novels would succeed if these houses gave them the backing they require, and you'd be right. But the truth of the business is that each editor is dealing with too many projects for every new novel to get the attention it needs and deserves. The publishing house knows that approximately 10 percent of its titles generate the revenues that pay for its entire list of new books. Most new books barely make back their advances, and the majority are out of print within eighteen months. If a book initially sells well, additional marketing may be developed. But if it fails to produce the expected sales figures, it will disappear quickly from the marketing department's radar.

Moderate-Sized Houses

Moderate-sized publishing houses have annual sales that fall between $10 million and $50 million, and produce over 100 titles a year. These houses tend to be well organized, but unlike the larger houses, they don't necessarily have a standard corporate structure. Many medium-sized houses have unique organizational structures and are managed by one or more individuals as private businesses or are run as family businesses. The secret to publishing with a medium-sized house, then, is to know who you are dealing with.

Just about any publisher will jump at the chance to sign on a published author whose previous books have a great history of sales—even if the new title is in an entirely different category of fiction. However, a published author whose novels have *not* done well is usually seen as a worse risk than a first-time novelist. Nielsen's BookScan—a rather expensive web service—allows publishers to check the US retail sales of just about any published book and determine an author's sales history.

The 90:10 Rule of New Titles

You may have heard of the 80:20 principle of work and finance—20 percent of the work you do generates 80 percent of the profits, and so forth. The publishing industry releases new titles according to a similar principle, only in this case the ratio is closer to 90:10.

In both large and moderate-sized publishing houses, about 10 percent of each season's new titles pay for the entire list of new books, 20 percent make a modest profit, 20 percent barely pay the cost of their own production, and the remaining 50 percent lose money. While nobody publishes a book expecting it to fail, the statistics show that more than half of new books do, year after year.

Acquiring Manuscripts

Just like his counterpart in a large publishing house, the acquisitions editor in a moderate-sized firm is given the task of acquiring a set number of titles each year, and a list of criteria that each title must meet. He still has to determine whether the novel fits the company's needs, and still must generate a dollar figure for the book's estimated sales. And just like the large-company editor, the editor in a moderate-sized firm must report to a supervisor—and sometimes to a committee—who can kill or green-light the manuscript. But in general, a novel doesn't have as many layers to penetrate, committees to win over, or corporate hoops to jump through on its way to getting signed.

■ Will the Novel Sell Enough Copies to Make a Profit?

Just as in the larger firms, the acquisitions editor at a moderate-sized house is usually responsible for signing on novels in a specific category. To do so effectively, he must remain up-to-date regarding the types of novels that have been selling well. He must understand why some books are winners, and others are not. Comparing a new manuscript to one that has been well received by the public is sometimes the best way he has of getting a go-ahead for a new title.

Although it used to be true that the profit-and-loss statement was less important at moderate-sized houses than at the major houses, today, the same number crunching typical of a large company is at play in a mid-sized firm. Acquisitions editors must estimate the size of a novel's audience and also predict the number of copies that can be sold. Each novel is expected to generate enough money to pay for its production costs, plus show a profit. If not, it will be very difficult for the editor to justify acquiring the novelist's second book. Editors who sign on too many novels that do not meet performance projections risk losing their jobs.

■ *Is the Novel Right for This House?*

An editor in a medium-sized firm, just like one in a larger firm, must consider if a novel is right for his company. This is accomplished by looking at how the novel fits its category as defined by that house, and judging whether the subject is one of current interest and whether the manuscript is in sufficiently good shape. A thoughtful review of the publisher's catalogue can help you determine the general editorial profile used by the house's acquiring editors.

A careful review of a publisher's book catalogue can help you determine the editorial profile used by the company's acquiring editors. This, in turn, can help you decide if the company might be interested in your project.

How a Manuscript Reaches an Editor's Desk

Just like the editor in a large publishing house, one in a moderate-sized firm may find books through an author's representative or through the unsolicited proposals that come in on a daily basis. In a house of this size, books written by previously published authors may play a more important role than they do in a larger house, especially when category fiction is involved.

Just like most of their major-house counterparts, many editors in mid-sized firms won't even open an unsolicited manuscript. But an unrepped manuscript has a better chance of getting read here than it does at the mega-publishers—as long as it suits the individual culture of that house. The publishing guidelines are extremely strict at some moderate-sized houses, and far more relaxed at others. Again, do your homework and get to know the company. If a house clearly isn't a good fit for your book, don't waste your time—or theirs.

Things to Consider When Working With a Moderate-Sized House

Some moderate-sized publishers are very well known in a specific category of publication. As with large houses, however, there are a number of positives and negatives to consider when evaluating a moderate-sized firm.

When investigating publishers for your project, consider asking about each company's editorial process—a process that varies from house to house. For instance, some mid-sized companies work closely with their authors to create high-quality novels, while others budget little time for editorial input.

Major publishing houses are known for paying out large advances. Some mid-sized houses pay generous advances, as well, but the majority pay much less money upfront than their larger brethren.

On the plus side, depending on the size and quality of its editorial staff, a mid-sized firm may encourage its editors to work closely with authors, carefully guiding them as they shape the manuscript. This can be a major advantage, as it may result in a higher-quality finished product. But not all mid-sized firms allow their editors to spend substantial amounts of time with their authors. That's why when investigating publishers for your project, it may be prudent to inquire about their editorial process.

Some mid-sized houses have distribution networks that rival those of giant houses. Over time, they have developed the relationships needed to get their books out to the public. And, like large houses, moderate-sized companies often have high visibility in specific marketplaces.

Some firms of moderate size have their own in-house sales groups. Others rely on outside sales forces to represent their titles. Still other houses have both. Some mid-sized firms even use the sales force of a large publishing house that carries titles other than those it produces itself. In general, you are likely to get better support from those houses that maintain their own sales force.

Many companies that use outside representatives often try to further encourage sales through direct mailings, telemarketing, and other promotional tools—anything that will help their titles stand out in the marketplace. But not all companies put forth this effort. Always try to learn how a company sells its books.

Just as in large firms, a book published by a moderate-sized house will be given a limited amount of time and exposure in which to perform. If the book sells well initially, additional marketing may be added to further promote the book. But books that don't sell well are generally relegated to backlist status, meaning that although they remain in print, they receive no further promotion. Occasionally, though not often, a mid-sized company will give such titles a second marketing opportunity. This depends on the strength of the company's commitment to a particular book.

Many mid-sized firms publish books using the same formulas employed in large houses. Approximately 10 percent of a company's new titles will generate enough revenue to pay for its entire list of new books; 20 percent will pay for themselves, plus make a reasonable profit; another 20 percent will just about break even; and the remaining books will lose money. If your book falls within the top 30 percent, it's doing well. If not, odds are that you won't make much more money than your advance. Some moderate-sized firms, however, may keep a slow-moving book in print for years, which is an important factor for many authors.

Small Houses

Smaller publishing houses have a sales volume of $10 million a year or less, and publish less than a hundred titles a year. (Some firms publish only one or two books annually!) They may run on some of the structural principles that characterize major houses, but many smaller publishers are loosely structured and run by only one or two individuals.

People start up small publishing companies for a variety of reasons. Sometimes, former employees of other publishing houses—editors, salespeople, copywriters, marketers, or publishers—establish small companies because they believe they've gained enough knowledge of the industry to run a successful business themselves. Sometimes, writers determined to get their own books into print establish a company, and then publish the works of other writers as well. Some companies are created to satisfy a specific niche market—a particular ethnic group, for instance. Some, to deliver a specific message. Some companies are even created as hobbies or as tax write-offs. Motivations for ownership of small houses are diverse, and it is this diversity that allows for their large range of organizational styles and their varied criteria for manuscript acquisition.

Today, the term *independent publisher* refers to any publishing house that is managed by its owners, as opposed to being publicly held or owned by a large publisher or business entity. While this term could be used to describe many moderate-sized houses, the true spirit of independent publishing clearly exhibits itself in the form of small presses. Overwhelmingly, small independent publishers are the ones that allow first-time authors to establish themselves as writers. Small publishers are often the risk-takers—the ones that give unknown authors the chance to pursue their visions.

Small publishing companies are not all alike. While some are run as hobbies and produce only one or two titles a year, others are highly successful businesses that publish close to a hundred books annually.

Small publishing firms are also mirrors of their creators. While it's true that they may provide great opportunities for unpublished authors, small houses may reflect not only the strength and vision, but also the shortcomings and weaknesses of the person in charge of the company.

Acquiring Manuscripts

In a small publishing house, because the staff size is usually minimal, only one or two people handle submissions, one of whom is often the owner. That person is also keenly aware of the company's financial limitations, so that the number of novels produced by the company may change each year based on the success of last year's list. The acquisitions person may also be responsible for other aspects of the production process, from editing the manuscript to designing book covers, and quite possibly managing publicity as well. Another employee might be in charge of sales and advertising, while the duties of another might include bookkeeping, order taking, and office management. In many cases, publishers may hire part-time employees or freelancers to handle some of these tasks.

The person or people making the decision about a manuscript submission in a small house follow the same guidelines employed by larger houses. They want to determine if the book will sell well and if the manuscript is right for their house.

■ *Will the Novel Sell Enough Copies to Make a Profit?*

Although small publishers are often willing to take a chance on new authors and new topics, they still have to earn a profit in order to stay in business. So just like larger companies, they must examine each manuscript critically and accept only those that they feel are a good fit for their firm.

Even smaller houses consider the size of the audience for each book, and most make a dollar estimate of potential sales. Profit is still an important concern—the publisher could not stay in business if it didn't turn a profit. But it may not be the only concern. Smaller houses that stand for quality writing—literary publishers, for instance—will stick with a book they believe in even if the anticipated profits are modest.

■ *Is the Novel Right for This House?*

Smaller publishers measure submissions against a set of guidelines just as major and moderate-sized houses do. But they often have more room for flexibility. They're more likely to consider a book that's slightly outside their realm—particularly if it's in great shape and doesn't need much editing. If the publisher gets really excited about a book, he may even consider expanding into a new category to accommodate it.

At a smaller house, the fact that an author is a new writer is not considered a hindrance. Smaller publishers simply don't have the budget to court established, best-selling authors. For this reason, the lack of an agent—who would work to get the author a larger piece of the pie—is less of a problem here than at larger firms. In fact, some small publishers won't accept manuscripts from agents. For the smaller publisher, an undiscovered gold mine of talent is the best client, so it's much easier for new writers to get a foot in the door.

How a Manuscript Reaches an Editor's Desk

Large or small, every publishing house receives hundreds of submissions a month, almost all unsolicited. Few agents will bother to send a manuscript to a small house because they feel the work required to secure a contract may not be worth their time, considering the small amount of money they'll earn on the deal. And small press owners tend to stay away from agents, too, believing that they can find the right author without an agent's help. That's why most submissions come to a small company "over the transom"—unsolicited.

In general, all manuscripts submitted to a small house are opened, which makes small houses an appealing option for authors who have never been published. Don't let this "open door policy" make you less careful about crafting your proposal, though. A good proposal that's addressed to the correct editor will make the best impression on the person who ultimately opens the envelope and makes the decision to accept or reject. Also be aware that because small-house editors do plow through all of the submissions they receive, it may take them as long as a year to get to yours, so it pays to be patient.

Things to Consider When Working With a Small House

Many first-time novelists immediately lose interest in smaller houses when they discover that they don't pay large advances or offer high-profile publicity. It is true that a small publisher cannot provide some of the benefits that a larger company can, but it can often offer many other advantages instead.

First and foremost, because a small publisher is willing to take chances on an unknown writer who has potential, it can provide that

Small publishers can offer a variety of benefits to the author, from ready access to staff members, to the generous investment of editorial time, to the ability to add new titles to their lists at the last minute.

all-important opportunity to be published. As an independent publisher grows in prestige in the publishing world, this can launch a long-term writing career. And when a writer makes a name for himself with a small company, it's pretty much guaranteed that the big guys will take notice.

Moreover, instead of giving you that juicy advance, a smaller publisher is more likely to invest that money in editing and shaping your book. What goes to print will have a better shot at success because it will be better developed. Plus, because your book is in the hands of a relatively small staff, you will have more access to the people who are working on it and, therefore, more control over the project.

Scheduling tends to be more flexible, too, in a smaller company. Whereas a major house seldom adds new titles once its list has been announced, a smaller house has the luxury of taking on a new title whenever something great comes its way. This flexibility can be a big plus for authors—especially when a book's quick release date can have an impact in the marketplace.

Very few small firms have their own sales forces. Few offer direct-mail promotions. Most do not have in-house telemarketing departments. And only a handful provide viable publicity. So how do they sell their novels? Some small firms have in-house sales directors, but most rely on outside systems of distribution and sales representatives for their titles. An outside sales force can be a group of independent salespeople who visit accounts on behalf of a company. It could also be an independent book distributor that sells books through its own catalogue and sales representatives. Some small houses utilize the sales force of a larger publisher that carries additional titles. And some rely solely on their own catalogues for sales. As an author, it is important to learn how effective the sales operation is of any small company.

One last word of caution is in order when dealing with smaller publishers. A business this small is a direct reflection of its managers and owners. If these people know what they're doing, they can create excellent and exciting vehicles for books. On the other hand, those who do not understand how to operate a publishing company correctly can be a source of nightmarish embarrassment for their authors. The lesson to be learned? Do your homework, and learn everything you can about a company before you sign a contract.

UNIVERSITY PRESSES

Earlier in the chapter, I said that nonprofit publishers such as university presses rarely publish works of fiction. While this is certainly true, "rarely" is not "never." So before we leave our examination of the business of publishing, it's worth taking a brief look at the world of university presses.

University presses are affiliated with institutions of higher learning, and for many years, their only market was the academic audience. In the last few decades, however, some university presses have become interested in projects of wider appeal. Most readers are familiar with Tom Clancy's *The Hunt for Red October* and John Kennedy Toole's *A Confederacy of Dunces*. Both of these novels were originally published by university presses—*The Hunt for Red October* by the Naval Institute Press, and *A Confederacy of Dunces* by the Louisiana State University Press. Clancy's book went on to mainstream publication, and later became a *New York Times* Best Seller and a major motion picture, while Toole's book garnered the 1981 Pulitzer Prize and won a paperback publication deal. Is it common for new novels to be published by university presses? No. Most academic presses avoid publishing original works of fiction. But if you come across a university press that publishes works in a field explored by your novel, or if you are able to find a champion among the editors of an academic press, there is a chance that your book will be one of those rare exceptions.

OTHER PUBLISHERS

This chapter has discussed traditional commercial publishing houses in some detail, and taken a brief look at university presses. You may also be aware of other types of publishers, such as vanity presses and electronic publishers. Vanity presses have been around for years, but are quite unlike the publishers discussed in this chapters, as they require substantial monetary investments from authors before publishing their books. As for the burgeoning world of e-publishers, they're all different. Some require payment from authors to place their books on a website; others charge to advertise the books online. These companies are discussed in detail in Chapter 9.

John Kennedy Toole, author of *A Confederacy of Dunces*, committed suicide in 1969 after years of struggling to get his book into print. After his death, his mother took up the cause and spent more than a decade promoting his manuscript. When his work reached the desk of Southern writer Walker Percy, Percy championed the story, eventually bringing it to the attention of L.E. Phillabaum, then director of the Louisiana State University Press. Despite the fact that Phillabaum expected the book to lose money, he published it. It took off, and Toole's work has not been out of print since its original publication.

IN SUMMARY

This chapter has covered the world of novel publishing. It has shown you that publishing houses can be large, moderate-sized, or small, and it has discussed the primary strengths and weaknesses of each. Hopefully, you now have a clearer idea of which size house you want to target. If so, you're fully prepared to tackle the question of representation. Should you try to get a literary agent or manager? If your goal is publication with a major publishing house, the answer is almost certainly yes. But if moderate-sized or, especially, smaller houses are your targets, you may decide to do without. In the next chapter, I'll discuss the pros and cons of having a representative on your side, and show you how to approach an agent when you're seeking representation.

PART TWO

*G*ETTING A NOVEL PUBLISHED

A writer has to do more than dream of success if she wants to see her novel in print. She has to get her book to the most appropriate publishers and present it in the best way possible. That's what Part Two is all about. It details the steps you need to take to get your novel into publication.

Every novelist is faced with a choice. Should she sign on with a representative or work directly with a publisher? If you plan to work with a rep, Chapter 4 guides you in finding the literary agent or manager that's right for your book. If you have decided to contact publishers on your own, Chapter 5 takes you step-by-step through the process of locating the most appropriate publishing houses for your project.

Whatever your decision regarding representation, you will need to prepare a winning submission package that presents both you and your novel in the best possible light. Chapter 6 lays it all out for you, from the crafting of a great cover letter and an attention-grabbing synopsis to the presentation of sample chapters. Following this, Chapter 7 offers a proven system for sending your polished package out to target publishing companies. If one or more publishers take an interest in your work, Chapter 8 is the next logical step, as it explains all the standard terms of a publishing contract and provides helpful guidelines for negotiation. Finally, in the event that the responses to your novel aren't favorable, Chapter 9 helps you both identify and solve possible problems, and discusses some great alternatives to traditional publishing.

In the following pages, you will:

■ Decide if you need and want a literary representative and—if so—learn how to find the best one for your novel.

■ Explore the many available market resource books and Internet sites, and use them to create a list of target publishers.

■ Discover how to prepare an effective submission package.

■ Master a system for sending out submissions that will maximize your chance of getting your novel into print.

■ Gain a thorough understanding of publishing contracts.

■ Learn from rejection, develop your writing skills, and explore new and exciting ways of getting your book into print.

It takes work to get a novel published. Part Two will guide your efforts, helping you navigate the maze of the publishing world and successfully reach your goal.

CHAPTER 4

$\mathcal{F}$INDING THE RIGHT REPRESENTATIVE

In Chapter 3, you learned that a manuscript which arrives at a major publishing house directly from the writer—in other words, without representation—has little or no chance of being read, much less seriously considered for publication. The same is sometimes true of medium-sized publishing companies. It's clear, then, that the issue of representation is an important one for novelists.

This chapter examines the question of representation. Do you need a representative, and if so, what kind of rep should you choose? The following pages will answer both of these questions, and will guide you in using available resources to locate the agent who can best serve you and your novel.

WHAT DOES A REPRESENTATIVE DO?

A representative first helps you prepare a professional submission package, including sample chapters, a sell letter, and other necessary components. She then makes the initial contact with a publisher on your behalf, and stands in for you during contract negotiations. Once the deal has been concluded, she follows up to see that the contract is fulfilled, and generally handles your business affairs so that you are free to write.

In sum, a good rep can open doors for you that you don't have the knowledge or connections to open for yourself, can shepherd you and your novel through what's often a tricky and frustrating journey from submission to publication, can increase your odds of getting the best possible contract from your publisher, and can help safeguard you against contractual problems further down the road. Most important for the new novelist, an agent can make the difference between your manuscript becoming a published book or remaining a pile of paper in your desk drawer.

DO YOU NEED A REPRESENTATIVE?

The best representative for a novelist maintains active contacts with publishers who buy fiction, keeps abreast of developments in the industry, and has considerable experience brokering book deals. Because of these day-to-day activities, she is a good judge of what is saleable and what is not. Nevertheless, only rarely do reps make suggestions for reshaping a manuscript. Most accept only those manuscripts that require little or no revision prior to submission to a publisher.

If a large publishing house is your target, you will probably need representation. As already discussed, few of the major houses will consider your novel if it doesn't come to them through a representative. The reasons for this policy are twofold. First, publishing houses fear litigation—specifically, they fear your bringing charges against them for using your story without your authorization. Second, because they are so swamped with submissions—most of which are inappropriate for their company or just plain bad—they need to have some kind of mechanism in place to assure that what's coming to them has passed at least the first few gauntlets of commercial appeal and professionalism.

Do any novels make it into publication with large houses without representation? It does happen. The fact is that publishing houses are made up of individuals, and even within a house that has a strict policy against reading unsolicited manuscripts, individual editors sometimes raid the slush pile—especially in category fiction, where the public's voracious appetite means that editors are always looking for new talent. Keep in mind, though, that this is an exception rather than a rule.

If you're planning to target medium and small houses, on the other hand, a representative may not be necessary. In fact, if you're approaching some of the very small houses, you might be better off without an agent. As explained in Chapter 2, some small companies would rather work with an unagented author, as they often feel that reps create an adversarial relationship between author and publisher. Furthermore, most agents would prefer to avoid small houses because the modest advances offered by these companies don't provide the reps with sufficient compensation for their work.

If you're an aspiring literary novelist, the community into which you're moving is so much smaller than the ones for mainstream and category fiction that, in this case, too, you might be able to get your book into print without representation. The publishers and imprints that court literary works do so out of sheer love for the craft. They're more likely to give a fledgling literary author a shot, whether she's represented or not. Still, when it comes to contract time and beyond, you'll probably want to have a knowledgeable representative on your side.

If at this point you are undecided about your need for a literary agent, it makes sense to check the submission guidelines of the publishers in which you're interested. These guidelines—which are available from the publishers themselves and also appear in certain resource books—will tell you whether each company accepts unagented authors. If most of the houses you're targeting do indeed accept manuscripts that have no representation, you have the option of going it alone. If not, your best course of action is pretty clear: You need to find an agent. Of course, you may not yet know which publishers you want to target. If that's the case, turn to Chapter 5, which will guide you in creating a list of the best companies for you and your book.

Even if you get started all by yourself, if you choose to pursue a career as a novelist, you will eventually find it advantageous to have a representative. The time and trouble a good rep can save you by virtue of her expertise will become more significant as your career develops. The good news is that once you have had a book published—even with a relatively small house—you will find it much easier to locate an agent who wants to work with you. Often, first-time novelists are unable to find an agent who is willing to sign them on. But agents know that it's much easier to "sell" a published author. Moreover, on those rare occasions when a larger publisher shows an interest in an unagented manuscript, the editor will often help the writer find a rep who can assist the author in completing the deal.

WHAT TYPE OF REPRESENTATIVE WOULD BE BEST FOR YOU?

By now, you may have decided that you would like representation, or that you actually *need* representation. Most novelists, you will find, use literary agents, but some use literary managers, and a few turn to lawyers. Which should you choose? Let's look at each of these reps in turn.

If you're uncertain about your need for a literary representative, check the submission guidelines of the publishers in which you're interested. If most of your target companies accept unagented manuscripts, you have the option of handling the submission process on your own.

Literary agents do exactly what we discussed earlier in the chapter. They create submission packages, target appropriate publishers, contact publishers, negotiate contracts, and work with you throughout the publication process and beyond. In rare instances, they also guide you in reshaping a manuscript to make it more marketable.

Literary managers do everything a literary agent does, but besides maintaining contacts in the publishing world, are also involved in the film production industry. In addition to helping you land a book contract and market your novel to Hollywood—both things that a literary agent can do—a literary manager can serve as a producer when your novel's making the journey to film. This can benefit you, because you will have someone present during the production of your project who understands your original vision.

If you decide to hire an attorney to help interpret your contract and negotiate better terms, look for an *intellectual property lawyer*— a lawyer who specializes in literary works and their inherent rights.

As I've already mentioned, some novelists are able to locate an interested publisher without help from an agent. Then, when the contract arrives in the mail, they feel that they need help in interpreting the agreement and securing better terms. At that point, they usually turn to a lawyer for help. Clearly, a lawyer has limitations as a representative. She does not have contacts in the publishing world, and cannot help the writer find a home for future novels. So most lawyers are useful only during contract negotiations. But if you prefer to go it alone up to the point of contract negotiations, a lawyer may be right for you. Just be sure to find one who is knowledgeable about the world of publishing and experienced in the negotiation of book contracts. Contracts in other industries are very different from those in publishing, and the family lawyer who is unfamiliar with the book industry can actually do more harm than good by making unreasonable demands or focusing on the wrong issues. Your best choice is an *intellectual property lawyer*—a lawyer who specializes in literary works and their inherent rights.

At this point, a word should be said about fees. Whereas a lawyer will most likely charge you a one-time fee each time you require her services, an agent or manager will take 10 or 15 percent of everything you make on your novel. She will take her cut off the front of your advance checks, and from every portion of your royalties. And she'll take the same percentage out of every right you sell, from audio books to book club rights to dramatic rights. Just keep in mind that while she'll be taking a bigger slice, she'll probably take it out of a bigger pie. You have to decide whether her expertise is worthwhile.

As mentioned earlier, most novelists choose to work with literary agents. They represent their clients from the submission of a proposal through production, and throughout the life of the book. So unless you intend to locate a publisher on your own—or your ultimate goal is to see your novel being reborn as a feature film, in which case, you might do better with a manager—an agent is what you want. Keep in mind, too, that many literary agents work in tandem with managers to help their clients' projects gain recognition in Hollywood.

Fortunately, it isn't hard to find agents. It's only difficult to get their attention. Let's look how you can both locate and secure a professional who will give your novel the best representation possible.

FINDING REPRESENTATION

You can find a good agent through several different means. It's always a good idea to ask people you know if they can recommend someone. If you have a mentor who's a published writer, you've probably already thought of asking her for a recommendation. But if you don't yet have contacts in the business, you can also find representatives in resource books, online, and through writers' conferences. Let's look at each of these options.

Personal Recommendations and Referrals

Nothing takes the place of a personal recommendation from an established writer, especially if she's willing to make the contact for you. Don't be bashful about approaching writers of your acquaintance and asking them for their advice regarding literary agents. I don't recommend asking them to read your novel—that's a different issue entirely, and usually produces a glazed look and an awkward excuse. But if your friend is willing to recommend you to her agent, or at least provide a referral, that will be a tremendous help.

Note the difference between a *recommendation* and a *referral*. The former implies that your friend has read your work, approves of it, and is willing to endorse it. The latter, only that your friend has provided you with the name of her agent. If your friendship is a close one, and/or you've prevailed on the writer to serve as your mentor, a recommendation to her favorite agent or manager is the best of all possible worlds. But a referral is a strong second best.

Don't hesitate to ask writers of your acquaintance for advice regarding literary representatives. When approaching agents with your proposal, nothing takes the place of a personal recommendation from an established novelist.

If your friend is providing only a referral, you can spring into action immediately and contact the rep as soon as you have put together a submission package. (See Chapter 6 for details on creating an effective package.) If you're fortunate enough to have your writer acquaintance recommend your work, don't send out the package until she has contacted the agent on your behalf, and the agent is expecting your submission.

Resource Books

A number of resource books present lists of literary agents and managers, and offer a variety of information about each agency. Some of these resource books are a bit more helpful than others to the new novelist. Look for the following books in your local library or—in the case of the less-expensive volumes—in your favorite bookstore.

Jeff Herman's Guide to Book Publishers, Editors, & Literary Agents

Published annually, this directory offers a list of over 130 literary agencies and management companies, as well as listings of publishers and editors. For most agencies, you will find the names of specific reps; contact information (address, phone number, e-mail address, etc.); information on the reps' education, career history, and personal interests; the reps' preferences regarding categories; the best way to initiate contact; rejection rates; commission percentages; the number of titles sold per year; and a list of representative titles. In most cases, the guide does not tell you whether the agency works with first-time authors.

In addition to the various listings, *Jeff Herman's Guide* also offers an extensive "Advice for Authors" section, with articles on writing the perfect query letter, dealing with rejection, working with a literary agent, the secrets of ghostwriting and collaborating, and more. Valuable lists of resource books and websites are also included.

Unlike other guides, this one takes a personal approach and uses a conversational tone. Designed for readers outside the industry, it fills you in on a lot of things that other resources ignore—why the rep became an agent, for instance, or what qualities the rep looks for in a "dream client." By providing this type of information in a highly accessible form, Herman enables you to get to know each agent a bit before you decide to make that initial contact.

This book is affordable, so you may want to buy a copy for yourself. If not, look for it in the reference department of your local library. Just be sure to use a recent edition, as this information becomes out-of-date quickly. (For guidance in using this book to research publishing houses, see page 90 of Chapter 5.)

Guide to Literary Agents

Written by Writer's Digest Books—which also produces *Novel & Short Story Writer's Market*, which you'll learn about in Chapter 5—*Guide to Literary Agents* lists over 400 literary agencies, as well as script agents, freelance publicists, and writers' conferences. Information on working with reps is included, as are lists of professional organizations and books and websites of interest.

Although it doesn't provide the personal insights offered in Herman's book, this resource is another "must have" for aspiring novelists, as it will allow you to double-check the information found in other books, as well as to locate additional agencies. Each entry in *Guide to Literary Agents* provides the name of a contact person, as well as other contact information; the agency's website; the year the agency was founded; the percentage of first-time authors; the percentage of novels handled; categories of interest; what the agency wants you to submit; the number of titles sold per year; fees or commissions charged; and useful tips and guidelines. Separate sections are devoted to fee-charging and nonfee-charging agencies.

Guide to Literary Agents is affordable, so you'll probably want to buy a copy. If not, look for an up-to-date edition in your local library. Like the other resource books discussed, it is revised on an annual basis.

Literary Market Place

Also published annually, the *Literary Market Place,* or *LMP,* provides an extensive list of literary agencies, as well as listings of publishers, editors, book trade associations, events, courses, awards, writers' conferences and workshops, and books and magazines for the trade. And that's just in Volume1! Volume 2 of this set offers lists of adver-

Jeff Herman's Guide offers information provided in no other book. For instance, many entries fill you in on an agent's education, hobbies, and personal interests, helping you get to know that person before you approach her.

tising, marketing, and publicity firms; book manufacturing companies; book distributors; services and suppliers; and more. A separate
edition—the *ILMP* (*International Literary Market Place*)—contains the
same information for the foreign market.

Each agency listing in the *LMP* provides contact information; the
agency's website; names of key personnel; the year the agency was
founded; the agency's interests—science fiction, romance, etc.; what
the agency wants you to submit; fees or commissions charged; and
what the agency may provide in terms of critiques. Unfortunately,
the *LMP* does not tell you whether the agency works with first-time
authors. Also note that this resource was designed for use by people
in publishing, and not for writers. You won't find any chatty tips
here—just the facts—and the book is certainly not user-friendly.
However, you will find a wealth of information that you can use to
piece together crucial profiles of both reps and publishers.

Since a copy of the *LMP* costs several hundred dollars, you'll
want to look for it in the reference section of your library. Again, use

WORDS FROM A PRO

Elisabet McHugh, Agent

Does My Agent Have to Be in New York or Los Angeles?

Not anymore. The Internet and email has changed all this. In the olden days virtually all agents were in NY, where they, presumably, sold most of their books while lunching with editors. These days, a surprising number of editors aren't even in NY, although the publishing houses they work for still are. They work from home, wherever that may be.

When I started my agency back in 1994, few editors had email and very few publishers had websites. This soon changed. Not surprisingly, the smaller publishers were the first to make their presence known and get their own websites. Some of the largest publishers took forever to get theirs. I believe Simon & Schuster was the very last one of the major houses to get their site up and running.

In the beginning, many of the editors didn't accept email queries—I think mainly because they weren't comfortable with their computers and all the new technology. Now, everything is done by email. Offers come by email and most contract negotiations are conducted by email. I sell books all the time without ever speaking to the editors on the phone. I have clients all over the US and in eight foreign countries—which, thanks to email, doesn't matter. And I sell a lot of books.

No, your agent doesn't have to be in NY or LA. He can live in the boondocks of Idaho and still find you a publisher.

the most up-to-date edition available. Or, alternatively, use the *Literary Market Place* online database, which is available for trial, weekly, or yearly subscription fees. (For guidance in using the *LMP* to research publishing houses, see page 93 of Chapter 5.)

Online Resources

The Internet provides the fastest of all resources for finding the right representative. At www.authorlink.com, you'll find a large database of literary representatives, with their e-mail addresses and query guidelines, which you can access for a reasonable annual subscription fee. In addition to this fee-based service, numerous sites offer free access to lists of representatives. Try www.writers.net/agents.html, www.author-network.com, and www.aar-online.org for a start.

If you've exhausted these websites and need more names of representatives, simply plug the phrase "literary agents" or "literary managers" into your favorite search engine, and the resulting list of sites will keep you busy for as long as you could possibly wish. Moreover, many of the larger agencies and literary management firms have websites of their own. Visit these before you contact the representatives so that you can arm yourself with the most current and accurate information available.

Take what you find on the Internet with a grain of salt. A number of "independent" sites print unexamined information about companies. Unless it's a website in which you have confidence, such as that of a well-known organization, double-check any information it presents by looking at the agency's website or directly asking questions of the agency. If a company doesn't give you a credible answer, cross it off your list. Actually, all information on representatives that you obtain from any resource should be double-checked before you send out your submission packages, just because addresses, key personnel, and so many other things can change so quickly in the world of publishing. Doing your homework early on will save you both time and money down the road.

Writers' Conferences

Writers' conferences provide a number of benefits, including advice on writing through workshops, discussions, and tutorials; insights

Can't get to a library or bookstore? To find names of representatives quickly and easily, log onto the Internet, where a search for "literary agents" will provide lists of possible candidates. Don't forget to check out the websites of the various agencies, too.

WORDS FROM A PRO

Carla Neggers

Author of *Just Before Sunrise* (Pocket Books)

In my experience, agents respond to vision, focus and professionalism from writers. Vision means you have a clear sense of what you write and where you want to go as a writer. Focus means you don't go flying off in different directions—you work hard to realize your vision. Professionalism means you listen to your agent's advice and respect his or her experience and point of view. A good agent helps you shape—not dictate—your vision and pinpoint your focus in light of the realities of the marketplace, so that your efforts make a difference now. And that'll make you happy as well as your agent.

into the publishing world; encouragement from both peers and professionals; and the simple but all-important reassurance that you are not the only novelist out there who's struggling to get her book into print. Best of all for the novelist seeking representation, many conferences invite three or four literary agents each year, providing writers with access to these professionals. Some conferences even offer attendees opportunities for one-on-one sessions with visiting agents and managers.

Before you attend a writers' conference, make sure that you're prepared to pitch your story. Pitching is simply the act of relating a story for the purpose of selling it to the person who's listening. First, create a *logline*—a single-sentence description of your story with which you can lead off. Then prepare a brief synopsis and a short statement about your credentials. Don't read this information off a card, as it will imply that you don't know your own work well enough to describe it. Instead, know your pitch by heart and practice it aloud, taking care to avoid a monotonous delivery. Your goal is to communicate your enthusiasm to your listener. You'll never get her jazzed unless you are.

Also create and carry with you a one-page "leave-behind" that presents the same information, along with your name, address, and phone number. Then, when you've finished your pitch, hand the sheet to the agent. If she's interested, you'll hear from her.

It's not difficult to find writers' conferences. The *Literary Market Place,* for instance, devotes an entire section to writers' conferences and workshops. And, of course, the Internet can guide you to these gatherings. Simply plug the words "writers conferences" into the search engine of your choice.

MAKING A LIST OF POTENTIAL REPRESENTATIVES

Now that you're familiar with all of the available resources, it's time to sit down with pad and pencil—or a blank computer spreadsheet—

and begin making a list of likely representatives. You'll want to read each listing carefully and make sure of certain basics. For instance, before writing down a candidate's name, you'll want to check that the agent works with new novelists. If not, there's really no point in contacting that rep. If your resource doesn't offer this information, pick up the phone and make a quick call. A thirty-second phone call costs less money and takes less time than writing, sending, and waiting for a response to a query letter that's doomed before it even leaves your printer.

Making Writers' Conferences Work for You

While it can be expensive to attend a writers' conference, many novelists feel that it's well worth the money. Through workshops and tutorials, these meetings can help you improve your writings skills. Just as important, a good writers' conference can give you the opportunity to meet both editors and literary agents. But you will have to put in some work if these conferences are going to work for you. The following suggestions should help you get the most out of the next gathering you attend.

- ☐ Dress in a professional manner to show you mean business. You may do your writing in jeans and a sweatshirt, but at a conference, you want to project a businesslike image.

- ☐ Target the people you want to meet, and learn what you can about them in advance by checking them out in the directories discussed earlier in the chapter, visiting their companies' websites, or performing an Internet search. This will give you a conversational edge if and when you get a chance to chat with them.

- ☐ Don't be shy, but—without being obviously pushy—do your best to meet the people you've targeted. Remember that one great contact is worth the cost of admission.

- ☐ Be prepared to make your pitch, and bring a handout that offers information about yourself and your book. (For more information on the pitch, see page 72.)

- ☐ Base your choice of workshops not only on the subject matter, but also on the instructors. Of course, you want to learn more about the craft of writings. But you also want to take advantage of every opportunity to meet agents and editors who might take an interest in your book.

- ☐ Collect business cards: Networking is what it's all about.

- ☐ Study the bookstore carefully. Not only will the store offer books on writing fiction and getting it published, but it will also be filled with novels of the conference's guest authors. Purchase a novel and get it signed, and you might pick up an ally along the way.

- ☐ Don't sell someone who's already sold: If an agent asks to see your work, back off. Sometimes less is more.

The representative you choose should have an active interest in, and a working knowledge of, your kind of book. Her vision of your future should be in sync with yours, and she should coach you toward being your best.

You'll also want to make sure that the agent is interested in your category of novels. Clearly, you're better off with a rep who has a great deal of interest and professional experience in your category. A rep who has sold dozens of romance novels, for instance, is probably on a first-name basis with the publishers who buy romances. She has the inside scoop on what they're after and how you can capture their attention. The more specialized your category is, the more important it is for your rep to have that specialization as well. Again, if your resource doesn't provide you with this information, call and ask.

Naturally, you'll also want to look at fees and commission percentages and, if available, lists of the publishers with whom the rep works and the number of books she sells annually. Remember that it's not enough to merely compile a list of agents. You want agents that are right for you and your book.

When you've decided that an agent might be a good match, write down as much of the following information as possible:

- The agency's name.

- The agency's address.

- The agency's phone number, fax number, website, and e-mail address.

- The name of the contact person and her title.

- The materials that should be submitted (query with SASE, for instance).

- The way in which the materials should be sent (e-mail, fax, or mail).

Leave a space on each rep's sheet to write in any new information you find, and to record the date and results of any contact you make with her. If any of the above information is not provided by your resource, look for the missing data elsewhere. You can, for instance, check another resource book, visit the agency's website, or—as discussed earlier—make a fast call to the agent's office. Just be sure to do your homework. Most reps take the trouble to make contact and submission information available. So if you send a full manuscript when the agent or manager you're targeting wants only a query, you will not make a good impression.

Once you've finished your research, go back through your list and prioritize it, placing the best candidate first on the list, the second best one in second place, etc. Ideally, your list should have at least thirty names. When you're ready to begin contacting potential representatives, you will have the data you need in a ready-to-use format.

CONCLUSION

This chapter has helped you decide whether you want to seek representation for your novel and, if so, how you can go about finding the best agent or manager possible. If you now have a list of possible reps, you probably want to skip to Chapter 6 and learn how to create an effective query package for submission to your prospects. If however, you have decided to find a publisher on your own, the next chapter will show you how to use some of the same resources we've just discussed—as well as a few additional ones—to home in on the most appropriate publishers for your project.

CHAPTER 5

FINDING THE RIGHT PUBLISHER

As discussed in Chapter 4, many first-time novelists are not able to find a literary agent or manager willing to represent them. Still other novelists actually prefer to work on their own, without outside representation. Whether you are representing yourself out of choice or necessity, this chapter was designed to begin your hands-on efforts to get your book into print. What if you have already secured an agent? In that case, you may still want to read through this chapter, as it will enhance your understanding of the market you hope to enter.

Almost 3,500 publishers are listed in the *Literary Market Place*, the bible of the publishing industry. Of these companies, about four hundred publish some type of fiction. Should you send your book proposal to each of these companies? Of course not! Aside from being prohibitively expensive and almost impossible to keep track of, a mass mailing of this sort would not increase your chances of getting your book into print. As you've learned from earlier chapters, all publishers are different, with different lines of books and different ways of acquiring manuscripts. Many may not have any interest in a book of your type. They may, for instance, produce mysteries and romances, while you have written a Gothic horror novel or a work of science fiction. Just as important, some companies may not be able to help you meet your personal goals. The trick is to zero in on those specific publishers that are right for you and your project—those that publish titles in your category and fit other requirements that are important to you.

This chapter will lay the foundation for selecting the most appropriate publishers for your work. The foundation will be laid in two steps. First, you will have to honestly assess your personal goals in getting your book into print, as well as your expectations regarding publishers. Once you've pinpointed both your motivation and your needs, you'll be able to move on to step two: creating that initial list of publishing houses. At that point, you'll find that an array of books, websites, and other resources are available to help you learn about the many companies that produce novels.

STEP ONE—KNOW WHAT YOU WANT

What's really driving you to get your work published? Do you want fame and fortune? Do you long to make a contribution to the world? Do you just want to see your name in print? All of these goals are valid, but more important, they are keys to choosing the best publishers for your work—firms that can meet your expectations.

What Are Your Personal Goals?

Every novelist in search of getting his work published is driven by different motivations. Status and income are probably the most common, along with wanting to make a contribution or to simply see your name in print. Of course, you may very well have more than one motivation. If that's the case, you'll have to consider which of them is a greater priority for you. Take a closer look at these aspirations to see which best matches your own.

I Want to Get Rich on Royalty Checks

If you're counting this among your goals, at least you're being honest with yourself—if not entirely realistic. Although there are novelists who get huge advances and hefty royalty checks, writers like these—John Grisham and Stephen King, for instance—are few in number, and make this money because they've been able to consistently produce bestsellers for their publishers. As you might remember from earlier chapters, the odds of your getting *any* money from royalty checks—especially for a first-time novel—are not all that great. It is important to realize that the average book published in the

United States sells approximately 5,000 copies, and the average author rarely sees more money than that offered in his advance.

But savvy writers can find good ways to maximize the income generated by their books. First of all, if authors know their markets, write decent books, and hook up with appropriate publishers, their odds of generating good sales will be enhanced. Remember that a book backed by a large publishing house must sell well initially, producing reasonable profits, or it is likely to find itself out of print very quickly. On the other hand, smaller publishers with strong backlists continue selling their titles for many years. This means that your backlisted title may continue generating income while you concentrate on your next writing project.

Your book may be able to generate literally hundreds of money-making opportunities. All you have to do is recognize them. There are some excellent books that can help you determine additional opportunities that are right for you and your novel. John Kremer's *1,001 Ways to Market Your Books* is an excellent and informative choice, as are *Guerrilla Marketing for Writers: 100 Weapons for Selling Your Work* by Jay Conrad Levinson, Rick Frishman, and Michael Larsen; and *Publish to Win: Smart Strategies to Sell More Books* by Jerrold R. Jenkins and Anne Stanton. More information on these books and other titles is found in the Resource List, beginning on page 293.

I Want to Have a Big-Name Publisher on the Spine of My Novel

Some writers believe that unless a high-profile company publishes their book, it doesn't count. For them, image is everything. If this is important to you, it's easy to understand why. Having your book published by a big-name company is prestige for you, and a seal of quality to potential readers. Unfortunately, for most first-time authors, the odds of securing a contract with a big-time publisher are very low. In fact, even writers who have already had a book published will face an uphill battle.

If you follow the Square One System described in this book, your odds of getting picked up by a well-known publisher will certainly improve. But this will not necessarily guarantee marketing success, fame, or fortune. It will only mean that the name of the company will appear somewhere in or on your book.

If you have your eye on a big-name publisher, be aware that most high-profile firms are not receptive to first-time authors. While smaller publishers may seem less "glamorous," they usually offer the best opportunity to new writers.

Remember, there are thousands of publishers out there. Some are famous; others, not so famous. But just because a publishing house doesn't have a familiar-sounding name doesn't mean that it won't do justice to your work. There are many fine medium-sized and small publishers, with more being established all the time.

While I don't want to discourage you from pursuing the prestige associated with big-name companies, I do encourage you to consider the possibility of contacting other houses. As you perform your research, you will come across many good companies that provide solid publishing programs, especially for first-time authors.

I Want to Make a Contribution

Does your novel have something important to say? The best often do. In that case, the most important factor to you may be getting your message out. If so, you'll want to look for publishers who have produced novels with similar themes.

A few publishers specialize in stories that promote a certain idea, like the triumph of ordinary people over extraordinary hardships, the beauty of a certain culture, or lost souls reuniting with God. Once you've located a likely company, read some of its novels to see if your book would be a good fit for that house. Even if a given publisher doesn't specialize in books with that message, if the company has ever published a book with a similar theme that's done well in the past, it might welcome another one.

I Just Want to Be Published

Some novelists simply crave the thrill of seeing their work in print. This is certainly a common and valid reason for wanting to get published. If this is your primary motivation, however, think about all of the time and effort you have put into writing your book. Shouldn't you consider going to a publisher that can do more than simply put your words into book form?

As discussed in Chapter 3, there are many different kinds of publishers out there. If you put forth some basic effort in researching the most appropriate houses for your work, you will not only increase your chances of seeing your book in print, but also give it an opportunity to sell in the appropriate marketplace.

What Do You Expect From a Publisher?

Now that you have given some thought to what you want to personally accomplish by getting your work into print, you can better pursue those publishers that can help you meet your goals. Of course, just because a publishing house produces books in your category, it is not necessarily the best one to represent your work.

I've heard too many horror stories from authors who, after seeing their books come out, discovered that the publisher did not live up to their expectations. To avoid surprises, think about the following criteria when analyzing publishers. A clear and honest assessment will help you put your expectations into proper perspective.

The Publisher's Specialty

No matter how big or how small, every publisher specializes in certain markets. Small and medium-sized companies usually have only one or a few areas of specialization, while large companies often publish in many areas through their various imprints.

It's vital to make sure that the publishers you contact print titles in your subject area. (I will show you how to do this later in the chapter.) This may seem like an obvious consideration, but the fact is that many first-time writers don't realize this, and waste time and money sending proposals to publishers who would never produce a book such as theirs.

The Age of the Company

Is it important for you to work with a firm that has been around for a number of years, or would you consider working with a younger company? Certainly, older companies have a proven track record, enabling you to check on their successes and failures. But newer companies may be hungrier for sales and more willing to take a chance on someone new. Therefore, the age of the company may be worthy of your consideration.

The Size of the Company

It is important to check out the size of any publishing house you may

While it's true that a publisher's catalogue won't allow you to actually handle or leaf through its books, it can tell you a lot about a company. Checking out the book titles and descriptions will give you a good indication of the publisher's area of interest. The catalogue will also reflect the investment the publisher makes in presenting his titles. Is the catalogue attractive and inviting, or dull and unimpressive? A catalogue can tell you reams about a company. (For more information on reviewing catalogues, see the inset "Reading a Catalogue like a Book" on page 144.)

be considering. A quick and easy way to do this, without going into a company's finances, is to find out how many titles the firm turns out each year. The fewer books produced, the smaller the company; the more titles, the larger the company. Will you be satisfied working with a small publisher, or is the status of a large well-known company what you really want? The answer is different for every author. Just keep in mind that, as you learned in Chapter 3, there are advantages and disadvantages to each size house.

The Quality of the Company's Work

To determine the quality of a publisher's books, nothing compares to a hands-on inspection. Visit your local bookstore or library, and examine the books' binding, paper, printing, and cover design. It shouldn't take long to determine if that company's work meets your standards.

Although initially thrilled to land a publishing contract, many writers end up disappointed with the finished product. How important is the overall "look" of the finished book to you? Do you want it to have a glossy, eye-catching cover? Do you have strong feelings about having your book printed on quality paper, with a crisp, professional typeface?

If your novel's appearance matters to you, take a trip to your local bookstore or library and handle some of the books published by the companies you're considering. You can expect the look of your book to be comparable.

While you're considering the quality of the book's paper, cover, etc., you may also want to consider the quality of the writing, which, to a degree, is a reflection of the editors employed by that house. If a book reads well and is free of typographical errors, you can be sure that the editor involved was both talented and conscientious. While a new writer can't choose his editor, a company that is found to consistently produce well-edited books will most likely do a good job on your manuscript, as well.

The Company's Marketing and Sales Forces

Getting your book out there—whether "there" is a bookstore, library, or website—is an important consideration when looking at publishing houses. That's why when you research each potential publisher, it's so important to get answers to certain questions. What kind of marketing and sales program does the company have? Does it have an in-house sales force to market its books, or does it employ the services of outside salespeople? In addition to promoting its books through catalogues, how else does the company sell its titles? Does it have a distributor? What marketplaces does it reach? Are the publisher's books available through Internet bookstores and other online sites? How much money and effort does the firm spend on advertising? How many bestsellers does it have within a marketplace?

To get answers to these important questions, you might begin by questioning the manager of your local bookstore. Your own powers of observation—a search of library and bookstore shelves and of online bookstores, for instance—may offer some answers as well. Finally, you might want to look through back copies of *Publishers Weekly*, which regularly runs articles about the book campaigns of various publishers.

The Company's Publicity Department

Closely related to marketing is publicity, which is the dissemination of information about books, authors, and the publishing company itself via magazines, newspapers, radio, and television outlets, as well as other media. Each publisher has its own methods of promoting its titles. During your research, it's important to ask questions concerning this facet of each company's operation. Does the company have a designated publicity department, or does it hire freelance publicists to work on a project-by-project basis? Is it run by one person or by a group? Does it have well-established connections with the media? Does it promote its books through media tours, book signings, or guest spots on radio or television programs? Are books reviewed in appropriate publications? How heavily does the company rely on its authors to generate their own publicity?

Again, you can start your search for information at your local bookstore, where the manager should be able to tell you which publishers routinely arrange book signings. Also read your local paper and check trade publications such as *Publishers Weekly* to see if the company's books are regularly reviewed. In all cases, writers today have to be willing to publicize their own books. But if the company puts a good deal of effort into publicity, it will certainly lighten your load and enable your book to get sufficient media exposure.

The Company's Offer

What type of advance or royalty payment do you expect to receive for your book? Not all publishing companies, particularly smaller ones, offer their authors advances. Since the money offered in an advance will be deducted from future royalties, this may not be an important issue for you as you search for a publisher. On the other hand, if you need the immediate income an advance provides, you should consider only those publishers that make such offerings. For more detailed information about the different types of offers that publishing companies make, see Chapter 8, "The Deal."

The Location of the Company

Don't be put off by the fact that a publisher is located on the other side of the country. These days, e-mail, faxes, and overnight delivery make it easy to work with any publisher anywhere.

Does the geographical location of a publisher matter to you? If your book has specific relevance to your region, perhaps a local publisher could best handle all aspects of publishing and promotion. In that case, I suggest that you first check out the publishers within the area related to your work. But if you simply want to work with a publisher in your city and state, consider that in this age of e-mail, faxes, and overnight delivery, every publisher—even a company on the other side of the continent—is as close as your keyboard. That's why in most cases, location should not be a factor in the selection of a publisher.

These criteria should be helpful as you search for potential publishers for your work. Add your personal requirements, and you will find yourself on the right path. Please don't skip this important step. Once you know what you want from a publisher, both personally and professionally, you will be ready for the next step—creating that initial list.

STEP TWO—CREATE THE LIST OF PUBLISHERS

You've already figured out why you want to be published and what you expect from a publisher, so now the time has come to roll up your sleeves, grab a notebook and pencil, and lay some important groundwork. How will you begin? You will start by compiling an initial rough list of possible publishers, which, depending on your category and subcategory (if any), can range anywhere from a few dozen to a few hundred names. This first list should include the names of publishers only—nothing else. Once this list has been created, you will take a closer look at the companies to see if they fit your personal criteria. Those that don't will be deleted from the list. Those that do will be placed on a new list along with some basic contact information, including street, e-mail, and website addresses; phone and fax numbers; contact name for submission proposals; and other pertinent information you come across during your search.

Finding Those Publishers

Where should you begin your quest for the best publishers for your work? Inexperienced authors may simply visit their local bookstore or library, jot down the names of the companies that produced the most bestsellers, and send their book proposals directly to them. Good idea? Let's just say that there are much more effective ways for prospective authors to find publishers. When looking for publishers of novels that meet certain criteria, it has been my experience that the most valuable references are the *Novel & Short Story Writer's Market; Jeff Herman's Guide to Book Publishers, Editors, & Literary Agents; Literary Market Place;* and *The International Directory of Little Magazines & Small Presses.*

Novel & Short Story Writer's Market

The best place to start your research is the *Novel & Short Story Writer's Market.* This reference lists hundreds of magazine and book publishers—including United States companies and publishers in Canada and other English-speaking foreign countries—and focuses on the fiction market only, so the weeding out of nonfiction-only publishers has already been done for you. Also included are articles and interviews featuring editors and writers, as well as information on literary agents, contests and awards, and conferences and workshops.

Novel & Short Story Writer's Market is updated annually. While you may be able to find it in the reference section of your library, the relatively small price tag makes it a wise purchase for any novelist—especially since you'll want to dog-ear the pages and highlight entries as your research various publishers.

One of the many benefits of using the *Novel & Short Story Writer's Market* is that it focuses on the fiction market only. This means that you won't have to spend time weeding out nonfiction-only publishers.

This book includes both a *Category Index* and a *General Index*. The one that will be most useful to you is the *Category Index,* in which you'll find nearly all the categories discussed in Chapter 2, including:

Adventure	Mainstream/Contemporary
Erotica	Military/War
Ethnic/Multicultural	Mystery/Suspense
Fantasy	New Age/Mystic/Spiritual
Feminist	Psychic/Supernatural/
Gay	Occult
Historical	Religious/Inspirational
Horror	Romance
Humor/Satire	Science Fiction
Lesbian	Thriller/Espionage
Literary	Western

Under each category, you will first find a list of magazines that publish fiction in that area of interest. This is followed by a list of book publishers.

Each entry in *Novel & Short Story Writer's Market* first provides standard contact information—mailing address, phone and fax numbers, e-mail address, and website, for instance. In addition, the entry includes the name of the editor who manages acquisitions, and usually, the number of books published each year. In some cases, you'll learn the percentage of titles that comes from debut (first-time) authors. Following this, under "Needs," the entry lists the types of books published by that company, and sometimes provides titles of books recently produced in each category. The publisher generally includes his requirements for manuscript submission and may inform you of his response time and state whether simultaneous submissions are acceptable. When included, a "Terms" section specifies royalty percentages and indicates whether advances are provided. Many publishers also offer a useful "Advice" section that clearly defines the kind of books the publisher is looking for and provides useful do's and don'ts. Finally, helpful icons indicate whether the publisher is actively seeking new writers, is seeking both new and established writers, or prefers working with established writers only.

The *Novel & Short Story Writer's Market* makes research easier by providing the names of those editors who manage acquisitions. Other important bits of information offered include the percentage of titles written by first-time authors, the types of books published, and the requirements for manuscript submission.

Using the Novel & Short Story Writer's Market

So now you know what the *Novel & Short Story Writer's Market* has to offer. But how do you use this reference to begin making your list? The best way to explain the process is by using an example. So here's a scenario: You have written a contemporary romance—a category romance that takes place in the present. With a free afternoon ahead, you open your copy of *Novel & Short Story Writer's Market* and turn to the Romance section of the *Category Index*. There, you find well over fifty publishers listed. Your first job is to record the names of all the publishers on that list. To save time, you photocopy the page.

Be sure to do your homework. Taking the time to research those publishers who seem best suited to represent your work will yield benefits as you pursue your dream.

Your next step is to get more information on the companies to see if they might be the right publishers to represent your work. For this, you turn to the A-to-Z directory of publishers. After reading through the information provided, you can remove the names of those firms that are not appropriate, and obtain contact information and other pertinent data for the companies that are.

Begin a new list for those companies you believe might be right for your book—the ones you might choose to receive your submission package. This list should include as much of the following information as possible:

- The company's name.

- The company's address.

- The company's phone number, fax number, and e-mail address.

- The company's website.

- The materials that should be submitted.

- The individual who should be contacted.

- The company's payment policy.

- The company's response time.

The last two items on the above list aren't necessary for contacting the publisher, but you'll want to have this information handy. The first is important because you'll probably want to have an idea of how much money you could earn. The last, because you'll want an idea of when you can expect to hear from the publisher after sending in your proposal.

You will be referring to this list later on when mailing out your submission packages, as explained in Chapters 6 and 7. While it is important to get as much pertinent company information as possible at this point, if certain info is missing, don't sweat it. You'll be filling in holes and verifying information later on, as detailed in Chapter 7.

Okay, let's get back to you and your rough list of publishers. When checking the companies out in the *Novel & Short Story Writer's Market*, you'll find that the information you need is usually fairly easy to locate and understand. In the next few pages, you'll find three sample entries—fictional versions of the types of listings you can expect to find for small, moderate-sized, and large publishers. Let's look at them one by one to see how you can use this reference book to assess each company's suitability.

By looking at the "Needs" section of Lilith's Garden Publishing (see the entry below), you can see that this press does produce contemporary romance novels. With an annual publication of twenty books, this is most likely a small house, which is another good sign, as small publishers are often willing to take a chance on new writers. Moreover, 50 percent of the company's books are by first-time authors! This is encouraging news. However, while your book does include some sexual scenes, you're not sure that it could be said to

NOVEL & SHORT STORY WRITER'S MARKET
SAMPLE ENTRY
SMALL PUBLISHING COMPANY

LILITH'S GARDEN PUBLISHING

6280 Berkshire Drive, Suite D, Los Angeles, CA 95118. (408) 555–2010. Fax: (408) 555–2014. E-mail: lilithg@tac.net. Website: www.lilithg.com. Estab. 2001. **Contact:** Lilith Surman, senior editor. Publishes trade paperbacks. **Published 50% debut authors within the last year.** Averages 20 total titles/year.

Needs Contemporary, erotica, horror, romance, suspense. All must be under romance genre. All must have erotic content or author must be willing to add sexual content during editing.

How to Contact Accepts unsolicited mss. Submit proposal package including 3 sample chapters, synopsis. Responds in 3 months to mss. Accepts simultaneous submissions.

Terms Pays 80–40% royalty on net receipts. Publishes ms 9 months after acceptance. Ms guidelines online.

Advice "Writers should familiarize themselves with our other books and visit our website before submitting material."

have "erotic content," and you're pretty certain that you don't want to add more graphic descriptions of love-making. So you keep Lilith's Garden on your list, but make a note to check out their books to see if yours would be appropriate for submission and—just as important—to decide if you want this company's logo on your book.

When you examine the listing for the mid-sized Little Black Dress Press, you are immediately heartened by the icon indicating that the company is actively seeking new writers. Clearly, this publisher is interested in contemporary romance, too, and you know that they'll like your story's urban setting. You feel that your book has the "hipness" and "energy" for which they're looking, so you keep this publisher on your list, along with all of its contact information.

 LITTLE BLACK DRESS PRESS

2040 W. 12th Ave., Eugene, OR 11732. (503) 555–2939. Fax: (503) 555–3723. E-mail: lblackdress@optagon.com. Website: www.lblackdress.com. Book publisher. Estab. 1999. **Contact:** Elizabeth Thomas, senior editor. "We launched Little Black Dress Press to provide stories that reflect the lifestyles of today's modern women." Publishes trade paperback originals. Averages 60 total titles/year.

Needs Adventure, confession, humor, mainstream/contemporary, multicultural, romance, contemporary women's fiction. Word length: 90,000–110,000 words. Published *Outside the Box,* by Matilda Bruno.

How to Contact Accepts unsolicited mss. Submit 3 sample chapters, synopsis, cover letter. Send SASE. Accepts simultaneous submissions. No electronic submissions.

Terms Pays 8–10% royalty. Offers advance. Ms guidelines online.

Advice "When you think Little Black Dress, think real life in an urban setting, with a touch of humor, hipness, and energy. Think fun and clever, but realistic."

NOVEL & SHORT STORY WRITER'S MARKET **SAMPLE ENTRY** MODERATE-SIZED PUBLISHING COMPANY

Empire Press is a large company that publishes approximately 400 books a year. A quick glance at the sample entry on page 90 shows that Empire produces adult fiction of all types, so it might very well consider a book like yours. However, you note that it's less interested in new authors than many of the other publishers you've considered—although it does publish some first-time authors. You also note that the majority of its fiction is agented. You realize that it's difficult to get a book proposal accepted by a large publishing house, but you've always admired Empire's publica-

NOVEL & SHORT
STORY WRITER'S
MARKET
SAMPLE ENTRY
LARGE
PUBLISHING
COMPANY

  EMPIRE PRESS

Mega Books Inc. 335 Barkley Street, Boston MA 02116–3942. (617) 555–3927. Fax: (617) 555–1014. E-mail: empire@empirepress.com. Website: www.empire press.com. **Contact:** Caleb Claiborne, publisher. Estab. 1941. Publishes hardcover and paperback originals and reprints. **Published some debut authors within the last year.** Averages 400 titles/year. Distributes titles through Baker & Taylor, libraries, Barnes&Noble.com and Amazon.com. Promotes titles through *Library Journal* and *Booklist*.

Needs Confession, ethnic, fantasy, feminist, gay/lesbian, historical, humor, literary, mainstream/contemporary (women's), multicultural, mystery, romance, short story collections, spiritual, general fiction.

How to Contact Query with SASE. Agented fiction 85%. Responds in 1 month to queries; 6 months to mss.

Terms Pays 5–15% royalty. Average advance: $1,000+. Publishes ms 8–12 months after acceptance. Ms guidelines online.

tions. You therefore decide to keep Empire on your list, along with all of its contact information.

By the time you've completed your work with the *Novel & Short Story Writer's Market,* you may still have around fifty publishers to contact, or you may have whittled your list down to half that number. Meanwhile, realize that as valuable a tool as this book is, it's important to check other resources as well. *Jeff Herman's Guide to Book Publishers, Editors, & Literary Agents; Literary Market Place;* and *The International Directory of Little Magazines & Small Presses,* which are discussed below, are excellent choices.

Jeff Herman's Guide to Book Publishers, Editors, & Literary Agents

Published annually, *Jeff Herman's Guide to Book Publishers, Editors, and Literary Agents* includes more than 400 United States and Canadian trade publishers, from major publishing houses to independent presses. The book is definitely affordable, too, so you can easily add it to your home collection of references.

Jeff Herman's Guide is divided into three major sections. The first, *Publishers, Editors, and Literary Agents,* includes separate sections on Publishing Conglomerates; Independent U.S. Presses; University

Presses; Religious, Spiritual, and Inspirational Presses; Canadian Book Publishers; and Literary Agents. The second section, *Advice for Authors*, offers helpful articles on such topics as writing the perfect query letter, how literary agents work, and time management. The third, *Resources for Writers*, includes Useful Websites, Books for Authors, a Glossary, and an Index.

If you read the above paragraph, you may have noticed that this resource doesn't include a separate category index. But if you examine the general index found in the back of the book, you will see that among its entries, it includes the following categories of fiction:

Adventure	Romance
Erotica	Science Fiction
Fantasy	Suspense
Horror	Thrillers
Mainstream Fiction	Westerns
Mystery	Women's Fiction

Included also are some categories—New Age and Humor, for instance—that are likely to include both fiction and nonfiction titles. Some categories have only a handful of entries, while others include a few dozen publishers.

All of the entries in *Jeff Herman's Guide* provide basic contact information—mailing address; phone number; and possibly e-mail address, website, and fax number. Most tell you when and why the company was originally founded, talk about its categories of interest, and provide a sampling of its titles so that you can easily find them online or in your local library and get a better feel for the company and its products. Most also briefly tell you what should be sent in a submission package—a query letter and SASE, for instance—and give you the name or names of the editors to whom the packages should be directed. Yet the occasional entry does provide more extensive information. Some, for instance, mention whether advances are likely to be large or "restrained"; talk about the press's success in advertising, promotion, and subsidiary rights; point to the company's awards, etc. Some entries provide considerable insight into the company's goals, point of view, and special interests. Others offer just a few basic facts.

A number of entries in *Jeff Herman's Guide* provide considerable insight into the publishing company's goals, point of view, and special interests. Use this information to determine the best houses for you and your book.

Using Jeff Herman's Guide

You already have a list of publishers from your work with the *Novel & Short Story Writer's Market*. *Jeff Herman's Guide* will allow you to further expand and refine this list.

As a first step, I suggest seeking out further information about some of the houses that are already on your list. As already mentioned, some of the entries in *Jeff Herman's Guide* provide a good deal of information about the publisher. This may help you decide whether a publisher might be a good fit for you and your book, or should be crossed off your list entirely.

Once you've learned a bit more about the publishers on your existing list, you'll want to locate any publishers that appear in this guide but are not included in *Novel & Short Story Writer's Market*. Again, we'll use the example of the contemporary romance novel. You turn to the general *Index*, and find over two dozen page numbers listed under the Romance category—no publishers' names, just the page numbers on which the entries appear. You jot down the numbers and start flipping to the entries. A fictitious entry, representative of one you might find in *Jeff Herman's Guide*, is printed below.

You're amazed to find the listing for Small City Press—a romance publisher that wasn't mentioned in the resource book you used earlier. Although it is a small company according to the entry, it has been in business for several decades, which is a good sign. Just as impor-

JEFF HERMAN'S GUIDE TO BOOK PUBLISHERS SAMPLE ENTRY

SMALL CITY PRESS
535 West Preston Street, Cobleskill, NY 12043
518-555-7344 fax: 518-555-7345
www.smallcitypress.com e-mail:info@smallcitypress.com
Established in 1980, Small City Press publishes some of the finest novels and stories in the fields of mystery and romance. Included is a growing number of fine contemporary romances. Its list is small but inspired.

Small City Press titles: *33 Chapters About 99 Women* by Figaro Stein; *Rose* by Amy Teller; *Yellow Butterfly* by Robert Miller; *Caught* by Patricia Borman; *Dancing Lights* by Michael McDowell; *Twisted Games* by Laura Bodine; *Sunday Sails* by Alexandra Michaels; *The Camera Obscurer* by Brett Saberhagen.

Small City Press distributes through a commission sales force. Query letters and SASEs should be directed to:
Diane Fitzpatrick, Editor

tant, it not only produces books in your category but also seems open to unagented manuscripts. So you add Small City Press to your list. A subsequent check of the publisher's website will be able to tell you more about Small City's contemporary romance titles.

Literary Market Place

While I suggest the *Literary Market Place*, or *LMP*, as your third stop for information on fiction publishers, this reference book is generally considered to be the bible of the publishing industry. A directory of United States and Canadian book publishers, the *LMP* lists about 3,500 publishers, both large and small. True, the scope and setup of the book makes it a somewhat unwieldy tool for our purposes. Moreover, a lot of the helpful information found in *Novel & Short Story Writer's Market* and *Jeff Herman's Guide*—the name of the person in charge of manuscript acquisition, for instance—is not included in the *LMP*. However, the *LMP* does list many fiction publishers not found in the other two resources. In addition, the *LMP* is a great means of exploring the business side of publishing companies. For instance, it will tell you whether the company in question has its own sales force, and it will show you whether the company sells foreign-language rights.

Because the *LMP* provides a good deal of information about business-related aspects of publishing companies, you'll want to use this resource to learn more about the companies already on your list. And, of course, the *LMP* is sure to guide you to a few publishing houses not found in other reference works.

As you learned in Chapter 4, the *LMP* is available in the reference section of your library. The cost of buying a copy is quite high, as is the cost of using the online version available at www.literarymarket-place.com. Fortunately, your local library's copy should be perfectly adequate for your needs.

Updated yearly, the *LMP* is published in two volumes, and it's Volume 1 that you—an author in search of a publisher—will find most helpful. Volume 1 is divided into subsections. For your needs, you will be focusing on the first section, which lists book publishers. This section begins with an A-to-Z directory of book publishers that are located in the United States. Each entry provides standard contact information—mailing address, phone and fax numbers, e-mail address, and website—as well as the types of books published by the firm. In addition, most but not all listings include the names of key personnel and information such as the year in which the company was founded, the number of books it publishes annually, and its total number of titles in print. Wherever applicable, an entry includes the publishing house's divisions, subsidiaries, and/or imprints, which are also cross-referenced and listed individually.

After the *LMP's* A-to-Z directory come the *Geographic, Type-of-Publication,* and *Subject Indexes,* which include listings of publishers by name only. As you might have guessed, in the *Geographic Index,* companies are listed alphabetically by state, which is useful if you are interested in working with publishers in a specific region. In the *Type-of-Publication Index,* companies are listed according to the type of books they print. Categories in this index include, for instance, children's books; directories and references; professional books; general trade books, including hardcover and paperback; scholarly books; and college textbooks. University and association (foundation) presses are also included in this index.

Finally, the *Subject Index* provides an alphabetical listing of over 100 subject categories. Under each subject heading there's a listing of the publishing houses that produce books in that area. These companies, which are listed by name only, include all types of publishers—trade, professional, college textbook, reference, etc.—but they are not identified as such.

In the *Subject Index,* under "Fiction," you will find a listing of several hundred publishers of fiction, presented in alphabetical order. This list provides company names only, but does not tell you the categories published by each house. However, you will also find separate listings for the following categories:

Erotica	Religion (divided by denomination)
Ethnicity	Romance
Gay and Lesbian	Science Fiction, Fantasy
Humor	Sports
Military Science	Western Fiction
Mysteries	Women's Studies

While some categories, such as Mysteries, are clearly fiction, others, such as Sports, may or may not include novels. If your category is one that potentially embraces both fiction and non-, you will have to do further research on each company listed to see if it might even consider a book of your type.

Using the LMP to Search for Publishers

Because you already have a preliminary list of publishers, you will be using the *LMP* to expand and refine this list.

As a first step, I suggest seeking out more information about those publishing houses already on your list—especially those companies about which you have some doubts. As already mentioned, the *LMP* is a great means of learning about various business-related aspects of a company. Does it sell its books in foreign markets? Does it have foreign offices? Does it use outside distributors? In most cases, the *LMP* will answer these questions, and will also tell you the year in which the company was founded, which is one way to judge whether it is a solid firm with well-established channels of distribution. Any new information provided by the *LMP* may help you decide which publishers might best serve you and your book.

Once you've filled in any information gaps about the companies already on your list, you'll want to locate those publishers that are listed in the *LMP* but were not found in the earlier resources. You'll find that a surprising number of companies are included in one source, but not the other.

Because the *LMP* does not focus solely on fiction, and does not recognize all of the fiction categories found in the books you've already used, you'll have to put more work into your search when using this book. Again, let's use the example of the contemporary romance novel. You flip the *LMP* open to the *Subject Index*, which is found in the first section of the book. Thumbing through the categories, you are happy to find the Romance category, which includes a list of fifty or so publishers. Only the names of the publishers are listed here—no other information is included. As you did when working with the other resource, you photocopy the page.

Your next step is to get more information on the companies to see if they might be the right publishers to represent your work. For this, you turn to the directory of *U.S. Book Publishers*. Just as you did when you gathered information from the previous resources, you read through the information provided on each company of interest. You can then remove the names of those firms that are not appropriate, and obtain contact information and other pertinent data for the companies that are.

While the *Subject Index* of the *LMP* does list certain categories of novels, such as mysteries and Westerns, it omits several others, including adventure books and novels of suspense. If your book's category is not among those listed in the index, you can first examine publishers that produce books in a similar category. For instance, if your book is a tale of suspense, it's a pretty good bet that many publishers who produce mysteries might also be interested in your work. If this strategy is not helpful, try examining the list of publishers in the broad category of fiction, and do further research on each company to see if it has an interest in your genre.

The *LMP* is an excellent resource because it lists so many well-established publishers. It does, however, have its limitations. As it is primarily a directory for use within the publishing industry, the *LMP* offers only basic statistical data and few details. But by understanding how to analyze the entries, you'll be able to determine company size, editorial interests, and a variety of other relevant facts. Then, if any companies seem promising, you can perform further research by visiting the company's website, sending for its catalogue, or perusing the shelves of your local library.

As you look through the directory of book publishers, you soon find that some entries are short while others are long; some provide lots of information while others offer less. In your search, you find the three listings presented below. Typical of *LMP* entries, these fictitious entries—representative of small, moderate-sized, and large publishers—have been marked with explanatory notes that guide you in pulling out the data you need. The samples also show how entry information varies from publisher to publisher. After analyzing all of the companies on your list, you will delete some and keep others.

A simple glance at Regency Romance (see entry below), and you can quickly eliminate it from your rough list of publishers. Why?

LMP SAMPLE ENTRY
SMALL PUBLISHING COMPANY

COMPANY NAME.	**Regency Romance**
THIS IS IMPORTANT CONTACT INFORMATION TO INCLUDE IN YOUR LIST.	3214 Hudson Dr., Phoenix, AZ 85014 *Tel:* 602-555-9900 *Toll Free Tel:* 800-555-5990 *Fax:* 602-555-9909
THE ONLY EDITOR IN THIS ENTRY IS MEGGIE ABRAMS. ADD HER NAME TO YOUR LIST. LATER ON, YOU WILL BE VERIFYING THAT SHE IS THE PROPER CONTACT.	*Key Personnel* Pres: Allan McConnach Ed: Meggie Abrams
AGE OF COMPANY.	Founded: 1975
SUBJECTS PUBLISHED.	Historical romance novels.
ASSIGNED INTERNATIONAL STANDARD BOOK NUMBER(S).	ISBN Prefix (es): 0-914846; 1-885590
ANNUAL NUMBER OF TITLES SHOWS THE SIZE OF THE COMPANY. FIFTEEN TITLES MEANS THAT THIS IS LIKELY A SMALL FIRM.	Number of titles published annually: 15 Print Total titles: 100 Print

LMP SAMPLE ENTRY
MODERATE-SIZED PUBLISHING COMPANY

COMPANY NAME.	**Pleasant Valley Publishing**
THIS SHOWS THAT THE COMPANY IS A DIVISION OF A LARGER COMPANY.	Division of Pleasant Valley Communications Inc

THIS IS IMPORTANT CONTACT INFORMATION TO INCLUDE IN YOUR LIST.	35 Frederick St, Fairfield, CT 06430
	Mailing Address:
	  35 Frederick St, Fairfield, CT 06430
	Tel: 203-555-3200 *Toll Free Tel:* 800-555-9868
	  Fax: 203-555-3220
	E-mail: info@pleasantv.com
	Web Site: www.pleasantv.com

THESE ARE NAMES OF COMPANY EXECUTIVES FOR YOUR LIST. YOU WANT THE NAME OF THE ACQUISITIONS EDITOR, BUT NONE IS GIVEN. SELECT THE NEXT LIKELY PERSON. IN THIS CASE, IT WOULD BE THE EDITORIAL ADMINISTRATOR— JESS CARA. LATER ON, YOU WILL BE VERIFYING THAT SHE IS THE PROPER CONTACT.	*Key Personnel* Pres: James F. Ciara Exec VP & Prodn Mgr: Deb Wilson Publisher and CEO: Gabriella Abrams Busn Mgr: Stephen Love Edit Administrator: Jess Cara Publicity: Elle D'Amico Intl & Subs Rts: Jason James
AGE OF COMPANY.	Founded: 1983
SUBJECTS PUBLISHED.	Adult contemporary romance, historical romance.
ASSIGNED INTERNATIONAL STANDARD BOOK NUMBER(S).	ISBN Prefix(es): 0-945257; 0-866224
ANNUAL NUMBER OF TITLES SHOWS THE SIZE OF THE COMPANY. FIFTY TITLES MEANS THAT THIS IS LIKELY A MODERATE-SIZED FIRM.	Number of titles published annually: 50 Print Total Titles: 400 Print
HAS ITS OWN SALES OPERATION AND OUTSIDE DISTRIBUTORS.	*Sales Office(s):* 35 Frederick St, Fairfield, CT 06430 *Distributed by:* The Chrysler Group
SELLS ENGLISH-LANGUAGE BOOKS IN FOREIGN MARKETS.	*Foreign Rep(s):* Merrimac Int'l
SELLS FOREIGN-LANGUAGE RIGHTS.	*Foreign Rights:* Fred Claus Agency
THIS INFORMATION IS NOT NECESSARY FOR YOUR INITIAL LIST.	*Advertising Agency:* Pleasant Valley Services, 35 Frederick St, Fairfield, CT 06430, Chauncey Masters, Tel:203-555-3500 Fax: 203-555-3520 E-mail: mmasters@aol.com *Billing Address:* 35 Frederick St, Fairfield, CT 06430 *Shipping Address:* Merrimac Dist Ctr, 400 Avery Dr, Edison, NJ 08837 *Warehouse:* Merrimac Dist Ctr, 400 Avery Dr, Edison, NJ 08837 *Distribution Center:* Merrimac Dist Ctr, 400 Avery Dr, Edison, NJ 08837

While this company does specialize in romance novels, it produces only historical romances—not contemporary stories like yours. Sending this company a submission package would be a waste of time, effort, and money.

By looking at the subject areas, you can see that Pleasant Valley Publishing does, in fact, produce contemporary romances. Perfect. This doesn't guarantee that it will take on your project, but it might. With an annual publication of fifty titles, this is most likely a moderate-sized house. That's another good sign for you as a prospective author. Moderate-sized houses sometimes are willing to take on new unagented authors. Final assessment? Pleasant Valley will go on your list, but you will later check the publisher's writer's guidelines to see if the company will, in fact, look at a manuscript submitted directly by an author.

Douglas International Publishing Group is a large company, publishing nearly 900 books a year. (See page 99.) A look at its subject areas shows that it does produce books on romance. Unfortunately, the listing does not specify the types of romance in which Douglas International has an interest. You're already aware of how difficult it is to get a book proposal accepted by a large publishing house, but you want to give it a try anyway. You decide to keep Douglas International on your list, along with all of its contact information. But before spending the time and effort to send this company your book proposal, it would again be wise for you to dig a little deeper. The company's writer's guidelines will let you know whether it will consider books submitted by unagented authors, and might tell you if it's interested in contemporary romances.

The International Directory of Little Magazines & Small Presses

If you're searching for a smaller publishing house, *The International Directory of Little Magazines & Small Presses* is an excellent resource. Starting out as a tiny compilation of presses in the 1960s, this directory grew to include over 4,000 small presses and journals. Most entries offer information such as payment rates, proposal requirements, and recent publications. Subject and regional indexes are also included. Copies of this affordable resource are available in libraries and bookstores.

When using the *LMP*, the long, impressive listings of big-name publishing companies are certain to attract your attention. Be sure to give equal consideration to mid-sized and small publishers.

LMP SAMPLE ENTRY
LARGE PUBLISHING COMPANY

COMPANY NAME.	**Douglas International Publishing Group**
THIS IS IMPORTANT CONTACT INFORMATION TO INCLUDE IN YOUR LIST.	2500 Third Ave, Suite 1500, New York, NY 10017 *Tel:* 212-555-2300 *Toll Free Tel:* 800-555-2704 *Fax:* 212-555-2333 *E-mail:* douglasint@tac.net *Web Site:* www.douglasint.com
PLACE BOTH THE VP/SENIOR EDITOR, DARLA STUART, AND THE MANAGING EDITOR, INGRID JUDD, ON YOUR LIST, ALONG WITH THEIR TITLES. YOU WILL BE VERIFYING THE PROPER CONTACT LATER ON.	*Key Personnel* Pres & Pub: Albert Will Douglas, Jr. Exec VP & Assoc Publisher: Tuesday Cirrus Exec VP & Gen Mgr Rts & Perms: Erica Rubin VP & Sr Ed: Darla Stuart Man Ed: Ingrid Judd Prod Coord: Roslyn Carl Mktg Asst: Joshua Shan Wilson
AGE OF COMPANY.	Founded: 1980
SUBJECTS PUBLISHED.	Mass market paperback originals: romance, fiction, westerns, general nonfiction, hardcover reprints, fiction & nonfiction, trade paperbacks.
ASSIGNED INTERNATIONAL STANDARD BOOK NUMBER(S).	ISBN Prefix (es): 0-4372; 0-7760
ANNUAL NUMBER OF TITLES SHOWS THE SIZE OF THE COMPANY. WITH 885 TITLES, THIS FIRM IS A LARGE ONE.	Number of titles published annually: 885 Print Total Titles: 21,000 Print
INDICATES THAT COMPANY DISTRIBUTES BOOKS FOR OTHER PUBLISHERS.	*Distributor for:* Christiana Press; Green Gables Ltd., Old World News Group; Rhodes Books
COMPANY SELLS BOOKS IN FOREIGN MARKETS.	*Foreign Rep (s):* Ashland Southampton (UK); Brightwaters Associates (Europe); Canadian Winston Group (Canada, UK); General Books (Europe, UK); Taylor & Taylor (Asia, South America, UK); Unity Press (Japan, Korea)
THIS INFORMATION IS NOT NECESSARY FOR YOUR INITIAL LIST.	*Advertising Agency:* Williams Roth Advertising *Shipping Address:* Douglas International Publishing Group, 77 Kingston Rd, Providence, RI 02904

Using the International Directory of Little Magazines & Small Presses to Search for Publishers

To use *Little Magazines & Small Presses,* you turn to the *Subject Index* and look under Romance. There, you find nearly three dozen publishers. You photocopy the page for easy reference.

The Importance of Writer's Guidelines

If editors could give writers just one piece of advice, it would be this: Find out what the publisher wants before submitting your proposal so that you don't waste everybody's time by sending the wrong materials to the wrong company. Fortunately, most publishers make this a fairly simple task. In their writer's guidelines, publishers tell you exactly what genres and categories they will and won't accept, as well as how they want to be contacted and what they want to receive. And they mean what they say. In fact, some guidelines bluntly state that they will return any proposal—unread—if it does not conform with the company's guidelines.

Writer's guidelines are not difficult to understand, and usually run only a page or two in length. The guidelines provided by a publisher of Westerns, for instance, might look something like this:

Author Specifications and Guidelines

Our Westerns are wholesome adult fiction, and are suitable for family reading. No graphic or pre-marital sex is allowed in our novels. Similarly, vivid descriptions of violence should be avoided, along with the overuse of alcohol. Suitable—but believable—euphemisms for profane words must be used.

All Westerns are historical fiction, and it is vital that they be carefully researched and highly accurate regarding background. But while it is important to use some "westernisms" in dialogue for authenticity, the overuse of dialect is to be avoided, as it slows the pace of the narrative.

The hero must be a strong moral-minded individual with good values. He is not overeager to use his fists or his gun, but is very competent with them when necessary.

The complete Western should be a minimum of 40,000 words in length and a maximum of 60,000 words, or about 160 to 210 pages. If the manuscript is truly exceptional, we will accept a slightly greater length.

We do accept unagented material and multiple submissions, but you must indicate that the proposal is a multiple submission. Please include a query letter, a two- to three-page (no longer) synopsis of the entire manuscript, and the first three chapters. (Please be sure to send the first three rather than random chapters.) All submissions must be typed and double-spaced. If we think that your

Your next stop is the A-to-Z publishers directory, where you can read about the companies you found in the index. Although the information in the entries may vary, for the most part, each listing provides the following: the name of the acquisitions editor, company address, year the company was founded, subject areas published, average print run, number of titles published in the previous year and number expected in the coming year, average copy price, discount schedules, average number of pages per book, average page novel might be suitable, we will contact you and request the entire manuscript. In case the manuscript is not suited to our needs, please include a stamped, self-addressed envelope for the return of your material. Be sure that the return envelope is large enough to hold your manuscript, and that you have attached sufficient postage for the weight of your manuscript. If these requirements are not met, your submission will be recycled.

Please allow at least three months for your manuscript to be considered. If you haven't heard from us after three months, and wish to make sure that your manuscript arrived, rather than calling, please write a letter stating the date of the submission and the title of the manuscript.

Please send submissions to XYZ Publishers, 222 Main Street, USA. Attention: Finley Haddock. We do not accept e-mail submissions.

Is that straightforward enough for you? This information is relatively easy to come by, too. The standard practice, used for years, is for you to obtain the company's name and mailing address from the resources listed elsewhere in this chapter. You then send the infamous SASE (self-addressed, stamped envelope) along with a note requesting the publisher's writer's guidelines. Within a few weeks, you should receive the requested information.

With the creation of the Internet, alternative means of acquiring the guidelines have become available, of course. By performing an Internet search for the publisher of your choice, you should be able to find the company's website. Once there, click on the writer's guidelines—and save yourself an SASE, as well as several weeks' waiting time. Another option is to use the handy searchable database of more than 1,500 writer's guidelines found at www.writersdigest.com. To use this database, though, you have to pay a small yearly fee to subscribe to WritersMarket.com.

Finally, although publishers certainly don't encourage phone calls, you can always try giving the company a call to request the guidelines. Usually, the person who answers the phone will jot down your address or other contact information and either mail, fax, or e-mail the guidelines to you. Be aware, though, that some publishers will not respond to requests made over the phone.

Remember that it's up to you, the author, to obtain and follow each publisher's guidelines to the letter. If you think that someone's requirements are too restrictive or difficult to follow, just cross that publishing house off your list. But when the time comes to mail out your proposals, you'll know that you have all the information necessary to send out the best submission packages possible to the most appropriate publishers for your work.

---

size, printing method, reporting time on manuscripts, payment or royalty arrangements, rights purchased and/or copyright arrangements, number of titles listed in the current edition of the *Small Press Record of Books in Print,* and membership in publishing organizations. A sample entry is provided on page 102.

Although the company discussed in the sample entry is very limited in the number of titles it publishes, you feel that your book may be of interest to the publisher. But you would like to learn more about the company first. So you place Shadow Box Press on your list, along with all of the contact information you've pulled out of *Little Magazines & Small Presses.* You plan to check the company's website to learn more about its books.

> **Shadow Box Press.** Mike Mansel, Senior Editor, PO Box 2445, Los Angeles, CA 90056, 213-555-6776; fax: 213-555-6777. 1983. Fiction, nonfiction, poetry. "We are currently looking for mainstream fiction and historic and contemporary romance. Submit 3 sample chapters, outline/synopsis." Avg press run 3–5M. Pub'd 4 titles 2005, expects 5 titles 2006. 21 titles listed in the *Small Press Record of Books in Print.* Avg. price, paper: $10. Discounts: for resale: 20–40% off; distributor discounts negotiable. 250pp; 6x9. Reporting time: due to volume, we cannot reply unless interested. Publishes 10% of manuscripts submitted. Payment: royalty only. Copyrights for authors. Memberships: Publishers Marketing Association (PMA).

Other Methods of Finding Publishers

While the *Novel & Short Story Writer's Market* and the other reference books just discussed are excellent resources for writers, they are not the only means of finding publishers that might be interested in your book. Depending on your goals, on the nature of your project, and on the time and money you are willing to commit to getting your book into print, a number of other resources should be considered.

Small and Independent Publisher Resources

You've already learned one place to find listings of small publishers: *The International Directory of Little Magazines & Small Presses.* There are, however, at least two other resources that can help you locate smaller houses.

The Resource Directory of Independent Publishers and Publishing Industry Vendors is printed annually by SPAN—the Small Publishers Association of North America. A nonprofit professional trade organization, SPAN was founded in 1996 to serve independent presses, self-publishers, and authors. The association's membership of 1,300 includes both one-book self-publishers and firms that have more than 1,000 books in print. All of these members are listed in the directory, with each entry supplying the publisher's address, phone number, fax number, e-mail address, website, areas of interest, and number of titles in print. Included are well over 250 publishers of fiction. A *Genre Cross-Reference Index* is included—along with a number of other indexes—allowing you to quickly home in on publishers with an interest in fiction. Publishers of romances and other categories of fiction are not identified, however. To find out if a company might be interested in a manuscript that falls within a specific category, further research is necessary.

The *Independent Publishers Resource Directory* is printed annually by the Publishers Marketing Association, or PMA. A nonprofit trade association founded in 1983, the PMA has a membership of over 3,800 independent publishers. All members are listed in the directory, with each entry supplying the publisher's address, phone number, and, when available, fax number, website, and e-mail address. Many entries also state the number of titles in print, the names of the company's distributors, and the year in which the company was founded. To discover which of these companies publishes fiction, you'll want to first turn to the *Genre Listing by Company* index, found in the back of the book. There, under Fiction, you'll find approximately 400 companies listed. Note that to learn which specific fiction categories are published by each company, you'll have to do further research. This information is not included in the directory.

As you flip through the SPAN and PMA resource directories, you'll want to keep in mind that some of the members listed are self-publishers, meaning that they publish only their own books. These will have to be weeded out through phone calls or other research. But if you've exhausted other resources and are open to working with a small to mid-sized company, you should by all means use these directories to find presses that may be listed nowhere else. Keep in mind, too, that self-publishers are sometimes willing to produce other authors' books.

Both the SPAN and the PMA directories are available only to group members. For a yearly membership fee, you'll receive the directory free of charge, as well as many money-saving benefits.

International Resources

With the exception of the *Novel & Short Story Writer's Market*, which lists publishers in several English-speaking countries around the

Resource directories printed by the trade associations SPAN and the PMA can guide you to hundreds of small independent publishers, some of which may be listed nowhere else.

world, most of the resources discussed earlier in the chapter offer information only about firms located in the United States and Canada. If you're interested in further exploring publishing houses in other English-speaking countries, you might start with Jeff Herman's *Writer's International Guide to Book Editors, Publishers, and Literary Agents.* Here, you'll learn of both publishers and literary agents in the United Kingdom, Canada, Australia, Hong Kong, Singapore, South Africa, and more. Herman also provides marketing suggestions and insightful essays from top literary professionals.

Yet another book you might want to check out is the *Writers' and Artists' Yearbook.* Like Herman's book, this resource homes in on English-speaking countries by including listings of publishers in the United States, the United Kingdom, Ireland, Australia, and New Zealand.

If you're looking for a comprehensive listing of worldwide publishers in both English- and non-English-speaking countries, you have two options. First, *Publishers' International ISBN Directory* lists well over 600,000 publishers in over 200 countries, regions, and territories, along with up-to-date contact information. Then there's the international version of the *LMP*—the *International Literary Market Place (ILMP).* The *ILMP* guides you to people, companies, and resources in more than 180 countries worldwide, including 10,500 publishers and literary agents.

Both Jeff Herman's international guide and the *Writers' and Artists' Yearbook* are affordably priced, so you may decide to add one or both books to your home library. The *Publishers' International ISBN Directory* and *ILMP* are quite expensive, though, so you'll want to look for them in the reference section of a large public library.

The Internet not only can provide lists of publishers in specific areas of interest, but also can help you research companies you already have in mind. A few clicks of your mouse will allow you to scan online catalogues, review writer's guidelines, and find information on distributors.

Online Resources

The Internet provides a wide variety of means to learn about new publishers, or to research publishers you may already have in mind. For starters, you may want to check out online bookstores such as Amazon.com or Barnesandnoble.com and browse subject areas of interest. Very likely, you will be able to get a listing of books in your category, along with their publishers.

Yet another directory of publishers is offered by Yahoo at www.yahoo.com/business_and_economy/shopping_and_services/

publishers. Click on "Literary Small Press," "Mystery," "Romance," or "Fiction, Fantasy, and Horror," and you'll find an alphabetical listing of links to publishers' websites.

Finally, don't forget that these days, most publishers have websites that include online catalogues, as well as guidelines for writers and information on their distributors. Don't hesitate to visit these websites as a means of judging if your manuscript would be a good fit for the company—and if the company would be a good fit for you.

Trade Shows

Trade shows—events designed to enable publishers, booksellers, writers, and other people in the industry to network, sell rights, and conduct business—provide another excellent means of gathering information about publishing houses. If possible, try to visit BookExpo America (BEA), which is the annual trade show for the publishing industry. Just about everyone associated with the book industry is in attendance, giving you the opportunity to meet representatives of many different publishing houses, and get a good sense of the types of books their companies produce.

Many editors and marketing representatives attend the BEA, and you might be able to steal a few moments of their time and discuss your project. Keep in mind that while your first instinct may be to approach a company's editors at one of these shows, you might be better able to gauge a firm's interest by speaking with someone from the marketing department. In many companies, an editor can't acquire a book unless the project has the support of marketing. (Remember that in Chapter 3, you learned that the number-one question most publishing houses ask before acquiring a book is, "Will it sell enough copies to make money for the company?") And if the people whom you contact don't feel that your project fits into their publishing program, they will often steer you toward a more appropriate house.

Another important trade show is BookExpo Canada—Canada's largest book industry event. A showcase of books in all formats and of all types, this convention is attended by thousands of industry professionals, and usually enjoys a good turnout of small publishers.

If you are interested in writing books for the Christian market, consider attending the annual convention held by the Christian Book-

Attending trade shows is a great way to collect information on various publishing houses. You can find announcements for upcoming shows in the *Literary Market Place* and *Publishers Weekly*. Another option is to check the Trade Show News Network at www.tsnn.com.

sellers Association, or CBA. This event attracts thousands of bookstore owners and buyers, literary agents, and media. Part of its expressed purpose is to enable publishers to meet new authors and artists.

Every year, Volume 1 of the *Literary Market Place* provides a comprehensive listing of worldwide industry-related conventions, conferences, and trade shows. *Publishers Weekly*, the book industry's trade magazine, also announces upcoming shows. You can also check out the Trade Show News Network (www.tsnn.com)—an Internet site that provides a listing of shows for a number of different industries, including book publishing. Finally, if you are interested in attending the BEA, you can visit www.bookexpoamerica.com for full information.

If you plan to attend a show, be aware that there will be an admission fee, which varies from show to show. Don't hesitate to call ahead and inquire about the cost.

MOVING ON

At this point, you have created a customized list of potential publishers for your work. Not only should these companies be the ones best suited to handle your book's category, they should also meet your personal criteria. If you've taken the time to develop this list carefully, it will increase your odds of getting published.

But you'll have to put that list aside for a short time. Your next step will be to prepare that all-important submission package, which you will be sending to the publishers you have selected.

CHAPTER 6

*P*REPARING THE PACKAGE

First impressions do count in the world of business and beyond. This is certainly true in the case of your submission package. This package will be your representative in the world of publishing, and the only means by which an editor or agent can initially judge you and your book, and decide if she wants to consider your proposal. That's why the components of your package must be treated with the same care you'd give to your appearance before a job interview.

This chapter was designed to guide you through the writing of a winning submission package—a package that will invite an editor's or rep's attention, give her the best possible impression of both you and your book, and provide her with all the information she needs to make an initial decision about your project. You'll learn exactly what should be included and, just as important, you'll discover what should never be included. Writing a winning package is probably easier than you think. As I explained in previous chapters, editors and reps know exactly what they want to see, and make that information available to you through their writer's guidelines. The problem has always been that most authors don't take the time to find out what that is. This chapter will let you in on industry secrets, and help you put together a proposal that will get the best possible results.

THE GOAL OF THE SUBMISSION PACKAGE

Before you begin work on your submission package, it's important to

Don't send an editor or
agent *one word* until you've
read the company's writer's
guidelines. (See page 100.)
Everything recommended
in this chapter should be
subordinated to the
specific guidelines provided
by your target publisher
or representative, as well
as your own creativity and
commonsense. If a publisher
or rep wants just a query
letter, send that, enclosing
no other material. If she
also wants a synopsis and
sample chapters, be sure
to enclose those materials
along with your letter.

understand the goal of the material you'll be writing. This goal is really threefold.

First, a winning package is designed to *get read*. That may sound ridiculously obvious, but many submissions are so poorly written, so confusing, or so overwhelming in size that they are destined to be "killed"—rejected, in other words—before the editor or agent even finishes reading the first paragraph. Above all, a winning package is so inviting that it maximizes the odds that the recipient will actually read enough of it to learn the merits of the project.

Second, a winning package shows the editor or rep that this is a viable project—a project with potential. It does this by demonstrating that the book fits into an existing category, and that it provides readers with a product in which they are interested. An important point to remember is that you're not only selling the idea of the book, but also selling yourself as the author. Reading your package, the editor or rep will have a chance to assess your writing ability. A good package can convince her that this book is a winner.

Finally, the winning package evokes a *positive response* from the editor or rep. If she is interested, she will probably send a form letter, asking for further material. If she is sufficiently excited, he might take the time to write a personal letter, send an e-mail, or even make a phone call to discuss the project.

THE COMPONENTS OF THE SUBMISSION PACKAGE

I've said it before and I'll say it again: You must obtain the writer's guidelines for every publisher and rep on your list, and then send in only what the guidelines request—no more, no less. If you already have the writer's guidelines from several companies in hand, or if you've simply read some of the "How to Contact" sections in *Novel & Short Story Writer's Market*, you know that the majority of representatives and publishers want to receive three items—a cover letter, a synopsis, and a portion of the manuscript. Some, however, want only one or two of these items—just a query letter, for instance.

If this seems confusing, relax. The remainder of this chapter will tell you how to craft each of these components. Throughout, you'll find samples that will keep you on track. By paying careful attention to each detail of your submission package, you'll maximize the chance that your package will prompt a positive response.

The Cover or Query Letter

Is there a difference between a query letter and a cover letter? Technically, yes. A cover letter is the letter that accompanies your full manuscript or a portion of your manuscript. A query letter is the letter you send to a publisher or agent to ask—to query—if she's interested in seeing the manuscript. Traditionally, publishers of fiction most often want cover letters, because they also want to receive at least several chapters of the completed work. But increasingly, to cut down on the amount of mail they have to plow through, some fiction editors are requesting query letters rather than full submission packages.

Although cover and query letters clearly have to be somewhat different, they have more in common than you might expect. In both cases, this letter is the first part of the package that the recipient sees, so it serves as an introduction to you and your book. It is therefore the most crucial portion of your submission package. Unfortunately, most of these letters miss some or all of the elements needed to capture the editor's or agent's interest and motivate her to read the remainder of the package. In other cases, the necessary information is there, but is presented so poorly that it casts serious doubts on the author's ability to write. Very few people will pursue a project further when the letter is poorly written.

In the real world of novel publishing, there's no set formula for the body of a query letter. The Square One letter I'm about to describe in detail shouldn't be regarded as *prescriptive*, but rather as *descriptive* of the information that an editor or agent needs and wants. With a few minor changes, this model letter can serve as either a cover or a query letter, as both of these letters must make the same major points about you and your book. It can also be easily revised to suit either a prospective publisher or an agent.

As you read the following material, keep in mind that the query is a business letter by nature, with the same structure as any other business letter. Sample a little of the letter's content, though, and you'll discover that it has an artistic gene somewhere in its family tree. This is because it also serves as a showcase for your writing talent. In writing your query, you'll have to call upon the same wellspring of creativity you drew upon when you wrote your novel. You'll be making decisions about the best ways to capture your reader's attention, pique her curiosity, and whet her appetite.

Because it serves as an introduction to you and your novel, the cover letter is the most crucial portion of the submission package. Make sure you've crafted a strong letter before moving on to the next component of your package.

Finally, remember that your letter should be kept to one page in length—single-spaced, concise, and professional. Editors and agents alike are looking for clear, thoroughly focused stories that are expressed with economy. The more succinctly you express your idea, the greater its chance of getting sold. Editors and reps are old hands at reading query letters. They can sniff out an unfocused idea or an illogical plot within seconds. A brief but compelling letter will suggest that your novel is a tightly crafted gem.

The following discussions were designed to guide you through the letter-writing process. You'll find a sample cover letter for a romance novel on page 111; a sample cover letter for a mystery on page 112; and a sample query letter for a mainstream novel on page 114.

The Salutation and First Paragraph

Every letter, of course, should begin with a salutation, such as "Dear Mr. Smith." Never send out a boilerplate letter that begins "Dear Editor," "Dear Agent," "Dear Sir or Madam," or "To Whom It May Concern." By placing the correct name at the top of the letter and, more importantly, on the outside of the package, you'll not only make sure that the package gets to the right person, but also demonstrate that you've done your homework. (More about getting the correct name in Chapter 7.) If the person's name makes her gender unclear—if the name is Robin Smith, for instance—use both the first and last names in the salutation: "Dear Robin Smith." And *never* refer to the recipient by her first name. Assuming familiarity isn't going to win you any points.

Below the salutation comes the first paragraph, which is the paragraph that introduces your novel. Ideally, this paragraph should be a hook that immediately captures your reader's attention and makes her want to know more. Remember that this letter is a selling tool—an ad campaign for your novel. The quicker you can interest your reader, the more successful your letter will be.

You can capture the editor's or rep's attention in a number of ways. One way is to make your lead sentence an intriguing statement about your book or its subject. (See the first sentence of the letter on page 111.) Or, if you prefer, open with a sampling of your protagonist's dialogue—particularly if it reveals something of the character's motivation or conflict.

25 Preston Street
Atlanta, Georgia 10013
Phone: (704) 555–9779
E-mail: rkline@hotmail.com

(Current Date)

Bonnie Blume, Executive Editor
Remarkable Romance Press
25 Preston Street
New York, NY 10013

Dear Ms. Blume:

How would you feel if you found yourself falling in love with a handsome Southern plantation owner whose family background is impeccable, but whose mysterious nighttime activities are the talk of the town? Everyone wonders if he is fully behind the Confederate Cause, or if his loyalties lie elsewhere. Now imagine that you are not a Southerner, but a Yankee, born and bred—and a spy for your uncle, a general in the Union Army. Thus begins *Heat at Four Oaks,* a completed 55,000-word historical romance set in Civil War Georgia. This story is targeted for Remarkable Romance's Southern Desire line. Enclosed, please find a synopsis and three sample chapters.

Eighteen-year-old Marianne Belgrave is dispatched by her Boston family both to nurse her ailing cousin Caitlan back to health and to gather information about the growing turmoil in the South. She plans to complete both missions quickly and return to the life she loves. What Marianne doesn't expect is the start of a war that will tear her heart in two as she tries to reconcile the political ideals of her New England upbringing with her concern for her cousin, who will soon need Marianne's help to keep her plantation afloat. Complicating this is Henry Morgan, a neighboring plantation owner who provokes first anger and then interest in Marianne, and whose puzzling actions cause everyone to question his loyalty to the South.

Romance is my first love. I've been reading romance novels since I was a teenager and have been writing for ten years. I am a member of both Romance Writers of America and Georgia Historical Romance Writers. Along with my husband, I am also a member of the Atlanta Civil War Reenactment Group.

If you're interested in *Heat at Four Oaks*, I will gladly send you the complete manuscript. A self-addressed, stamped envelope has been included for your convenience, or you may contact me at the above phone number. Please note that this is a simultaneous submission. Thank you for your time and consideration.

Sincerely,

Rachel Kline

Rachel Kline

18 Washington Drive
Boonsboro, MD 21998
Phone: (301) 555–7887
Email: JerAm@hotmail.com

(Current Date)

Terry Holyfield, Managing Editor
Twilight Books, Inc.
74480 Albom Avenue
New York, NY 10011

Dear Terry Holyfield:

It was a pleasure to meet you at this year's Mystery-Maker's Book Fair in Saint Louis. Per our brief conversation and your website's instructions, please find enclosed a three-page synopsis and the first three chapters of my mystery novel, *Stealing Back Shiraz*. This completed 113,000-word manuscript won Burdette College's Mystery Writer's Award last year, and an excerpt was recently featured in my hometown paper, *The Boonsboro Messenger*.

The day he was foaled, Shiraz was already worth two million, and he has never lost a race. He's the pride and joy—and sole companion—of his reclusive billionaire owner Percy Gentry. But now he has vanished. *Stealing Back Shiraz,* a mystery set in such exotic locales as Casablanca, Mombasa, Bombay, Kyoto, and Perth, traces Percy Gentry's desperate struggle to track down the thieves who have stolen this remarkable stallion. As Percy emerges from seclusion to search for his beloved companion's abductors, Shiraz reappears at the last second to run the most prestigious races across the globe before being whisked away again. The thieves taunt Percy by mailing him strands of the animal's cherry-colored mane, along with clues to the date of Shiraz's next race. Percy, who hasn't left the confines of his mansion in more than eight years, finds himself drawn farther and farther away from everything safe and familiar.

I'm an avid mystery reader and charter member of the Mid-Atlantic Mystery Writers' Guild. To create *Stealing Back Shiraz,* I combined my master's degree in creative writing from Penn State with my lifelong love of horses. I was raised on a farm that bred Standardbreds for the racetrack. During my first career as a sports journalist, I traveled to each of the locales featured in the book.

I will send you the full manuscript upon your request. I've included a self-addressed, stamped envelope for the return of my materials. Please feel free to contact me by phone or email with any questions, and please note that this is a simultaneous submission. Thank you for taking the time to consider my novel.

Cordially,

Jerome Adashek

Jerome Adashek

Another way to start the letter is to refer to a recent accomplishment of the letter's recipient. For instance, if through attendance at writers' conferences or through research you've discovered that the editor has a new imprint or was recently promoted, you could refer to that: "Congratulations for being named senior editor of XYZ Books." Perhaps you've read a quote by her or learned that five of the books for which she served as editor recently won awards. It's a smart move to show that you follow the industry. But be genuine in all you write, and be sure to get your information correct!

Finally, if you have a personal connection to the editor or rep, or if a writer friend has suggested that you send your manuscript to her, lead off with that information. But do this only if you have a genuine contact with this person; don't name-drop. Also avoid waxing poetic about how much your writer friend loved your work. Editors and agents like to make up their own minds.

If your first line was a statement about the book, use the next line or two to expand on it. If your first line was about the editor or agent, use the next line or two to introduce the book. In the last or second-to-last line of the paragraph, be sure to state the title of the novel, to define its category, to indicate the approximate length of the book either in double-spaced pages or an approximate word count, and to assure the letter's recipient that the manuscript has been completed. If you've found that your book would be perfect for that publishing house because it fits beautifully into a specific line of books or imprint, this would be a good place to mention it. Such a statement will not only show that you've done your homework, but will also help the editor better identify the book's audience. Finally, when writing a cover letter, also mention what you have enclosed—three sample chapters, for instance.

If a writer friend has recommended you to her agent or editor, be sure to mention this fact in the first line of your letter: "Vincent Dressman told me he spoke to you about my novel, Drive Down to Dixie, which he was good enough to read. Enclosed, per your writer's guidelines, are the first three chapters along with a five-page synopsis."

The Second Paragraph

Now that you've introduced your novel, use the second paragraph to tell your reader more about the book. Although there's no set formula for this paragraph, you'll want to make sure to include the most important details: main characters, setting, theme, and action. The type of novel you've written will dictate which of these elements you spend the most time explaining. A serious literary work should focus more on style; a mainstream novel, more on character; a mystery or suspense story, on story line.

233 Silvertone Blvd. Suite 52
Nashville, TN 37203
Ph: (615) 555–3147
email: JSTL@earthlink.net

(Current Date)

Dr. Ken Atchity
A. E. I.
9601 Wilshire Blvd., #1202
Beverly Hills, CA 90210

Dear Dr. Atchity:

Can a man ever truly outrun his past? In my new mainstream novel, *Deadly Green,* Wall Street powerhouse Griffin Scott has rebuilt himself as a philanthropist and runaway financial success, and has managed to put his past behind him. But on the eve of his greatest financial coup, cuttingly sarcastic CEO Aemon Parrish, who helped send Scott to prison years ago, arrives and threatens to expose him as a liar, a thief—and a murderer. *Deadly Green,* which takes readers on a thrill ride into the coveted, often dark, upper echelons of the financial world, is inspired by Victor Hugo's classic *Les Miserables,* and is 340 double-spaced pages complete. I believe it is a perfect match for your company, as I understand you are actively seeking modern retellings of classic stories.

Protagonist Griffin Scott is that rare individual who can cut billion-dollar deals without breaking a sweat, yet will still take the time to make the office cleaning lady feel like a princess. But his nemesis, Aemon Parrish, sees his grace and generosity as a sham. He remembers a different Griffin Scott, one who would kill to achieve success. And Parrish doesn't believe murderers are entitled to second chances.

I'm a teacher of literature and creative writing at Harding Community College and a lifelong devotee of the written word. My short fiction has been published in various anthologies since 1993.

I would greatly appreciate your consideration of my novel for representation. Upon request, I will send a synopsis and the first three chapters, per the guidelines on your website. I've enclosed an SASE for your reply, or you may contact me by email or phone. Please note that this is a simultaneous submission. I look forward to hearing from you and thank you in advance for your time.

Sincerely,

Jeremy Katz

Jeremy Katz

When creating this second paragraph, describe your book in an enticing manner using a spare amount of words, like the copy found on book jackets and in catalogues. In fact, if written well, this copy will be used by the publisher in all promotional materials. Many writers find that these words follow them throughout the life of their book!

The Third Paragraph

The goal of this paragraph is to establish your credibility as the author of your book. Here, you can mention a variety of credits, from educational background to work background to hobbies. The key is to mention only relevant experience. For instance, if you've written a novel set in the Civil War and you're a member of a Civil War reenactment group, that would be relevant information. If your educational degree is relevant to the book—if you majored in biology and your main character is a microbiologist—that, too would be important to mention. You also want to mention any writer's groups of which you're a member, or anything else that would show that you're a serious writer who has studied her craft.

But it's equally important to avoid citing irrelevant accomplishments, however important they may be to you. For instance, if you have written a Civil War novel, there would be no reason to mention that you're the commodore of a local yacht club. On the other hand, if you have written a mystery in which a character is killed in a boating accident, your boating experience *would* be pertinent.

Of course, the best credential of all is having had something published, be it a book, a short story, a magazine article, or even an article in a local paper. (Don't bother mentioning the publication of a poem, though, as it won't be viewed in the same light as prose.) If any of your writings have been in print, certainly mention this within the third paragraph, as it will show that your work has already been approved by another editor and that you are capable of completing a project. But keep in mind that while it's a plus to be published, it's not a prerequisite to having a winning submission package.

What if you don't have any experience relevant to your project? In that case, skip this part of the letter. Whatever you do, don't tell the agent or editor about your *lack* of experience. Don't say that this

Make sure that your cover or query letter reflects your best writing. Since words are your medium, think of the letter as a free sample of your merchandise, and use it to showcase your talent as well as your professionalism. Be businesslike and concise, but don't be afraid to show a little personality.

If none of your work has yet been published, consider submitting a short story to a regional or local newspaper. If your submission is accepted, it will establish you as a published author.

is the first novel you've ever written, and don't mention how many people have already turned your novel down. In other words, don't tell the reader what she doesn't need to know.

The Fourth Paragraph and Closing

The purpose of this concluding paragraph is to wrap up the letter and close on a cordial note. Express your appreciation for the editor's or agent's consideration and, if appropriate, offer to send any addi-

Multiple Submissions

Because of the high rate of proposal rejections in the publishing industry, I highly recommend that you send out *multiple submissions*—in other words, that you submit your proposal to several publishers at the same time. These days, most editors recognize that it can take months to get back to a writer about his proposal, making it unfair to expect a writer to wait indefinitely for a response, only to have to go through the same process again and again, in most cases. At that rate, it could take years for the average writer to learn the fate of his proposal!

Some publishers still do demand exclusive submissions, and that's a consideration you'll have to keep in mind if a company's guidelines include a statement such as, "Will not consider simultaneous submissions." But even though most companies don't like the idea of multiple submissions because of the possibility that more than one house may end up competing for the same contract, they do understand that most authors send their proposal to more than one editor.

Although multiple submissions are now acceptable, it's important to inform each editor that you are sending your submission out to other companies. It is *not* good etiquette to imply

through omission that the editor is the only one receiving the proposal. If and when you have the good fortune to be offered a deal by two publishers, and you have to reject one in order to accept the other, you won't be making any friends at that second publishing house. This may not seem important to you now, as the idea of being offered a book contract is so exciting. But remember that people in publishing tend to move from company to company, so the rejected editor may become part of your life down the road. And editors do talk to other editors from other houses. It will be to your advantage to keep all of your business relationships positive and on the up-and-up.

As discussed on page 117, the best course of action is to include a sentence at the end of your cover or query letter, stating that you are sending out multiple submissions. In addition to keeping your business dealings honest, this statement will show your savvy about the submissions process. Just as important, it will add a sense of urgency by giving the impression that another editor at another house may snap up your manuscript at any moment. So by including this one simple statement, you will do quite a bit to increase the impact of your letter.

tional materials. Also indicate that you've enclosed an SASE or self-addressed, stamped envelope, and if you desire, specifically mention other ways in which you can be reached. If you plan to send out multiple submissions, this is the section of the letter in which to indicate that you'll be doing so. Finally, add your complimentary close—"Cordially," "Yours Truly," or "Sincerely" are all appropriate—and type your name, placing your handwritten signature above it.

Contact Information

Although it may be hard to believe, many authors fail to provide the information the editor or agent needs to contact them by mail, phone, fax, or e-mail. If the submission package is truly outstanding, the recipient may try to track down the missing information—but don't count on it! The very fact that this information was omitted is a red flag to the editor or rep, who may then have serious doubts about the writer's commonsense and organizational abilities.

Years ago, an author simply typed her address at the top of the letter. But now that so many methods of contact are available, a number of options are considered acceptable. I strongly suggest that you invest in business stationery that shows your name, address, phone number, and fax number and e-mail address, if any. If you do not choose to make this investment, but you own a decent printer, consider creating your own letterhead. If neither of these options seem right, simply place your contact information at the top of the letter; place it beneath your typed name at the end of the letter; or work it into the last paragraph of the letter.

The Synopsis

A synopsis is a concise description of your novel's story line—a summary of your book. In their writer's guidelines, most representatives and publishers ask that a synopsis be included in the submission package. If by chance a synopsis is not mentioned in the guidelines, call to find out if the company prefers one. Most of the time, it does.

Write your synopsis as a narrative in third person, present tense, using brief, attention-grabbing paragraphs. Emphasize the way the protagonist drives the plot, focusing on the *action*. Use the same style of writing you used in your book. If your book is serious and literary,

It may seem unnecessary to offer advice on the correct way to end a letter. But it's amazing how often publishers receive letters with bizarre endings or no signatures. So this is a helpful reminder to wrap up your winning letter with a winning close.

Although you don't want your synopsis to recount every event of your story, you also don't want to tease the editor by stating that if she wants to learn what happens, she'll have to read your manuscript. Editors don't like guessing games or surprises. Be sure to clearly indicate where the plot is going, but paint the picture using broad strokes— not minute detail.

your synopsis should be, too. If your book is chatty and humorous, make sure that your synopsis is, as well. Don't include any dialogue, and don't present the story in outline form.

Be sure to introduce your main characters in the synopsis, weaving the descriptions of the characters into the narrative. Don't list the characters separately. Do, however, make sure that their conflicts and motivations are clearly defined, and that they are to some degree sympathetic. Avoid any unnecessary adjectives and adverbs, though. The editor or agent doesn't care about eye or hair color—unless that information is essential to the plot.

Don't feel that you have to include every character or every scene, plot twist, or subplot in your synopsis. You should, in fact, avoid side plots and minor characters, and focus instead on the pivotal scenes, making sure to resolve all important conflicts and answer all questions. This means that you can't omit the ending and tell the editor or rep that she'll have to read the manuscript to learn what happens. Remember that the recipient of your package is reading the book for professional reasons, not just for pleasure. She has to be assured that you know how to successfully end your book. So if a character has a secret identity or the action of the book turns out to be the imaginings of a lunatic, this should be made clear in the synopsis. Don't hold anything back.

Advice varies regarding the length of the ideal synopsis. Some authors aim for three pithy pages, and some produce twenty. My first advice to you is to check the writer's guidelines to see if a length is specified. If it is, give the company exactly what it wants. If the synopsis length isn't specified, use the size of the finished book to help determine the size of your synopsis. For instance, if your novel is 50,000 to 70,000 words in length, aim for a five- to seven-page synopsis. If your novel is longer, you may need as many as ten pages for an adequate summary. One rule of thumb is to include one synopsis page for every 10,000 manuscript words.

Although the rules for formatting your synopsis are not set in stone, you will want the document to have a neat and professional appearance, and to provide all of the information needed by the editor or rep. With this goal in mind, type your synopsis single-spaced, using the same typeface used for your cover letter—preferably, Courier New. (See pages 119 to 126 for a sample synopsis.) After leaving a 1-inch top margin, type the book title, centered, in all uppercase

THIS ISLAND, MADE OF BONE

a novel by

Stuart Connelly

On the dark, glassy Chesapeake, a sleek police boat drifts across the Bay in the moonlight. On deck, eighty-year-old Virginia border patrolman Nils Buchannan lies in a pool of blood, a steel gaffing hook sticking out of his head. The boat jerks, stops, heels around, hits something. Nils' eyes peel open one last time to see a rusty sign jabbing up out of the water that reads "MD-VA Line." With the still propeller of his outboard tangled in crabpot lines, he's held like a fly in a web on the north side of the marker, and his last thought flutters by: dying isn't so bad, it's dying in Maryland that's hard for a Virginian to take.

On a damp night a year later, twenty-five year-old Bridget Marquez heads up the steps of the death house in Annapolis, Maryland. She's approached by Dr. Claire Miller, her former psychologist, who pleads with her that it's not too late, the wrong man is being put to death for Nils' murder and Bridget is the only one who can stop it.

But Bridget ignores Claire and heads inside to take her place in the witness chamber. There, awaiting the execution, she relives the events of the past year.

It begins in Richmond, when Bridget's boss asks her to represent the Virginia Department of Interior during Maryland's investigation of Nils' murder. This is not who Bridget is; she's frail, eager to please and be liked, she's not in law enforcement but in wildlife conservation. Yet her boss feels she's perfect for this job: to go to enemy territory—Maryland—where Nils' body, technically, was found and act as a kind of auditor to make sure there isn't a witch hunt or the local police aren't protecting one of their own and

Connelly/This Island, Made of Bone   2

railroading some outsider. The old man had been an employee of Bridget's division, hired to make sure the Maryland crabbers (or watermen, as they refer to themselves) stayed on their side of the state line and left the Virginia crabs to the Virginia watermen. But steady Baltimore pollution has kept the crabs migrating south over the years, to the point where the watermen of Smith Island, only miles from the MD-VA line, had to cross the border just to scrape together a living. This is really a border war being fought, Nils was a casualty of war. Someone patrolling Virginia against poachers was a threat to their very livelihood and conversely, the death of that man was a cause for celebration. Since Nils was found in Maryland waters, the case was being handled by Maryland police, and since a Marylander was likely responsible, there is some question whether justice will be served. Bridget has been picked to level the playing field on Smith Island.

Intimidated, Bridget first refuses the assignment, but Claire tells her it would be healthy to go into a situation where there's no possibility of being liked, of getting someone else to take over, of running away. The therapist's opinion carries a lot of weight, and Bridget finally decides to go.

She flies to Crisfield, the mainland Maryland town closest to Smith Island. Sheriff Laird, the man in charge of the Buchannan investigation, is not happy to meet Bridget, and as he briefs her, he tries to align her thinking with his own, towards the man he thinks is responsible, the documentary director who's been filming on the island since the beginning of crab season. When Bridget suggests the possibility that a local might be responsible, Sheriff Laird is offended. It's hard for him to imagine there are bigger stakes than a documentary film that is lucky enough to stumble onto a grisly murder, the first since the island was settled in the 1600s. But he claims if one of his people did it, he'll bring them to justice. Bridget wonders.

She arrives in Tylerton, the most isolated of Smith Island's three towns—a restaurant and a four-room motel—and the one where Nils Buchannan

Connelly/This Island, Made of Bone   3

was last seen alive. She's told the motel's been taken over by the director and his film crew and the owner suggests a particular waterman, very unsuccessful, could use the money if she wants to rent a room. Bridget finds Clay Tyler, a young man who has taken over his father's crabbing business after his parents' death, is happy to rent his old bedroom to her. Surprisingly, she finds an ally in him. Like Bridget, he feels as if he's an outsider in Tylerton, ineffective on the water and blamed by his neighbors for his parents' death. Clay makes a crab feast for dinner and afterwards, begins to suspect Bridget is bulimic.

The next day, Bridget kicks off her shadow investigation of Buchannan's death at the motel, interviews film director Victor DeBassey, who recounts his story about filming Nils at Tylerton's one restaurant, Kitchings, where the patrolman often ate with and talked among the locals, and later, stumbling across Nils' body by the dock with his crew, capturing the sight on film just as the boat started drifting away. Bridget wants to see the film, and DeBassey tells her the sheriff has already asked. Someone is bringing a videotape dub of the reel the next day.

That someone, Greg Rabidoux (a shifty city boy who's been hired to shuttle fresh, exposed and developed film between a Baltimore processing lab and Tylerton) sits with a film tech working—on DeBassey's orders—to create a video dub of the reel shot of Nils on the boat that cuts off the first few crucial minutes of the reel.

In the schoolhouse the next day, Bridget, the sheriff, DeBassey and his crew watch the video dub of the reel of film. It's eerily silent (Reg Verlaine, the sound man, explains the sound is recorded on a separate machine and the tape wasn't there at the lab to sync up), but what the film shows is truly horrific. The jittering movie lights awkwardly illuminate the inky Bay night, pausing here and there to catch sight of Nils, the blood pouring out of his head like it's sprung a leak.

Connelly/This Island, Made of Bone   4

Sickened, Bridget demands to know why the film crew didn't try to moor
the boat before it got too far from the dock. DeBassey retreats with the old
photojournalist line—our job is to document, not interfere. But Bridget
suspects that the real reason they didn't stop the boat was much more self-
serving: it's just so damn cinematic this way, drifting out of reach of the
lights, moving beyond. So Oscar-worthy.

Afterward, Bridget tells Sheriff Laird she thinks they're at a dead end,
but he's all fired up to go after DeBassey for murder. Bridget asks for more
time to be sure.

Meanwhile, Verlaine has invited DeBassey into his motel room. They share
a few lines of cocaine and then Verlaine blackmails the director, threatening
to turn over the audio tape that matches the reel Rabidoux tampered with,
where in those opening moments, DeBassey can be heard talking about making it
look good for the film, where he can be heard saying "Gimme that hook," heard
burying the gaffing pole into Nils' temple with a wet thud. Verlaine demands
to get co-director credit on the Smith Island film, or he'll turn the tape
over to the media and destroy DeBassey's reputation as a documentary
filmmaker. Reluctantly, DeBassey agrees.

In Baltimore, Rabidoux gets a call from DeBassey, who tells him Verlaine
has become a problem. Rabidoux suggests the next batch of cocaine he's been
supplying could be laced with something deadly. He knows just the thing.

That night, over too many drinks, Bridget starts feeling close to Clay.
He talks about his guilt over his parents' death—he shirked his crabbing
duties one day when he was a teenager, so his father took his mother out to
bring in the catch. A bad storm came up and his parents drowned.

It's hard for Bridget to imagine the shallow Bay water like that the next
morning, when Clay takes her out and they spend a golden morning crabbing. He
tells her the Chesapeake is deceptively deep. She learns how he knows which
traps are his—each of the cork buoys in a waterman's operation are painted

the same in a different pattern than everyone else's—and she doesn't even mind the poaching in Virginia. She's falling in love.

But that night they fight, Clay turning his observations into simple truths about her she can't bear to hear. Bridget packs her things and spends the night in the schoolhouse. Unable to sleep, she goes back to the video of Nils. She keeps replaying it until she has a breakthrough: there's no leader on the tape, it simply starts with the camera moving over Nils' body.

The next day she gets a hold of DeBassey's original film reels and dubs. She confirms her suspicion: all the other tapes, even the one from earlier the night of the murder, they all open with black leader, film that was threaded through the camera and exposed to light. Something was cut off the front of the film during the dubbing, but it's still on the reel.

Bridget finds a 16mm projector in the school and watches the film. After the leader, it starts with Nils lying in the boat, apparently asleep. Then suddenly, DeBassey comes into the frame. He slips on a pair of work gloves, grabs the gaffing hook and brings it down with both hands into Nils' skull. Then they untie the boat and the film catches up to the footage she's already seen.

Back at the motel, Rabidoux arrives with cocaine he's laced with a poison that he says will make it seem as if Verlaine dies of a heart attack. DeBassey has just pocketed the coke when Bridget and Laird storm in. Laird takes the cocaine they find on him, but they're accusing him of murder. When he realizes he has no room to maneuver, DeBassey admits that he stabbed Nils with the gaffing hook. But, he insists, only after they found him dead. Just for cinematic value, something to shoot. A guy who dies of something inside just doesn't play on film.

Bridget is disbelieving, but DeBassey brings them over to "co-director" Verlaine's room. Verlaine plays them the sound reel, which he turned on running even before the camera started shooting. On the tape, it's clear

Connelly/This Island, Made of Bone　　　　　　　　　　　　　　　　6

they stumbled across a dead body and took actions just for the film. Bridget
is disgusted, but the story definitely seems to hold together.

Now the question has become, if Nils didn't die getting his skull
pierced, how did he die?

The Crisfield M.E. reexamines Nils and learns he was poisoned by a
chemical compound known to create symptoms of heart failure, given to him
maybe an hour before he died. That gets Bridget thinking about the night at
Kitchings. She threads up the reel shot at Kitchings earlier that night, just
before Nils was found. She watches as the whole town, now knocked off for the
day, enjoys a meal with their sworn enemy. Nils Buchannan walks among them,
shows, in his own way, that he's one of them. People chat with Nils, someone
even buys him a beer . . . Clay does. She stops the film, rewinds, and just
there in the background, slightly blurry, she watches Clay pouring a vial
of white powder into Nils' beer bottle.

While Clay is on the water, Bridget turns his house upside down looking
for the poison. She fights against a rising stomachache as she hunts, a fever
blistering inside her. Just as she's virtually incapacitated, she finds the
small vial. Has he poisoned her too? She tries to throw up but Clay comes
home, stopping her. She accuses him of killing Nils as she falls, unable to
move, overcome with a debilitating pain, at his mercy.

Clay carries Bridget down to the dock as a storm swells in the Bay, and
it's unclear whether he's trying to get her to the hospital, or simply get rid
of her.

When Bridget wakes up, she's on the deck of the skipjack, staring up at
Clay, who's holding the vial of poison he's taken from her pocket. Clay
confesses, explaining that he poisoned Nils in an effort to give the Smith
Islanders a chance at a full harvest. Bridget thinks he's trying to get rid of
her, too, but he insists he fully expected to get caught. He wants to be a kind

of martyr for his island, which he'd let down so consistently. But that, of course, doesn't explain why Bridget is dying.

The wind comes up suddenly, tossing the skipjack around, the same type of wild storm that took Clay's parents down ten years earlier. Clay tries to fight the elements, but he can't do it alone. They need each other now.

Barely able to move, Bridget nevertheless gets to work, a steely will Claire had always sensed beneath her mild exterior coming into sharp focus. She overcomes the crippling pain to help Clay with the sails. Together, they keep the skipjack from tearing itself apart and going under but Bridget looses consciousness again just as the storm fades.

When she comes to, she finds herself in post-op. She wasn't poisoned; she'd been crippled by appendicitis, brought on by a swallowed piece of jagged crab shell lodged in her appendix. Against medical advice, she leaves the hospital and heads back to the island.

Meanwhile, Laird leans on Rabidoux, trying to link the poison to DeBassey. Rabidoux tells the sheriff about DeBassey's plans for Reg Verlaine, but then says where he got the idea for the poison—it's the same stuff Clay Tyler asked him to get a few weeks earlier. Bridget and Laird both know the situation: Clay, one of Smith Island's own, murdered Nils.

But something's been nagging at Bridget's subconscious. Among the information Laird provided her that first day is a photograph, taken the morning the boat was found. She'd been particularly haunted by the fact that Nils' eyes are wide open in the picture. She gets it out, then cues up the film DeBassey shot the night before. In the movie frame, the old man's eyes are closed. In the photo, they're open. Proof positive that Nils was still alive when the hook went into him.

It seems the outsider is responsible after all. Never mind that Clay poisoned him and Nils was just about to die. Laird considers this

Connelly/This Island, Made of Bone   8

technicality long and hard, then tells Rabidoux to forget any services he
provided Clay Tyler. For a rat like Rabidoux, it's not a problem.

Laird arrests DeBassey while his crew films. On the boat back to
Crisfield with DeBassey in custody, Bridget says she feels seasick, but when
she moves to the stern out of the sheriff's sight, she digs through the
confiscated film. She pulls one reel out, holds up to the moonlight: that
night at Kitchings, when Clay bought Nils a beer. Slowly she feeds the film
overboard, patient as a waterman lowering the crabpots down. Into the black
water, the film sinks out of sight, lost forever.

Back inside the death house a year later, Bridget watches. She is
sitting next to Reg Verlaine, who has taken over DeBassey's film and is
completely in the dark about how close he came to death himself.

As they give DeBassey the lethal injection and the moment for Bridget to
interfere slips past, she thinks, technically he was the one that killed
Nils. It's all just technicalities—Nils getting stuck in Maryland was a
technicality; the line itself, separating two states drawn on water, is a
technicality. Life is a technicality, Clay keeping his, DeBassey giving his
up. So what, you play them to your advantage or you don't ever win.

Outside, Claire watches from her car as Clay approaches her former
patient. Clay has become a kind of folk hero on Smith Island, his tarnished
reputation made whole. Everyone in Tylerton knows he murdered Nils Buchannan,
and everyone knows he did it for them. Turns out he's one of them after all.

He begs her to marry him, but she refuses. Bridget is cast anew,
confident and trusting in herself. But no longer the kind, sweet girl she
was. Now strong, manipulative, a grown-up, she disappears alone into the
foggy night reborn.

letters. Then space down twice, and type "a novel by." Space down once, and type your name. Begin the text two spaces below your name, flush left. On each succeeding page, place your last name, followed by a comma or a slash (/) and key words from the title of your novel, in the upper left-hand corner. Place the page number in the upper right-hand corner of the page.

Remember that the purpose of the synopsis is to sell your story to the representative or editor. The synopsis should therefore hook the reader with the first paragraph, and, by the end, should have her eager to read your sample chapters or request the full manuscript. If the synopsis reads like a textbook, it won't do its job.

The Sample Chapters

Most publishing companies, literary agencies, and management companies request that several sample chapters be included in the submission package. If so, make sure to provide exactly what the company asks for in its writer's guidelines. If the guidelines request the first three chapters, send only Chapters One, Two, and Three. If they specify the first 100 pages, send as close to that number as possible, making sure to submit complete chapters even if that means including 115 pages. If the size of the sample isn't specified, send the relatively standard first three chapters.

Be aware that when you're writing nonfiction, it sometimes makes sense to send nonsequential chapters. For instance, you might send Chapters Four, Ten, and Twelve if you felt that they did the best job of showcasing your book. But this won't fly with fiction. Give your reader the first three chapters rather than random chapters. The first three are the most crucial chapters. And if the editor or agent isn't hooked within the first twenty-five pages, you've probably lost her, anyway.

At this point, it should go without saying that your sample chapters should be flawless in terms of spelling and grammar, and should display your abilities as a writer. Review the chapters several times to check for errors, and refer to the *Chicago Manual of Style* (see the Resource List) to answer questions of punctuation, abbreviation, numerical style, and so forth. Don't fool yourself into thinking that your concept is so unique that an editor or rep will jump at the chance to buy your work even if the text doesn't read as well as it

When sending sample chapters, be sure to follow each publisher's writer's guidelines to the letter and submit exactly what's been requested.

On the Brink of Bliss and Insanity

By Lisa Cerasoli

All Inquiries:
Ken Atchity (AEI)
212-555-0256

Cerasoli/Brink of Bliss   1

Chapter One

My advice to the world: If you make only one worthwhile decision in your

entire pathetic life, decide to never mess with an eleven-year-old

girl. Don't be her first bad day, her first tear, her first swear word,

her first drink. Don't be the moment she realizes her parents don't

know what they're talking about. And do not be the alpha ghost that for

the first time rises from that happily dormant corner in her mind to

tell her that she's shit. You'll live to regret it, because if she

actually survives the blow, she'll make sure of it. I'm not taking any

chances. I smile nicely.

First floor, second door on the left just past the drinking

fountain—I get to the door. Room 13. Room 13. That's one twisted

inside joke. I can handle it, no big deal. What the hell was I worried

about? The lecture is going to be a snap, a breeze; I could do this with

my eyes closed. I know, I'll stand here and think of every clichéd

Cerasoli/Brink of Bliss   2

phrase known to man used to describe "things that are easy," then I'll

make my grand entrance. Piece of cake. I could do this with one hand

tied behind my back; *both* hands tied behind my—*oh get over yourself*.

You're an adult. I am an adult. I'm in my thirties for Christ's sake. I

have a Ph.D. in Psychology, surely that's proof. What the hell? Hey, at

least I'm more of an adult today than I was yesterday, I have to be,

I'm twenty-four hours older, right? Okay, breathe, blink, and pretend

to behave yourself.

I look down, briefcase in hand. I prop the case up on one knee and

snap it open to reveal the book inside: *On the Brink of Bliss and*

Insanity, by Dr. Rosie Meadows. Seeing it enchants me. I sweep two

fingers lazily across the title, as if to fondle it. Okay, book inside

briefcase. I glance slyly at my cleavage (it rocks), pat my tummy, and

reach for the doorknob. I'm in. My first reunion in thirty years with

St. Mary's Secondary School for girls is about to begin.

This is the story of my fairy tale romance exactly as it occurred.

Sort of. I mean, it's not exactly a fairy tale, and some of you might

not even find it very romantic, but that's why we'll be referring might. While this could be true, it's more likely that the reader will use the sample chapters as a means of judging your abilities, and will turn the project down if your skills as an author aren't up to snuff.

While the editor or rep probably won't toss out your proposal if the format of your manuscript pages isn't perfect, it is important to provide certain basic information on the first page of your sample chapters, and on each page that follows as well. No matter how many sample pages you're sending, make sure to include a title page. About a third of the way down the page, type the title, centered. Space down twice, and type your name, preceded by the word "By" ("By Emmanuel Angsten"). Then go down to the bottom margin, and space up just enough to single-space your address, phone number, and e-mail address, if you have one. (Note that when an agent submits the chapters on behalf of the author, the agent includes her own contact information rather than the novelist's.) Do *not* place a page number on the title page.

Begin each chapter on a new page. Place your last name, followed by a comma or slash (/) and key words from the title of your novel, in the upper left-hand corner of every page except the title page. Place the page number in the upper right-hand corner of the page. Type the chapter title—or simply Chapter One, Chapter Two, etc., if appropriate—a third of the way down the page, centered. Double-space twice, and begin the actual text of the chapter flush left, without an indent. Indent all subsequent paragraphs five spaces. On all subsequent pages of the chapter, double-space twice beneath the header that shows your name, book title, and page number, and start typing your text. Within each chapter, break sections with two double-spaces, and don't indent the first line of a paragraph after each break. If in doubt about how to format dialogue and so forth, pull your favorite novels off the shelf and model your format after theirs. For additional format guidelines, see "Getting the Mechanics Right" on page 137. Also see the sample manuscript pages starting on page 128.

The Self-Addressed Envelope

As a courtesy to the editor or agent, it's important to always include a self-addressed stamped envelope (SASE) in your submission package. If you don't, a number of things will happen. First, you'll reveal

By including a self-addressed stamped envelope (SASE) in your package, you'll help ensure that you receive a response to your proposal. Just as important, you'll show that you're a savvy writer who's aware of standard submission procedures.

Ten Common Submission Package Errors

Over the years, I've seen literally hundreds of submission packages. Some of them inspired me to immediately request more information from the author, while in other cases, I couldn't get the package off my desk quickly enough. Throughout this chapter, I've mentioned several submission package don'ts, but these warnings bear repeating as long as authors keep making the same mistakes. If you avoid the following errors, you will, at the very least, avoid raising a red flag. Here are ten errors that, believe it or not, I see all the time.

1 The query letter is printed on brightly colored stationery using weird fonts, bold text, and capital letters. Use only standard-size white bond paper for all your submission package materials, and print in a standard font, such as New Courier 12. In other words, employ standard business formats. The best way to capture the recipient's attention is with great writing—not gimmicks.

2 The author mentions fees, advances, and/or royalties in the letter. This isn't the time to discuss money. First of all, you don't want to seem greedy. Second, you don't want to seem cocky—as if you're sure that the editor or agent will want to make a deal. Finally, if the amount mentioned is too high or too low, you may wreck the deal before the editor or rep even learns whether your book is a mystery or a fantasy.

3 The author seems worried that the editor or rep will steal her work. Don't ask a rep or editor to sign a release form before you let her read your work. If you do, she will immediately assume that you're difficult to work with. (See page 135 for information on safeguarding your words *without* alienating your editor or agent.)

4 The author makes negative comments about herself. Don't recite your shortcomings in your letter. Don't mention that this is the first time you've ever submitted a novel, and don't say, "I'm not a professional writer." Instead, include only positive statements and let your writing shine.

5 The author makes irrational promises in her cover letter. Don't tell the rep or

a lack of understanding of standard submission procedures. Second, you'll imply that you don't want your work back, which is a bad message to send. Third, you'll decrease the chance of receiving a response.

It's a good idea to leave your submission package open when you take it to the post office so that the postal worker can weigh the package. You can then enclose the proper postage with your SASE—an envelope large enough to hold the returned manuscript; fold your SASE; and tuck it inside the submission envelope before sealing and mailing the package. Preferably, attach the stamps to the envelope with a paperclip rather than pasting them onto the envelope.

editor that your novel will make her rich. People in this industry hear that all the time—generally from the least professional of writers.

6 **The author promises that she can re-write the book to the agent's or publisher's specifications, or requests advice from the editor or rep.** While it may seem that such an offer would make you sound flexible and helpful, it will actually make you sound as if you lack confidence in the quality of your writing. While you don't want to seem arrogant, you do want to appear confident in your talent as a writer.

7 **The author mentions all the other books she's written—and hasn't managed to sell.** Information of this type will immediately prompt the editor or rep to ask herself, "Why haven't all those other books been published?" In such a case, less is more. On the other hand, if you have a second novel in progress, you should mention that, as it will give the impression that you're a serious writer with a wealth of creative ideas.

8 **The manuscript proposal is filled with spelling errors, grammatical errors,** **and awkward sentences.** Don't send a rough draft hoping that the editor or rep will edit it, and don't believe that your plot is so outstanding that she will be willing to overlook sloppy writing. Once you've read the section "Perfecting the Language" on pages 134, 136, and 137, you'll know what to do. Take the time you need to make the package as good as possible.

9 **The submission package is sent to the wrong type of publishing house or agency.** Authors have been known to submit their literary novels to companies that publish only science fiction, and to send romance novels to nonfiction houses. To avoid wasting both your time and theirs, do your homework and send your submission package to the appropriate person at the appropriate company.

10 **The package doesn't follow the rules presented in the company's writer's guidelines.** This is critical, so I'll say it yet another time: Read the writer's guidelines and send in only what the editor or rep wants. If you submit the appropriate materials and address them to the correct person, you will greatly increase your chance of seeing your novel in print.

You won't always get all of your contents back. In fact, some editors and agents will use the large-sized envelope, complete with extra postage, just to send back a one-page rejection letter. But most of the time, you will receive everything but your cover letter.

POLISHING THE PACKAGE

All along, I've emphasized how all the details of the submission package are worthy of your attention. Since this package is your calling card—your one chance to make an editor or rep sit up and take notice—it's important to take a little extra time and make sure that your package is the best it can be. This involves two steps: checking your material for spelling, grammar, clarity, and flow; and making the materials attractive and professional in appearance. Let's look at each of these in turn.

Perfecting the Language

As a literary manager, I'm always amazed by the many poorly written query letters I receive on a day-to-day basis. In addition to typos, a good number of these letters contain rambling paragraphs and poor grammar. Almost always I determine that I don't have time to work with someone who can't present the core of what they do in a professional, polished manner.

Are book editors likely to be more forgiving than reps? Undoubtedly not. That's why it's so important to perfect the language, spelling, and grammar in every component of your submission package. Just keep in mind that even if the language is reasonably perfect, editors are likely to make changes. Editors have to follow their in-house style guidelines. Moreover, because they have the benefit of objectivity, they can sometimes see how to better phrase a sentence. Nevertheless, it's vital to demonstrate that you can produce copy that is well organized and clear. You also want to show that you're a careful and conscientious writer, who can and will do any work that is necessary to bring the book to completion.

After you've drafted your letter and the other components of your package, read through the materials carefully. Don't forget to do the same for your manuscript or sample chapters, if these are to be included. Check for spelling, grammar, and organization. Even if everything seems fine to you, run a spell-check on your computer. Then carefully check any changes you made per your computer's advice. Sometimes computers *don't* know best, and will replace a correct word with an incorrect homonym, substituting "they're" for "their," for instance. While the spell-check is a good tool, like all tools, it must be used with care.

Be aware that the more familiar you become with your work by reading it over and over, the more likely you are to become blind to it. So once you've perfected your package as much as possible, put it aside for a day or two. This will place a little distance between you

It's important to create your submission package—your letter, synopsis, and sample chapters—on a computer rather than a typewriter. Most publishers and reps will view a lack of computer access and/or skills as a major problem, and will immediately toss the package into the kill pile.

Protecting Your Work

When you send out copies of your submission package, you may wonder if any of the editors or agents you're contacting might be so unscrupulous as to steal your idea. Or perhaps this notion won't occur to you until an editor requests sample chapters and you worry that your painstakingly worded text might end up in someone else's book!

If you start to get a little overprotective, you're not alone. The fear that someone, somewhere, will steal or modify your work is a common concern for the writer who's just starting to submit queries and manuscripts to publishing houses or literary agencies. Keep in mind that this rarely if ever happens, simply because an editor is most interested in finding a writer who can produce a marketable book—not just an idea that might someday be developed into a book. Most serious professionals have neither the inclination nor the time to steal. Most frequently, writers only *think* their ideas were stolen when it's really a case of multiple invention—of several people coming up with the same idea at the same time. This is understandable, as we're all exposed to the same media stimuli in this increasingly homogenized world. But if the possibility of theft remains a concern, you'll be glad to know that there are two good ways to protect your work.

Register a Copyright

You may have noticed that every commercially printed book contains a copyright notice on the back of the title page. What you might not realize is that unpublished works can also be registered as copyrighted.

What does a copyright mean? It means that you exclusively have the legal right to publish, produce, sell, or distribute your intellectual property—the words you have written. United States copyright law protects that right from the moment you put the words down on paper, but that alone is often not sufficient to protect you, because it's difficult to prove that you, rather than someone else, wrote the material. When a copyright registration is issued in your name by the United States Copyright Office, you will have protected your legal right by creating evidence that's admissible in the event of a lawsuit. In other words, once your copyright claim is registered, you can prove that you claimed copyright and submitted your claim for registration on the date of your application.

With or without registering your copyright, no one else will be legally allowed to print your work unless you formally grant her the right to do so. But if anyone does violate your copyright by publishing part or all of your work, the formal registration will speed up legal battles and avoid complications. And if the work is registered with the copyright office within three months of its appearance in print or before any violation of your rights occurred, and the court decides that your claim and registration were valid, you'll be awarded the money to pay for any attorney expenses, as well as compensation for the theft of your intellectual property.

It's simple to register your copyright with the United States Copyright Office in Washington, DC. And you can register the work at any time—even years after your manuscript is written. First, you will have to fill out an application form, which can be downloaded from the Internet or obtained through the mail. (See the Resource List for further information.) You will then send the completed application, the manuscript, and a check covering the copyright registration fee to the Copyright Office. The office will mail you a certificate of registration once your application has been reviewed and accepted. Be aware that neither the fee nor the manuscript will be returned to you. The manuscript will be stored along with your registration as evidence of your claim to that manuscript.

One last point should be made. When a copyright is issued in your name, only your actual *words* are protected. It's impossible to copyright a concept, be it the central idea of a book or a unique format or method of presentation.

Obtain a Notary Public's Stamp

A notary public is a person who has been officially authorized to certify or witness the placing of a signature on a document, and to confirm that the paper was signed on a given date. Every notary has an exclusive ink stamp that contains her identification number. Therefore, when you have your work notarized and then, at a later date, someone prints your work, the notary seal will prove that this work was in your possession on the recorded date.

It's easy to have your work notarized and thereby establish visual proof of possession. If you

don't know a notary public, you can find one at a bank, a financial office, or a professional office. Bring with you the manuscript itself, as well as two forms of identification, one of which must include a photo. In the presence of the notary, place your signature on the first page of each chapter—it's unnecessary to notarize more than this. Then, for a small fee, the notary will stamp, sign, and date each signed page. Keep the notarized documents in a safe place.

A Final Caution

Either of the methods described above should allow you to protect your work as you send it out to one or several editors or literary representatives. But do keep one important point in mind: The material you submit should not actually bear a copyright notice or notary seal. Why? Simply put, such practices are insulting to the recipient of the package, as they give the impression that you don't trust her integrity. Perhaps just as important, such practices demonstrate that you lack experience and professionalism. Keep the copyright certificate and the notarized pages in your home records, and send the editor or agent an unmarked copy of your material. That way, you'll both protect your work and project a professional image.

and your work so that the next time you review the material, you'll have a fresh perspective and a bit more objectivity. Correct any further errors that you find.

Finally, consider asking someone else to read through your package and provide an appraisal of your work. If you can find someone in the publishing industry or another skilled writer to read your proposal, that's best. If not, a teacher, librarian, or someone else who is well-read and has a good ear for language will fit the bill. But make sure this person isn't going to just tell you the nice things you want to hear. She has to be willing and able to provide an honest response.

When you hand the material to your "reader," explain that you want her to read the material through for clarity, organization, spelling, and grammar. Also mention what the package is supposed to contain. Then walk away. You don't want to stand over the person's shoulder, figuratively or literally, and you don't want to even inadvertently give her your "take" on the material. Then, when she's finished, make sure you're willing to listen with an open mind to any comments or criticism. Did she tell you that your package is clear, logical, well written, and interesting? Did she find anything misleading or offensive? Did the cover letter grab her and hold her attention, or did it or bore her silly? Did the synopsis make illogical leaps, without explaining how the plot got from point A to point B? Keep in mind that you don't have to change everything the reader mentions, but chances are that if something you've written jars one person, it could easily bother an editor or rep. Thank your reader politely and make those suggested changes that you can live with and that are in line with your objectives.

Consider asking a friend to read through your submission package. Someone in the publishing industry, a teacher, or a librarian would be a good choice.

Getting the Mechanics Right

Once you feel that you have perfected the wording of your submission package, you'll want to make the package as attractive and professional in appearance as possible. This serves two purposes. It makes the copy easy to read, and it shows the editor that you understand what a publishing company expects from a prospective author.

Some of this will sound very basic. But because many not-yet-published novelists don't know about these basics, they bear repeating.

First, choose 8½-x-11-inch white paper. Standard photocopying paper will do fine, but a nice white bond is even better. Use 1- to 1½-inch margins and type—don't handwrite—all of the submission package materials. The only handwritten element in your package should be your signature on the letter. Everything else should be printed on a computer, even if you have to borrow your friend's computer.

If you have letterhead, you can, of course, use that for the query or cover letter only. But please don't use cutesy images or typefaces.

To maximize the readability of your submission package and ensure a professional appearance, you'll want to use 8½-x-11-inch white paper—preferably, a nice white bond—and select a basic no-frills typeface like Courier New or Times New Roman.

If you ordinarily have little rainbows or kittens on your letterhead, skip the letterhead and use the plain white paper on which you're printing the rest of the submission materials. Editors are professionals, and writers should be, too.

Your ink should be basic black, even if you have a color printer. Black is clear, legible, and professional. Similarly, if you have a choice of typefaces, you'll want to choose a basic, readable font. I personally prefer 12-point Courier New for all submission materials, although some people opt for 12-point Times New Roman. Avoid fancy or exotic typefaces, as editors generally don't appreciate hard-to-read copy. And make sure that your ink cartridge is working well so that your printout doesn't have feathery, blotchy, or fading type.

Start each new part of the package—the letter, synopsis, etc.—on a new sheet of paper. If you're sending several sample chapters, also start each of these on a new sheet. Single-space the cover letter and synopsis, but double-space all the other materials. Set the material ragged right. Don't justify the right-hand margin or otherwise try to make the material look typeset. This won't impress the recipient of the package, but will merely mark you as an amateur.

One last caution is in order regarding the appearance of your package. Many editors and reps confirm that they receive proposals that have been stained by food or coffee. As you may imagine, this is not an attractive sight. If there's one time to keep the coffee mug or buttered roll off the table, it's when you're preparing your submission package! Professionalism always wins points.

CONCLUSION

If you have prepared each component of your submission package with thought and have carefully selected the publishing houses or agencies to which you will submit your work, you have greatly increased the chances that your proposal will elicit a positive response. In the next chapter, I present a proven system for sending your package to the companies you've chosen. This system will help you keep your costs down and capitalize on any feedback you receive, all the while maximizing your chance of success.

CHAPTER 7

USING THE
SQUARE ONE SYSTEM

Chapter 6 guided you through the preparation of a query or cover letter, synopsis, and sample chapters. Hopefully, your submission package is now polished to perfection and ready to send to the appropriate publishers or literary agencies. If you are like most novelists, you want to immediately mail a copy of your package to each and every company on the list you created in Chapter 5. But believe it or not, there are several reasons why a mass mailing may not be the best course of action.

Consider what's involved in sending out thirty to forty submission packages all at once. First, the copying and mailing costs involved are likely to be sizeable. Moreover, as you'll learn later in this chapter, the job of gathering the data you need to complete the mailing can be a daunting task if you decide to research every company in one fell swoop. Finally, it's important to keep in mind that although most publishers and agents are likely to respond to your package with form letters, some may offer valuable feedback. If your letters are sent out all at once, you'll receive this helpful feedback only after the people on your list have been contacted, so you won't have the opportunity to fine-tune your package during the submission process.

What about the alternative of sending your proposal out to only your "dream" publisher or agency? While this may seem cost-effective, it's certainly not time-effective. It can take four months or more to receive an answer from a company. If that company does *not* opt to give you a contract, do you really want to wait that long before sending out additional submissions? At that rate, over a year may pass before you receive any positive word about your proposal!

The Square One System for proposal submission is a carefully planned program that guides you in sending out your proposal in groups, with the first group going to those editors or reps who best meet the criteria you established in earlier chapters. Therefore, this program can save you time and money by having you first contact those companies that you favor most highly. (If the publisher or agent you really want to work with accepts your proposal, there may be no need to contact those at the bottom of your list.) This system also breaks the submission process into small steps, each of which can easily be managed, and enables you to benefit from any feedback you receive along the way. But most important, the Square One System maximizes your chance not only of getting your manuscript into publication, but of getting it into publication with a company that will work with you to produce a book of which you can be proud. This chapter will show you how it's done—step by step.

STEP ONE:
PRIORITIZE THE COMPANIES ON YOUR LIST

Earlier chapters guided you as you put together a list of likely publishers or literary representatives. You should now have a list of at least thirty candidates. But chances are that all of these companies are not equally appealing. You may, for instance, favor only smaller companies or companies found in your area of the country.

Now it's time to prioritize the candidates on your list. Start by selecting the five companies that you feel best meet your criteria, and write the names of these A List companies at the top of a piece of paper. Look at your long list again, and choose the next ten companies that appeal to you. Write the names of these B List companies below the A List. Finally, write the names of the remaining firms— the C List—at the bottom of the page. Your prioritized list should, of course, contain all the companies that appeared on your original list, but should name them in order of preference, with the most promising and desirable ones appearing at the top. In Step Two, you'll work with the first five publishers or reps, verifying the information needed to send out your first submission packages.

STEP TWO:
VERIFY YOUR CONTACT INFORMATION

Earlier in the book, I mentioned how important it is to direct your package to a specific editor rather than to the company as a whole or, for instance, to "The Romance Book Division." Publishing companies are busy places, and everyone from the receptionist to the publisher usually has more work than he can comfortably handle. For that reason, you can't assume that the person who opens your package will take the time to forward your proposal to the appropriate editor. To prevent your manuscript from remaining in the so-called slush pile for days, weeks, or months, you need to find the name and title of the appropriate editor and send the package directly to him. And, of course, to make sure your package reaches that editor, you'll have to find the correct address—the address of the building that actually houses the editorial department and not, for instance, the company's corporate headquarters or warehouse.

The same is true if you're sending your submission package to literary representatives. Agencies and management companies, too, are busy places. Moreover, companies of every type can change their location, making resource directories dated before they even roll off the press.

When you composed the list of publishers or reps, you jotted down the appropriate contact information for each company, including the address, phone number, and—to the best of your ability—the name of the person who should receive your submission package. Even if you feel that your research provided you with exactly the information you need, you must double-check it through a phone call. And, of course, if your source books were unable to provide you with the name of a likely contact person, a phone call to the company is your best bet.

If you're intimidated by the idea of calling an editor, relax. You don't want to speak to the editor at this time, as most won't discuss a project with an unknown author until they have a submission package in hand. You simply want to ask the person who answers the phone—probably an editorial assistant—if your proposal for, say, a Western novel should be sent to the address and editor you have noted. If you're in luck, the person you contact will politely provide you with the information you're seeking. You should then

Even if you managed to find complete contact information in your resource books, you'll want to double-check it through a phone call. The publishing world is one of rapid change, and the acquisitions editor of yesterday may not be the acquisitions editor of today.

confirm the spelling of that editor's name, his title, the name of the publisher (in case it has changed since you composed your list), and the mailing address. Don't be surprised, though, if the staff member refuses to give you the name of the appropriate editor. Many publishing houses are very protective of their editors and try to screen them from unwanted phone calls and unsolicited manuscripts. But don't cross a publishing house off your list simply because the person who picked up the phone isn't especially cooperative. Just verify the address, and direct that particular package to the editor of the appropriate division—the Western Book Editor, for instance—so that when it arrives, those who route the mail will deliver it to the correct person.

Occasionally, even though your initial research indicated otherwise, the editorial assistant may tell you that the company is no longer accepting unsolicited manuscripts. This is most likely to happen after a company or division has been inundated with submissions. In this situation, just remove that company from your A List and place it on the B List. In a couple of months, contact the publishing house again to see if it has reversed its policy. If not, move it to your C List. Eventually, that publisher may have to come off your lists altogether, but for now, don't rule it out.

If you happen to get an editor on the phone, try to make the best of this rare opportunity. Briefly describe your book and confirm that he's the person who should receive your submission package. Then modify your cover letter so that the opening line mentions your phone conversation.

Every once in a while, you may actually get an editor on the phone. While this may be unnerving, try to make the best of this wonderful opportunity. Although this isn't the time to launch into a five-minute speech about your book proposal, you could quickly indicate, in ten words or less, the type of book you're sending, and confirm that he's the person to whom you should address the proposal. If so, be sure to modify your cover letter so that it leads with the words, "As we discussed in our phone conversation of April 5. . . ." Sometimes an editor will tell you that your proposal sounds interesting. At other times, he might reject it outright, possibly saying that he's just signed on a book with a similar theme. If he's even remotely encouraging, thank him for his time and ask if you can send him your next proposal. Then be sure to keep his name and number on file.

At the end of each phone call, be sure to request a company catalogue. Why? A catalogue can tell you a great deal about the company that produced it, and therefore may be useful later, when you may have to choose which of several companies you want to publish your book. If the person on the phone gives you a choice, ask for the specialty catalogue—in other words, a catalogue that contains only those titles in your area of interest. If a specialty catalogue isn't available, ask for a full catalogue and a frontlist catalogue. (For more information on this, see the inset "Reading a Catalogue Like a Book" on page 144.)

If you're calling a literary agent, your approach should be similar. Be polite to the person who answers the phone, as the tone of your initial contact will probably be reported to the representative with whom you're seeking to do business. In the long run, the assistants at both publishing houses and reps' offices are likely to be your strongest allies—or enemies. Identify yourself as a writer seeking to submit a novel to the agency, and explain that you want to double-check the information you found in a resource book, on a website, or wherever. Give the name of the representative, and ask the person either to connect you to his office or to verify the correct spelling, the person's title, and the address of the agency. If you're in luck—that is, if the agency is accepting material—the person who answers the phone will provide you with the information you need. If you're feeling confident and the person is friendly, you can ask further questions, such as, "Is your company still looking for minority authors?" or "Is it true that you like books with film potential?" Ask the person's name, and be sure to end the call by thanking him by name. If the person you speak to tells you that the company isn't now accepting projects, remove the company from your A List and place it on your B List. And don't be afraid to ask, "Shall I try again in a few months?" Most people respond favorably to politeness, and you may make yourself an "inside contact."

STEP THREE:
FILL OUT YOUR TRACKING CHART

You now have all the information you need to send your submission package to the first five companies on your list. But instead of rushing out those first packages, take the time to fill in the information on your Tracking Chart. (See pages 146 to 147.) At this point, of course, you'll be able to fill out only the first two columns: the company's name, address, phone number, and other contact information, including the name and title of the appropriate editor or rep; and—in the case of a publisher—the date that you requested the catalogue. As you actually

If possible, create your Tracking Chart on the computer. This will enable you to easily add information as you receive responses to your proposal.

Reading a Catalogue Like a Book

Before writing your book, you may have received book catalogues in the mail from time to time. Perhaps you leafed through them to see if they contained anything of interest. What you probably didn't realize is that a publishing company's catalogue provides the reader with far more than a listing of its books. As an extension of the company's marketing department, it is a clear reflection of how that company packages and markets its products—not only through its catalogues, but through all its marketing tools.

Depending on various factors, a company may offer only one catalogue at any given time, or it may produce several, each of which serves a different purpose. Some companies—especially small companies—may produce only a *full catalogue*. This catalogue includes both frontlist titles, which are new releases brought out for the current selling season, and backlist titles, which were published prior to the current season. Most companies offer both a full catalogue and a *frontlist catalogue*—a catalogue that presents only new books. Some companies also offer *specialty catalogues*, which include books in a specific area of interest. For instance, a company may produce a separate catalogue of mysteries.

When you receive one or more catalogues from a publishing house, first look at the covers. Are they attractive and enticing, or dull and unappealing? Are they printed in full color, or black and white? Some companies invest a great deal of time, money, and care in their catalogue covers so that their catalogues will be noticed and read. Others, unfortunately, farm the cover design out and use whatever is given to them—even if the result is unattractive. As a writer, you want your book featured in a catalogue that invites the reader to pick it up and look inside.

Now, open the catalogue and examine its listings. Note whether the interior is printed in black and white or in color, whether the covers of the books are displayed, and whether the format invites you to look further or lulls you to sleep with its ho-hum layout.

Pay special attention to the titles of that company's books. Some publishers work hard to

mail out packages and, later, receive the responses from the various companies, you can fill in the Date Catalogue Received, Date Package Sent, Date Response Received, Outcome, and Feedback columns.

If you choose to recreate the tracking chart on paper and write the information in by hand, be sure to leave space between the different entries so that you'll have room to fill in the information as you receive responses and review catalogues. Another option is to create a table in your computer and fill it in as appropriate during the submissions process.

You may wonder why it's desirable to keep track of your mailings and responses. Although you may be one of the lucky authors who immediately receives a positive response from the company at choose book titles that are both appropriate and catchy—that both tell the reader what the book is about and engage his interest. Don't underestimate the power of a title. When your book is displayed on the shelf of a bookstore, it is often the title that determines whether the consumer takes the book off the shelf to examine it or leaves it there to gather dust. A title can make or break a book.

Now read the book descriptions. The quality and length of these descriptions can vary widely from catalogue to catalogue and from company to company. In the catalogue you're examining, are the descriptions full or skimpy, lively or boring? Do they give you a clear idea of what each book is about, or do they fail to provide any useful information? In other words, do they make you want to order the books, or do they make you want to toss the catalogue into your recycling bin?

Finally, compare the company's presentation of its frontlist books with that of its backlist books. While most companies devote a little more space to a frontlist title than to a backlist book, some nevertheless feature both frontlist

and backlist titles in full-color pages, display the book covers of all their titles, and provide well-crafted and intriguing descriptions of every single book. Other companies, unfortunately, give their backlist titles little attention. They may, for instance, merely list their older books in a lackluster black-and-white section, and omit both a photo of the book cover and a description of the book. If you work with a company that will give your book only one chance to be a frontlist success, and then relegate it to an unappealing backlist, chances are that sales will die quickly. But as many small publishing companies have shown, continual promotion of an older title can lead to a long life—and a profitable one.

When you have finished reviewing a catalogue, don't forget to note your impressions in your Tracking Chart and to put the catalogues away for safekeeping. You have learned how to "read" a catalogue, and this skill will serve you well as you review the responses to your submission packages and—if you're lucky!—pick and choose among the positive responses, selecting the company that will provide you with the most rewarding working relationship.

the top of your list, chances are that it will take some time to actually go to contract. In the meantime, you'll probably be sending out a lot of letters and receiving a lot of letters in return. A conscientiously filled-out Tracking Chart will allow you to quickly check when you sent the submission package out to a particular company, when—and if—you received a catalogue, and when you received a response to your proposal. The data on your sheet may also provide clues about the target company itself. For instance, if the catalogue you requested fails to arrive or arrives only after you've made several follow-up phone calls, you'll have learned something about the operation of that company. This, like the catalogue itself, will help you select the company with which you ultimately choose to work.

TRACKING CHART

Company/Editor or Agent/Contact Information	Date Catalogue Requested	Date Catalogue Received
Little Black Dress Press Elizabeth Thomas, Senior Editor 2040 W. 12th Avenue Eugene, OR 11732 Phone:503-555-2939 Fax: 503-555-3723 E-mail: lblackdress@optagon.com	November 13	November 26 Black and white; boring.
Small City Press Diane Fitzpatrick, Editor 535 West Preston Street Cobleskill, NY 12043 Phone: 518-555-7344 Fax: 518-555-7345 E-mail: info@smallcitypress.com	November 14	December 1 Full color; well written.

STEP FOUR:
MAIL THE FIRST FIVE SUBMISSION PACKAGES

And now the moment you've been waiting for—the release of your creations into the hands of the five companies at the top of your list! Before you send your packages out, though, finalize the five letters by adding the date, the name and address of the publishing company or agency, and the editor's or agent's name and title. (See the sample cover and query letters on pages 111, 112, and 114.) Remember that unless you know the person to whom you're writing, this is no time for informality. The salutation should read "Dear Ms. Jones" or "Dear Mr. Jones," for instance—not "Dear Susan" or "Dear Bob." Do not use the titles "Mrs." or "Miss" unless you know that this is how the editor prefers to be addressed.

Experience has taught me that if you're using a computer template to generate your cover letters, you have to take special care to make all the changes necessary in each of the individual letters. That

Date Package Sent	Date Response Received	Outcome (yes/no/maybe)	Feedback
November 20	December 20	No	None
November 20	January 2	Maybe	Liked concept. Asked for remainder of ms.

means that if your first letter is to Mr. John Smith and your second is to Ms. Ellen Randolph, you must remember to change the name not only in the address field but also in the salutation, and you have to make sure that any references to the person or company that appear within the body of the letter—as well as references to the materials being enclosed—are changed as well. Never send anything to an editor or rep until you've read it over several times and you're certain of perfection.

Take the time and care to spell the names of both the company and the contact person correctly. Remember that spelling counts in every element of a submission package. I can't tell you how many letters I have received addressed to "Ken Achity" or "Ken Atchisy." While I didn't toss the packages out, these errors certainly didn't assure me that the author was a careful and conscientious writer.

Make a copy of each cover letter and place it in a file. Then type out the envelopes using the correct name, title, and address. Again, be careful. This is no time to make a careless error. (For more guidelines regarding this final step in sending out submission packages, see "Your Submission Package Checklist" on page 149.) If your package is only a few pages in length, a standard white #10 envelope—one that is $4\frac{1}{8}$-x-$9\frac{1}{2}$ inches—is just fine. The package's recipient will find it easy to handle, and it will look businesslike. Of course, you'll have to fold the letter and other materials in thirds, and the self-addressed stamped envelope in half so that everything will fit in your envelope. If your sample chapters, if any, run more than a few pages in length, though, you'll want to use a 9-x-12-inch envelope or one large enough to comfortably hold your materials. Although this will increase your mailing costs by a few cents per package, it will accommodate the bulkier enclosures and enable everything to lie flat. In my opinion, it also looks neater when it arrives in the editor's or agent's hands.

I highly recommend that you use regular mail to send out your submission packages. Registered or overnight mail may get the envelope there sooner, but it's not going to get your submission read any faster. And avoid faxing anything to an editor or agent unless you're specifically instructed to do so. Faxed materials can easily be lost, and even if they aren't, they're never as attractive and readable as originals and photocopies. You want to put your best foot forward, so do all you can to ensure that your package is as neat and attractive as possible.

Finally, fill in the Date Package Sent column of your Tracking Chart. You can sit back and relax now, or better yet, get to work on your next book.

STEP FIVE: BE PATIENT

Now that your first five submission packages have been sent out, you may be tempted to start checking your mailbox every day, looking for a response. But it may take weeks or months for some of the editors or agents to even open your package, so try to cultivate patience during this time. The responses will arrive; they just won't arrive as quickly as you might want them to.

Some authors call the recipient of each package a few days after the mailing. They hope that if the editor or agent has already looked at the package, he will discuss it with them, and that if that person has *not* yet opened the package, the call will inspire him to do so. I

Do your bank account a favor and use regular mail to send out your submission packages. Although overnight mail may get the envelope to the editor sooner, it won't get the package read any faster.

Your Submission Package Checklist

Throughout this chapter and Chapter 6, I present some important submission package do's and don'ts. As you begin mailing your packages out to publishing houses or literary agencies, keep in mind that all this information is intended to help your package receive a positive response. The following checklist can ensure that the all-important details will not be forgotten. As you prepare to mail out your packages, be sure that you:

- ☐ Include a cover or query letter, as well as any other materials requested in the company's writer's guidelines, such as a synopsis or sample chapters. Send these materials "loose"—unbound and unstapled—and be sure to enclose a self-addressed, stamped envelope (SASE) in every package.

- ☐ Type, rather than handwrite, all the various elements of your package, including the mailing label.

- ☐ Place the elements of your package in order, with the cover or query letter on top; followed by the synopsis and sample chapters, per the writer's guidelines requests; and, finally, the SASE.

- ☐ Address both the letter and the envelope to a specific editor or rep by name, or at least to the editor of the appropriate division. Make sure to spell the names of both the company and the contact person correctly.

- ☐ Make a copy of each cover or query letter for your files and fill in your Tracking Chart with all the appropriate information.

- ☐ Place your materials in a plain envelope—either a #10 business-size envelope or a 9-by-12-inch or larger envelope, as the bulk of your mailing requires.

- ☐ Avoid "protecting" your package by enclosing it in plastic wrap or sealing it with packing tape. The envelope should be neat in appearance and easy to open.

- ☐ Make sure to use the proper amount of postage on both the outgoing envelope and the SASE. You don't want your package to arrive on the editor's or agent's desk marked "postage due."

strongly suggest that you avoid making these phone calls. The editor or rep will get to your package as his workload allows, and probably won't appreciate your efforts to hurry him. And if he's already reviewed the package, there's a very good chance that he won't remember your proposal simply because he sees so many of them.

During this waiting period, is there anything you can do to increase your chance of getting your book published? You can, of course, begin performing the research needed to send out the second group of proposals. And you can review any catalogues that arrive so that you can start learning more about your target publishing companies. (Don't forget to record everything you receive on your Tracking Chart.) If you haven't already examined books published by the companies on your list, this would be a good time to visit your local bookstore or library. Pay particular attention to those books that are in the same category as yours and examine them as critically as possible. Are the covers attractive? Do the books seem to have been well edited? (In other words, do they read well?) Is the typeset page pleasing to the eye? Does the publishing company ever highlight its books by arranging for special displays in bookstores? The answers to these questions will tell you a great deal about each of the publishing houses.

As hard as it may be, I suggest that you wait at least six weeks before sending out the second wave of submission packages. That's the minimum time that most editors and agents say it takes to get to the proposals on their desks. During that time, you'll probably receive responses to some or all of the initial five packages. Perhaps one of the people you contacted will even request to see the full manuscript. If so, consider yourself fortunate, and respond in as timely a manner as possible, submitting a package that's just as crisp and professional as your query packet. Write a business letter addressed to the rep or editor who asked to see the manuscript, stating that this is a full submission, "as requested." Include an SASE for the manuscript's return and a copy of your original query letter to make it easier on the recipient. Then place the manuscript and cover letter in an envelope or manuscript box—marking "Requested Material" on the outside—seal securely (but not *too* securely), and send it off. Note that if you included sample chapters in your original submission, you should still send the entire manuscript, sample chapters included, so that your fate won't depend on the recipient's organizational skills or memory.

Remember that an expression of interest in your novel is not the same as a signed contract, so don't stop sending out submission packages just because an editor or rep has requested additional material.

Even if someone requests additional material, don't stop sending out submission packages! I can't overemphasize the fact that a letter expressing interest in your project is not the same as a signed contract. Many writers have received these requests only to find a rejection letter in the mailbox a few weeks later. Sometimes, after seeing the additional material, the editor or rep may decide that the project isn't right for his company. And, of course, after learning more about the company, you may decide that you'd be happier working with someone else. When the wrong person says no, it's always a good thing, even though it may not seem that way at the time.

If you don't receive a positive response from this first group of companies, don't be discouraged. Keep in mind that most writers have to send out quite a few proposals before they elicit any interest on the part of an editor or rep. AEI, my company, was the forty-eighth agency that Steve Alten contacted before we sold his book to Disney and Doubleday Bantam.

When an editor or agent decides that he's not interested in a project, he usually responds to the author via a form letter. But occasionally—and I do mean only occasionally—the recipient of the submission does provide the author with some feedback on the proposal. For instance, the editor might say that the book is too long for that particular genre, or that the main character isn't sufficiently sympathetic. If you're lucky enough to receive such feedback, try to consider any recommendations with an open mind—especially if you receive the same comments from several people. You may decide that they are just what your book needs to make it more marketable—or you may find the suggested changes very unappealing. Regardless of your opinion, I suggest that you call the editor or rep and thank him for his comments. During your conversation, remind him of the letter he sent and ask if he would be interested in the book if you made the recommended alterations. If he answers in the negative, ask if he knows of another company that might be interested in your book. Though this may strike you as a rude question, it can actually be quite fruitful, as editors and agents get to know other editors and agents in the course of their work. Whatever the response, thank the editor or rep graciously for his time. In this business, if you actually manage to talk to someone on the phone, you're light years ahead of most first-time novelists, the vast majority of whom get nothing more than an impersonal form-letter rejection.

WORDS FROM A PRO

Jonathan Karp

Former Vice President and Senior Editor, Random House

One thing I've never understood about submission packages is why they're so difficult to open. There have been occasions when I spent more time trying to extract the manuscript than I did reading it. In terms of on-the-job hazards, excessive use of adhesive tape and staples finishes a close second to anthrax. So, if you want to begin your editorial relationship in the right way, my advice is to submit the manuscript the way many of the best literary agents do: in a folder or cardboard box, with no more than one rubber band. Insert the folder or box in a padded envelope. Seal and send. If your manuscript won't fit in a box, or if your box is so big it won't fit in an envelope, you might want to consider cutting the manuscript before you send it.

Occasionally, an editor or agent provides feedback on a novel in his letter of rejection. If you're lucky enough to receive such feedback, and if the comments make sense to you, consider changing your package before mailing out the next round of submissions.

Finally, if the editor's or agent's comments make sense to you, make any necessary changes to your package before finalizing and mailing out the next round of submissions. Maybe the modifications will lead to a more encouraging response from the remaining editors or reps on your list.

STEP SIX:
MAIL OUT THE NEXT TEN SUBMISSION PACKAGES

Six weeks or so after sending out the first wave of proposals, prepare and send out submission packages to the next ten companies—the B List. Be sure to follow Steps Two, Three, and Four carefully, researching names and addresses, filling out your Tracking Chart, and finalizing each package by adding the appropriate information.

As discussed earlier in this chapter, if you received feedback from any of the editors or reps on the first mailing list, you may want to amend one or more portions of your submission package. If you decide to do that, be sure to take the same care you took when preparing the original package. Read through the new letter, synopsis, and other package components, checking for spelling, grammar, punctuation, flow, organization, and style. It should go without saying that any change made in one portion of the package should be reflected, as necessary, in all the other portions. For example, if an editor suggested that the book's protagonist be more sympathetic, this may affect not only your sample chapters, but also your synopsis.

If you feel that you benefited from the comments and suggestions of the friend who read your original submission package, by all means ask that person to review any subsequent revisions. And as the catalogues and letters arrive in response to your phone calls and submissions, be sure to keep your Tracking Chart up-to-date.

STEP SEVEN:
MAIL OUT THE REMAINING SUBMISSION PACKAGES

After you mail out the second group of packages, wait at least another month. Then repeat all the steps necessary to send out the remaining packages.

E-Mail Submissions

As we all become more computer savvy, it can be tempting to save yourself the time and expense of mailing your proposal the old-fashioned way by opting for an e-mail submission. After all, your submission package elements—the cover or query letter, synopsis, and sample chapters—can easily be sent as attachments. And they'll get there so much faster than they would by snail mail! In addition, wouldn't an e-mail lend some measure of urgency to your proposal?

Well, it all sounds good in theory, but there's no guarantee that an e-mail submission will receive prompt attention—or any attention—from an editor or agent. Why? Many people in the field complain that e-mail has only made their job harder because now in addition to submissions sent by regular mail, they have all those e-mails to worry about. As a result, some admit to ignoring a good number of their e-mails. Think how you feel when your message in-box is filled with e-mails from people you don't know. Your first impulse is to treat them like junk mail and delete them unread.

Also realize that if an editor or rep were to open your attachments, he would still need to print them out so that he could review a hard copy. That takes time as well as money in the form of paper and ink. Editors and agents are also understandably concerned about opening attach-ments, which could carry viruses. So, you see, as nice as the idea may be, there are many reasons why your proposal won't get the red-carpet treatment if it arrives by e-mail.

I recommend e-mailing your proposal under only two conditions: if the writer's guidelines specifically say that it's okay to do so, or if you've made contact with an editor or rep who has given you permission to send an electronic sub-mission. In either case, be sure to follow all guide-lines to the letter. For instance, my company accepts e-mailed queries as long as they are brief. If a query is longer than a paragraph, it's likely to be deleted unread. Other companies request that their e-mail submissions include a standard cover letter, synopsis, and sample chapters. Some will open attachments, and others specify "no attach-ments."

If an editor or rep has specifically asked you to send a proposal by e-mail, make sure your subject field says something like, "Requested proposal materials for *Murder in Singapore*." This will pre-vent your proposal from being deleted as an unsolicited message.

Increasingly, companies are accepting or even *preferring* e-mailed queries. But never assume! As always, it's imperative to check each company's preferences and provide exactly what the editor or rep wants in exactly the form he wants it.

What if you've already received some positive responses to your earlier packages? If they came from companies that were high on your list, and you've already sent out the full manuscripts, there's no need to continue your mailings until you hear from these A-List prospects. If the editors or reps decide the book isn't for them, you can always continue the submission process where you left off.

STEP EIGHT: REVIEW YOUR RESULTS AND ASSESS YOUR OPTIONS

At this point, you've sent proposals to every publisher or rep on your list. Now is the time to assess the results of your efforts.

Maybe you've received positive responses from one or more publishing companies who are prepared to offer you a contract. If so, congratulations! You should now turn to Chapter 8, "The Deal," to learn about publishing contracts. You'll want to understand all you can to make the most of this important document.

Possibly some editors or agents had requested additional materials, but after reviewing the complete manuscript, they rejected your project. I know how disappointing this can be. But don't take it personally, as there may be absolutely nothing wrong with your book. Many factors beyond your control can affect an editor's decision, from personal bias against a topic to poor timing. Sometimes writers are simply in the wrong place at the wrong time. Maybe the editor has recently been inundated with historical novels set in the 1940s, so that no matter how unique your book is, he can't get beyond the topic to give it a chance. Or perhaps the sales department determined that the book wouldn't earn the company enough money. Whatever the reason, it's fine to give the editor or rep a call at this point. Once someone has become sufficiently interested to request further materials, he may be willing and able to provide you with feedback. If what he says makes sense, you'll be able to use it as a guide for reworking your book into a more marketable project.

If you didn't receive any positive responses to your proposals, you need to analyze the reason for this result. While the Square One System is designed to increase your odds of eliciting a positive response from editors, when there's a problem with the package itself, the system isn't likely to work. To help determine if the package may be the problem, turn to Chapter 9, "When It Doesn't Happen." This chapter is designed not only to guide you in pinpointing any flaws, but also to help you rectify them so you can enjoy more positive results with later submissions. In addition, it looks at a number of proven alternatives, including self-publishing.

Maybe you feel strongly that your package isn't the problem. Or maybe you've already revised it and believe that it's ready to meet the needs of the companies in which you're interested. What are your options now? First, consider waiting six months to a year from the time you began the submissions process, and resubmitting the package to the publishers or reps on your original list. The types of stories that are in vogue change all the time, and a novel that people are ho-hum about today may be the same one they'll be dying to get their hands on next spring. The reason for all those rejections might be a simple question of timing.

But both editors and reps are affected by far more than just their company's publishing program. Each one is an individual who is influenced by many factors, from the people he knows to the television shows he watches to the books and magazines he reads. Many times, an editor or agent will simply become excited about a subject because of a story or a bit of information that he heard or read somewhere along the line. Then, when a proposal for a book on this topic lands on his desk, he can't move quickly enough to contact the author and request further material. While you may find this a bit maddening—do you have to pray that an editor develops an interest in turn-of-the-century Boston before he receives your submission package?—it does mean that a door that was once closed to you may suddenly open. The result may be that your book, once rejected out of hand, may now be in great demand.

Is any other option open to you at this point? Consider creating an entirely new list of publishing houses or literary agencies and sending your submission package to them. Literally thousands of companies dot the United States, with new ones cropping up all the time, so it's highly unlikely that your initial list of companies included every one that might be interested in your book. Maybe when you were compiling your first list, you didn't seriously consider the many small firms that are more likely to accept the works of first-time authors. If so, now is the time to look into these smaller companies. Or perhaps you didn't sufficiently home in on the publishers or agents that focus on books in your particular category. By creating a new list of prospects and following the system outlined in this chapter, you will greatly increase your odds of finding the right company for your project.

Finally, don't give up! Stay positive and keeping working towards your goal. Many authors receive scores of rejection letters before landing a contract. As you have already gathered, this doesn't mean that you should indiscriminately send out proposals to every

The types of stories that are in demand change all the time, as do the publishing programs of various companies. That's why it often makes sense to wait six months to a year from the time you began the submissions process, and resubmit your package to the publishers or reps on your original list.

publisher or agency large and small, regardless of the company's areas of interest and the quality of its books. (If this book has taught you anything, I hope it's taught you the importance of zeroing in on the firms that are right for you and your project.) But it does mean that it may take longer than you expected to find someone who appreciates the special merits of your manuscript and has faith in you as an author. By following the Square One System with care, consistency, and perseverance, you will greatly improve your chances of ultimately making contact with the editor or agent who will champion your project and work with you toward the realization of your dream.

SAVOR THE MOMENT

Whether your feedback to date has been positive or negative, take the time to congratulate yourself. Your novel is out in the world, making the rounds. You should be proud of that because most people who set themselves the task of publishing a novel never get that far. Do you realize that putting your work in the mail was the one crucial action that stood between you and the possibility of getting published? It can happen now—it can happen any day.

So now that you're in that awkward state between wannabe and published pro, it's a great time to begin preparing yourself for what will, with any luck, be your next move. In Chapter 8, I'll walk you through a standard publishing contact.

CHAPTER 8

THE DEAL

If you now have an offer from a publisher in hand, by all means, celebrate the moment. In a world filled with as many frustrations as opportunities, it's important to rejoice over every achievement.

Whether the offer came directly to you or through your agent, attorney, or manager, be aware that this is a crucial step in the publishing process, and one that you should understand and fully take part in. I constantly hear writers say, "I'm hopeless when it comes to business," claiming that their only abilities lie on the "creative side." Most writers consider reading their contract a chore, or even a terror. While you, too, may hate business and wish to avoid plowing through your contract, it's imperative that you understand at least the basics of your publishing agreement. This is essential for two major reasons. Most obviously, you want to make sure that your contract is a fair and equitable one that provides you with appropriate compensation for your work. Just as important, though, your publishing agreement spells out not only your rights, but also your responsibilities, so that only by understanding your contact will you know what is expected of you at each stage of the publication process.

This chapter was designed to explain the standard publishing contract and to make you aware of the types of terms you're likely to encounter. By the time you finish this chapter, you'll have a greater understanding of the rights and responsibilities conferred on you by the agreement, and you'll know the warning signs that can alert you to a publisher who may be less than scrupulous in his dealings.

The majority of publishing agreements are relatively standard. Although they may vary in length, in the wording used, and in the order in which the topics are covered, all of them cover pretty much the same subjects and offer similar terms.

Please be aware that this chapter is not intended to provide you with legal advice. If you feel that legal advice is necessary, contact a lawyer. In fact, this is one of the first topics I'll cover. But with the help of this chapter, you'll be in a better position to figure out the terms of your agreement and—either alone or with the help of a professional—to ask appropriate questions so that you can make an informed decision regarding the details of your contract.

SHOULD YOU HIRE A LAWYER OR A LITERARY AGENT?

Upon receiving their publishing contract, many authors' first question is, "Should I hire a lawyer to review this?" The decision to hire a professional to represent you in negotiations with a publisher is one that is largely based on personal preference. Some authors prefer to manage any negotiations themselves rather than giving a piece of the pie to a lawyer or agent. Others feel that only a lawyer or agent can get them the best possible terms.

If you're not sure whether you want to finalize your contract on your own or with professional help, there are a few facts you should consider. First, while a smart and aggressive attorney can, to some extent, negotiate profitable changes in the agreement, unless he's an *intellectual property lawyer*—one who specializes in literary works and their inherent rights—he can wind up doing you more harm than good. As I first mentioned in Chapter 4, publishing contracts are different from those of other industries. A lawyer who's unfamiliar with publishing contract terms could make unreasonable demands on a publisher or focus on the wrong issues. This could result in your starting off your relationship with the company on the wrong foot.

Second, although an experienced literary agent may be capable of getting a larger advance, limiting a publisher's rights, and even assisting you later in the publishing process—if, for instance, you need someone to interpret a baffling royalty statement—you must pay a high price for this service. While a lawyer may be compensated with a one-time fee, an agent usually works on commission, garnering 10 to 15 percent of both your advance and your royalties. And these payments are expected for the life of the agreement. When you consider that most books don't earn any money for the author beyond her advance, that could be a high price.

If you *do* decide to hire someone to represent you in negotiations, keep in mind that in addition to being experienced, your representative should be someone with whom you feel comfortable working. This is particularly important if you use a literary agent, as this person may continue to represent you for years to come. Also remember that you should never remove yourself from the bargaining process, leaving the fate of your contract in someone else's hands. Instead, read your contract carefully and discuss your "wish list" with your representative before negotiations begin. Let her know exactly what's important to you. You may well care about issues that were of little concern to the authors she worked with previously. Only by developing contract literacy through the reading of this chapter and by staying involved in negotiations will you insure that the terms of your publishing agreement are consistent with your wishes.

Be aware that many representatives will charge you a smaller commission if they don't make the sale for you, but only negotiate your contract. Don't hesitate to discuss this possibility with a potential rep.

THE CONTRACT

The first sign that a contract may be on its way will probably be a telephone call or e-mail from one of the editors to whom you submitted your proposal and, perhaps, subsequent material. "I read the novel," the editor might say, "and I'm just calling to find out what's happening with it." The editor first has to ascertain that the book is still available. Once she learns it is, a period of discussion will follow. During this time, the editor may or may not discuss the broad strokes of a possible contract with you. While editors always make a verbal offer in discussions with representatives, they sometimes skip this step when dealing directly with authors. But whether or not the editor covers contract terms, if all goes well during your conversations, your contract will eventually arrive in the mail.

The period between your initial conversation with an editor and the arrival of a contract can range anywhere from a few days to a few months. In smaller companies, only one person may have to approve the acquisition, making the process relatively fast. In larger companies, approval may have to be obtained from an editorial board, as well as marketing and sales departments. This, understandably, can take time.

Usually referred to as the "Author/Publisher Agreement," your contract may be five pages or twenty-five pages in length. It may be couched in impenetrable legalese, or it may be worded in relatively plain English. But chances are that much of your contract is "boilerplate"; that is, it follows a formula used throughout the publishing industry, covering the same conditions treated in most publishing agreements. This certainly has been true of the many contracts I've dealt with during my career.

If the editor made a verbal offer to you in earlier conversations, your first task will be to read through the contract and make sure that it accurately reflects the terms you discussed with her. You will then want to read the document through again so that you understand every word.

The remainder of this chapter will lead you step by step through a standard publishing contract, explaining the terms and examining the issues to be negotiated. As you read through the following material, please keep in mind that although most publishing contracts deal with the same subjects, these subjects are discussed under different headings in different contracts. Similarly, the order in which they appear can vary. For ease of understanding, I've tried as much as possible to discuss the various issues in the order in which they appear in *most* contracts, and to choose headings that define the issue being discussed. When possible, I've also indicated the headings under which they may be discussed in your own publishing agreement.

Please note that it's virtually impossible to consider every element that may be included in your contract. Some publishing contracts go on for many pages, detailing every situation that may be encountered in the life of the agreement. My intention is to cover only those terms that are most common and/or most important. Should you encounter terms that you don't understand and that cause you concern, don't hesitate to request clarification from your editor or from legal counsel.

Identifying the Parties and the Work

Before you get into the body of your contract, you'll encounter an introductory paragraph whose purpose is to identify the parties and the property to which the contract pertains. Your name will appear, along with a statement that identifies you thereafter as "the Author." (If you're writing for hire—in other words, if you're a ghostwriter—you will instead be termed "the Writer"). The publishing company will be referred to as "the Publisher." If an agent is involved, she will either be referred to as "the Agent," or she will simply be named. The title of your novel will appear, with the notice that it will thereafter be referred to as "the Work." Note that the publisher will have final control over your title, and that the title which appears in your contract is the working title, and not necessarily the final title of your book.

Rights

According to the current Copyright Act, the author is the owner of all rights to the literary work, including the right to publish the work in book form. The author may grant one, several, or all of his rights to the publisher, but such a grant *must* be in writing. The various rights that pertain to the publisher's production of, direct use of, and direct sale of the book are generally covered in a section called "Rights," "Publishing Rights," "Grant of Rights," or "Author's Grant." (For those rights not covered in this section, turn to "Subsidiary Rights" on page 162.)

One of the issues generally defined in this section is "the Territory"—the geographical location in which the publisher has the right to sell this book. This territory can be the United States and its possessions, North America, and/or the world.

The contract also generally defines the form of the work to which the publisher's rights extend. For example, it may grant the publisher sole rights to produce the work in book form and/or electronic data form—tapes, disks, diskettes, databases, networks, CD-ROMs, etc. The contract may also specify that the rights include both this edition and future editions, and may state that they extend to hardcover, trade paperback, and/or mass market paperback form. Be aware that if the contract does not specify a form such as hardcover, but does grant rights to print, publish, distribute, and sell the work in any form throughout the world, this means that the grant extends to all possible book forms, from hardcover to CD-ROM.

Usually, the contract specifies the language or languages to which the publisher's rights extend. It could extend to publication or reproduction of the English language only, or it could be for "all languages," meaning that the publisher has been granted all translation rights. Stay alert when reading this section of the contract, and make sure that you're not going to be charged a fee for the translation of your book into other languages. Some small houses now charge authors who can't translate their own works. While having your book published in Spanish, for instance, may increase your sales, you may not want to have the translation performed at your own expense. Do your best to negotiate terms that you find acceptable.

Finally, the contract usually defines the time in which the grant is extended in terms of the copyright, which is in effect for the author's life and fifty years thereafter. For instance, the contract might state

You'll make the task of understanding your contract a simpler one if you keep in mind exactly what it is you're selling. You, as the author, own all the rights to your novel, until you choose to part with one, some, or all of them, for a specific period of time and a specific purpose. Your publisher wants to obtain one, some, or all of those rights—and will almost always pay you for these rights according to the number of books that the company can sell.

that the rights are granted "for the full term of all copyright and renewals of copyrights." Rarely does the grant extend for less than the term of the copyright.

Subsidiary Rights

The "Subsidiary Rights" section of the contract grants to the publisher certain rights not referred to in the earlier "Rights" portion of the contract. Depending on the "Rights" section, this may include periodical or newspaper publications, either prior to publication of the book (first serial rights) or after publication of the book (second serial rights); condensations and abridgements; book club publications; foreign-language publications; English-language publications not covered in the "Rights" section; reprint editions; motion picture, television, radio, and stage interpretations, often referred to as "dramatic rights" or "performance rights"; audio recordings; electronic recordings; public reading rights; Braille, large-type, and other editions for the handicapped; and calendars, greeting cards, posters and other "merchandising/commercial" applications of the work.

Why are the above rights covered sometimes in the general rights section of the contract and sometimes under subsidiary rights? The general or primary rights covered in the first section are those rights that the publishing house itself intends to exploit, and therefore are often limited to different editions of the book. The secondary or subsidiary rights are those rights that the publisher intends to license to a third party, such as a motion picture company or a software company. So a publisher that owns an audio books company will probably cover audiocassettes in the primary rights section of its contract, while a publisher that doesn't own an audio books company will cover the same topic in the subsidiary rights section.

In the case of each of these rights, the contract—either under "Subsidiary Rights" or in the "Royalties" section—generally specifies the allocation of the money received by the publisher from the grant of these rights to third parties. In most cases, the proceeds are shared with the author in a fifty-fifty split.

The Manuscript

Whether called "the Manuscript" or "Delivery of Manuscript," this section of the contract spells out your obligations regarding the delivery of the completed manuscript to the publisher. The contract specifies the date by which the manuscript must be delivered, as well as the length of the manuscript in terms of words. For instance, the contract may spell out that the manuscript should be "approximately 70,000 to 100,000 words in length." The contract generally also states the desired form of the manuscript—usually a floppy disk in Word, in English, with a printed-out hard copy as well.

Either within this section or within a section called "Publishing Details," the contract may specify the party that will bear certain costs and complete certain tasks relevant to the completion of the manuscript. For instance, the author may be charged with the responsibility of obtaining written permission to reprint any quotations from outside sources. Some contracts specify that any expenses for such permissions will be paid by the publisher. Others state that these permissions will be obtained "at the Author's expense." In the latter case, it's expected that the author will pay for the permissions out of his royalty advance.

All contracts state that the delivered manuscript must be "acceptable to the Publisher" in content and form. In some cases, they also specify that certain items must be included—usually, at least a title page and acknowledgments. On rare occasions, an editor has been known to refuse a manuscript because she felt that its content wasn't up to snuff. Normally, the editor then gives the author a month or so to fix whatever she thinks is wrong. If it isn't rewritten and delivered within that time—or even if it is rewritten, but still doesn't meet the editor's standards—the contract may then become null and void, and the company may demand a return of the author's advance. While this is unlikely to happen if the full manuscript has already been received and read by the editor, in today's troubled times, it is happening more and more often. For this reason, it's important to send in a manuscript only when you're sure that it's in the best shape possible.

Editing, Proofs, and Publication

The publisher's rights and obligations regarding the editing, typesetting, printing, binding, pricing, and marketing of the book, as well as the author's rights and obligations in this regard, may be addressed

Some authors try to edit their manuscripts to fit the exact word count stipulated in their contract. Be aware that this word count is provided as a guideline, and that it's perfectly all right if your book is a couple of thousand words under or over. What the publisher wants to avoid is a book that's *significantly* shorter or longer than the target length.

under a heading such as "Publishing Details," "Publication," "Editing and Proofs," or simply "Proofs."

The publisher normally reserves the right to copyedit the manuscript in accordance with her house style of punctuation, spelling, capitalization, and usage. In some cases, the contract states that the meaning of the text will not be materially altered during this copyediting. Often, the contract also states that the edited manuscript will be sent to the author, who will have a chance to make revisions and corrections, but then must return the revised manuscript within a specified period of time. Even when the contract does not include this last statement, it's a standard practice in publishing to submit the edited manuscript to the author for her input.

The contract also normally details the author's rights and obligations regarding the book's *proofs*, the typeset version of the book that is produced after the manuscript has been edited. The author is permitted to review and correct the proofs and "other production materials." Sometimes, the contract specifies the time period in which the proofs must be returned. The contract may also state that any author's alterations other than corrections of errors made in typesetting will be made "only at the Publisher's discretion," and may be paid for by the author if they are in excess of a stated percentage of the cost of typesetting—usually 10 to 15 percent. This last term is generally included to prevent the author from rewriting the book after it has been typeset, and therefore incurring extra costs as well as possible delays.

> Once your novel reaches the proof stage, it will be too late to make substantive changes unless they are of the utmost importance. Even if your publisher approves such changes, you may be required to pay for them.

Normally, the publisher reserves the right to determine the so-called "details of publication"—the format and design of the book; the paper, printing, and binding; the title and price; and the advertising, promotion, and distribution of free copies. Sometimes, the contract specifies the form of the book, whether hardcover or paperback. It also may specify time constraints—for instance, that the edition shall be produced "within 18 months from the date of the Publisher's acceptance of the manuscript." And it may specify the imprint under which the work will be published—provided, of course, that the company is large enough to have imprints.

The Author's Copies

In a section entitled "Author's Copies," "Publication," or simply "Free Copies," the contract may specify the number of copies that will be given to the author free of charge upon the book's publication. Generally, the author is offered ten to twenty-five copies, although some authors receive as many as a hundred free books. If the book is to be published in both hardback and softcover editions, the contract may specify that the author will receive X number of hardback copies and X number of paperback copies.

The contract may also state the discount the author will receive if she chooses to purchase additional copies. Usually a discount of 40 to 50 percent is given, depending on the number of copies bought.

Be aware that if a contract does not spell out what your discount is to be on purchased books, the publisher may choose to give you only a minimal discount—or no discount at all. As an author, make sure you know what the price will be if you choose to purchase copies of your own novel.

The Author's Promotional Responsibilities

Another subject that may be covered in the contract is the author's responsibility regarding the promotion of the book. For instance, the contract may state that at the publisher's request, the author must participate in a promotional tour of a stated duration—say, two weeks. It may also state that any expenses incurred during such a tour will be paid by the publisher. Publishers who make such stipulations often explain that the author's participation in publicity activities was a "material inducement" to the publisher to enter the agreement. But other publishers don't specify such activities in writing, although they may verbally request—not demand—that the author involve herself in publicity tours, newspaper and television interviews, etc.

It should be noted that even if such a clause appears in your contract, it's rarely enforced in the case of first-time novelists. The reason for this is simple: Experience has shown the industry that tours are not an effective means of selling books, especially in the case of unknown authors. Rather, they are a way to promote good will among booksellers.

What if your contract does *not* include a clause on the topic of promotion, but you want one as a means of insuring that your book will, in fact, be publicized? It's unlikely that the publisher will add this term to your agreement. But this doesn't mean that you should not request the clause. Make your wishes known, and if your request is denied, ask the publisher for a letter outlining the proposed marketing program. This will allow you to review the company's promotional plans and understand the program as it moves forward.

The Out-of-Print Provision

Most likely, your novel will go out of print during your lifetime. The good news is that at that point, the rights will probably revert to you. Just make sure that the definition of "out of print" is clearly stated in the contract. If not, you may have trouble regaining your rights.

Under a heading such as "Publishing Details," "Out of Print Provision," or "Reversion of Rights," the contract should define the circumstances under which the book will be taken out of print—in other words, will no longer be published by that company. The publisher, for instance, may state that the book will be taken out of print if the book "shall cease to be profitable," if sales fall below a certain number of copies per year, or if the publisher doesn't reprint the book within a specified time after the existing inventory has been sold. Once the book has been taken out of print, the publisher usually offers the remaining copies to the author at cost—that is, at the unit print cost for each book—or at a specific discount, plus shipping. If the author chooses to not purchase the remaining copies "within a reasonable period of time," the publisher reserves the right to destroy the copies or *remainder* the book—sell it for a price that is below the manufacturing cost.

Generally, the contract specifies that the rights to the book will revert to the author when the book is declared out of print. If your contract doesn't include this statement, you should make sure that such a provision is added. Remember that if the contract doesn't specify when a book will be declared out of print, the publisher may retain the rights to the book in spite of the fact that she no longer stocks, markets, or sells it.

Royalties

Most authors are understandably interested in their *royalties*—the money they will receive based upon the sales of their book. Because this subject is one of both great concern and some complexity, it makes sense to explore it in some detail.

A royalty refers to the money paid to the author for the sale of each book. Royalties can be calculated in two ways. First, they may be based on the *retail price* of the book. This price is easy to determine in the case of trade books, as the retail price is almost always printed on the back of the book. Because customers aren't always charged the retail price, royalties are sometimes based on the *net price* of the book, which is the price actually charged by the publisher to the customer. When the book is sold by the company directly to an individual consumer, the net price is usually the same as the retail price of the book. But in other cases, books are usually discounted. For instance, when books are sold to bookstores, the discount may range from 20 to 40 percent of the retail price. (In other words, the bookstore pays 80 to 60 percent of the retail price.) When sold to distributors, the discount may range from 50 to 60 percent. (The distributor pays 50 to 40 percent of the retail price.)

When royalties are based on the retail price of the book, they generally range from 5 to 10 percent. (In other words, if the book's retail price is $10.00, the author makes $.50 to $1.00 per copy.) When royalties are based on the net price of the book, they generally range from 5 to 15 percent. (The author receives $.50 to $1.50 per book.) Traditionally, publishers of trade books have paid royalties on the full retail price of the book, but it's become increasingly common for publishers—especially smaller ones—to base royalties on the net price. Although this isn't ideal for you, it's not unusual, and at the beginning of your career, it may be the best you can do.

It's important to be aware that your contract may base your royalties on the retail price in some cases, but on the net price in others. For instance, a trade publisher may base royalties on the retail price if the discount given to the customer is less than 50 percent, but switch to a percentage of the net price if the discount is equal to or greater than 50 percent, or if the book sells to an outlet other than a bookstore—to a wholesale club, for instance. In such cases, the contract must spell these terms out.

A number of other variations may be found in a single contract. For instance, the publisher may use a sliding scale so that the royalty percentage increases as sales increase. As an example, the publisher may pay 10 percent of the retail price for the first 5,000 copies sold; 12.5 percent of retail for the next 5,000 copies sold; and 15 percent of retail for any sales in excess of 10,000 copies. The sliding scale may work in two different ways. When computed on an annual basis, the sliding scale begins at ground zero at the start of each year. When computed on a cumulative basis, all books sold over the years are included in the calculations.

The concept of paying an author part of a book's profits was devised by American publishers in the mid-1800s. English poet Elizabeth Barrett Browning was one of the first authors to be offered a royalty by an American publisher. Before that time, publishers simply gave the writer a fixed sum in exchange for all the rights to a book. It is no wonder that so many well-known writers of the past—authors like James Fenimore Cooper—chose to publish their own works.

Depending on the publisher's plans for the book, the section on royalties may include a staggering number of possibilities. The contract may, for example, list different royalty percentages for hardcover copies, trade paperbacks, mass market paperbacks (sometimes referred to as rack-size paperbacks), large-print hardcover copies, large print paperback copies, low-cost hardcover editions, audio recordings, and more. The royalty percentage may also vary according to the territory in which the book is sold. For instance, the royalty percentage may be 7 percent for books sold within the United States, but 10 percent for books sold outside the United States.

Some contracts include a section on "holdbacks" or "reserves." This requires some explanation. The publishing industry is unique in that bookstores can send their unsold copies back to the publisher, in which case the money paid for the books is credited to the stores. Because these returns can be large, some publishers hold back between 20 to 60 percent of the royalty payment until a specified date, at which point the balance is sent to the author. Others simply state that royalties will be paid "on sales, less returns." If your contract allows the publisher to hold back more than 20 percent of the royalty payment, it would make sense to try to negotiate a smaller percentage.

Some contracts also state the royalty percentages for subsidiary rights—those rights, such as performance rights, that aren't covered in the basic "Rights" section of the contract. (See page 162 for a full discussion of subsidiary rights.) In most cases, the author receives 50 percent of the proceeds from the sale of such rights, but the author may receive more or less for certain specified rights.

Either in the "Royalty" section of the contract or in a special section on accounting and payment, the contract also specifies *when* the publisher will calculate and pay the royalties to the author or authors. Generally, royalty statements are issued every six months. Be aware, though, that a posting date isn't the same as a payday. The actual payment may arrive months after the end of the royalty period.

The "Royalty" section often concludes with a statement about royalty-free copies—copies of the novel on which no royalties will be paid. Depending on the contract, these royalty-free copies may include author's copies; copies damaged or destroyed; copies furnished gratis for review, publicity, or promotion; books licensed for printing in

Braille, or produced as mechanical audio recordings or visual recordings for the blind or other physically handicapped people; and copies sold at or below manufacturing cost. In contracts with larger publishing houses, royalties are often not paid on sales by the publisher to its parent, subsidiaries, affiliates, or related divisions for resale.

The Advance

Although the advance is usually specified in the "Royalty" section of the contract, it's so important to some authors that it merits its own discussion. It's been my experience that some authors are actually more concerned about their advance than they are about the terms of their royalty. Sometimes, this is due to stories they have heard about authors' receiving huge advances. In other cases, the author actually needs the advance in order to live—especially if she must take a leave of absence from her job to rework the manuscript.

It's important to note at the start that an advance is more properly called an *advance against royalties.* In other words, the advance is not additional to the royalty, but is a prepaid portion of future royalties. So if you receive an advance of $1,000, this amount will be taken out of any future royalty payments.

Advances are usually paid in installments, with the payment schedule varying from publisher to publisher and according to the size of the advance. Smaller companies, which generally provide smaller advances, often pay half upon signing of the contract and half upon "delivery and acceptance." Larger companies, which offer more sizeable advances, usually prefer four installments, with the first quarter being paid upon signing of the contract; the second, upon submission of the completed manuscript; the third, upon publication of the hardcover edition; and the fourth, upon publication of the paperback version. Most contracts specify that any portion of the manuscript received must be in "satisfactory" form as judged by the publisher before the corresponding portion of the advance is paid.

It's possible that, along the way, the publisher will exercise her right to not publish your book and ask for a return of your advance. While this rarely occurs, *rarely* is not *never*. In order to avoid this problem completely, request that the advance be paid out on a nonreturnable basis.

Always keep in mind that the advance is not *additional* to the royalty payment, but is a prepaid portion of future royalties. Therefore, any money you receive as an advance will be deducted from your royalty check.

To avoid future problems, request that your advance be paid out on a nonreturnable basis.

Accounting

Either under the heading "Accounting" or a heading such as "Royalty Statements and Payments," all publishing contracts include details about the publisher's records on the contracted book. In general, the publisher agrees to keep records of payments due the author, and to send statements of such payments to the author at times specified in the agreement. The contract may further detail exactly what these statements must include—for instance, the number of copies sold, the list price, the royalty rate, and the royalty amount.

Most contracts also state that the author or a representative of the author has the right to examine the publisher's records for the novel during normal business hours at the author's expense. The contract may or may not specify how often such an audit may be performed. If an error of 5 percent or more is found in the publisher's favor respecting a royalty statement, the money must be promptly paid to the author, and the publisher must contribute to or cover the cost of the examination. It should be noted that if the author or the author's representative accuses the publisher of underpaying the author, the publishing company can take issue with the author's interpretation of the accounting records. So accusations of underpayment don't necessarily result in additional royalties for the author.

Warranty and Indemnification

The publisher must rely upon the author to produce an original work that has never before been published. So in the "Warranties" or "Warranty and Indemnification" section of the contract, the author guarantees that she is the sole proprietor of the work—in other words, that she did not plagiarize material from other sources—except in those instances in which she quoted material with written permission of the copyright owner. (For more on this, see "The Manuscript" on page 162.) The author may further guarantee that she has the full power to enter into this agreement and grant those rights granted within the contract, and that the work doesn't contain any material that is libelous or that violates any right of privacy, is not legally obscene, and is not unlawful in any way.

Either in the same section of the contract or in a separate "Indemnities" section, the author usually indemnifies the publisher—that is, protects her—from any loss, damage, or expense that may be incurred if the author is, in fact, convicted of breaching any of her warranties. It's worth noting, though, that most publishers have an omissions and errors insurance policy that covers the company if it is sued for libel, copyright infringement, or invasion of privacy. To make sure that you're properly protected, you should request the addition of a clause which formally states that if any action is brought against you, you will be covered by the publisher's insurance policy. This is a standard change to which most publishers will agree.

Reserved Rights

Some publishing contracts include a "Reserved Rights" paragraph, which simply states that any rights not granted to the publisher in the agreement are reserved by the author, but that the author will respect the rights granted to the publisher within the contract. While it may seem a little strange that this clause doesn't simply spell out the rights to which it is referring, the clause does actually serve a purpose.

As you learned earlier in the chapter, in a standard publishing contract, the author grants the publisher the specific rights in which a publisher is usually interested—the rights to sell paperback and hardback editions of the book, for instance. But, according to this clause, should a new area of rights emerge—think CD-ROMs and electronic books—this new area will be controlled by the author.

Copyright

Sometimes within the "Rights" section of the contract, and sometimes within a special "Copyright" section, the publisher is charged with the responsibility of registering the book for United States copyright. In most cases, the contract states that the copyright will be taken out in the name of the author, who is the owner of the work. The contract may specify that the publisher will print a copyright notice in every copy of the book. But since doing so is standard practice, the omission of such a statement should not be viewed as a problem.

Sometimes the contract also specifies that in the event of any infringement of the work, the publisher "may employ such remedies as it deems advisable." The contract may even specify whether the

Most publishers have an insurance policy that covers the company if it's sued for libel, copyright infringement, or invasion of privacy. To make sure that you're protected, request the addition of a clause which states that if any action is brought against you, you'll be covered by the publisher's insurance policy.

author, the publisher, or both parties will pay for any such litigation, as well as how any recovered funds will be divided between the parties. The standard practice is for the publisher to advance the costs, even if the author must bear some of them.

Option

Some contracts give the publisher an option to acquire the author's next book before it's offered to another publishing house. This is referred to as the *right of first refusal*. Usually the publisher is given a specified amount of time—sixty days, for instance—in which to examine the new manuscript and determine whether she wants to acquire it. If she doesn't offer to publish it within the period specified, the author may show it to other parties and sign a contract with the publisher of her choice. The author may also offer it to other parties if the publisher *does* wish to produce the book, but the author and publisher are unable to agree on financial terms within a stated period of time.

Sometimes this clause gives the first publisher the opportunity to match the terms offered by another publisher competing for the next book. If the first company does offer the same terms, that company is entitled to the publication rights.

Occasionally a contract will stipulate that the publisher has the option to publish not just the author's next book, but her next two books or all subsequent books. While this may not seem significant to an author signing her first contract, it's important to understand both the pros and the cons of the option clause. If your first book is doing well with the publisher and you enjoy your relationship with her, most likely, you'll want her to publish any subsequent books. But if you're not happy with that publisher—perhaps because you feel that your current book has not been marketed properly—you probably won't want her to handle your next book. For this reason, it's usually prudent to request that the option extend to your next project only—or that the option clause be entirely eliminated from the contract.

> Some contracts stipulate that the publisher has the option to produce all of the author's subsequent books. In case your relationship with the company ends up falling short of your expectations, it's usually wise to request that the option extend to your next project only.

Rights of Termination

Some contracts include separate sections that spell out the circumstances in which the author and publisher can terminate the publishing agreement. For instance, if the publisher doesn't publish the work within a specified time, or if the work is out of print and the author sends the publisher a written request for a reversion (return) of rights, the contract may state that the publisher must return all rights to the author.

On the other hand, the publisher may have the right to cancel the agreement—and therefore not publish the work—if the author does not deliver the manuscript by the specified date or if a requested revision isn't judged to be acceptable by the publisher. The contract may further state that under such circumstances, the publisher has the right to recover any advances already paid to the author under the agreement. As stated earlier, it's important to request that the advance be paid on a nonreturnable basis.

Proceedings

Under a heading such as "Proceedings," "Arbitration," or "Applicable Law," the contract may specify that any major problem or disagreement relating to the contract, or to a breech of contract, will be settled in a specific manner, through legal proceedings or arbitration, and in a specific location—usually in the city or state in which the publishing company is located. For instance, the contract may specify that any legal proceedings will be governed by the laws of a particular state and be venued—in other words, take place—in that state. Or it may specify that any controversy or claim shall be settled by arbitration in the specified state. In the latter case, the contract may also state who shall bear the costs of the arbitration.

Because the financial resources of a publisher are generally greater than those of an author, publishers prefer to resolve differences in a court of law if they can't resolve them through direct negotiation. For the same reason, in most cases, it's in the author's interest to seek a remedy through arbitration rather than legal proceedings.

Be sure to note how any contract-related disagreement between you and your publisher will be settled. As an author, it will be to your advantage if differences can be resolved through arbitration rather than a court of law.

Benefit

Under a heading such as "Benefit" or "Assignment," the contract usually states that if the publishing company is sold or acquired, the terms of the agreement will continue to apply to the new company or its successor. Similarly, it states that if the author is deceased, the terms of the contract will apply to the author's executors, administrators, or assigns (anyone to whom the author legally transfers the rights to the book).

Bankruptcy

Although the standard bankruptcy clause may make you *feel* more secure, be aware that it will provide little actual protection in the event that your publisher declares bankruptcy.

The bankruptcy clause itself is relatively straightforward. It states that if a publisher becomes insolvent and petitions for or goes into bankruptcy, all rights to the book will revert to the author. Who could argue with that? Unfortunately, a great many people do.

In truth, when a publisher declares bankruptcy, his contracts are viewed by the court as company assets. This means that the rights in these contracts can't be reverted to the authors no matter what the bankruptcy clause states. Usually, if a buyer can be found for the publisher, the rights to the books are transferred to the buyer. If the company goes under reorganization—if it remains a working company with all contracts in place—it's protected under the bankruptcy laws. For authors, this means that the bankruptcy clause is unenforceable.

If you want actual protection in the event that your publisher declares bankruptcy, you might consider another option. One clue that a company is having financial problems is its failure to send out royalty checks. By incorporating a clear statement under the "Royalty" clause or the "Rights of Termination" clause that provides for the reversion of rights if the publisher doesn't make timely royalty payments, you may be able to protect the rights of your book. But if the publisher seeks relief from the bankruptcy court before the appropriate reversion procedure is concluded, even this may not work.

The good news is that this issue doesn't come up often. However, it does highlight the benefits of working with a publisher who has a proven track record and a solid history.

Force Majeure

Many publishing contracts include a section on a so-called *force majeure*—an unexpected event that can't be controlled. In such a section, the contract usually states that the failure of the publisher to publish or reissue the work will not be considered a breech of contract if it's caused by events that are beyond the publisher's control. These events may include restrictions imposed by governmental agencies, labor disputes, terrorist acts, and an inability to obtain the materials necessary for the book's manufacture. In such a case, the publication of the work would simply be postponed until the events no longer posed a problem.

The Agent

When the author has an agent, the contract clarifies the relationship of the agent, publisher, and author under a heading such as "Agent" or "Author's Literary Manager." Sometimes, this portion of the contract identifies the agent as sole and exclusive agent with respect to all rights to the book. The agreement may also clarify the commission that will be received by the agent—15 percent of all monies payable to the author, for instance. Even in the briefest of contracts, it's at least stated that all sums paid by the publisher to the author will be paid directly to the agent—not the author. In other words, the publisher will send advance and royalty payments to the agent, who will then pass the money—minus the agent's commission—on to you.

THE NEGOTIATIONS

I hope you now understand most or all of the terms of your contract. If you have any questions about the meaning of any portion of the publishing agreement, don't hesitate to speak to the editor or publisher with whom you've been dealing. She should be able to explain any and all of the terms to your satisfaction. And, of course, if you're working with an agent or a lawyer, she'll be able to interpret the contract for you.

You may, at this point, find the terms of your agreement satisfactory, or you may wish to change some of them. The following discussion explores the negotiations process. Be aware that it is beyond the scope of this book to look at every possible contract term and then discuss if and how it might be changed. Rather, I hope to provide you with some insight into the "dance" of negotiations, as well as a closer look at a few important terms that are of interest to many authors. For a more detailed look at publishing agreements, refer to Martin P. Levin's *Be Your Own Literary Agent*, which includes a term-by-term review of a standard book contract, or *Kirsch's Guide to the Book Contract* by Jonathan Kirsch, a detailed clause-by-clause discussion of the publishing agreement.

Even if you've been lucky enough to find representation, it pays to understand the negotiation process so that you will know the kinds of terms that can be changed and the kinds of terms that are likely to remain unchanged. Keep in mind, though, that first-time novelists have little clout. As your career builds, you will enjoy greater success in getting the terms you desire.

What Terms Can Be Negotiated?

Once you understand all the terms of your contract, you may recognize a fact that is well-known in the industry: Most contracts are weighted on the side of the publisher. The reasons for this are pretty clear. First, it's the publisher who actually creates the contract. Second, it's the publisher who invests the money needed to edit, typeset, print, bind, warehouse, ship, and market the book. Naturally, the publisher feels that she deserves the lion's share of the profits.

On the other hand, it's also true that *most* terms are not set in stone. Virtually any term—from the territory in which the grants apply to the subsidiary rights—can be amended. But also keep in mind that for every publisher, certain points are not negotiable. Which terms are not open to change in your case? You'll have to discover this yourself through discussions with your publisher.

Before beginning negotiations, I suggest that you determine which points are most important to you. Maybe you'll have to take a leave of absence from your job to rework the manuscript, and therefore need an advance of a certain size. Or maybe you want to retain certain subsidiary rights. Once you decide the specific changes you'd like to make, you'll be better focused and more likely to get what you want—as long as the terms you wish to amend are among those that the publisher is willing to change, and as long as your requests aren't truly outrageous. In any case, don't be afraid to at least request those changes that are important to you. The worst your publisher can say is "no."

While most publishers do expect some give and take and do allow for a period of negotiation, be aware that negotiations don't always have a happy ending. If you insist upon changing a specific term, and if the publisher is equally determined to leave that term as written, that term may prove to be a deal breaker. Similarly, if the negotiations drag on too long, the contract may be withdrawn. But if you are just breaking into publishing, my advice is this: *Make the deal.* And remember that your first deal is highly unlikely to be the best one you'll ever make.

Important Bargaining Points

In the many years I've participated in contract negotiations, I've found that the contract terms which authors seek to change vary rad-

> Before beginning contract negotiations, determine which points are most important to you. This will help you maintain focus during the negotiations process.

ically from person to person. One author may refuse to extend the publisher's rights beyond the United States. Another may demand a greater number of author's copies. But in addition to any special concerns such as these, most authors are interested in four issues: advances, royalties, subsidiary rights, and author's discounts. Let's look at each of these in turn.

Advances

Everyone has heard stories about authors' receiving outrageously large advances. But remember that large advances are the exception rather than the rule, and are usually given to known authors. Standard advances—if any can be said to be "standard" nowadays—range between $2,000 and $25,000. And some authors get no advances at all.

> Don't allow your hunger for a large advance overshadow your perspective. In the vast majority of cases, hefty advances are awarded only after a writer has produced *several* successful novels.

What dictates the amount of the advance? Many factors come into play, including the policies of that particular publishing company, the company's strength of interest in your manuscript, the size of the market for which your book is intended, and your need for money in order to complete the manuscript. For instance, if the potential audience for your book is small, it wouldn't make sense for the publisher to offer a large advance, as the sales will never pay for that advance.

If you're dissatisfied with the amount of your advance, don't hesitate to discuss it with your publisher. But in addition to considering the factors mentioned above, keep in mind that while your advance may provide you with ready income, this income is not additional to the royalties. Rather, it's a prepaid portion of the royalties that your book will eventually earn, and will be deducted from your royalties.

Royalties

Royalties are another issue that, quite understandably, is of interest to most authors. As explained earlier in the chapter, standard royalty percentages range from 5 to 10 percent of the retail price, and from 5 to 15 percent of the net price. While this may appear satisfactory on the surface—especially if your contract specifies 10 percent of retail—you do want to watch out for a common pitfall of many contracts. Earlier in the chapter, I explained that some contracts reduce the royalty amount when the discount given to the customer is equal to or greater than 50 percent. What these contracts don't state—and what the publisher who offers such a contract isn't likely to explain—is that most books aren't sold directly to the bookstore, but are sold through distributors *at discounts of 50 to 60 percent.* As a result, most of the royalties you collect are likely to be based on the smaller percentage listed in such a contract, rather than the more generous percentage.

What can you do to avoid such a pitfall? Now that you're aware of this potential problem, request that the percentage and the basis for the percentage (net or retail) remain the same based upon discounts up to *60 percent,* not 50 percent. This is a point worth negotiating for, as it will have a marked effect on any earnings you enjoy from the sales of your book.

Subsidiary Rights

As discussed earlier in this chapter, subsidiary rights are those rights derived from the literary work other than the primary right to publish the work. These rights are a common point of negotiation. Many authors want to retain various subsidiary rights, from the right to publish their book in a foreign language to the right to movie adaptations of the work.

> If you're thinking of retaining one or more subsidiary rights, realistically consider if you'll be able to sell them on your own, or if the publisher will be able to do a better job. If the publishing house has personnel devoted only to selling subsidiary rights, it may be in your best interests to let the company represent you.

If you wish to retain one or more of the subsidiary rights, consider if you are truly able to sell them on your own. If these rights are granted to the publisher, she'll be committed to presenting your work to interested parties. Many publishers have personnel devoted strictly to selling subsidiary rights. And, of course, your publisher will divide any resulting proceeds with you as detailed in your contract. But if you retain these rights for yourself, your publisher won't have a vested interested in contacting such parties, leaving you to your own devices—unless, of course, you employ a literary agent to represent you in this regard. A literary agent is almost certain to reserve at least the dramatic rights, and to handle them either directly or through a correspondent agent in Hollywood. If the agent happens to be strong in another rights market—audio books, for example—she may retain those for you as well, and market them on your behalf.

I would be remiss if I didn't emphasize that some publishers—and some agents, as well—are better equipped than others to find parties interested in buying various subsidiary rights. If you're considering retaining any rights, it makes sense to explore your publisher's abilities and past performance in this regard. Let's say, for instance, that you want to retain the rights to foreign-language editions. Ask your publisher about her track record in selling foreign rights. Are her books internationally distributed? Are her books represented by agents in foreign countries? Does she attend the Frankfurt Book Fair and the London Book Fair—two shows at which publishers often make contacts with publishers from other countries? Does she attend BookExpo America (BEA), another show at which foreign rights may be sold? By asking appropriate questions about your area of interest, you'll be able to judge who can best represent you in the selling of subsidiary rights.

Author's Discounts

Novelists are almost always concerned about being able to buy their books at a discount from the publisher, either to distribute to friends and family, or to sell through workshops and lectures in nonbookstore venues. Generally, the publisher allows the author a discount of 40 percent from the list price of the book, but if the author orders the book in significant numbers—and the definition of *significant numbers* varies from publisher to publisher, by the way—the discount can rise to 50 percent or even higher.

If this issue is of concern to you, and if you are offered a discount that's below the standard, don't be afraid to negotiate this point.

Tips for Negotiation

At this point, you probably have a good idea of the contract terms you can live with, the terms that make you a bit uneasy, and the terms that you are determined to change. But what's the best way to go about persuading the publisher that these revisions should be made? Is any strategy particularly effective?

Regardless of the area of the contract you wish to negotiate, I've found that the best way to discuss any of these changes is to start with one or two points that are of *least* importance to you—say, the number of author's copies that will be coming your way. These are the terms that you can graciously accept if the publisher insists on

Is This Publisher Right for You?

Throughout this book, I've emphasized the importance of seeking out a publisher who will meet your personal criteria as established in Chapter 5, produce a high-quality book, market your book aggressively, and deal with you fairly and honestly. In reality, you may be offered a contract by only one company. But if you're lucky enough to elicit the interest of more than one publisher, the following steps may help you choose the one that will provide you with the most rewarding relationship.

☐ Request and review the publisher's catalogues to see how the company markets its books. (For tips on assessing catalogues, see page 144.)

☐ Examine the publisher's novels—especially those books that are in the same category as your own. Be critical, and look for specific things. Are the book covers inviting? Are the titles catchy and clever? Is the typeset page appealing? Unless your goal is simply to get your book into publication, you want a company that will produce an attractive, high-quality edition. Any books already published by the company will give you a fairly good feel for how your own work will be treated.

☐ Ask the publisher how she distributes her books in the relevant market. Also ask her how many sales representatives the company employs, how many books the company has produced in that category, and how many copies have been sold of each title. The answers to these questions—and to any other questions that occur to you during your conversation—will indicate how aggressively the company will market your book, and how much success they've enjoyed in the appropriate marketplace.

☐ Ask to speak to two or three of the authors who have published their books with this company. If the company is reputable, your publisher will gladly give you the names and numbers of some of her authors. Or you can get the names right off the company's published novels and contact the authors via the Internet. You'll then be able to ask these authors about their experiences with the company. Has the publisher made good on her verbal agreements? Has the author's book been effectively marketed? Was the editing of good quality? Have the royalties been paid on time? Although the publisher will probably choose those authors with whom she feels she has the best relationship, the authors will nevertheless provide you with helpful insights. (Some of these insights might surprise the publisher if she heard them!) And, of course, if the publisher refuses to put you in touch with her authors, you'll have a pretty good inkling of how she's treating them.

the original contract wording. Then, by the time you start discussing the areas of the agreement that you really want to change, you'll be seen as a reasonable person, and the publisher will be more likely to negotiate.

What if the publisher calls your bluff and immediately agrees to those extra author's copies? Take it as great news, since you can always use extra books. Besides, I'm not suggesting that you ask for something you don't want, as that would be a waste of time and energy. Moreover, the editor's ready agreement may indicate that she would be amenable to the more important changes you have in mind.

Finally, always keep in mind that your publisher is taking a big gamble on you, a first-time novelist. In Chapter 3, I mentioned that publishers have been estimated to spend an average of $25,000 to $35,000 to turn a manuscript into a printed book. And they have no assurance that they'll make any money back on their investment. For this reason, they can be quickly scared off by an author who demands a large advance or asks for other terms that are generally considered unreasonable for a debut novel. This isn't to say that you shouldn't negotiate. But do temper your requests with a respectful knowledge of the realities of the industry.

> Don't be afraid to at least request those contract changes that are most important to you. Just be sure to temper your requests with a respectful knowledge of the realities of the industry.

If More Than One Company Offers to Buy Your Book

If two companies are interested in publishing your book, you're in an excellent position to compare terms and to use the publishers' interest in your project as a bargaining tool.

First, be sure to avoid comparing apples and oranges—for example, don't compare royalties based on retail price with royalties based on net price. What you do want to compare are the amounts of the advances, as well as when the advances are to be paid out; the royalties; when the book will be published; and how each publisher intends to market the book.

Once you've examined the terms offered by the two companies, don't simply choose the publisher who offers the biggest advance or who has agreed to make the most changes in the contract. Instead, consider the big picture—your career goals, your present situation, and your personal motivations—and choose the contract that best fits your overall objectives. Then, once you receive the contract, you'll be able to negotiate the smaller issues.

A FINAL WORD ON CONTRACTS

In its most basic form, a contract spells out your rights and responsibilities as an author, and the company's rights and responsibilities as the publisher of your work. This chapter has provided you with an

Know the Warning Signs

With any luck, you'll be satisfied with the terms of your contract, or you'll be able to negotiate better terms—at least regarding the issues that are most important to you. Remember, though, that any contract is only as good as the parties who sign it. How will you know whether the publisher you're dealing with will honor the terms of your contract and treat you honestly and fairly? While there is no sure-fire method of gauging a company's character, there are certain warning signs that should alert you to a possible problem. You may want to contact a lawyer or resume your search for a reputable publishing company if:

☐ The contract is so full of legalese and so convoluted in wording that it's impossible to understand without the help of a lawyer.

☐ You ask the publisher or acquisitions editor for clarification of some of the terms of the contract, but she never gives you a straight answer.

☐ You attempt to negotiate the terms of the contract, and find that there's no give and take on the part of the publisher.

☐ Other authors who have worked with this publishing company report that the publisher is late with royalty payments and that she rarely makes good on verbal promises regarding marketing or other aspects of the publishing process.

☐ The contract states that the author will pay the publisher for one or several aspects of the publishing process. This is a bad sign *unless* the payment is expected to come out of the royalty advance—a practice that is acceptable and used by many legitimate companies. Any company that expects the author to pay for editing, typesetting, printing, or warehousing may be a vanity press masquerading as a commercial publisher.

understanding of your responsibilities, and will help you negotiate for those rights that are most important to you.

Years of experience have taught me that the best thing you can do for yourself throughout the negotiation phase is to keep up with your writing. Lay the groundwork for your next success while you're putting the finishing touches on this one. It will do wonders for your perspective.

CHAPTER 9

WHEN IT DOESN'T HAPPEN

After sending out a submission package, the future sparkles with promise. It's almost impossible to stop yourself from imagining the hefty royalty checks, the fan mail, the appearances on talk shows—maybe even a movie option. All that disappears when you open your mailbox and spot your own SASE—a sure sign that the publisher isn't interested in your book. It's pretty hard not to take a publisher's rejection personally. And it's pretty hard not to feel bad.

What can you do to lift your spirits? First, think about all the now well-known novelists who were rejected time after time before they got their first break. Frank Herbert's *Dune* was rejected twenty times before it became a science fiction classic. Elmore Leonard's *The Big Bounce* got the cold shoulder eighty-four times, but sold on its eighty-fifth submission and later became a Gold Medal Original. Almost every major modern-day author, in fact, has received his or her share of rejection letters. So you're in good company.

Second—and most important—take steps to accurately diagnose where the problem may lie. In earlier chapters, we discussed a few possible roadblocks to success. For instance, you know that by failing to target the right publishers, you can significantly decrease your chance of finding an interested editor, and may even totally sabotage your efforts. And you know that a poor submission package can also prevent you from reaching your goal. Your story concept, your timing, and your approach may also be "off."

If the task of diagnosing the problem, let alone fixing it, seems more than a bit overwhelming, take a deep breath and relax. This chapter was designed to help you analyze where the problem may exist, and then choose the course of action that is most likely to get your book into print. It will also provide you with some intriguing possibilities, including that of self-publication. In fact, you may be amazed by the number of options available to you—options that will allow you to reach your goal of seeing your novel move from manuscript to printed book.

IDENTIFYING THE PROBLEM

Short of a concerted plot to stop you from getting your work published, there are only a few basic reasons why manuscripts get rejected: the subject, the approach, the timing, the choice of publishers, the submission package, or some combination of these. Let's first briefly consider each of these possibilities so that you will be in a better position to pinpoint your problem. Later in the chapter, we'll look at what you can do to overcome these roadblocks.

Your Subject

Many companies, including mine, offer lists of those subjects that are now selling well, versus those that are a tough sell. Log onto www.aeionline.com, and click first on "News" and then on "Market Trends." There, you'll find What's Hot/What's Not lists. But exercise caution in using the "What's Hot" material to select a subject for your next novel. Some subjects are of interest for only a short time.

Your choice of subject matter can greatly influence your chances of getting published. If you've chosen a subject that has a very limited audience—one that is too esoteric—you may have created a project that is simply too hard to sell to a commercial press. On the other hand, if you've selected a topic that everybody is writing about, titles like yours may have already saturated the marketplace. Publishers may be reluctant to put out any more books on the subject—at this time, at least. Finally, if you've presented your topic in a manner that is unclear or that fails to demonstrate the project's marketability, you have definitely reduced your odds of being picked up.

Your Approach

Let's assume that the subject of your book is solid, with a good-size audience and a very reachable marketplace. Still, you're not getting any nibbles. The problem may center on the way you've presented or explored your subject—in other words, on your approach.

Let's say that you've written a contemporary romance that you feel would be perfect for a particular line of books and a particular audience. But instead of writing in the style characteristic of that genre, you have chosen a very literary style with sophisticated language, complex sentence structure, and detailed character development. The reality is that the style you've chosen isn't appropriate for that category. So your approach—to use a literary style in a romance novel—is a problem.

Or perhaps you've written an action-packed Western, complete with realistic Western vernacular and settings, but your manuscript is twice as long as the longest novel in that category. Here, again, your approach may have caused a problem.

Something to Laugh About

It's easy to allow rejection letters to make you doubt your worth, as well as your ability to get your book into publication. To gain perspective and to enjoy some much-needed laughter, spend an afternoon leafing through *Pushcart's Complete Rotten Reviews and Rejections*. This book includes hundreds of scathing comments directed at authors whose works are now regarded with respect and, in some cases, with reverence. As you read the following remarks—culled from both rejection letters and reviews—think of the joy the reading public would have missed if these writers had meekly accepted the editors' comments as gospel instead of continuing their search for the right publisher.

Anna Karenina
Leo Tolstoi, 1877
Sentimental rubbish. . . . Show me one page that contains an idea.

Lord of the Flies
William Golding, 1954
It does not seem to us that you have been wholly successful in working out an admittedly promising idea.

Animal Farm
George Orwell, 1945
It is impossible to sell animal stories in the U.S.A.

Lady Chatterley's Lover
D.H Lawrence, 1915
For your own good do not publish this book.

Catch-22
Joseph Heller, 1961
I haven't really the foggiest idea of what the man is trying to say.

The Adventures of Huckleberry Finn
Mark Twain, 1884
A gross trifling with every fine feeling. . . . Mr. Clemens has no reliable sense of propriety.

The Time Machine
H.G. Wells, 1895
It is not interesting enough for the general reader and not thorough enough for the scientific reader.

A Confederacy of Dunces
John Kennedy Toole, 1980
Obsessively foul and grotesque.

Timing

Closely related to the problem of subject is that of timing. When I talk about timing, I'm referring to the specific time an editor receives your submission. This topic was first explored in Chapter 7. (See page 155.) But if you haven't yet found a publisher who's interested in your proposal, the subject is well worth revisiting.

Timing can be everything. Your proposal can be wonderful, and you may submit it to the perfect house. Then one week before you send in your proposal, the house may sign an agreement with another author for a similar novel. Odds are you'll never know of the earlier project. All you'll know is that "the perfect house" said no. This is bad timing.

Your book might have come onto the market just a hair too late, on the heels of a departing trend. Or it might have appeared on the editor's desk a little too early, on the leading edge of a soon-to-be-hot topic. You tell the editor how this subject is going to be really popular, but the editor doesn't agree. Being ahead of a trend may result in continuous rejections from editors who don't share your vision. This, too, is bad timing.

Or imagine that an editor rejects your manuscript because the house isn't looking for a book in that category. Two months later, at an editorial meeting, there's a radical shift in editorial direction that might now make your project a prime target for publication. The editor vaguely remembers receiving your proposal some time earlier, but can't locate a copy of the rejection letter, and so is unable to contact you. Sound bizarre? Things like this happen all the time. You may have a great idea for a book, but if your timing is off, it's not going to happen.

Your Choice of Publishers

Choosing a publisher raises a number of challenges. Let's first assume that you sent your proposal out to appropriate houses—companies that produce the type of novel you are writing, and that are willing to consider unsolicited manuscripts. Why hasn't your book been snapped up? If no other problems exist—if your approach, subject, and other elements are all what they should be—it may just be that you haven't yet found the editor who will judge your proposal exciting and intriguing.

On the other hand, you may have unintentionally targeted inappropriate publishers. For instance, although your topic may be perfect for a small literary publisher, you may have targeted only major New York houses because you want your book produced by a company with "a name." If you've followed your heart's desire—or anything else—instead of following the advice provided in Chapters 3 and 5, you may have virtually guaranteed a stream of rejection letters.

Your Submission Package

Now let's assume that your topic is fine, your timing isn't a problem, your approach is flawless, and you've carefully selected the publishing houses to which you mailed off your submission package. Nevertheless, either no one has asked for further materials, or one or more editors did request materials, but no one followed up with a contract.

Now it's time to take a step back and consider if the problem may be with your submission package. Most likely, if your manuscript is being held back by a problem found within the submission itself or within any follow-up materials you sent, you should be looking for at least one of two possibilities. Either the writing of the submission package or of the materials sent subsequently is lacking in necessary quality, or you have not identified the audience and marketplace for your book in a way that favorably impressed the editor. Let's look at each of these in turn.

Writing Quality

As discussed in Chapter 6, "Preparing the Package," your submission package not only provides information about your book, but also serves as a sample of your writing style. A number of writing-related problems can turn an editor off. In any type of writing, of course, poor grammar, lack of clarity, and lack of organization can cause an editor to reject the project. In the case of a novel, though, you also have to consider if there might be flaws in character development, dialogue, plot, structure, and "voice" or style. Any of these difficulties signals the need for hours of rewriting by a capable editor. And in an industry in which the bottom line is all-important, few if any editors are interested in rolling up their sleeves to save a potentially good story that needs a lot of work.

Never forget that your submission package not only informs the editor about your novel, but also serves as a sample of your writing. That's why it's so important to make your package is as good as it can be before sending it off to the publishers on your list.

Too often, writers send out what is, in effect, their first draft. Any writer will tell you that it's difficult to determine when something is ready for submission, but for most successful authors, the rewriting stage takes longer than the creation of the first draft. The revision process is a necessity because as sterling as we all think our work is, chances are that it needs at least some polishing before it's presented to an editor.

If you didn't think that it was necessary to revise your submission package, or if you thought that a once-over was enough, consider the possibility that your package was sent out too soon.

Painting the Right Picture

When assessing your submission package, keep in mind that although your book may have been painstakingly tailored for its intended audience—and even for a specific imprint— if your package doesn't convey this fact to the editor, he won't be likely to give your novel a chance.

If your submission package doesn't provide the editor with the information for which he is looking, there's little chance that your proposal is going to make him sit up and take notice. Maybe your letter doesn't adequately identify your category or subcategory. Or maybe although you tailored your manuscript to a specific imprint, you haven't communicated this fact to the editor.

It's easy to understand how such omissions occur. Often, in our enthusiasm, we assume that the editor will immediately perceive all the wonders of our book—without being told. But the fact is that if you don't clearly provide the editor with the information he seeks, it's possible that no one will ever know just how great your book is.

Strategies for Pinpointing the Problem

You now know that there are a handful of problems that may be holding your project back. During your reading of the above discussions, you may have identified the problem. If you're still in the dark, though, there are a number of things you can do to pinpoint the flaws in your project.

Look for Clues in Your Rejection Letters

Although most rejections are frustratingly uninformative form letters, some editors do take the time to mention the reason for the rejection in their responses. Sometimes it's a line scrawled on a form letter; other times, it's a separate note.

If you receive such feedback, consider it a gift, and use it to correct any problems in your submission. (See the inset below for more details on this strategy.)

Enlist Some Help

If your rejection letters failed to provide any clues, consider showing your submission package to one or two people who you feel can be both discriminating and honest. Ask them for their opinions, and try to consider their comments with an open mind. You might want to provide them with a list of the pitfalls we've just discussed, and ask them if they believe that any of these problems may be holding your project back.

How to Profit From Rejection

If you're lucky, at least one of the rejection letters you received was not a form letter, but actually mentioned the reason for the rejection. Maybe an editor noted that your story was unfocused. Or perhaps he felt that the character development wasn't adequate for a mainstream novel. This is not to suggest that the editor was necessarily correct in his evaluation. Every editor is a human being, after all, and if the inset on page 185 proves anything, it proves that editors can be dead wrong. But if a busy editor has taken the time to note his impression of your project, it would be foolish not to take a long, hard look at your materials. Then, if the editor's criticism does make sense to you, by all means make any necessary revisions and send the revised package back to him, along with a personal note of your own.

If you decide not to make the changes that the editor has suggested—or if the rejection was due to a factor beyond your control, such as the editor's recent acquisition of a similar book—you should nevertheless send a note thanking him for his interest and expressing hope that your next submission will better suit his needs. It's always smart to be as polite and courteous as possible. As I've said before, editors move around from house to house all the time, so you never know when you'll run into that editor again.

If none of the editors shared his thoughts with you, you may be tempted to call some of them up and ask the reason for their rejections. While this may seem like a simple, commonsense approach, as I explained in Chapter 7, your calls aren't likely to yield helpful answers. Most acquisitions editors sift through so many queries on a daily basis that they probably won't even be able to remember your proposal, much less offer useful comments and suggestions. On the other hand, if an editor was sufficiently impressed by your submission package to request further materials, and if he sent a rejection letter only after reviewing those materials, it would make sense to give him a call, as he may now be both willing and able to provide you with the feedback you're seeking.

If you took the advice presented in Chapter 6, you've already shown your submission package to one person. This time, try to choose different people so that you can get a new perspective. As before, it would be helpful if your reviewers had solid English skills, as well as experience with novels. A high school or college English teacher would be a good choice, for example, as would anyone who does a great deal of writing in his job.

If your chosen reviewers haven't provided you with the answers you're searching for, you may want to look outside your circle of friends and acquaintances. Writers' groups and writers' workshops can be found throughout the United States. Through these groups, you may be able to find other writers who can look at your work objectively and offer valuable criticism. Similarly, writing courses can put you in touch with other writers and, perhaps more important, with instructors who are both able and willing to critique your work. Objective advice may be exactly what you need to pinpoint problems in both your proposal and your actual manuscript. (More information on these resources is provided later in the chapter.)

The Writer's Lifeline, Inc. (www.thewriterslifeline.com) is one of the companies that can provide a written assessment of your project's strengths and weaknesses, focusing on action line, character, dialogue, setting, and tone. Log onto their website and click on "Services," then "Novels," then "Launch Analysis" to read a sample assessment.

Another constructive option is to find a good freelance editor who can help you identify your problem and work towards a solution. Choose someone who has experience with novels, and have him perform an analysis, pointing out flaws such as undeveloped characters or faulty structure. This alone might be enough to guide you, or you may want the editor to work with you in improving the novel. Be careful in your choice of editors, though. There are plenty of self-styled "book doctors" out there who are not qualified to do what they're promising.

It's not difficult to find an experienced freelance editor. The "Editorial Services" section of the *LMP* is one good source, as are ads in periodicals such as *The Writer* and *Writer's Digest*. Another option is to simply type "editorial services" into your favorite Internet search engine. Note that many of these services offer free sample edits and critiques, which will give you a chance to determine if that service is the right one for you and your book.

Learn More About Your Category

If the cause of your problem still eludes you, you may want to carefully examine published books that are in the same category as yours, be it mainstream fiction, fantasy, or adventure. Look at books that are similar to yours in genre, and pay special attention to the more popular titles. Your goal is to note the difference between your own book and other books in the same category. Compare the vocabulary, dialogue, pacing, character development, and action line. If you find marked differences—if the protagonist in your book isn't as well developed as protagonists in other novels of that type, or if other books in that category have far more (or far less) action—you may have located the source of your problem.

When investigating possible problems with your novel, it often pays to compare your book with published works in the same category. If you find marked differences between the two—if the protagonist in your book isn't as well developed as protagonists in other novels of that type, for instance—you may have found your problem.

If your search yields no published book similar to yours, that alone may be the problem. Editors may be interested in a unique approach to an old idea, but for the most part, they want books designed for an existing category and an eager audience. On the other hand, your search may have turned up dozens and dozens of similar books. You now know that you've chosen a subject or genre of interest. But the glut of competing books may mean that the market is already saturated with novels like yours. That, too, isn't good.

How Much Are You Willing to Change?

Just as it might someday be necessary to revise your work so that it's acceptable to your editor, it may now be necessary to make changes to get that first contract. And these changes can be difficult—even painful—to make.

Before I move on to suggest ways of remedying any problem found, I want to point out that it's not necessarily in your best interest to do anything and everything to get your book into publication. If you wrote your novel from the heart, and you're confident that it says what you want it to say, you might actually diminish it by revising to suit a fickle market. But you should seriously question if the uniqueness of your book is a necessary and essential component of the work, or if it's an expendable feature that may be keeping you from getting published.

As just mentioned, with the exception of the handful of companies that publish "experimental fiction," editors aren't looking for something that has never been done before. They're looking for a book that fits into an existing category, has an existing and accessible audience, and meets the needs of that audience in established ways. Your book may prove to be the exception—a sports novel that uses

Many novelists, while acknowledging the need to revise their book, make only a few superficial changes rather than reworking the manuscript at an appropriate level. If you have determined that your novel needs a rewrite, take the time to do it properly.

the language typical of a literary work, but nevertheless appeals to its intended readers. Chances are, though, that if you insist on a truly unique approach, you will greatly decrease your odds of finding an editor who's willing to champion your project.

If you do decide to revise your manuscript in order to make it more marketable, make sure to rework it at the appropriate level. Some writers, while acknowledging the need for change, try to effect it with a few keystrokes here, a couple of deletions there, when what's really needed is a deep, systematic rewrite.

SOLVING THE PROBLEM

By now I hope you've identified the likely culprit that's standing between you and a publishing contract. Your next step is to revise your materials in a way that makes them more appealing to prospective publishers. Depending on the nature of the problem and your skills, you may choose to go it alone, or you may want to enlist the help of others.

Going It Alone

Depending on your writing skills, you may be able to make many types of changes on your own, without the help of either a more experienced writer or further training. Let's look at some of the problems discussed earlier in this chapter to see what action you can take to clear the path to success.

Your Subject

The solution to a subject-related problem will depend on the exact difficulty caused by your topic. If, for instance, you've chosen a subject with a very limited audience, and have therefore kept the novel from being judged sufficiently profitable for a large commercial press, consider focusing on smaller presses with a similar subject focus, or on an academic publisher.

If there appear to be too many books on your subject, try waiting six months or even longer, and resubmitting your writing to the publishers on your original list. As time passes, many of the other books with similar themes will disappear from the marketplace, possibly

Your Novel Might Not Be the Problem

If the desk in your home office is now piled with rejection letters, you may have begun to doubt the worth of your work. If so, the following story should help put things in perspective.

In 1969, well-known writer Jerzy Kosinski won the National Book Award for his novel *Steps*. In 1975, freelance writer Chuck Ross decided to test his theory that unknown writers don't have a chance to get their novels published. So he typed out the first twenty-one pages of Kosinski's novel and submitted it to four publishers, using the pseudonym "Erik Demos." All four houses rejected the sample. Two years later, Ross typed out the *entire* book and sent it to ten publishers and thirteen literary agents. Again, he received only rejections—including a form rejection from the publishing house that had originally produced *Steps*. That made a total of twenty-seven rejections for a novel that had earned an important literary award!

leaving room for yours. (For more about this strategy, see "Timing" on page 194.)

Finally, reread your cover or query letter. Is the subject of your book clearly spelled out? Have you made the book seem marketable? By demonstrating that your book has an existing and accessible audience, you may stimulate interest in your project.

Your Approach

If you've decided that the flaw in your novel lies in your approach to the topic, you may very well be able to rework your sample chapters and other submission materials to reflect a new and more marketable approach.

For a moment, let's return to the contemporary romance novel written in a literary style. If you've determined that the vocabulary and sentence structure should be revised to suit your chosen genre, start reworking it. Just be sure to thoroughly familiarize yourself with other books in your category so that the appropriate language of the contemporary romance novel is clear to you before you begin your rewrite.

Remember the Western that was much too long for a formula novel in that catagory? Try to determine how your story can be pared down without robbing the book of its flavor or having a negative effect on the plot.

Computers make it easy to experiment with different ways of presenting material. Don't hesitate to pull your book apart and put it back together again in a new way, to rework the dialogue, or to add and delete scenes. Just be sure to save your original document so that if you finally decide that your first approach was best, you'll have the original draft intact.

There are many more ways to change your approach. Just don't be afraid to pull your book apart and put it back together in a new way. Computers make it easy to experiment with different ways of presenting material. Simply save your original document and create a new one that you can "play" with until you find the best approach possible. If you ultimately conclude that your first approach was best, you'll still have the original document intact.

Timing

Timing is a unique problem in that you can't solve it by reworking your cover letter or taking a new approach because the problem isn't in the proposal or the project. What you *can* do is adopt one of the strategies suggested earlier, under "Topic." Simply wait six months to a year, and send out another set of submission packages to all the publishers on your original list. You can begin your cover letter by stating that this is a resubmission, and that you hope the editor will reconsider your project in light of changing editorial needs.

Does this strategy work? Based on experience, resubmissions do hit their marks—not always, but enough times to make this a worthwhile option. Within six months or so, a company's ownership can change hands, editors may be replaced, editorial programs can change, new subjects and themes can catch on—dozens of things can happen to turn your project into a strong candidate for publication. Resubmitting your material will keep bad timing down to a minimum.

Your Choice of Publishers

If your problem is related to your choice of publishers, a couple of solutions are worth considering. If you feel that the publishers on your original list were appropriate, keep in mind that you've probably sent out your proposal to only about thirty publishers, while there are *thousands* of book publishers in the United States, with new ones cropping up all the time. That's why within Chapter 7, I suggest that if you don't find an interested editor among those on your first list, you put together another list of companies. If you haven't already done so, give this strategy a try, making your criteria as liberal as possible. You may be able to find as many as a hundred additional publishers who may show interest in your book.

After you've put together your new list of publishers, go back to Chapter 7 and use the Square One System to send out submission packages to these new companies. Perhaps your new list contains an editor who will appreciate your project and personally guide it through the editorial process all the way to publication.

What if you suspect that you didn't select the best publishing houses for your original list? Chapter 3, "The Business of Publishing Novels," and Chapter 5, "Finding the Right Publisher," will guide you to the most appropriate companies for your project. This time around, though, you may have to be a little more realistic in your selection, and carefully consider each and every company before adding it to your list.

Your Submission Package

Depending on your skills, you may be able to solve various problems with your submission package once these problems have been identified. For instance, although you may not initially have recognized that your protagonist wasn't developed in sufficient detail, now that you've found the problem, you may be more than capable of reworking your sample chapters to more fully explore the main character's personality and background. Similarly, once you realize that your cover letter fails to clearly define your category, you may be able to easily integrate the missing information in your package. But if these tasks are currently beyond your reach, if you suspect that your grammar or general writing skills are weak, or if you're unable to invest the time needed to bring your proposal and manuscript up to par, you might benefit from outside help. The following discussion will guide you to a variety of resources that may be able to provide the help and support that you need.

Finding Training, Support, and Other Assistance

It can be frustrating to find that despite your passion for writing—and, possibly, despite a wealth of wonderful ideas—you lack the expertise necessary to revamp your submission package and/or your manuscript. Be assured that some skills come with time and practice. As you exercise your writing "muscles" by writing and rewriting, and as you immerse yourself in the world of fiction, your skills will

New publishing companies open every year, and older houses establish new imprints. That's why it often makes sense to check the most current editions of resources such as *Novel & Short Story Writer's Market*, and make up a new list of potential publishers for your project. All you need is one interested editor to get your book from the desk drawer to the bookstore.

become stronger. But everyone can use some support, especially when they're first starting out. Fortunately, there are many resources available to the writer in need. Some are designed to get your skills up to speed, while others involve finding an individual who is capable of performing the rewrite for you.

Writing Classes, Groups, Conferences, and Workshops

Earlier in this chapter, I mentioned how writing courses, writers' groups, and writers' workshops can put you in touch with people who have the judgment needed to critique your submission package. These same groups and courses can also help you hone your craft.

If you've determined that your grammar skills are in need of improvement, a grammar course at a local college will be your best bet. These courses, which generally take you step by step through a grammar workbook, cover a variety of important topics such as parallelism, tense, and verb and noun agreement—areas that baffle many aspiring novelists. Just as important, most teachers are happy to address any specific questions you have, and may even be willing to read through your work and offer constructive criticism. Night courses are usually available, and some colleges have continuing education programs designed specifically for adults who want to improve their skills.

If you wish to develop your writing skills in general, and your fiction-writing skills in particular, consider taking a creative writing course, also available at most colleges. In any good writing class, you'll learn to arrange words to form a structured whole. If you're lucky enough to find a course that focuses on fiction writing, you will also learn specifics about character development, structure, dialogue, and other elements of a good novel. Your writing will then be submitted for criticism to your teacher and, possibly, your classmates. Afterwards, you'll rewrite your work, taking any comments and suggestions into account. You may also be asked to offer constructive criticism of your fellow students' writing—a process that will help you sharpen your ability to identify strengths and weaknesses. Contact those colleges and adult study programs near you and see what they have to offer. And keep in mind that, like any instruction, a writing class will give you only as much as you put into it, so be prepared to work hard if you're serious about improving your skills. Just be sure to sign up with an instructor who has the right credentials for that particular course. A teacher of creative writing should himself be a published writer or editor of fiction.

Writing can be a lonely business, and even published authors sometimes seek out writers' groups for the camaraderie they offer. Newer writers often find that involvement in a writers' group can provide the support of people who have objectives similar to their own, and are eager to share writings, tips, and encouragement. To find a local group that is being formed or is trying to fill a chair, check advertisements in local newspapers; scan school bulletins and writers' websites; and read coffeehouse, bookstore, and library posting boards. Be picky, and don't hesitate to leave a group that you feel isn't giving you the help and support you want. For a writing group to be productive, the members have to get along well, trust one another, care about one another, and be compatible in intelligence and focus. It may take some time to find a group that can provide you with the constructive criticism you need.

Yet another option is to join an online writing group. These groups don't foster the companionship and trust that "in-person" meetings might, but if you don't have the time or opportunity to attend such a gathering, an online group is a good alternative. (See pages 301 to 302 of the Resource List for some helpful sites.)

You might also wish to consider attending writers' conferences and workshops. Depending on their focus and format, these gatherings can provide you with advice on writing through workshops, discussions, and one-on-one tutorials; insights into the publishing world; and encouragement from both peers and professionals, including book editors, literary agents, and published authors. Some writers have even been able to forge useful relationships with editors and agents at such events. (See pages 71 to 72 for more information about meeting agents and editors at conferences.)

If you're looking for a local workshop or conference, flip through regional magazines and newspapers, and contact your local and state arts councils; your Town Hall; and your local schools, libraries, and community centers. For instance, YMCAs across the country sponsor YMCA National Writer's Voice Centers. These centers host a variety of events, including workshops and writing camps.

Maybe you'd like to combine your training with a trip to another part of the country. A number of gatherings are listed in the *Novel &*

Some writers' groups are nothing but egos and neediness; others are overflowing with talent and professionalism. Choose carefully to find a group that will give you the support, encouragement, and constructive criticism you need to develop your skills.

Short Story Writer's Market and the *Literary Market Place (LMP)*, each of which devotes an entire section to writers' conferences and workshops. Also look through the ads and events listings in magazines such as *Writer's Digest* and *The Writer*. And, of course, the Internet can provide you with listings of numerous writers' gatherings. Simply use the search engine of your choice to look for "writers conferences."

Working with a Ghostwriter

Most ghostwriters require an advance before they begin work on a project. Some, however, will allow you to delay payment until you have a signed contract in hand.

If, for any reason, you feel that you cannot rework your submission package and/or your manuscript as necessary, you have another great option—a ghostwriter. A ghostwriter can organize your ideas, thoughts, and writings into a readable book. You provide the ideas for the characters and story line, and your ghostwriter provides the writing. A talented ghostwriter can even "mimic" your writing voice. Your name will still appear alone as author of the book, as the ghostwriter will not be credited as an author. He will, however, be compensated through a percentage of the royalties or a flat fee, which can range anywhere from $5,000 to $100,000 per novel, depending on the work required and his credentials.

Where can you find a competent ghostwriter? To start, writers' workshops and conferences are good places to find candidates for the job. (Don't forget that the teachers of most writing courses are themselves writers, and may be interested in your project.) The "Editorial Services" section of the *LMP* lists a number of companies that provide ghostwriting. Finally, magazines like *The Writer* and *Writer's Digest* contain numerous advertisements of editing and rewriting services.

Whether a ghost has been highly recommended by a friend or was located through an ad, you'll want to do your homework and make sure that he is a skilled writer. Ask the ghost about his background. What kinds of books has he written? Has he been published? Ask to see some of his work, and read it critically. If in doubt, ask other people to read it, too. You want to make sure not only that he can write, but also that he can write books in your category, whether that category is science fiction or horror. Finally, make sure that this is a person with whom you can work. Collaboration can be a positive experience. It can also be instructive. Your own writing may improve as you see what your ghost does with your material. But collaboration can be a nightmare if you don't choose your ghostwriter carefully. You and your ghost should be able to work well together.

Using an Editorial Service

Earlier in the chapter, I talked about finding an editor who could pinpoint any problems in your submission package. In exchange for a flat fee, a skilled editor can also correct problems in syntax, grammar, usage, style, and punctuation; help you with plot, pacing, characterization, and dialogue; and provide helpful feedback and suggestions. An editorial service is not, of course, credited as an author. (See the earlier discussion on page 190 for tips on finding an editorial service.)

OTHER OPTIONS

What can you do if, despite your best efforts to rework the material, your book still hasn't found a publisher? What if you feel that it would not be in your best interest to change your work to meet the needs of a commercial publisher? Not every author wants or needs to get his work edited and produced by a standard commercial press. Maybe you simply want to make your story available to the public. As you'll soon see, this is still a very realizable goal.

Don't despair if despite your best efforts, no publisher has offered you a contract. There are other ways to make your novel available to potential readers.

Self-Publication

Are you passionately committed to becoming a successful writer? Is your belief in the merit of your work ironclad? Are you blessed with an entrepreneurial spirit? If you can truthfully answer "yes" to all three of these questions, you may choose to dispense with traditional publishers for now and publish your novel yourself.

The uninitiated often think that self-publishing and vanity publishing are one and the same, but in truth, there's a *huge* difference between the two. While a vanity house takes care of the whole publication process—albeit, for a hefty fee—in a self-publishing program, you literally do everything yourself. You edit the book or hire someone else to do the editing for you; design the layout and either typeset the text or hire a typesetter to do so; proofread and correct the copy; design the cover or arrange to have it professionally designed; arrange to have the book printed and bound; warehouse the finished book; and even do your own marketing and publicity. You then sell your book to individuals, bookstores, libraries, or other outlets. Finally, you do your own billing and collections.

While this may sound overwhelming, self-publishing is, in fact, an old and honorable practice. If you decide to take this path, you'll be in good company. Mark Twain, William Blake, D.H. Lawrence, Edgar Allan Poe, Nicholas Sparks, Zane Grey, Mary Baker Eddy, Pat Conroy, Walt Whitman, and many other now-famous writers got their start by publishing and promoting their early works on their own. So self-publishing doesn't involve the stigma associated with vanity publication. This means that once your book is in print, you'll have a good chance of getting it into bookstores and of getting it reviewed.

WORDS FROM A PRO

James Michael Pratt
Author of The Last Valentine *(St. Martin's Press)*

In 1993, I became a statistic in the California Real Estate crash. I owned property worth less than it cost to buy and build. I was wiped out, financially and emotionally.

We moved to Utah to get a fresh start. No money, just a pad of paper, a pen, and dreams. Writing solely for my own enjoyment, I penned the novel *The Last Valentine* with the coaching of a local instructor. After garnering rejection slips from five agents, I approached three regional publishers—two of whom, to my surprise, offered me contracts. But after I analyzed the extent of their distribution, I determined that I wanted to play in the "bigger game," New York. I rejected their offers.

Following the example of Utah author Richard Paul Evans, who had succeeded hugely with his novel *Christmas Box,* I hired an aggressive distributor who saw my book's *national* potential. I borrowed $12,000, spent $8,000 to print the first 4,000 copies, then used the rest—judiciously—for publicity. I tagged along with the distributor to the 1996 BookExpo America in Chicago, and handed out 1,200 autographed copies. I went to book signings where nobody showed, courted local news articles, and reinvested every penny.

It began to produce results.

The publicity, coupled with my distributor's efforts, made it happen. I can't emphasize enough how important the distributor is in the life of a book.

When I'd sold 15,000 copies, I decided to try again for a representative. One of my top choices was Ken Atchity of AEI in Los Angeles. I was thrilled at his enthusiasm. We agreed to go forward.

Four novels later, I *still* work hard to build my readership. But the rewards are worth it. Would I self-publish again, knowing the hard work and unwavering self-confidence it requires? Absolutely.

Some authors have actually been able to make more money self-publishing their novels than they would have made by working with traditional publishing houses. More than once, I've consulted with writers who have a built-in method of ongoing distribution for their self-published books. Some are members of huge organizations, and others are constantly on the lecture circuit, with captive audiences who are offered the book for purchase. If you have an existing system such as this, or any other type of public presence that you can tap into to promote your book, your self-publishing enterprise will have a ready-made launch pad.

Self-publishing can even land you a contract with an established publishing house. It's become increasingly popular for novelists to publish their own work, establish a solid sales record, and use their sales figures to prove their work's audience and profitability. Many authors produce between 500 and 5,000 or so copies of their book, and then send some of these copies to reviewers and otherwise work to garner a readership prior to approaching publishers. Then, instead of mailing out submission packages, they send printed books to their target publishing companies, enclosing any positive reviews and sales figures. Publishers are more likely to take a chance on a book that already has a proven track record. Self-publishing also allows these authors to establish a fan base of their own design, while gaining invaluable experience in the industry.

When self-publishing is handled intelligently, it has the added benefit of generally being much less expensive than publication through a vanity press. Thanks to computers, laser printers, and publishing software, authors can get their books and promotional pieces ready for printing without the numerous costly production steps that used to be necessary. Many small-run printers will print as few as 300 copies of the book—a far cry from the 5,000-book run demanded by many vanity presses. Naturally, prices change all the time, and your own costs will depend partly on the manufacturers with whom you deal. But, in general, authors who shop for the best prices can save thousands of dollars by choosing self-publication over vanity publication. (To learn more about vanity publishing, see the inset on pages 208 to 209.)

Yet another benefit of self-publishing is that it will allow you to market your book for as long as you desire. As discussed in earlier chapters, most of the larger traditional publishers abandon a book

Since the late 1990s, when savvy authors began to successfully market their books on the Internet, several dozen self-published novels have been picked up by major publishing houses.

within a few months if it's not selling well. But as a self-publisher, you'll be able to continue your marketing and distribution efforts indefinitely. In fact, some writers choose self-publishing over more traditional routes not because they can't elicit a conventional publisher's interest, but because self-publication will allow them to retain control over marketing, distribution, and every other aspect of the publishing process. They can also keep a greater percentage of the profits from each book they sell.

But in order for your self-published novel to succeed, it must be a high-quality book in every regard, as well as one that generates appreciable—and auditable—sales. To achieve this, you must invest in quality production, including editing, interior layout, and cover design; establish significant distribution through some of the major wholesalers or distributors, like Baker & Taylor or Ingram; and effectively market the book to both retailers and consumers. For many authors, this is a daunting challenge, demanding the same amount of work performed by an entire company in a traditional publishing scenario.

When designing your self-published book, visit a bookstore and choose a book that's similar to yours. Then use the commercial book's typeface, layout, and cover as inspiration for your own design choices. You want to make sure that your book is in the same league as the competition.

If you're interested in self-publishing but are intimidated by the idea of seeking out cover designers and printers, you might want to consider print-on-demand publishers. Found online, these companies often offer a variety of services, from copyediting to cover design to marketing. You can choose all of the offered services, or you can choose just a few. Most important, the companies keep an electronic version of your book on file, and print and bind copies of the book as needed for a relatively small fee—from less than $100 to about $2,000. You retain the copyright, receive a certain number of bound copies, and earn a royalty rate of about 25 percent of the retail price on sales. Just remember that if you opt only for printing and binding, you'll still be responsible for other aspects of your new business, such as marketing. Also keep in mind that you'll be bound by the terms of your online agreement, so before you hit "send," you'll want to make sure that you're getting only the services you want—and that you're retaining the rights to your book. Finally, be aware that traditional booksellers won't stock POD books and that commercial publishers are unlikely to accept them for republication, so if your objective is to distribute your novel to major retail bookstore chains or to land a publishing contract, POD publishers won't help you realize your goal. If you simply want to see your book in print, though, POD is a viable alternative. To find these services, simply perform an Internet search for "print on demand," and a number of websites will pop up.

Whether you decide to manage every aspect of self-publication on your own or to enlist help from POD publishers, it's essential to thoroughly investigate the self-publishing option before you make any commitments. A number of books can familiarize you with the process and provide you with valuable tips. For starters, take a look at *The Self-Publishing Manual* by Dan Poynter, which I regard as a leader in the field. Another excellent resource is that bible of the publishing world, the *LMP*. The "Book Manufacturing Section" of the *LMP* includes listings of typing and word-processing services, art services, and printing and binding services. Many of the printers spe-

Is Self-Publishing Right for You?

If you've been unable to find an established publisher for your book, or if you are too independent-minded to cater to the demands of a commercial publishing house, self-publishing may help you realize your dream of seeing your book in print. But self-publishing isn't for everyone. When you commit yourself to self-publishing a book, you're really starting your own business. To see if you have what it takes, ask yourself the following questions:

☐ Is the publication of my book so important to me that I'm willing to invest both thousands of dollars and countless hours of time?

☐ Am I willing to accept the fact that I may never again see the money I invest?

☐ Am I willing to investigate typesetters, printers, and other manufacturers and services to find companies that can give me what I need for a reasonable price?

☐ Am I thick-skinned enough to face the possibility that bookstores may refuse to carry my book?

☐ Am I thick-skinned enough to face the possibility that the media may ignore or criticize my book?

☐ Will I really do the homework necessary to learn about book distribution, publicity, and marketing?

☐ Once my book has been published, will I really spend all of the hours and money necessary to properly distribute, publicize, and market my book?

☐ Do I have both the motivation and the self-confidence it takes to continue to promote my book despite any rejections and setbacks I encounter along the way?

Self-publishing involves hard work, but if you answered yes to most of the above questions, this option may be just what you're looking for.

cialize in short-run book manufacturing, and the majority of entries state the company's minimum run, which in some cases is as small as 300 books. And because your job as a self-publisher doesn't end when your book is in print, you'll also want to examine John Kremer's *1001 Ways to Market Your Books*.

You can also learn a great deal about producing, marketing, and selling your book by joining one or two trade groups: the Publisher's Marketing Association (PMA) or the Small Publishers Association of North America (SPAN). Founded in 1983, PMA has a membership of 3,400-plus United States and international publishers, including many self-publishers. Created in 1996, SPAN has a membership of over 1,000 publishers. This also includes many self-publishers.

Through their individual newsletters, publications, and services, the PMA and SPAN can guide you to reputable typesetters, printers, editors, and more; inform you of worthwhile publishing fairs, seminars, and workshops; and otherwise provide you with the information you need to be a successful player in the publishing world. (See the Resource List for further details.)

> It's not always easy to discriminate between a vanity press and a legitimate print-on-demand publisher. Organizations like the PMA and SPAN will steer you towards reputable firms that can help you in your self-publishing endeavors.

Electronic Publishing

If you've had trouble up to this point getting a traditional publisher interested in your book, but you're leery about undertaking self-publication, you may be considering e-publishing as an alternative. If you're nodding your head as you read this, make sure you understand both the pros and the cons before plunging ahead with that decision.

What is e-publishing? E-publishers convert existing bound books or unpublished original works into electronic formats that can be downloaded by Internet users. Consumers can then read the books on-screen or print them out on home computers.

E-publishing is still in its infancy. So far, skepticism has outweighed interest on the part of the publishing world because e-publishing sales to date have been consistently low. But that could change. Like the rest of us, publishers know that the Internet is the wave of the future, and that the enormous potential of a medium like e-publishing might soon be a force to be reckoned with. The number of reputable e-publishers is growing larger every day.

Be aware, though, that there are different types of e-publishers. Some companies function much like traditional "paper" publishers.

They review submissions and if they like them, they pay the author for the rights to sell his book. They then edit and produce the book, underwriting their own costs and paying the author a royalty on copies sold. Because they don't have to invest money in printing, warehousing, and shipping, and don't have to worry about returns, these e-publishers offer good royalty percentages—from 24 to 75 percent of the retail price.

Other e-publishers are really closer to electronic vanity presses. A quick search of the Internet will turn up several companies that will sign you up, convert your manuscript into the appropriate electronic format, and provide a place on their site for your book to be reviewed and sold. Most pay a royalty on works sold. Some charge you a monthly fee to maintain your book, usually for a minimum of one year. Others charge all the traditional costs of print vanity publishers, from a $50 set-up fee to line-by-line editing fees. These companies may show a profit, but since the download fee for most books is about $4.95—and so far, readers aren't swarming to their sites—profits generally come from selling the use of their sites to authors.

Clearly, unless you're willing to pay dearly for the right to post your book on someone's website, you'll want to look for a "traditional" e-publisher. But even here, you'll want to beware. First, keep in mind that although copyright law extends to cyberspace *in theory*, enforcing it is like upholding the law in the Wild West. If you still need a scare, just think about Napster, which allowed people to download millions of digital musical works from the Internet without paying the copyright holders a dime. Anyone, anywhere can download your book, print it out, and do whatever they like with as many copies as they're willing to print. This has already happened to many titles, and the authors of these books will probably never be able to determine who's doing the publishing—if they even discover that they've been published. Good old-fashioned physical media, either paper or audiotape, keeps pirating at least somewhat controlled by its physical limitations.

Second, be aware that even though a legitimate e-publisher does pay a considerable royalty, the majority of writers who have made e-publishing work for them are authors whose readership is already established, like Stephen King. As I said earlier, although e-publishing shows promise, sales of electronic books have been low.

Different from print-on-demand presses, which store books electronically but ultimately produce a bound book, e-publishers produce an electronic version of a book that consumers can read on-screen or run out on home printers.

If you decide to make your novel available in electronic form, be sure to investigate each potential e-publisher just as you would investigate a conventional publishing house. As a first step, visit each company's website and review it critically, noting the relative ease with which you can navigate the site.

If you do choose to publish online, and you want to find a legitimate publisher to help you do so, you can simply do an Internet search for "e-publishing." You might be better served, though, by following the advice presented in books such as Victoria Rosenborg's *ePublishing for Dummies* and Harold Henke's *Electronic Books and ePublishing: A Practical Guide for Authors*. Once you compile your list of e-publishers, visit each company's website and review it critically, noting the relative ease with which you can navigate the site and locate submission and ordering information. If a publisher appeals to you, order a book from the company and evaluate the way in which it handles the order. Was your order confirmed? Was it filled promptly? Was the book—whether downloaded or on disk—easy to read? Your answers will tell you a great deal about the company's operation and about the ease with which your readers will be able to access your work.

Of course, you'll want to check the formats in which the books are made available by each e-publisher. Some can be downloaded, and some are produced on disks. And some, but not all, companies make their books available through online bookstores. Obviously, there are a variety of factors, including the contract, that may make one company more appealing than another.

One final caveat is in order. Generally, selling your novel to an e-publisher drastically reduces the odds of selling it to a traditional publisher at a later date. True, e-publishing contracts often state that the publisher is acquiring only the electronic rights, leaving all other rights to you. But unless your track record is truly extraordinary, a traditional publisher probably won't be interested in making a deal with you because you can no longer offer *him* electronic rights, which are becoming more and more important to the traditional publisher. So if you do decide to sign an e-publishing contract but you're interested in some day making your novel available in bookstores, make sure that the agreement gives you the right to pull your book back at a later time. This may or may not open the door to traditional publishing.

Of course, there's a way to make your book available electronically without dealing with any contracts at all. Simply e-publish your novel yourself. If your book is already in electronic form, all you need is an Internet connection and a web page. Set up your page so that visitors to your website can download your novel, and you're in business! If this sounds like an interesting option but you don't know how to create a web page, and don't know anyone who can do it for you, a number of books can guide you through the process, starting with Bud E. Smith's *Creating Web Pages for Dummies*.

Once you make your book available online, you can provide it free of charge (the exposure it gets is your "pay"), or demand a fee for each download through a service such as PayPal, which will charge your customer's credit card. You could also ask for a mailed donation; a few electronic self-publishers have made a decent profit this way. Whichever route you choose, make sure your customers receive a copy they can download and print. Customers want something real for their money, which is probably why "pay-per-view" e-books haven't been a success. There aren't many people willing to pay for the eyestrain of reading a book on a web page.

Yet another computer-related option is print on demand, or POD, publishing, which was discussed on page 202. As you've already learned, these publishers keep an electronic version of your book and print copies as requested, shipping them directly to purchasers. Just keep in mind that traditional bookstores won't carry POD books.

Unless you feel strongly about e-publishing your novel right now, my advice is to adopt a wait-and-see approach. Wait until some of the greatest drawbacks—like copyright abuse—have been resolved, and learn what successful writers are doing to make e-publishing pay off. In the meantime, keep an ear out for publishing developments in the cyberspace frontier. Sooner or later, we'll probably all be boarding that shuttle.

> Once your novel is online, refer to a book like Rusty Fischer's *Ebook Marketing Made Easy* for tips on maximizing the sales of your e-book.

Selling Your Novel to Hollywood

If you haven't yet managed to sell your story as a novel—and even if you have—here's another option you should think about. You may be able to sell your story to film or television. This is probably your best bet for making *serious* money from your writing. And contrary to what many people think, you don't have to wait until your novel has been sold to a publishing company to pitch it to an agent or a producer. Approaching Hollywood with your story is an excellent way to fill the time between submission chores.

Your first step is to adapt your novel to a *film treatment*—the detailed story of a film, usually told scene by scene from start to fin-

What About Vanity Presses?

This chapter presents a variety of ways in which you can get your book into print or otherwise make it available to your intended audience. Is vanity publishing yet another way to get your manuscript published? Well, yes and no. A vanity press can certainly take your manuscript and turn it into a printed book. But at what price?

A vanity press—also called an author-subsidized publisher, subsidy publisher, author-investment publisher, or cooperative publisher—requires the author to pay for the cost of production and distribution. Usually, the fees charged by a vanity press are high. For the 5,000-copy printing that is often considered a minimum run by these presses, the publisher may charge as much as $35,000, sometimes more! For this fee, the company will typeset, print, and bind your book, and may even edit it. Generally, the press will also warehouse half of the print run; you'll have to store the rest of the books. Some vanity presses may offer to market your novel; most will send copies of your book to reviewers.

What's wrong with this picture? First, be aware that vanity presses make their money through the fees they charge their authors, not from the income made via book sales. So they have no great commitment to produce a quality product or to market it. As a result, many vanity presses claim to edit manuscripts, but in reality do no editing at all or perform only superficial edits. According to *Writer's Digest* magazine, most also fail to deliver the promised promotion. Any efforts they do make, whether in the areas of editing, printing, or marketing, are generally subpar.

Second, keep in mind that because of the well-known low or nonexistent standards of vanity publishers, having your book produced by such a company can negatively affect your credibility as an author. The accepted belief of the book publishing, book reviewing, and bookselling industries

ish. *Writing Treatments That Sell*, which I cowrote with my partner Chi-Li Wong, first guides you through the process of converting your novel's story to a marketable treatment, then guides you through the process of marketing the treatment to producers and representatives in motion pictures and television.

Screenplays are very different animals from novels and treatments, but several good books have been written to lead you through the script-writing process. I particularly recommend Syd Field's *Screenplay: The Foundations of Screenwriting*, and Linda Seger's *The Art of Adaptation: Turning Fiction Into Film*.

Once your screenplay has been written, you'll want to go about selling it. At this point, *How to Sell Your Screenplay* by Lydia and Joan Wilen can help you prepare an effective query letter and lead you through the subsequent steps necessary to get a television or film deal.

is that vanity presses will publish any book by anyone, without regard to quality. Even if your book is well written, it probably will be perceived as being substandard just because it was produced by a vanity publisher. When vanity-produced books get sent to reviewers, they're almost never reviewed. In addition, most bookstores won't carry titles produced by a vanity press, which is one reason why vanity press books rarely return even a fourth of the author's investment. Moreover, if you later send the printed book to a regular publisher or agent in hopes of having it acquired, the editor won't seriously consider the title. Most people in the field, from agents to editors to bookstore owners, recognize the names of the major vanity firms. And even when they're not familiar with a company, they recognize the product of a vanity press from the poor production quality—and they avoid the book as if it's carrying the plague.

How can you tell a vanity publisher from a company that will legitimately assist you in self-publishing? As discussed on page 204, certain organizations—the PMA and SPAN—are familiar with many vanity presses and can help steer you away from them. But you'll often be able to discriminate between these two types of businesses on your own. A company designed to assist you in self-publishing is very direct about the fact that it charges certain fees for certain services; it doesn't masquerade as a publisher. But a vanity press disguises itself as a publisher, and often offers hefty royalties—as much as 40 to 45 percent. Then, either from the start or when the manuscript is submitted, the press asks for "a commitment"—money, in other words. The result is that you're left with a big bill, an enormous number of books that you have to warehouse yourself, and a lot of broken promises.

Years ago, many authors, unable to sign on with a traditional publisher, felt that their only recourse was to work with a vanity press. But as this chapter has shown you, novelists now have far more—and far better—options.

Keep in mind that this isn't an either/or situation in which your story can be either adapted for the screen *or* published as a book. If you do sell your screenplay and the movie is a success, most publishers will be much more inclined to offer you a contract—for this novel and, most likely, the next one, too.

Another Novel

If self-publishing requires more time and money than you care to invest, and e-publishing is too high-tech and dangerous for your taste, there's yet another way to enter the world of publishing. Simply put the manuscript for your old book away, and begin a new one. While this might make you feel as if you're abandoning your original project, it's often a great idea. Why? For starters, this time you can select a category and/or subject that has proven to be more mar-

Whether you realize it now or not, you've done a tremendous amount of learning throughout the process of writing your first novel, creating a submission package, researching publishers, and assessing the results of your queries. You've acquired knowledge and skills that no one can take away from you. That hard-won experience will be an asset in all your future writing endeavors.

ketable. Also, if your second book is accepted by a publisher and does well in the marketplace, doors will open to you, and you will have a greater chance of getting your first book into publication. To a writer, a completed manuscript is like gold bullion that's been tucked away in a bank vault, quietly growing in worth.

If, in fact, you want to start a career as a novelist, your efforts to sell your work and promote your career should consume no more than a third of the total time you've set aside for your writing. The other two-thirds, of course, should be spent doing the actual writing and revising—one-third writing, two-thirds revising. Whether you continue marketing your first novel or decide to put it on the shelf, keep working on the next book, then the next. This positive daily action—even if you only manage to complete a single page each day—will help you avoid the career doldrums that plague people in every creative field.

IN CONCLUSION

You've now come to the end of this chapter, and perhaps you're still not sure what the problem is and what you want to do about it. Is it you? Is it them? Is it the project? Should you revamp your old proposal or start an entirely new book? If your path isn't clear at this point, I strongly suggest that you put the project aside and forget about it for a month—longer if necessary. Once you've had time to relax and gain some perspective, return to this chapter and reread it. You may discover that it offers an option which will work perfectly for you.

In Part Three, you'll be looking towards the future. First, you'll learn a little more about the book business, and—if you now have a contract in hand—you'll learn about the steps you'll follow from signing to publication. You'll then explore ways in which you can perfect your craft. Finally, you'll learn how you can promote your current book and build your career as a novelist.

PART THREE

BUILDING A WRITING CAREER

While some writers are interested in getting only one novel into print, others dream of establishing a writing career. If you are determined to build a career as a novelist, Part Three is the place for you.

For those of you who have been lucky enough to win a publishing contract, Chapter 10 shows you the physical stages your book will go through between signing and publication, and details your responsibilities during this important phase of your novel's production. Chapter 11 then takes you beyond your present novel by helping you perfect your craft with an eye towards writing a great novel with commercial appeal. And because in this competitive world, authors have to be both willing and able to promote their books, Chapter 12 helps you formulate and implement an effective marketing plan, complete with publicity packets, websites, personal appearances, and more.

In the following pages, you will:

- Learn about the phases of book production, including revision, copyediting, design and typesetting, page proofs, advance reading copies, printing and binding, and marketing.

- Discover how to effectively work with editors and other publishing pros.

- Learn to use the novelist's toolbox of character, action, structure, theme, setting, narrative voice, and dialogue.

■ Master the art of research.

■ Find tips for budgeting your time and keeping the creative juices flowing.

■ Set up achievable marketing goals and a realistic marketing plan.

■ Design a publicity packet that will capture the media's attention.

■ Discover the benefits of creating your own website.

■ Learn how guerilla marketing techniques can help you achieve maximum results with minimal resources.

A writing career can be both personally and professionally rewarding. If this is your dream, the following chapters can help make it a reality.

CHAPTER 10

$\mathcal{F}$rom Signing to Publication

Once, it was just you and your computer screen. You dreamed of getting your novel into print, but both your dreaming and your writing were solo occupations. Now that your book has been accepted and your contract has been signed, you'll be working with a whole team of people to prepare your story for its audience. What exactly will happen to you and your masterpiece before the book's actual release?

From this point on, your novel will undergo several distinct phases, including revision, copyediting, design and typesetting, page proofs, advance reading copies, printing and binding, and marketing. If you're new to the world of publishing, this chapter was designed to fill you in on the steps that lead from signed contract to printed book. It also provides tips on working in harmony with the publishing pros so that the finished product is everything that you and your editor want it to be.

REVISING YOUR MANUSCRIPT

No matter how beautifully you've crafted your novel, your editor is going to request some changes before the book goes into print. As a writer, you may have always thought that your job was simply to write, but that's really only half your job. Your job is first to write, and then to *rewrite*, and the second task is no less important than the first. During this phase, you'll work closely with your editor to revise and polish your book.

What's In a Name?

From the time you first start investigating the world of publishing, you'll find that publishing houses are staffed by people with a bewildering number of titles. Publisher, senior editor, acquisitions editor, copyeditor—what do all these terms mean? Job titles in book publishing mean different things in different companies. The responsibilities of a senior editor, for instance, can be extensive in one house and minimal in another. Generally speaking, though, the titles of the editors who may be working on your book can be loosely described as follows.

At the top of the chain of command is the **publisher.** In charge of a company or company imprint, the publisher oversees the operation of every department, including editorial, art, marketing, and sales.

An **acquisitions editor,** sometimes called an **editor, senior editor,** or **editorial director,** is responsible for bringing new projects to the company. When she comes across a book proposal that catches her attention and strikes her as marketable—one that she believes will be profitable for the company—she typically presents the proposal to either her department head or an approval committee. This committee, which includes the publisher and, often, marketing and administrative personnel, ultimately decides whether or not the book can find its audience and make money for the company.

A **managing editor** or **production editor** has responsibilities that are largely administrative in nature. In most houses, she oversees the timely coordination between departments—editorial, art, typesetting, and advertising, for instance—to maintain a smooth production process. She makes sure that schedules are made and deadlines are met.

In many publishing companies, an **executive editor** is, in reality, an acquisitions editor who spends her time seeking out new projects. In other firms, she's the head of an editorial department, responsible for assigning projects and overseeing the work of the project editors—**editors, associate editors,** and **junior editors**—who are involved in the actual shaping of the manuscripts.

Once the manuscript has gone through the organizational stage, it's then sent to a **copyeditor.** It is this editor's job to make any changes necessary for stylistic consistency and grammatical accuracy. She's responsible for correcting typographical errors, grammar, and spelling; checking cross-references; and creating consistency; and is also accountable for the accuracy of any factual material presented in the manuscript.

Generally an editor-in-training, the **editorial assistant** helps the editors as required. Depending on a company's specific needs, this editor's responsibilities can range from making copies of manuscripts and filing to proofreading typeset copy.

Once again, editorial job titles and their responsibilities differ from company to company. Major companies tend to be departmentalized, with specific editors responsible for very specific jobs. In smaller houses, on the other hand, one or two people may assume several or all of the editorial responsibilities involved in the production of each book.

Some say that writers and publishers are at cross-purposes. One is concerned with quality writing; the other, with making money. Think of your editor as the bridge that spans the gap between creative work and marketing, making sure that the integrity of your work is preserved, but also that the book will meet the expectations of its audience.

Many authors find the revision phase far more grueling and ego-bruising than the original writing and submission phases. The editor usually provides the author with a rigorous set of notes detailing all the changes she'd like made before the book goes into typesetting. These notes may be scrawled on a hard copy of the manuscript, written on separate sheets of paper, or typed into an electronic version of the novel. Similarly, the editor may request that the author handwrite the changes on a hard copy or that she work in an electronic file, using the "Track Changes" function so that the editor can readily see the alterations when the file is returned to her.

It's certainly difficult for most of us to take criticism, even when it's constructive and offered in a relatively gentle manner. But if you're going to be a professional novelist, it's important to be open to your editor's input and to realize that a good editor can enhance both the quality and the marketability of your writing. She can help you focus your ideas, improve your style, cut out the deadwood, and gear the story for its readership. She can offer suggestions for improving your work while maintaining your unique voice. She may even help you *perfect* your voice.

A good editor tries to remain true to the author's vision, and regards her job as helping the writer make that vision shine as clearly to the outside world as it does within the writer's mind. Her goal is to make what's there on the page equal or excel what was in the mind of the novelist. My personal inspiration, both as a teacher and an editor, is the statement by German philosopher and playwright Johann Wolfgang Goethe: "If you treat people the way they are, you make them worse. If you treat them the way they ought to be, you make them capable of what they ought to be." Most good editors know how to offer criticism frankly but gently. You can trust them to mean what they say; they're neither flatterers nor harsh judges. It's often hard for new writers to take criticism of any kind, no matter how gently it's offered. This is understandable as writing is so personal that it makes you feel vulnerable. But handling criticism is one

Most writers find it difficult to accept an editor's criticism. But if you hope to be a professional novelist, it's important to objectively review your editor's comments and requests, and to address her concerns both thoroughly and thoughtfully.

of the most important skills you can develop if you're going to be a professional novelist. Constructive criticism is extremely rare in the professional world, partly because so few novelists know how to deal with it, and editors, when met with resistance, often decide that life is too short, and move on.

As you review your editor's comments, you're likely to find at least some notes that simply say, "Call to discuss," or just "Discuss." An editor often writes this when a point requires some give-and-take on your part, when she must have some clarification from you before she decides how you should proceed, or when she feels that she can make her point better verbally than through written comments. Whatever the reason, if the note directs you to call, call. Don't worry about bugging her when she's actually asked you to bug her.

Whether reading written notes or talking to your editor over the phone, try to be receptive to her comments and suggestions. Even if you disagree strongly, never refuse to rewrite something the moment it's requested. If you're not sure how to respond, simply say, "Let me think about that one."

If you truly think that an editor's suggested change would have an adverse effect on your novel, carefully explain your point of view. But avoid reacting in an emotional and defensive manner.

This doesn't mean, though, that you shouldn't resist politely when, after giving the matter some thought, you feel that resistance is in the best interest of your novel. If you truly believe that the editor's suggested change would have an adverse effect on the story, plainly state why you feel that your way is better. But continue arguing your point only if you continue to believe that your course of action would be better for the book.

Whatever you do, don't react to criticism in an emotional and defensive manner. Many a novelist who might otherwise be on the road to success has sabotaged her own efforts by refusing to rewrite, thereby preventing her book from becoming commercially viable. Acknowledge your pain quietly, to yourself. Then let go of it and knuckle down to the business of rewriting.

Be sure to give your rewrite the time and effort it deserves, addressing your editor's concerns both thoroughly and thoughtfully. Nothing slows down the production process like a hastily rewritten draft that simply creates the need for another round of notes from your editor, followed by another rewrite from you. Such a draft shows a lack of pride on your part, and a lack of respect for your editor's time and efforts. Worst of all, it throws a wrench into the production process.

If you made your corrections in a computer file, print out a fresh copy of the manuscript, setting it up with the same care you used when formatting your sample chapters. Even after a painstaking rewrite, additional revisions may be required. Eventually, though, the editor will approve the draft and it will be sent to the publishing house's copyeditor, who will comb through the manuscript, looking for any remaining errors of spelling, grammar, syntax, or logic.

A Word About Acknowledgments

As you are putting your final touches on the manuscript, you'll probably want to include an Acknowledgments section. If you haven't written it already, your editor may request it. So difficult is the process of getting published that it's become customary, as well as considerate, to thank your editor and your representative, if any, along with anyone else who helped you with the novel—for instance, a librarian who performed research vital to your book's completion. This is one of the few ways you can "give back" to those whose support and expertise got you to this point. If you're not sure how to word this section, look at Nelson DeMille's *Night Fall* for a good example of how a professional novelist handles acknowledgments.

Believe it or not, many authors forget to recognize the vital contributions of the people with whom they've worked to get their book into print. Keep in mind that it costs you nothing to acknowledge the efforts of those who helped you. And don't think for a moment that even the most experienced of agents and editors is beyond feeling slighted if she is not mentioned and, conversely, feeling pleased by heartfelt gratitude. Everyone appreciates being thanked.

Finally, realize that it's not only nice, but also politically wise to recognize those who have helped you on your way. Do you want to publish another book with that house? If so, it's vital to show your gratitude.

COPYEDITING

Now that a new draft of your novel has been handsomely put together, it's about to be torn apart again—this time by your copyeditor, who will rout out even the tiniest flaws. Does your hero's eye color change from steel blue to velvet brown in Chapter Twelve? Did you

Did your local librarian assist you with the research for your novel? Did your editor help you focus your ideas? Did your spouse check the proofs for typos? The Acknowledgments section of your book will allow you to graciously thank everyone who contributed to your book.

In some publishing houses, the copyeditor is a staff member. In others, she's a freelance editor. Whoever she is and wherever she works, her job is to rout out grammar and spelling errors; contradictions and ambiguities; anachronisms; numerical style that does not conform to company guidelines; incorrect names, places, and dates; and more.

spell the world "travelled" with one "l" at the beginning of the book and two at the end of the book? Did you mistakenly state that the Battle of the Bulge ended in 1944 instead of 1945? A good copyeditor will catch all of these problems and more. She will check grammar, punctuation, spelling, word usage, and consistency. In addition, she will make sure that the book conforms to the publishing company's in-house style and will identify any potential legal issues. She will then return the copyedited work to your editor, who will double-check all of the corrections and, if necessary, refer issues to the company's legal department.

What type of material might result in legal problems? As an example, best-selling crime novelist Patricia Cornwell was sued when a couple claimed that her 1992 book *All That Remains* provided details of their daughter's murder. Cornwell had been privy to the information when working in the medical examiner's office. The details of the crime, presented in the autopsy report, had never been made public because the case was never solved. Since so many novels include information about real people, real places, and real events, the potential for a lawsuit often exists.

Once your editor has reviewed the copyeditor's work, she will forward the manuscript to you and grant you a week or two to review changes and correct any errors. Again, depending on the practices of that publishing house, these corrections may be written on a hard copy of the manuscript or typed directly in a computer file. Because all of the major revisions, if any, were made in your work with your editor, this part of the production process should be far less demanding and time-consuming than your earlier work. Just be sure to follow instructions closely regarding how your corrections should be made. With any luck, the next time you see your novel, it will be in typeset form.

DESIGN AND TYPESETTING

Once you've returned the copyedited manuscript to the publishing house, the manuscript will be finalized and your editor will move it into the design phase. In smaller houses, the art director may create your novel's interior and cover designs herself or may send the book out to freelance designers. In larger houses, the art director heads a department that creates these designs in-house.

The Importance of Shepherding

If a publisher has accepted your work, it's important to understand and appreciate the role of the sponsoring editor—the person in charge of overseeing your project through its various stages of production. In many cases, this is the acquisition editor who initially believed in your book enough to propose it to the company. In other instances, this may be a project editor who has been assigned the job. Of all the people in a publishing house, the sponsoring editor is the person who has real interest in having your book succeed—she's the shepherd, the champion, the advocate of your book. And it's important to maintain a good working relationship with her.

What happens if this person gets transferred to another department or leaves the company altogether? Suddenly, your project will find itself "orphaned" and in a precarious situation. More than likely, one of two things will happen. Either it will be assigned to another editor immediately, or it will be temporarily shelved. In either case, your project will no longer be under the watchful eye of the person who first believed in it.

While it's true that you may be limited in controlling the fate of your book at this point, you can still proactively intervene on its behalf. If your book has been transferred to the hands of a new editor, make it your business to contact her. Call and ask to schedule a few minutes of her time to introduce yourself and discuss a few important aspects of your book. Remember that an editor's time is limited, so be prepared to make your points quickly and professionally. Your objective is to get the new editor to familiarize herself with your book and make a connection with it.

If you discover that your project has been shelved temporarily, try to contact the person responsible for reassigning it. This could be a senior editor or executive editor. Inquire about the plans for your book, and again, try to share its obvious assets.

Whatever you do, don't allow yourself to call the editor ten times a day, five days a week. This is the quickest way to alienate yourself from anyone involved in the process. Keep your frustration and worry from overcoming your good sense.

Interior design involves the typeface font and size, the size of the margins, the location of the folios (page numbers), and every other aspect of page design. If your novel is part of a specific line, such as a line of romance books, interior design may be determined before you even go to contract. If not, a number of factors may affect design decisions. For instance, if it's been determined that your book's audience is "mature," the company may choose a larger type size to accommodate an older reader's eyes.

Most authors are understandably interested in the design of their novel's cover. I say *"understandably"* because it's well known that a book's cover is a significant sales tool—especially in the case of unknown authors. The fact is, though, that although your editor may have input in the book's design, unless you have a good deal of clout you probably will *not* be consulted; and even if you are, your contract won't grant you design approval. If you find this upsetting, keep in mind that only the best-known authors—writers like Michael Crichton—have design approval. Remember, too, that the publisher's success in selling your book is proportional to the booksellers' reaction to the novel's appearance, and no one's more aware of this than the publisher. This doesn't mean that you shouldn't voice any objections you may have to your book's design. But do allow your editor to explain why a specific design was chosen. Many times, for instance, decisions are made with full knowledge of the book's competition, which is often an important consideration.

Once the page design has been approved, your editor will move your book into the next stage of production—typesetting. Shortly following this, you'll receive your pages proofs.

PAGE PROOFS

Years ago, typesetters keyed in every manuscript by hand and ran off *galleys*—long sheets of typeset copy, which were corrected, cut into pages, and pasted onto paper boards. Now, typesetters are given books in electronic form and use a computer program to quickly create typeset pages, completely skipping the galleys phase. These pages, properly known as *proofs* but sometimes still referred to as galleys, are then given to the editor and author for review.

The typesetter, also known as the compositor, uses a computer program to follow the designer's specifications and transform the edited manuscript into the typeset pages called *proofs.* These proofs—which look very much like the pages of a printed book—are then given to the editor of the project, who keeps one copy for in-house proofing and forwards another copy to the author for proofing.

When you receive your novel's proofs, you'll be asked to check them over for any *minor* problems that were not caught during the editing phase, as well as any problems that crept in during typesetting, such as incorrect word breaks and crowded lines of type. Do not go overboard and start editing! While this is, of course, your last chance to rectify problems, as explained in Chapter 8, most publishers reserve the right to charge you if you make too many changes during the proofing process. Changes at this point are quite costly and can result in significant production delays.

Once you've returned the corrected proofs to your editor, your job will be over for a while. The editor will review your changes, combine them with the in-house proofreader's corrections, and send the proofs off to the typesetter. The resulting corrected proofs will, of course, be read in-house to make sure that no problems remain, but in most cases, they won't be sent to you.

ADVANCE READING COPIES

Once the proofs have been finalized—and sometimes *before* the proofs have been finalized—advance reading copies (ARCs) of the novel are produced by the publisher. These no-frills publications are bound versions of the page proofs with plain paper or cardboard covers, usually not in color. Note that ARCs aren't intended as merchandise but as marketing tools, and are sent to book reviewers, feature writers, booksellers, radio hosts, and sometimes people in the film industry who track new novels for motion picture or television potential. Most publishing houses will provide you and/or your representative with ARCs, and early in the production process, will ask you how many you'd like to have. Authors use these ARCs to approach foreign publishers, if they've retained foreign rights; to have their novels read by television and film buyers; and to send out review copies to personal contacts, either directly or through their publicists, if publicists are on board.

Whether or not you're asked about it, make sure to request a number of ARCs in advance, as they are expensive and therefore printed in limited numbers. Just be aware that they may still contain some errors. In fact, ARCs usually include a statement advising the reader that the book is unproofed and should not be used for the purpose of quotations.

Be sure to request a number of your novel's ARCs in advance, as they are expensive and therefore printed in limited numbers. These no-frills publications are great marketing tools.

PRINTING AND BINDING

When all the problems and errors in the book have been corrected, your novel is shipped to the printer. Just a few decades ago, printers actually photographed each page, created film, and used the film to create the plates needed for the printing process. Nowadays, most printers receive a digital file and, skipping the film phase completely, burn the text directly from the digital file onto a plate. Then the plates are used to print the book.

Based on a number of variables, including the printer's schedule, the printing process can take anywhere from five to eight weeks for a softcover book, and seven to ten weeks for a hardcover book. As part of this process, the printer makes another proof—a set of loose or bound pages—that is quickly reviewed by the production editor shortly before the presses roll as a means of finding and correcting

For many years, the proofs provided by the printer were called *bluelines* or, more commonly, *blues* because they were printed in blue on yellow photosensitive paper. These days, though, most proofs are printed in black ink on white paper, just like the final book. Nevertheless, many people in the book business still refer to them as blues.

any technical errors that may have emerged in the printing process. These printer's proofs are not provided to authors, as a trained eye is required to detect any problems at this stage.

Once all the pages have been printed, they're folded, cut to final size, and bound. Although this step is sometimes performed by a separate bindery, more and more printers now have their own binderies. Finally, the finished books are boxed and shipped to the publisher.

Shortly after the books are printed and bound, you'll receive a case or two of your novels—whatever number is stipulated in your contract. While this will certainly be a moment for celebration, be aware that the book won't be landing in the store at the same time you receive the author's copies. As explained in earlier chapters, most bookstores and libraries order their books from distributors. For that reason, the vast majority of newly printed and bound books travel first to the distributor's warehouse, and only then are sent out to the booksellers, libraries, and others who placed orders for that title. This process of shipping and reshipping takes time, and in most cases, anywhere from three weeks to two months will elapse before the finished book is made available to its intended audience.

MARKETING PLANS

Although this is the last subject we're covering in this chapter, the marketing plans for any book really start being forged as soon as the acquisitions editor finds a manuscript of interest. In larger publishing houses, the decision to acquire a book can't be made, in fact, unless the marketing and sales department feels that they can sell the book. In smaller houses, it's possible that only one editor—who may be the owner of the company—is needed to acquire a manuscript. Whatever size house you're working with, though, once your book is entered into production, marketing activities will be planned.

One of the first marketing activities—which in larger houses is performed in close consultation with the sales department and the editor—is scheduling the month in which the book will appear. Most fiction companies have between two and four selling seasons—spring and fall; or winter, spring, summer, and fall. They therefore put out two to four catalogues a year, as well as any specialty catalogues. It's usually the publisher herself who decides exactly which books are scheduled for which season and catalogue, and who makes a determination about your novel's release date based on that knowledge. Obviously, you don't want to have your book competing head-to-head with the company's favorite author for fear of its being neglected. Your editor will remain your advocate during this process by helping to position your book for maximum exposure, even if it means frustrating you in the short range by postponing it from one season to the next. More than anyone else, she knows that your book has only one chance to come out for the first time, and she knows it's her responsibility to you and your novel to maximize that opportunity—even over your protests.

At some point, your editor will let you know that an in-house publicist—generally, a member of the publisher's marketing department—has been designated as your book's "point person." If your book's profile is high enough at the company, you and/or your representative, if any, may have a face-to-face meeting with the publicist. If not, you will probably be able to at least talk to her on the phone. This is an extremely important event in the life cycle of your book. Many books end up being neglected simply because their authors cease to be proactive once the contract is signed. You'll want to request this conversation or meeting, and you'll want to prepare for it, too. Often, the publicist will ask the author if she has any contacts that could be helpful in the marketing of the book—if she knows someone on a newspaper staff, for instance. The publicist may also ask for the writer's "wish list" of publicity events. You may, for instance, want to set up a book signing at your local bookstore. Be sure your publicist knows about this, and be sure to offer your ideas of how your audience can be reached. Be aware, too, that as you talk to your publicist, she will be gauging your ability to handle radio interviews and the like, as well as your willingness to self-promote your book through events that *you* arrange. It is, of course, to your advantage to come across as a confident and capable speaker, as well as someone who is willing to go that extra mile.

If you're like many first-time novelists, you may now be dreaming of book signings, publicity tours, and television interviews. But be aware that for the majority of first-time authors, marketing activities are limited to the sending of advance reading copies (see page 221) to reviewers and booksellers, the sharing of sales sheets with booksellers, and the distribution of catalogues that include informa-

A *sales sheet* is a one-page handout that offers promotional copy on a forthcoming title, including a description of the book, information on the author, and book specifications such as trim size and page length. This promotional tool is used by the company's sales representatives in meetings with booksellers.

tion on the new book. As discussed earlier in the book, most publishing houses have neither the time nor the budget to create a full marketing campaign for a debut novel. But there are exceptions to this rule. For instance, when an editor is really impressed by a forthcoming novel, she will often take steps to create a buzz—both within the company and among bookstore buyers—by sending advance reading copies of the novel to department heads throughout the company. In turn, company representatives will sometimes take ARCs to bookstores to pique the buyers' interest. If this results in sales, the company may plan further marketing and publicity activities for that book. I can't overemphasize, though, that this sequence of events doesn't occur very often.

Does this mean that your finished book is doomed to sit in a warehouse gathering dust? Absolutely not. The fact is, though, that should you want to do that local book signing or that interview, you'll probably have to arrange it yourself. That's why in Chapter 12, I address the topic of self-promotion. There's a great deal you can do on your own to create that "buzz." Chapter 12 will show you how it's done.

MOVING ON

As soon as you cut open the carton of author's copies and hold your novel in your hand, you'll realize that your status has changed. You are no longer dreaming; you are a *published author.* This is a moment to celebrate. Pour yourself a glass of your favorite celebratory beverage and congratulate yourself for realizing your dream—a dream that millions of people have, but only a small number see through to fruition.

But even as you savor the moment, it's important to recognize that if you want to build a career as a novelist, you'll have to follow this book with another, and then another. And with each new novel, you'll want to develop your talents. That's what the next chapter is all about—perfecting your craft as a novelist so that each book is better than the last.

CHAPTER 11

PERFECTING YOUR CRAFT

---

legendary New York story has a lost tourist asking an elderly
lady on the street, "How do I get to Carnegie Hall?" The lady
replies: "Practice, practice, practice." Nothing takes the place
of practice. Good writing requires more than raw talent; it requires
the honing of skill and technique. But practice is productive only
when a writer understands the elements of a good novel and learns
how to use them to create a riveting tale.

This chapter discusses the novelist's "toolbox," explaining how
each instrument can be used to best effect. It also offers proven tips
for getting over the rough spots that all writers encounter and
improving yourself as a commercial novelist.

THE NOVELIST'S TOOLBOX

Whether writing a formulaic romance or a literary novel, the writer
uses a variety of "tools," including character, action, dialogue, structure, theme, setting, and narrative voice and tone. From the alchemy
created by the artful joining of these elements, a story emerges. Let's
examine each of these elements in turn.

The Main Characters

Character is by far the most important element of a novel. To the
extent that your readers are "on board" with your protagonist—the
"hero" of your novel, who serves as the focus for the story's themes

In a novel, the *protagonist* is the central character who serves as the focus of the story's themes and incidents. The *antagonist* is the major character who works against the protagonist. In Cervantes' *Don Quixote*, for example, Don Quixote is the protagonist, and Sancho Panza is the antagonist.

and incidents—they will stay committed to your story. An unforgettable protagonist, like Atticus Finch in Harper Lee's *To Kill a Mockingbird* or Birdy in William Wharton's *Birdy*, is made up of just a handful of key components, even though he might seem quite complex. These components include motivational conflict, mission, obstacles, relatability, and change.

Motivational Conflict

What makes your main characters—your protagonist and antagonist—tick? What does each one want? Each major character must be struggling with one or more of the major motivating human drives, like love, hate, fear, anxiety, vengeance, rage, jealousy, ambition, or greed—ideally, with two of these drives in conflict with each other. In Wharton's *Birdy*, Birdy's primary drive is ambition, the desire to *be* a canary. His conflicting drive is the desire to fit in, to please. In Miguel de Cervantes' *Don Quixote*, Sancho Panza's primary drive is to prove that Don Quixote's missions are foolish; but beneath this is the opposite motivation—his need to believe in miracles. In Lee's *To Kill A Mockingbird*, Atticus Finch is conflicted between civic duty and personal duty. Although he wants to "do the right thing" by helping Tom Robinson receive the fair trial he deserves, he also wants to protect his children, who are bearing the brunt of the town's bigotry-driven hatred of Robinson. In Charlotte Bronte's novel *Jane Eyre*, the protagonist is torn between two powerful drives—her own sense of morality, which won't allow her to be involved with a married man, and her all-consuming attraction to Rochester.

Your readers know these motivational drives, have experienced these conflicts, and will respond to them in your novel. For this reason, it's important to identify one drive for each of your major characters and develop that character's motivational conflict by finding a second a drive that works against his first. Note that in real life, people run a gamut of emotions and have many drives. But this is not true of well-constructed fiction. The beauty of the "what if" pattern—what if a woman with a strong sense of morality fell deeply in love with a married man?—is that it allows us to isolate and explore the actions of a character who is driven by opposing motivations that influence every word and deed.

Mission

Your protagonist needs a job to do—a goal that tests his motivational conflict to the utmost. If it's greed you've chosen, you may want your protagonist to be the man who's driven to become the top player on Wall Street, the woman who has cornered the oil exploration business, the couple that wants to have more money than anyone else at their country club. Opposing these drives might be, for example, love—a man's love for his father that stops his greed short when he finds himself crossing his father's interests; a woman's need for love that interferes with her conquest of the oil fields; or the couple's love for their Jewish son-in-low, whose exclusion from the country club makes them question their suburban values. It doesn't matter whether the character chooses to undertake the mission himself, or if the mission is thrust upon him. Once Atticus Finch is charged with defending Tom Robinson, his mission is to prove Robinson innocent and enable him to return to his family, even though it would be far easier—and far less dangerous for Finch's children—if he allowed the man to be portrayed as a villain in court.

In every novel, the mission must be involved enough to sustain the story for the duration of the book. It must lend itself to challenges, both in the form of obstacles and in the form of an antagonist—the force that works against the hero's mission. Protagonist Don Quixote's mission is to defeat the dragons of his imagination and thereby prove that the "ideal" world he prefers to the "real" world is actually the only important one. Antagonist Sancho Panzo, however, is driven to prove that Don Quixote's missions are foolish.

The antagonist need not be a bad guy; there's nothing bad about Sancho. In fact, he need not even be a person. In Sebastian Junger's novel *The Perfect Storm*, nature is the antagonist. It's the storm itself that foils Captain Billy Tyne's mission to come home with a boatload of swordfish. In Steve Alten's *Domain*, the antagonist is the otherworldly dragon creature that rises from the bottom of the Gulf of Mexico after lying dormant for millions of years. In *To Kill a Mockingbird*, although Bob Ewell can be viewed as an antagonist because he works against Finch's attempts to free Robinson, the greater antagonist is racial bigotry and prejudice.

> Every protagonist needs a mission—a goal he has to reach. And this mission must be involved and challenging enough to sustain the story for the duration of the book.

Obstacles

Action occurs when your hero struggles against obstacles to his mission, as when Don Quixote is faced with Sancho's doubts. The obstacles with which you choose to confront your protagonist must be appropriate for him. Don't pit Thomas the Tank Engine against the Third Reich. In addition, the obstacles should be arranged in a progression of ascending and descending scenes, so that the tension rises and falls rhythmically throughout your story.

Ideally, your obstacles should relate to one another in a pattern that gives your novel symmetry. The smaller obstacles should come earlier in the story, followed by the greater obstacles. In a trek through the jungle, mosquitoes (an obstacle) should come first, not last—before, not after, the lions, tigers, pythons, and cannibals. Placing the mosquitoes last would only make the audience laugh at your storytelling ineptitude. Successful novels are stories that rise and fall with an overall story arc. If you think about each obstacle as a story in itself—with a beginning, a middle, and an end—you'll be off to a good start, and you'll also be much less anxious about writing.

The obstacles faced in the novel must feel real to the protagonist, must challenge him greatly, and must engage the sympathies of the reader. If not, the reader won't be able to empathize with the main character.

Relatability

Although your protagonist doesn't have to be likable, *he does have to be* sympathetic—*meaning that readers must be able to feel pity and sorrow for him. If not, your audience won't get involved in your story.*

Above, I touched on the idea that the reader must be able to empathize and identify with the protagonist. If not, he's not going to be able to involve himself in your story. This doesn't mean, though, that the reader has to *like* the protagonist. The protagonist of Jerzy Kosinski's *Cockpit* is hateful from the opening page. When beginning writers are told that a protagonist should be "sympathetic," they sometimes mistakenly think the term means "likable." In actuality, when used in this context the word *sympathetic* indicates a sharing of feelings. In other words, we should be able to feel pity and sorrow for the character—to suffer along with him and relate to his point of view. In John Kennedy Toole's *A Confederacy of Dunces*, Ignatius O'Reilly may be a hopelessly introverted nerd, but we hunger for his redemption because we can sympathize with nerds. In Nelson

DeMille's *Night Fall,* John Corey may be abrasive and cocky, but we root for him to learn the truth about TWA Flight 800. And although we may be horrified by Raskolnikov's determination to prove himself a "superman" by committing a gratuitous murder in Fyodor Dostoevski's *Crime and Punishment,* we nevertheless long for him to confess his crime and find personal peace.

Change

Over the course of the story, ideally, your protagonist—and, again ideally, your antagonist as well—must face his shortcomings, his doubt or fear, or whatever it is that's keeping him from achieving his

---

WORDS FROM A PRO

Shirley Palmer

Author of *Danger Zone* (Mira)

Have you ever closed a book feeling dissatisfied? The plot was intricate, the writing style was good, the research was impressive, but even so, nothing quite gelled?

Chances are, it was because there wasn't a character in the story you really cared about. When writing a novel, the writer has to keep a lot of boats afloat: structure, narrative drive, prose style, dialogue, pacing, rhythm—to name just a few. But without strong, believable characters, what you have is a near-miss.

The question is: What makes strong characters?

They have to be true to themselves. That does not mean they have to be likable—think Hannibal Lector, Thomas Harris's great and ghastly creation—but strong characters have a complexity that is uniquely theirs.

In my own work, I never know what the characters are really about until they reveal themselves in the course of the first draft. In my novel *Danger Zone,* the character of Michael O'Malley is repellent, becoming more so with each appearance. Becoming more himself. Only in the last scene do we find that he has any redeeming quality whatsoever, but throughout the book that teasing voice is there, just below the surface of the character.

Every character you create contains a part of who you are. A writer is constantly asking, "How would I behave in this situation?" or perhaps more honestly, "How would I like to *believe* I would behave?" Or, "How would I *never dream of behaving* in such circumstances?" The answers are often a complete surprise.

In a good novel, characters tell the story. If the characters are there merely to serve the plot, you have a lot of machinery clunking around, forcing the book onward.

The writer's job is to understand each character—even the most minor—to know them more than they know people they have come to understand, to love, or perhaps loathe.

And the writer rejoices.

The five elements of motivational conflict, mission, obstacles, relatability, and change should be present in your protagonist. And all of these attributes should be directly related to your novel's action. In a good story, the action happens as it does *because* of who your protagonist is. In turn, your protagonist develops as he does because of the way the action unfolds. Action and character drive each other, and the resulting tension explains what makes a good novel a "page-turner."

mission. He must grow into his ability to meet the goal you've set for him. In real life, human change is nebulous, messy, and imprecise. In fiction, it should be more clear-cut. Although exceptions abound, generally the best novels are those in which your character's change progresses in a logical, clear series of steps. His motivational conflict provides the engine for his change.

Revealing Back-Story

Before we leave the subject of main characters, a word should be said about revealing *back-story*—everything of relevance that happened before the opening of the novel. Many new writers, seeking to show exactly why a main character is the way he is or does the things he does, dump an enormous amount of back-story into the first chapter of the novel. The crucial thing to remember is that too much back-story provided too soon impedes the forward-moving action of your novel. The reader should always be hungering for more. If all of the back-story is provided at the beginning of the novel, the reader loses interest in the book, since the pleasure of reading lies in imagination and discovery.

Construct your characters clearly, and their words, gestures, and actions will speak for themselves. Let the suspense build and the reader speculate. He will then have to keep reading for more clues so that he can see if his supposition is correct. Wait until the reader *needs* to know the back-story, and then supply only as much as he must have at that point—preferably, through the thoughts, actions, memories, or dialogue of the characters. When back-story is provided in this way in a book I'm reading, I know I'm in the hands of a professional novelist.

Supporting, Minor, and Function Characters

Earlier, I explained how the protagonist drives the action of the novel. This is actually true for *all* the characters that populate your novel, to an extent that diminishes as the characters move down the ranks from major to supporting to minor to function. Every character belongs in your story only to the extent that he serves the action line.

Supporting characters usually display a single attribute—sometimes known as a "tag"—that defines them and makes them memorable. Any supporting character that *isn't* memorable should be instantly thrown out. A character's "tag" can be just about any attribute—greed, lechery, vanity, etc.—but he has just one tag, not two or three. Don't spell the tag out, though. If a character is absent-minded, show this feature in action, thought, and dialogue so that the reader comes to an understanding of the character on his own. Don't *you* use the phrase "absent-minded," or you'll condescend to your reader.

In addition to having a tag, the supporting character changes—although the change is recorded on the single note of his tag. Perhaps a needy character learns he can fend for himself, or an ambitious character learns that ambition can be destructive. But the change is superficial because the supporting character doesn't have the motivational conflict that makes the protagonist the primary focus of your story.

Like a supporting character, a minor character has a defining tag. Unlike a supporting character, though, a minor character doesn't change during the course of the novel. Instead, he remains static.

Function characters play an even less important role than minor characters. They perform a single function without being as complex as a major character, or having a tag like a supporting or minor character. They ride in at sunset to deliver the fateful telegram, they serve the drinks, they drive the cabs. Unlike your other characters, they're *supposed* to be forgettable.

Keep function characters simple. If you spend too much energy on them, your readers will start to think they're more significant than you meant them to be. Then, when the character disappears, your readers will feel as if you left them dangling or, worse, that you misled them.

Always keep in mind that your characters—whether major, supporting, minor, or function—are not real people, but devices that you invent for the sole purpose of capturing and holding your reader's attention. As such, it's your primary responsibility to make sure that their characteristics serve your novel's purpose. The best way to do that is to give them something significant to *do* whenever they appear. The most successful commercial writers don't get wrapped up in the complex psychological machinations of their characters—much less their own psychological hang-ups. They write to satisfy their readers' expectations of being entertained by a good yarn. To the best storytellers, the only important psychology is the psychology of their audience. More than anything, your audience wants to see

Function characters are designed to perform a single task, such as driving a cab or delivering a telegram. Keep them simple, or your reader may be confused when they disappear from the scene.

how your protagonist gets out of the corners you paint him into. How can you write a best-selling book? *Don't disappoint your readers!*

Plot and Action Line

Everyone is familiar with the word "plot." But what exactly does it mean? The *plot* is the unified structure of incidents in a novel, including all of the motivations behind the actions.

The action line is different from the plot. The *action line* consists of what your characters do and say, the two aspects of drama being *action,* from a raised eyebrow at one extreme to a nuclear explosion at the other; and *dialogue,* the only purpose of which is to move your story forward.

When Peter Feibleman was struggling with his novel *Charlie Boy,* playwright Lillian Hellman advised him, "Write it one more time, and throw away the plot." Many new novelists dwell too much on plot instead of concentrating on action. Action is the focus around which the plot is constructed. Concentrating on plot is like focusing on the edges of a picture instead of the picture itself.

The action line is the direction in which your story moves. If you're writing a tragic novel, like Charles Dickens' *A Tale of Two Cities,* your story has to move from happiness to unhappiness. If your novel has a happy ending, you have to put your protagonist in a hole and make him dig his way out. Whatever the case, there has to be a change. Your story has to move actively from one state to another. If it doesn't, the story will meander, sputter, and lose its drama.

In order for the action line to work, it has to have some fundamental components. Let's look at each of these.

Conflict

Conflict occurs when your protagonist encounters obstacles to his mission—whether those obstacles are physical, psychological, emotional, or moral, and whether they take the form of your antagonist, other characters, or an entity such as a storm. A car *chase* is dramatic only because a conflict is involved, with one character in pursuit of another. An ordinary *race* is generally not dramatic.

The best novels are filled with conflict on every level, internal as well as external. Whether the protagonist succeeds or fails in a given conflict depends on where he is in his developmental arc—the arc that tracks his change from the beginning of the story to the end. If your story has a happy ending, it's inevitable that your character will succeed in your novel's final conflict. If your novel's ending is tragic, your protagonist will fail in his last conflict.

The shape of your novel's action line is created by one conflict after another, whether it's the conflict of characters locked in mortal combat or of characters involved in heated arguments. All well-constructed conflicts have this defining characteristic: They alter the character's future.

Turning Points

During the natural course of the story, your protagonist will encounter *turning points* in the action, so called because they are events that literally spin the story's action off in a different direction by forcing the protagonist to make a decision. A private detective who has become disenchanted with his work is closing his office for good, for example, when a woman walks in, claiming she's the sister he didn't know he had, and asking him to find their missing parents. The detective, who minutes before was ready to retire, now finds himself on a new and critical case.

Your protagonist should come to the first turning point early in the story. It's the event that launches him on his mission. In Nelson DeMille's *Night Fall,* the first turning point is the discovery that the investigation of Flight 800 may have involved a coverup. This pushes the protagonist to launch an investigation of his own.

The most dramatic turning point in a novel comes toward the end of the story. It sets the stage for the ultimate confrontation that will culminate in your story's climax. Remember that all the turning points in your story are intimately connected to your protagonist's motivation—as when the protagonist of Peter Benchley's *Jaws,* who's afraid of water, realizes he must grapple with his greatest nightmare in order to protect the people he loves.

There's no rule about the number of turning points a novel should have. There should, however, be a minimum of two: the opening one, which might be called the "inciting incident," and the final one, often called the "climax," which leads to the story's conclusion. (To learn more about the climax, see page 234.)

A turning point literally spins the story's action off in a different direction by forcing the protagonist to make a decision. It's the first turning point that launches the protagonist on his mission.

Plot Twists

Not every novel includes a plot twist—an unexpected turn of events that accelerates the action. But a cleverly crafted plot twist can make the story far more exciting and memorable.

A *plot twist*, also called a reversal, is exactly what it sounds like: an unexpected turn of events, or revelation, that accelerates the action. Your novel doesn't have to contain twists—many novels don't—but they do make the story more exciting and memorable. Often, the second turning point is a twist, although the twist can happen at virtually any time. The twist in Orson Scott Card's *Ender's Game* comes at the very end and gives the previous climax scene an entirely different meaning. The twist in Daphne DuMaurier's *Rebecca* comes relatively near the end, when the heroine is startled to find out that her husband didn't love his first wife, Rebecca, at all, but detested her!

The trick to writing an effective twist is to fashion it so that your readers don't see it coming, but when they look back on it, they can't imagine it happening any other way. In *Rebecca*, for instance, every conversation between the characters leads the reader to believe that Rebecca was universally adored, and that Maxim de Winter was so distraught after her death that he attempted suicide. When we find out that this was not the case, though, many of the story's events are clarified.

Climax

As the book progresses from its beginning, action accelerates and the protagonist's obstacles get tougher and tougher. But the obstacle faced at the climax blows all the others away. The climax is the moment of greatest emotional tension in a novel. Will the good guy beat the bad guy? Will the hero save the heroine from the impending explosion? Will the detective solve the mystery of his mysterious sister before the evidence is destroyed? This is what the reader is dying to know, and the climax must answer these questions in a riveting scene. If the protagonist can rise to the occasion and face this ultimate challenge, his problems are resolved and his mission is achieved. After the climax—the high point of the action—the action falls.

Dialogue

Earlier in the chapter, I explained that the action line is made up of action and dialogue. Now that we've discussed action, it's time to discuss dialogue.

Dialogue is one of the most important tools the novelist has at his disposal. It not only provides a great deal of information about the story's characters and events, but also moves the plot forward. Good dialogue also sets the tone of the novel. Elmore Leonard's novels create their comic tone primarily through dialogue, for example. Finally, through speech patterns and vocabulary, dialogue conveys a sense of time and place and defines your characters' motivational conflicts.

How, though, do you make your dialogue effective, interesting, and believable? To start, always make sure that the dialogue fits the character. Is the character a truck driver who never graduated from high school? A Harvard professor? A girl who grew up on a farm? A sophisticated city dweller? A nineteenth-century small-town sheriff? A fourteenth-century sailor? Clearly, each of these people would have their own way of speaking. This is not to say that every truck driver is alike—or every college professor, for that matter. But it's unlikely that someone with a doctorate in literature, for instance, would speak in grammatically incorrect sentences using street talk. And it's equally unlikely—though not impossible—that a truck driver would command a sophisticated vocabulary and make numerous references to classical literary works in the course of his conversation. Everything a character says should reflect who he is and where he is. If it doesn't, the dialogue won't be believable—and neither will the character.

In addition to getting the dialogue right for each character, when appropriate, you'll want to use *dialogue tags* to tell the reader *how* the words were said, as well as *action tags,* which describe any accompanying physical motion. Consider, for example, the same bit of dialogue used each time with different tags:

> "I love you," he said, flipping open his newspaper.
> "I love you," he said, clenching his fist.
> "I love you," he grinned.
> "I love you," he murmured, ducking his head shyly.

In each case, the tags enhance the spoken words, providing the reader with a bit more information about the character. Just don't overdo it. Whenever possible, the dialogue itself should convey the speaker's intent. Overuse of dialogue tags is the sure mark of a novice.

Dialogue is one of the novelist's most important tools. Well-written dialogue helps set the tone of the novel, provides information about the story's characters and events, moves the plot forward, and conveys a sense of time and place.

Use slang when appropriate, but, again, try not to overdo it. When used properly, slang can convey character, time, and place. When used improperly, it can make speech seem artificial. It can even make it difficult to read and understand the text.

Although dialogue should be natural, it should not mimic real-life conversation in every way. Remember that the purpose of dialogue is to move the story forward. If you listen carefully, you'll hear that real everyday conversations are often repetitive and boring. People often talk about the weather or current events just to have something to say. In a novel, though, dialogue should never be meaningless. It should always help develop the character or advance the action. And it should avoid the all-too-common but irritating repetition of words and sounds such as "Well," "Uh," "Um," and "Like."

How else can you make dialogue work? Consider the following tips:

■ As much as possible, rely on rhythm and vocabulary—not phonetic spellings—to convey accent or dialect. If you feel that dialect would be useful in showing where a character came from, use it once or twice. Then drop it, as repeated use of dialect can be boring and even irritating.

■ When writing a contemporary novel, use contractions to make speech sound more natural.

■ Avoid the use of clichés, as they can make the dialogue seem tired and stale.

■ Keep your dialogue relatively brief. Paragraph after paragraph of "speech" seems unnatural and forced.

■ When stating a character's exact unspoken thoughts, use *italic type*, unless "he thought" or "she thought" immediately precedes or follows the character's words.

When you've finished writing the dialogue, read it out loud to see if it sounds natural, if it flows, and if it has the desired effect—to make the character seem angry, for instance, or to develop a conflict between two characters. If you detect a false note or if the dialogue doesn't do what you intended, rewrite it until you're satisfied.

Although the dialogue in your novel should sound natural, it should not mimic real-life conversation. Real-life conversation sometimes serves no purpose except to pass the time or fill an awkward silence. But in a novel, dialogue has to move the story forward.

To evaluate the dialogue you've written, try reading it aloud. If the words are stilted or if they don't have the desired effect, you'll probably be able to hear it immediately.

Structure—Acts and Scenes

"Where shall I begin, please, Your Majesty?" Alice asks the King of Hearts in *Alice in Wonderland*. "Begin at the beginning, and go on till you come to the end: then stop," the King sagely replies.

Fiction, unlike life, has a dramatically clear-cut beginning, middle, and end, often referred to as acts. Each act has its own shape, nature, and function.

The first act of a novel takes the reader from the protagonist's initial introduction and the setup of the situation to the first turning point that launches him into his mission. The middle or second act—the most challenging portion for many writers—shows that the protagonist is developing as he tackles an ever-escalating series of challenges, or obstacles, to his mission. The third act has the protagonist facing his ultimate obstacle in the climax of the story; overcoming the ultimate obstacle or failing to overcome it; and either achieving his mission or failing to do so. After this point, the rising action reverses and falls.

Every act unfolds scene by scene, with each scene ideally ratcheting the story along one step. Because of this, a novelist reveals his artistic talent most clearly in the scenes he composes. Compare, for instance, the sprawling, sometimes exhausting scenes written by William Faulkner to their polar opposite—the bullet-point scenes of Kurt Vonnegut.

Every scene centers on a conflict, the resolution of which moves the story forward one way or another. Whatever its size and tone, a fictional scene—just like the novel itself—has a beginning, middle, and end. In the beginning of the scene, the character is placed in a setting. In the middle, something dramatic happens—a challenge leads the character to act through this new conflict to a happy or unhappy resolution. At the end of the scene, the character either overcomes the obstacle or is defeated by it.

One of the ways to determine if your scenes will create the structure you want is to use index cards to plot the book's events. On each card, write down a scene or turning point in the major action line. Place the cards in order and gradually add cards to fill in gaps and introduce subplots. Then read through the cards to see if that sequence creates the structure of increasing tension followed by climax and resolution. If not, change the order of the scenes—or add and delete them—by manipulating the cards.

If the technique of using index cards to plot the action is helpful, by all means, use it. But if this system stops your creative process in its tracks, feel free to abandon it. Not all writers plot out all their scenes before they begin writing. Some leave the end to suggest itself along the way. Some turn to cards only when they get stuck.

Two of the scenes that you'll want to choose carefully are the beginning and ending scenes of the book. "Where to begin?" is a question that all writers must ask. Keep in mind that true drama—the kind that leads to bestsellers lists and a long writing career—begins only when something compelling happens. Aristotle said that Homer's greatness was that he began "in the middle of things," and novelist-screenwriter William Goldman counsels writers to start their scenes as far into the action as they can. What about the end of your novel? Does it satisfy the reader's expectations, or at least defeat them in a surprising way? Does it tie up all the loose ends, making sure that every piece of the puzzle you've laid out is fit into place? Whether or not an ending leaves the reader thinking, it must leave him feeling that the ride he's paid for has come to its appropriate end. I remember the frustration I experienced when I finished reading John Fowles' *The French Lieutenant's Woman*, which offers several possible conclusions so that the reader can choose the one he prefers. The unwritten contract between storyteller and audience requires the storyteller to provide the ending; that's your job as a novelist, not your reader's.

The first and continuous question you must ask yourself as you shuffle the file cards is, "How will my readers respond if I tell the story in this particular order?" The second is just as important: "Do I want them to respond that way?"

Theme

A book's *theme* is its main idea—the message that the author is trying to convey. A book may have one theme, or it may have several themes of different degrees of importance. Usually, the theme is about life, society, or human nature.

"To write a mighty book," Herman Melville wrote, "you must have a mighty theme." And in *Moby Dick,* Melville has several, including man's search for control over nature and the universe as hostile. Anyone who's read the novels of Joyce Carol Oates understands her infatuation with the theme of despair, fate, and futility. The theme of Joseph Heller's *Catch-22* is the absurdity of warfare; of John Scott Shepherd's *Henry's List of Wrongs,* that it's never too late to mend your ways. The best stories take a single, profound theme and plumb its depths through all the characters like variations on a musical theme. The worst stories skim the surface of many different themes, leaving their readers lost, confused, and unsatisfied.

Although much commercial fiction today appears to thrive relatively themeless, the novels that stand out—that receive strong reviews and awards—do so because their writers have something important to say and some insight into the human condition that *moves* the reader and somehow changes his life. If you're becoming cynical about love and romance, take Gabriel García Márquez's *Love in the Time of Cholera* to the beach with you on your next getaway. Its theme: True romance conquers time and space, and triumphs in the end. If you want to better understand the amorality of our times, read Jerzy Kosinski's *Cockpit*, an exploration of the borders and edges of morality and sociopathic evil. Again, the best novels are *unified* in theme as well as action, with theme hovering like an aura over action.

Setting

Every aspect of a novel is important to the success of the book. It should come as no surprise, then, that setting is a crucial element of the novel.

Many writers specialize in a location they know intimately: John Irving's New England, Pat Conroy's North Carolina, Anne Rice's New Orleans. You may choose to explore your own geographic roots this way, but don't let anyone tell you that you're limited to your origins or your place of residence. If that were true, there'd be no science fiction or fantasy.

A setting is far more than a location where the book's action takes place. Setting can infuse the book with atmosphere and mood. In some cases, setting is central to the characters and action. Think of Edith Wharton's *Ethan Frome*. The bleak New England town, battered by harsh winters, is an integral part of the plot and helps make the characters what they are. The same can be said of the oppressive southern heat of William Faulkner's *As I Lay Dying* and the exotic backdrop of Rumer Godden's *Black Narcissus*.

Before setting your story in a real location, perform meticulous research on the area even if you think you know it inside and out. When New York residents read a Nelson DeMille novel, they find the names of real towns, streets, and buildings—names that they instantly recognize. If the names were wrong or the relative positions of the streets and

Your setting is the backdrop of your novel, and is composed of many details. You may want to set your novel in a place that you already know, such as your home town. If you choose a location that's less familiar, though, be sure to perform meticulous research on the area so that all of the details are correct. This will help make your story more convincing.

towns were faulty, DeMille's story would be much less convincing. Consider how Dan Brown's *Angels & Demons* would fall apart if the details of the city of Rome and ecclesiastical architecture weren't accurate.

If setting your story in an invented location such as the make-believe world of a fantasy or sci-fi novel, the sky's the limit—as long as you create a world that is consistent and believable. If the temperature of your made-up planet is 200°F, how does that affect the creatures that live there? What kind of vegetation is possible? Everything has to fit.

Be careful, though, not to overdo research and details. Too many details can kill the vitality of a novel and make the reader lose track of the story, or at least lose interest in it. Unless research is necessary to evolve the plot (see the inset on page 241), I recommend that you do this research *after* you've finished your first draft, relying on your imagination for the first draft. This will prevent you from overloading your book with details that detract from, rather than add to, the story's impact.

Narrative Voice and Tone

Someone in your novel has to tell the reader that the sky is darkening or that the protagonist is running along the beach. That someone is the narrator. The narrative voice can take three basic forms: first person, second person, or third person. First-person and third-person narratives are common, while second-person narratives are extremely rare.

In *first-person narrative*, the story is told by one of the characters of the novel. This person—who is often the protagonist—can report only what he knows, and he cannot know everything at every moment. But because everything he recounts must have happened already, he's able to weave some of his "eventual knowledge" into his description of events as they occur. A first person narrative might read:

> I walked down the hotel hallway and paused at the elevator, wondering whether to push the button or return to my room and wait until morning. I remained there for several minutes before deciding to retire for the evening. If I had pushed the button, I'd have known then that the elevator had been sabotaged.

In *second-person narrative*, an omniscient narrator, who knows everything that is going to happen in a godlike way, addresses the protagonist as "you." Often, this type of story has the narrator speak-

WORDS FROM A PRO

Steve Alten

Author of *Domain* (Forge)

The Role of Research in the Writing Process

So you've decided to become an author. You've got the basics of your story, perhaps a few characters and their arcs, somehow you've made it to page thirty, and now . . . you're stuck in neutral. Is it that infamous "writer's block"? No, it's called lack of research.

Research is the elixir that reinvigorates your storyline, opens your chapters, and liberates you when you've written yourself into a suffocating closet. It makes you an expert in things you know diddly about, and elevates you from a wannabee to an author.

So how do we begin?

Preliminary Research: First, let's start with a basic premise. In my third novel, *Domain,* I began with a "what if?" What if the asteroid that struck Earth 65 million years ago, killing the dinosaurs, *wasn't* an asteroid. . . . Step One: Access the Internet.

The Internet is an incredible tool for authors, leading you down paths you never knew existed. In researching the asteroid, I was led to the Chixulub Impact Crater off the Yucatan Peninsula, to the Mayan homeland, to the Mayan folklore, to the Mayan Calendar and its 2,000-year-old prophecy that predicts humanity will perish on December 21st in the year 2012.

Whoa . . .

Refocusing on the Mayans, I found similarities in other cultures. The Incas. The Egyptians. Now I'm researching pyramids and other mysteries, and my mind is swimming with the ingredients of a real thriller. I now have a starting point (65 million years ago) and end (the day of doom in 2012), and now my characters can be re-created to move the storyline forward.

Continuing Research: This happens once the words start hitting the paper (or monitor). Where should I begin the intro to my main character? After many misses, I finally hit upon a mental asylum in Miami. Back to research. I need a mental disorder, asylum details, some terminology that makes me sound as though I know what the hell a paranoid schizophrenic is—voilà . . . and Chapter One is drafted.

Is it that simple? Hell no, but research simplifies the process.

Domain takes place in the year 2012. Back to research. What is the near-future like? Buildings, cars, roadways, economy . . . who is the President? When is the next election? Damn, this is getting complicated . . . but the novel is growing. I am not stuck in a dark closet with my basic plot and nowhere to go, I am adding flesh to my story, letting it take me to places that I had no inkling were there for the taking. A scene with the new President? Okay, but do I need to stop by the Oval Office? No, just a click on my computer, and I have schematics that detail the White House. An alien encounter? More difficult, but I have collections of "alien artwork" to help inspire my imagination. (The Internet is great, but it's not everything. My real-life visit to Chichen Itza definitely made an impact.)

Bottom Line: If the devil is in the details, then it is research that exorcises him.

ing to a younger version of himself. Most modern books don't speak directly to the reader, and most writers find this narrative form extremely difficult to use. If you took the previous narrative and rewrote it in second person, it might read like this:

> You walked down the hotel hallway and paused at the elevator. You couldn't decide whether to push the button or return to your room until morning. You remained there for several minutes before walking away. Had you pushed the button, you'd have discovered that the elevator had been sabotaged.

In a *third-person narrative*, the narrator is not a character in the story, but an outside observer who knows everything and is therefore able to explore all of the characters and events in the novel. If you took our sample narrative and wrote it in third person, it might read like this:

> He walked down the hotel hallway and paused at the elevator, wondering whether to push the button or return to his room and wait until morning. Another hotel guest, on the way from the soda machine to his room, stared at him as he stood there indecisively. But John didn't notice anyone else in the hall, so focused was he on his decision. Finally, he turned towards his room, visibly shaken. Had he pushed the button, he'd have realized that the elevator had been sabotaged.

I generally recommend that novelists stick to writing in third person during the early part of their careers. As I said earlier, second person is hardly ever used and extremely difficulty to pull off convincingly. And creating a convincing first-person narrative is much trickier than it may sound. New writers often struggle with the nuances of "voice" in their novels, blurring the line between author and storyteller. I advise you to leave these explorations for a later phase of your career. At that point, you may want to consult Orson Scott Card's *Characters and Viewpoint*, which offers solid information about each point of view, as well as advice on creating characters and other elements of storytelling. Another valuable reference is Percy Lubbock's essay "Picture, Drama, and Point of View" in his book *The Craft of Fiction*.

How is *tone* different from narrative voice? While narrative voice tells you *who* is speaking, tone displays an attitude toward the events being described and the world in general. Of course, tone is deter-

The third-person narrative is the most common form of narrative in fiction—and the easiest to manage. Moreover, when the narrator is omniscient, he is able to relate the thoughts and feelings of any character, to insert editorial comments, to move around to different times and places, and to fill in back-story whenever it's needed.

mined to a point by the identity of the storyteller. If the narrator is the protagonist of the story, for example, the tone is a reflection of his attitudes, which may or may not be your own.

Many different types of tone can be used, with each having a specific effect on the reader. Do you want to preach to the reader? To offer your story dispassionately? To communicate sorrow? Do you want the reader to trust you, or do you want to arouse suspicion? Anything is possible through the artful manipulation of tone.

You may never have thought about tone before, but at this point, you might want to revisit some favorite novels and see how other authors have handled this aspect of novel writing. The narrator of *Don Quixote*, for instance, is an enchanter with a playful elusiveness. The narrator of *Moby Dick* is the straightforward seaman Ishmael. Choose a voice that you believe is right for your book, and try using it for a few pages to see if it feels natural and works with your story. If it doesn't, let it go and try a different tack. Often, writer's block is caused by the novelist's failure to find the right tone for his story.

> It's vital to find the right tone and the right narrator for each piece of fiction you write. Experiment to see how you can use different tones and narratives to better tell your stories.

The Importance of Unity

You now know the essential building blocks of any story: character, action, dialogue, structure, theme, setting, narrative voice, and tone. But a novel is more than a collection of separate elements. A good novel has *unity*.

Aristotle addressed this issue more than two thousand years ago, saying that in the best stories, all the components support a single plot line. That's what makes good fiction so satisfying. It has a single clear mission and a definite conclusion.

In the interest of unity, I recommend that you work out the many "tools" of fiction in your mind before you start to write. For that purpose, long walks in the mountains or desert are often far more useful than sitting in a chair, staring at your computer screen. Beginning writers put in too much—too many characters, too many subplots, too many different tones, too many viewpoints—because they haven't yet identified the one line of action that everything else must serve. Generally this bad habit comes from premature writing—forcing yourself to sit down and begin your tale before you know what you're going to write.

Writing style varies from author to author. The creative process varies, too. But in *every* great novel, every element works together, with the characters moving the action along, the action developing our understanding of the characters, the dialogue serving both action and character, the characters and action supporting the theme, and the narrative voice and setting establishing the tone.

FICTION-WRITING TECHNIQUES AND TIPS

Once you've thought out the different elements of your novel, it's time to start writing. Whole books have been published on the craft

---

WORDS FROM A PRO

Steve Alten

Author of *Meg: A Novel of Deep Terror* (Bantam)

On a hot Saturday in August 1995, I sat down at my desk in front of an old word processor (that only saved 3 pages at a time) and began to write the manuscript that would be sold by AEI a year later as *MEG: A Novel of Deep Terror*. I worked from ten at night until two or three in the morning, and often fell asleep at the keyboard. I thought about my novel nearly every waking moment and kept paper and pen by my bedside just in case I dreamed an important story point. I had no prior writing experience, save for a master's thesis and dissertation, and no clue or contacts to help me get published, but I had two things going for me:

1. I knew how to set goals.

2. I refused to quit.

If you have these qualities, then the rest will come to you . . . *if* you have the ability to block out the naysayers. You know who they are, those "helpful" family members and friends who want to "save you" from wasting all that time writing because "it's nearly impossible to get published."

That's where goals come in. Determine now, *before* you start, how many pages you will average a night, a week, a month, and when you will finish the manuscript. Add another 30 days for editing, then a game plan for finding a literary agent. Remember, nothing gets done with a "wish-list." Goals require proper planning.

I've found that writing, like most skills, gets better with practice—assuming you endeavor to improve. I'm still learning—and proud to admit it—because when the learning process stops, the dying begins.

Persist. Along the way you'll find the help you need. Remember, what goes around comes around, so give back if you want to receive. Luck is a residue of hard work, but no matter what your chosen endeavor, no one is truly successful without the help of others. Pray, toil, but keep the faith and keep working at it, and good things will happen, often when you least expect it.

of writing in general, and novel-writing in particular. While this chapter doesn't provide the room needed to present all there is to know about writing, it's useful to review some important writing techniques as well as some tips for budgeting your time and keeping the creative juices flowing.

Chapters and Paragraphs

Earlier in this chapter, you learned that the dramatic action in novels forms acts and, within the acts, smaller scenes. But as anyone who ever read a novel knows, in a printed book, the acts and scenes are presented in chapters, which are further divided into paragraphs.

Basically, the chapter is a unit that gives the reader a sense of progress and of pause. Many new writers want to know how long a chapter should be. Chapter lengths vary from author to author. Some writers compose long chapters; others, short chapters. Some novelists vary chapter length for dramatic emphasis. Perhaps most of their chapters are twenty or so pages in length, but the occasional chapter—one that presents a suicide scene, for instance—is only a page in length for effect. There are no rigid rules for determining chapter length, so you'll want to do what works best for your novel.

Chapter beginnings and endings are crucial moments in a novel, but again, different novelists handle this differently. Some use a chapter to introduce a conflict and end the chapter after the conflict is resolved, giving the reader a sense of intermission and accomplishment. Others close a chapter before a conflict has ended or even after a new one has begun, thereby building suspense and impelling the reader to keep turning the page. Again, you'll want to do what best serves your story.

Like chapters, paragraphs aren't governed by hard-and-fast rules. But you'll find that by using paragraphs wisely, you can add clarity to your book, make it more accessible to your reader, and create dramatic emphasis.

To enhance clarity, start a new paragraph when a new character begins speaking or when your narrative switches from one character's viewpoint to another. Note how this technique is used in the following text:

> Anthony sat in his office, e-mailing his wife LeAnne. Although his desk was covered with stacks of manuscripts that

Chapter beginnings and endings are crucial moments, and should be chosen carefully. Do you want to give your reader a short intermission from the action? Do you want to build excitement and suspense? All this can be achieved by carefully crafting the beginnings and endings of your chapters.

cried for attention, Anthony felt the need to make contact after their early-morning argument.

The door opened at the end of the hallway and Jackie strode in, late as usual and flushed from her morning workout. She tossed a "How are you?" in Anthony's direction and, without waiting for a reply, continued down the hall, cappuccino in hand.

Learn to use paragraphs wisely. Smart paragraph breaks help clarify the action, turn large blocks of type into reader-friendly text, and add dramatic emphasis.

Also use paragraphs to break up large blocks of type and thus keep your text reader-friendly. The modern eye, no doubt thanks to web-browsing, has become conditioned to taking input in smaller and smaller bites. Large blocks of type are often intimidating, while smaller paragraphs seem friendly and appealing.

Finally, use paragraphing for dramatic emphasis. The successful commercial novelist uses every trick at his command to dramatize his writing, and sometimes short paragraphs—even as short as one sentence or a single word—can add dramatic emphasis to the narrative. Read the following example:

Looking out the window, he saw Amy walking absent-mindedly across the street. On her back was a worn knapsack, heavy with books from her English lit class. As usual, she seemed oblivious to her surroundings—lost in some internal conversation.
She never heard the car speeding around the corner.

Beyond these general principles, remember that as a writer of fiction, you should feel free to take license and use both chapters and paragraphs in your own way. As Humpty-Dumpty told Alice: "When *I* use a word, it means just what I choose it to mean—neither more nor less."

Writing What You Know

Everyone has heard that it's best to write about what you know, and certainly, many fine fiction writers have found inspiration in their own lives or in the news. Harper Lee based much of *To Kill a Mockingbird* on recollections of her childhood in Alabama. Ernest Hemingway's work as a World War I ambulance driver inspired his novel *A Farewell to Arms*. Patricia Cornwell used knowledge gained while working in a medical examiner's office to create her character Kate Scarpetta, a medical examiner who solves crimes. Nelson DeMille's *Night Fall* explored the 1996 crash of TWA Flight 800.

Your life—your upbringing, your work, your romances, your town, and your family and friends—may well prove to be a treasure-trove of plots and ideas. Moreover, by writing about what you know, you may find it far easier to create believable characters and realistic settings for your book. Just keep in mind that basing your novel on real life has its problems as well. Let's look at two major hazards.

First, the events in your life occur, quite obviously, in chronological order—not in dramatic order. Some writers feel that when basing fiction on personal experiences, they must relate the events in the order in which they occurred and *exactly* as they occurred. But this can result in a deadly dull book. That's why your life should be used as inspiration—not as a blueprint for your novel. Feel free to move events around in time, deleting and adding incidents as necessary to create a fascinating tale. Your readers won't know or care if the story doesn't exactly follow the events on which your story is based. They just want to read a great story.

Second, while it's all right to turn your relatives and acquaintances into characters, you must proceed with caution. People have a right to their privacy, and when they feel that their privacy has been invaded or that their reputation has been damaged, they can sue. Every writer taps the reservoir of his own personal acquaintances to garner material for his characters. How else could he create them? But the trick to doing this effectively, legally, and ethically is not to borrow too much from any given real person, but to use bits and pieces from each to assemble your own characters. Look for the characteristics that make the most dramatic combination and that, above all, serve your story's action.

Creating a Space, Finding the Time

Perhaps you have a great idea for a novel but somehow have never found the time to write it. Or perhaps you sat down to write your novel only to find yourself so plagued by interruptions that you couldn't get past Chapter One. Is there a solution?

Professional writers succeed not only because they have the requisite talent and skills, but also because they create an efficient workspace and carve out a time to write. You can do the same.

Begin by finding an area—whether it's a corner of your bedroom or a separate study—in which to work. The area you select will depend not

Many great novelists have written about what they know best. If you choose to draw upon your own experiences, be sure to use your life as inspiration only. Don't hesitate to change the order of events—or the events themselves—to make your story more exciting.

only on the space available, but also on the schedules of family members. If you choose to work while the kids are at school, you can probably get away with writing at the dining room table. But if you work while others are in the house, you may need a more secluded area where you can shut yourself away for a few hours.

Once you've chosen your writing area, gather everything you need—notebooks, pens, computer, etc.—in that space so that you won't waste time each day searching for the essentials. Just as important, try to eliminate any items that might distract you from the task at hand. If the TV set seems too tempting, move it out of the room or simply choose another area of the house. Also exclude piles of new and interesting magazines, and anything else that might pull you away from your work.

Once you have the space, choose the time. Successful writers set aside a certain time of day just for writing. If you're a stay-at-home mom with a baby, your child's naptime might work. If you work nine to five in an office and you're an early-morning person, try fitting in an hour or two before leaving for your job. If you're a night owl, block out your time in the evening. If possible, adjust your schedule so that you can write during the time of day that is most creative for you. Then do your best to write on a regular schedule. Make writing a habit—like brushing your teeth—and let family and friends build their routines around yours so that interruptions are kept to a minimum.

WORDS FROM A PRO

Kathryn Falk
CEO/Founder *Romantic Times*
Book Club Magazine

Tricks of the trade? Get up early in the morning to write, rather than late at night when you're tired. Leave your last sentence unfinished for the next day (Hemingway did this). Some writers compose in the first person, then translate it into the third (most editors prefer third person). Writing the last chapter first seems very difficult, but a few savvy writers manage it with positive results.

Beating the Middle

Many writers begin a new story brimming with ideas and enthusiasm. For a while, everything proceeds beautifully. And then they hit the second act—the middle.

The middle portion of a novel seems to be the toughest part for writers to handle. Many novels fizzle out midstream because the writers have lost their perspective. Writers get exhausted and sometimes mistake this normal, natural exhaustion for depression. They begin to second-guess their decision to undertake the project, and their fatigue soon colors their judgment. Pretty soon, they've convinced themselves that the novel isn't worth finishing, and they abandon it.

How can you beat the middle doldrums? First, realize that this drop in enthusiasm is a normal part of the writing process—one that you should anticipate and prepare to deal with before it cripples your efforts. Second, take vacations from your work. Take lots of vacations, in fact. Plan to take them at regular intervals and at any time you feel the writer's doldrums starting to get you down.

Does the prospect of walking away from your project for a week or two fill you with anxiety? Good. That's part of the idea. By stepping back from the process whenever it starts to bog down, you'll place a healthy pressure on yourself and feel that much more compelled to use your time productively when you do get back to work.

Stepping away from the project will also give your mind a chance to work out any plot problems. Many writers find that their most creative ideas come not when they're sitting in front of their computer, but when they're walking the dog, vacuuming the carpet, or jogging through the park. Should the hero learn his father's true identity through a computer search or through a heated confrontation? Should the heroine return to her husband or start a new life with her love interest? The answers to these questions are often found during "down" time, when you're relaxed and your mind is free to wander.

Finally, by dividing the novel-writing task into small chunks, you will make it feel less like a monster and more like a joy. Keep plugging away at this series of manageable tasks until the rush of adrenaline that comes toward the end of a project energizes you, carrying you to the finish line.

Are you stuck in the middle doldrums? Try taking a vacation from your writing. Frequent breaks will give your mind a chance to work out plot problems and will divide the novel-writing task into smaller, more manageable pieces.

Breathing Life Into Your Work

Your novel is finished and you feel great—until you read through your work. Somehow, it seems dead. Lackluster. You have carefully plotted out the action, created your characters, and chosen your setting. Your research was meticulous and your theme is strong. What, then, might be the problem? Often, it lies in your choice of words.

No matter how wonderful your characters and plot may be, dull words and phrases will make for a dull book. But once you've finished your novel, it's relatively easy to replace dreary wording with vibrant terms that will breathe life into your work. This doesn't mean that you should grab your thesaurus and come up with ten-dollar terms designed to impress the reader. It does mean that your words should be used to paint a vivid picture of your characters, their actions, and their environment. Consider the following phrases:

Dull	Lively
Her blond hair was beautiful.	Her hair fell in sheets of liquid gold.
Tired, he seated himself on the couch.	Groaning with exhaustion, he flopped down on the threadbare couch.
Hungry, he ate quickly.	He tore into his sandwich.
She could hear the wind blowing outside.	She could hear the wind howling like a creature of the night.
He drove quickly down the street.	Gunning the engine, he wheeled around the corner.

> If you're at a loss for ways to bring your characters and settings to life, revisit your favorite authors and see how they describe characters, actions, and settings.

While you want to use strong words and phrases that bring your work alive, at the same time, you want to avoid overly florid descriptions or long descriptive passages that slow down the action. You don't have to use a lot of words to paint a vivid picture. You do have to choose your words carefully.

IN CONCLUSION

You now should be aware of the elements that make up a great novel, as well as a number of techniques that can help you in your writing endeavors. But most successful novelists agree that in these highly competitive times, an author simply can't afford to limit his work to the actual writing of the book. As explained in Chapter 10, the vast majority of publishers do little if any marketing for a debut novel, other than the distribution of catalogues and the like. That's why it's so important to get involved in the promotion of your book. Fortunately, there are many things that you can do on your own to bring your book to the attention of sales representatives, distributors, and booksellers—the people who will make your book available to its readers.

CHAPTER 12

PROMOTING YOUR NOVEL

Some say that a book's success is determined more by its marketing than by the quality of its writing. Yes and no. If your book doesn't receive the marketing necessary to make the public aware of its existence, no one will ever get the chance to discover how good it is. But if your book isn't good enough, all the marketing in the world won't turn it into a bestseller with "legs." The fact is that you need both good-quality writing *and* good marketing to have a truly successful book.

If you're now thinking, "But isn't the publisher responsible for marketing the book?" you're lost in a bygone era, when publishers had the budget to aggressively promote their books. Now, the vast majority of publishers have a smaller marketing budget for *all* books, and do little or nothing to market a novel from a first-time author. If the publishing house does make efforts in addition to your own, or if they eventually jump on the marketing bandwagon that you have created, consider it icing on the cake. In the meantime, I urge you to take your novel's fate into your own hands.

Before we start discussing specific marketing goals and strategies, it's worth noting that when most first-time writers think of their book's customers, they think only of the readers. But the reading audience is only the last in a long series of "customers" that you need to buy your book. Between them and you stands a veritable conga line of sales reps, distributors, librarians, and bookstore owners. In order to have an opportunity to make your book available to the public, you've first got to sell it to each link in this chain.

If this sounds as if it involves a lot of work, well, it does. But it's certainly not impossible. This chapter will lead you through the steps you can take to promote your book.

YOUR GOALS AND OBJECTIVES

Although every novelist would love her book to be a *New York Times* Best Seller, this is not a realistic goal. Instead of shooting for the *Times*, try to get your book reviewed by as many recognized review outlets as possible.

Before you outline a marketing plan for your novel, it would be helpful to think carefully and, most of all, *realistically* about your overall goals. Every novelist wants her book featured in bookstore displays and listed among *The New York Times* Best Sellers. But if these are your expectations, you're setting yourself up for disappointment. Instead, set goals that, with hard work and some luck, can be reasonably achieved. A worthy and achievable set of goals includes:

- To get your novel reviewed by as many recognized review outlets as possible.

- To get your novel and/or yourself chosen as a subject of one or more feature articles or interviews, in print, on radio or TV, or on the Internet.

- To maximize sales of your book. (To keep things in perspective, remember that the average book sells about 5,000 copies, and sales of 25,000 hardbacks unofficially give a book "bestseller" status.)

- To learn about and enjoy the process of promoting your novel.

Now that you know your goals, you'll want to start working toward achieving them through a multi-step plan that will gradually increase your novel's visibility in the book world.

YOUR MARKETING PLAN

If you're going to maximize the sales of your book, you've got to start well in advance of its publication date. As soon as you've turned in your last set of page proofs, start putting together a marketing plan for your novel. As much as possible, coordinate your plan with your publishing house and—if you have them—with your representative and publicist. But whether you have a whole crew on board or you're both captain *and* crew, make sure that *you* are the engine behind the plan.

Your marketing plan should begin with research. Identify who your largest group of readers will probably be. Look at the markets for books similar to yours. What age groups read them? Which gender prefers them? Where do the largest groups of readers live? What interests do they have?

Let your research be your guide. It will tell you how to put your book in the kind of light its readers will find most attractive. It will tell you the types of publications and venues your advertising should target as your publication date approaches. And it will help you design a selling "package" that everyone who's marketing your book can use.

If you're lucky enough to be part of a large, supportive organization, you might be able to sell a good many books within that one group, either through preorders from them or through a speaking program that will get you in front of enough members so that you can personally make those sales. Utah novelists, perhaps the most entrepreneurial of them all, are fortunate to have a built-in support group in the Church of Latter-Day Saints. With organization, and the right novel, a Utah novelist can sell 50,000 copies within Utah alone. Let's say you're not a member of a church such as this. Are you a pilot? Do you belong to a professional nursing organization? To a veterans group? If so—and especially if the subject of your book ties in with the focus of the group—by all means contact the organization and see if some arrangement can be made to let members know about your upcoming novel. Also consider speaking at meetings and conventions so that you can talk about your book in person.

When you have a sense of your target audience and how best to approach it, draw up a marketing plan that lists the steps you will take to make your book known among booksellers and the media. You may or may not choose to look into every means of getting your book in the public eye, but the more exposure you give your book, the better. The following is an effective plan of attack that you can use as a basis for your own marketing efforts.

1. At least six months before your book's publication date, identify people who might be willing to provide a blurb—a celebrity endorsement—that can appear on the book cover. Send out proofs or advance reading copies (ARCs).

2. Research and compose a list of target venues—both print and

Never stint on research. Only after you've identify your potential readers—who they are, where they live, and what publications they read—will you be able to target the magazines, newspapers, and television and radio shows that might be interested in reviewing your novel.

electronic media—that might review your book, print an article about you or your book, or conduct and/or print an interview.

3. Design and put together a publicity packet for distribution to the media.

4. Create a website for yourself and your book. Make sure the website includes all of the information in your press kit, a schedule of speaking events and signings, excerpts of interviews, and links that will allow interested consumers to purchase your book.

5. Interview a publicist if desired.

6. If your publisher doesn't send out advance reading copies (ARCs) to trade journals, mail out ARCs to *Publishers Weekly*, *Kirkus Reviews*, *Library Journal*, *ForeWord*, and *Booklist* at least four months before publication. Make follow-up calls to determine if they were received.

7. Once the book is printed and in distribution, send out final copies to all other target reviewers, and make follow-up calls.

8. Once the book is printed and in distribution, send out publicity packets to print and electronic media, and make follow-up calls.

9. Contact appropriate websites that might review or sell your book.

10. Arrange book signings, readings, and lectures, and attend conventions.

11. Launch a book tour in coordination with earlier contacts with print and electronic media. (See Step 8.)

12. Arrange for offbeat advertising and promotion.

Once you've put your marketing plan together, it will be time to fill in the publicist and marketing people at your publishing house. If you've hired your own publicist and/or are working with an agent, try to arrange a meeting at which you can all share ideas and coordinate your efforts. Don't be surprised, though, if your meeting is carried out over the phone and through e-mails. However you make contact with the publishing company, let the staff know what you're planning and try to get them on board. An important part of this meeting involves finding out just how much they'll be doing on your behalf so that you can avoid duplicating their efforts. If the publisher will be sending out ARCs to trade journals, for instance, you should *not* send copies out on your own. Just be grateful that the company has shouldered one of the tasks on your list. Similarly, if the publisher is preparing a publicity packet for your book, be appreciative and ask for copies—or a single copy that you can have duplicated—for use in your own marketing efforts.

Also make sure that in the course of your marketing efforts, you avoid doing anything that could create havoc in the publishing house. For instance, if the publisher isn't set up to sell books directly to consumers, it won't be appropriate during interviews to direct listeners or readers to contact the company for copies of your novel. Instead, refer your audience to the appropriate chain bookstores or to your website.

Be aware that the publicist may react with alarm when she reads your plan and sees what you intend to do independently. Since most publishing houses now do so little marketing, this reaction may seem strange. But if you keep the publishing company in the loop on your marketing and promotional activities, and solicit the staff's input, they'll probably get behind you. Just use all your diplomatic skills to get them invested in your effort so that they'll support you whenever possible.

Perhaps you now have drafted your own personal marketing plan. Or perhaps you're still staring at the list presented above, wondering how you're supposed to put together a publicity packet when you have no idea what a publicity packet *is*! Relax. The remainder of the chapter will discuss each of the steps outlined in the plan and help guide you through the marketing of your novel. And at the end of the chapter, I'll recommend some great books that are devoted entirely to the subject of marketing.

OBTAINING BLURBS

A *blurb* is a celebrity endorsement of a book that's printed on the novel's cover. For instance, a famous mystery writer might enthusiastically endorse a new mystery with the words "It kept me on the edge of my seat!" Clearly, a blurb like this is a great boon to a debut novel.

Once you've drafted your marketing plan, be sure to fill in the publicist and marketing department at your publishing house. During your meeting, you'll be able to discover how much they'll be doing on your behalf so that you can avoid duplicating their efforts. Just as important, by always keeping them in the loop, you may win valuable support. Over time, you might even inspire them to launch marketing efforts of their own.

Unfortunately, many novelists blow their shot at getting endorsements by trying to get them too late. The ideal time to solicit blurbs is six months before the book appears, as this will allow the celebrity time to read the book and respond before the novel goes to press. It should come as no surprise that a blurb from an established writer—especially one who works in the same genre and would be immediately recognized by your potential readers—is most desirable. But if you can't get an endorsement from a writer, rest assured that a blurb from *anyone* with name recognition would be great.

How can you go about getting these blurbs? Obviously, if you have an entrée with a writer or other celebrity, that would be your best bet. Simply ask that person if she would be kind enough to supply a blurb and if she agrees, give her an advance reading copy or a set of proofs. If you don't already know someone suitable, network. Speak to your editor and your publicist to see if they work with any authors who might be willing to help you out. Speak, too, to friends and acquaintances—including your hairdresser or barber, your accountant, and your dentist. Do you plan to attend a writers' conference or workshop? Take your advance copies with you and see if you can grab a moment with an established writer who's giving a talk or teaching a workshop. Be proactive and *never* be afraid to ask.

If networking supplies no leads, simply make a list of appropriate writers, identify each writer's publisher or literary agent, and send an advance reading copy of your novel care of the publishing company or rep. Enclose a polite letter asking for a blurb, and hope for the best. You never know.

You can often find the name of a novelist's literary agent on the acknowledgments page of her novel. Just be sure to check the *latest* novel, as writers sometimes switch from one agent to another over time. Then use one of the directories listed in Chapter 4 to locate the address of the agency.

MAKING LISTS OF TARGET MEDIA

Your advance reading copies, I hope, are now in the hands of various people who are willing to supply enthusiastic endorsements of your book. So it's now time to research the trade journals, magazines, newspapers, and television and radio shows that might be interested in printing a review, conducting an interview, or writing a feature article.

I've already mentioned the trade magazines that include reviews of books—*Publishers Weekly, Kirkus Review, Library Journal, ForeWord Magazine*, and *Booklist*. If your publisher is not planning to send advance reading copies of your book to these publications, you'll want to do it yourself at least four months ahead of time.

All publications other than those listed above should get copies of the final printed book, and should be contacted only after the book is in distribution. Why? The periodicals mentioned earlier go to the trade—to librarians and booksellers, among other people in the book world. You want these folks to learn about the book *before* it's in print so that they can preorder it. But other magazines and newspapers are read by the general public—the reading audience—and you want your book in the store when your readers learn of it so that they can run right out and buy a copy. If your novel isn't available when your audience first learns of it, it's highly unlikely that they'll look for it again when it's actually in print.

When locating likely magazines, try to focus on those that will appeal to your reading audience. If your book is a romance novel, for instance, look for women's magazines that print book reviews, as well as magazines designed especially for romance readers, such as *Romantic Times.* Clearly, it's very important to understand your audience so that you can be a better judge of how—and where—you should approach it.

When making a list of newspapers that might be interested in your book, look first at local papers, including town newspapers, as these are the ones most likely to review your work. Budget permitting, target major city newspapers next, as they often print book reviews.

Although you may dream of making an appearance on *Oprah,* I can't overemphasize the fact that you must first target *small local* television and radio shows. First of all, these are the ones that are most likely to grant an interview to a new writer who has no previous experience with electronic media. Second, all larger television shows, and some larger radio shows as well, demand tapes of previous interviews so they can judge your performance. For this reason, you'll want to tape any interviews you do get, not only for submission to larger venues, but also as a means of judging and perfecting your own interview skills.

As any publicist can tell you, the best time to address a radio audience is during "drive time"—that period between 6:00 or 7:00 AM Eastern Time and 8:00 or 9:00 AM Pacific Time. This, of course, is when people are in their cars, listening to their radios on the way to work. Some publicists offer a service that will have you speaking in ten-minute intervals on different local shows, one after the other. If you can afford to pay a publicist to do this, it may be worth the price.

Although trade journals should be contacted before your novel is in print, you'll want to contact all other magazines and newspapers only *after* your book is in distribution. Why? If your novel isn't in the stores when interested readers learn of it through a review or feature story, they probably won't look for it again when it's finally in print.

But if you can't afford this service, you may be able to arrange the interviews on your own.

Where can you find the names and contact information for print and electronic media venues? When it comes to print media, you'll be able to find a good deal of what you need on the Internet. But when searching for radio and television shows, you'll need to turn to the Bacon's Media Directories, which are available in the reference section of most libraries. Bacon's produces separate directories on magazines, radio, newspapers, and TV/cable. Venues are divided by category, so you can home in on the ones most appropriate to your book. Each entry provides complete contact information, all of which should be added to your list.

CREATING A PUBLICITY PACKET

Once you've outlined your plan and identified your target venues, you'll want to put together a slick, professional-looking publicity packet for your novel. While this packet won't be sent to media when you're seeking reviews, it will be sent when setting up interviews or suggesting an article. In the latter instances, it serves to grab the attention of the reader and to introduce both the novel and the author.

A publicity packet should include:

- A full-color copy of the book cover.

- A photo of yourself.

Even if you've already sent your Q & A sheet to a radio or TV station, take an extra copy or two with you when you go for your interview. Don't assume that the host has read your book, and don't assume that she'll have the sheet on hand. Make sure that the host has what she needs to give the best interview possible.

- A two- to -three-page teaser for the novel. (This can be based on the synopsis, but should exclude anything that would ruin the "read"—the solution to a mystery, for instance.)

- A brief but interesting biography that's no longer than one page.

- A question-and-answer page.

If you have a friend who's a graphics whiz, see if she's willing to design a folder in which you can place the materials that compose the packet. If not, keep it simple and businesslike by using a plain folder that displays your name and the title of your book in attractive type. Although you'll usually send out printed packets, be sure to create an electronic version, as well, for your Internet marketing needs. (You'll read more about this on pages 269 to 271.)

While most of the components of the publicity packet are fairly self-explanatory, you might be wondering why you need a question-and-answer sheet. The purpose of this do-it-yourself Q & A sheet will become crystal clear as soon as you experience your first interview with a radio or television host who's never even laid eyes on your book, let alone read it. For this type of host, the Q & A sheet will serve as a guide, helping ensure that the interview goes in a direction that's favorable to your book. The Q & A sheet will also help you land more interviews to begin with, because it's concrete evidence that you have something interesting to talk about, and because the media people will see that you've already done a big chunk of their work for them. So it's worthwhile to sit yourself down and compose and answer eight to ten questions that interviewers might ask—questions like, "How did you come up with the idea for your novel?" (See the sample Q & A sheet on page 262.)

Have your publicity packets ready to go as early in the process as possible, but keep adding to the packets as your book's publicity gains momentum. Over time, you'll be able to slip in copies of favorable reviews, little articles on public appearances, feature articles, and so forth, as they become available. You might even want to include a giveaway of some sort, such as a bookmark. (See the Sample Publicity Packet on pages 260 to 264.)

> During any interview, make sure that the conversation remains focused on you and your novel. If the interviewer digresses from the topic to discuss something of personal interest to her, tactfully but firmly pull her back to the subject of you and your book.

SETTING UP A WEBSITE

By now, you may have heard horror stories about books that appeared on major television talk shows, garnered fabulous reviews, and compelled thousands to rush out to their local bookstores—only to find not a single copy on the shelf. Sound like a fluke? This happens far more often than you'd think. But fortunately, there is something you can do right now to avoid singing the out-of-stock blues later on. Set up a website so that readers can order your book directly from you or through an active link to an online retailer like Amazon.com.

A website is one of the cheapest and most effective forms of advertising available. Ninety percent of Americans have online access, which means that once you create a site, nearly anyone will be

Sample Publicity Packet

Your publicity packet should be brief but intriguing, and serve to pique the reader's interest in your novel. Your "teaser" can be based on your synopsis. Unlike the synopsis, though, it should not include any information that would spoil the story for the reader. Instead, reveal just enough of the plot to give the reader a good feel for the book and to hook her into exploring both you and your novel more fully. (See the sample teaser, which begins on the right.)

When reviewing the sample publicity packet on pages 260 to 264, keep in mind that your final packet should also include a full-color copy of the book cover and a high-quality photo of you. Over time, you'll want to add further materials as they become available. Copies of favorable reviews, feature articles, and articles on public appearances will make you and your novel an even more attractive interview subject. Finally, consider enclosing a giveaway of some type, such as a bookmark that bears a photo of your book and/or quoted excerpts—anything that will catch the recipient's eye and capture her interest.

For Immediate Release

Contact: Marybeth Adams
Adams Entertainment
Phone: (818) 555-0101

DANGER ZONE

By Shirley Palmer

Maggie Cady is living the perfect life. She has a home in suburban New Orleans, which she shares with Sam, her husband, lover and soul mate, and their adored son, four-year-old Jimmy. They even have a dog, Max. She has the family of her dreams.

Then one quiet Sunday morning the dream is shattered. While Maggie is at Mass, a storm of bullets rips across the front of the house. When the gunfire ends, Max is dead in the driveway, and Sam races upstairs to find his son's bed empty. Their idyllic world has exploded in a violent attack that has Sam—and the police—baffled.

But not Maggie. She knows exactly who has penetrated the shield that was built around her, and around her son. And to find Jimmy, she must become the hunter in a world from which she once barely escaped with her life. She must return to the danger zone.

Maggie writes a note for her husband: *"Sam, I love you. Don't follow me. I have gone to get Jimmy."* Then she leaves the safety of New Orleans and returns to New York to embark upon a search that she knows will lead her into the depths of a world of violence and deceit.

Upon arrival at Kennedy Airport, she calls a number she has not used for six years. A familiar and once much loved voice answers, "This is Father Patrelli."

"Bobby," she says. "This is Andrea. I want you to meet me at the place we saw each other last."

While waiting to meet him at St. Saviors Cemetery, she runs her fingers over the most recent names carved on the Bellini family tomb. *Salvatore Bellini. Giacomo Bellini.* The dates of birth are a generation apart but the date of death is the same, six years earlier. When Father Patrelli arrives, she asks him to take a message to Michael O'Malley, the leader of an Irish gang with whom her father and brother were meeting when they were cut down in a bloodbath that left seven men dead, including O'Malley's twin brothers.

Page Two/DANGER ZONE

When, reluctantly, Bobby agrees, she knows Father Roberto Patrelli is still what he always was, a negotiator for the mob.

In New Orleans, Sam is devastated by the disappearance of his son and his wife, and bewildered by the note left by Maggie. Although the FBI is working the case, as an ex-cop, Sam is not without resources. But while following a lead passed to him by his former partner in the New Orleans Police Department, Sam is embroiled in a shoot-out, and when the smoke clears, two men are dead, shot in the head by an unseen marksman.

Hunted now by the FBI for the murders, and armed only by hunches and a faded black-and-white photograph he found when searching Maggie's things, Sam tracks his wife to a shabby parish church in Manhattan. As he moves closer to the elusive Maggie, Sam discovers that the woman he thought he knew, the woman he loved, is a stranger whose name is Andrea Bellini, the daughter of Salvatore Bellini, head of the notorious Bellini Crime Family.

Although carrying the Beretta her brother Giacomo taught her to use, and ready to kill to find her son, Maggie is snatched from the street in front of the church and taken to see Michael O'Malley. He plays a tape of Jimmy's voice, and tells Maggie that he knows Salvatore did not die that day when his own twin brothers were cut down. And he offers a deal. *"Your son for your father."* He gives her 24 hours before he'll start to deliver her son to her—one piece at a time.

Of the handful of people who knew that Salvatore Bellini, although wounded, survived and went into hiding, and that his coffin held only sand, most have met a violent death. And only her mother knows that her father has never forgiven her for unwittingly leading the FBI to the meeting place in upstate New York in a desperate attempt to save him and her lover, Bobby Patrelli. Although she was once the child of his heart, Salvatore Bellini has never again spoken to his daughter.

Now she must persuade him to come out of hiding to save her son.

Racing against time, Maggie must locate her father before it is too late. She must beg his forgiveness and convince him to put his own life at risk.

But as the clock is ticking, both Maggie and Sam begin to realize that in the shadows behind O'Malley lies an enemy more deadly than either of them could have imagined.

Points for Teaser

☐ Base your teaser on your synopsis, but don't include any information that would ruin the story for the reader.

☐ Use white bond $8\frac{1}{2}$ x 11-inch paper.

☐ Use 1-inch margins on top, bottom, left, and right.

☐ Set in 12-point Courier New or Times New Roman typeface.

☐ Double-space your text.

☐ Justify the text on both the left and right sides.

☐ On the first page, include your contact information in the upper right-hand corner, and center the novel title and your name. (See sample teaser on page 260.)

☐ On all succeeding pages, place the page number and the novel title in the upper lefthand corner.

The question-and-answer page is an essential part of any publicity packet. By doing a good deal of an interviewer's work for her, the sheet will help you land more interviews. It will also serve as a guide for the interviewer and help ensure that the conversation stays on track.

Try to write eight to ten questions, crafting them so that they underscore important points about you and your novel—information that you feel will interest both the packet's recipient and your potential readers. These questions will, of course, vary from author to author. Possibilities include: When did you know that you wanted to become a writer? Where did you get the idea for your book? Did you draw from your own personal experiences? Did you draw your ideas from the news? Did you base your characters on people you know? Did you base the setting of your novel on your home town? What message are you trying to convey to your readers? Are you presently working on another novel?

Follow each question with a short but informative reply. Remember that you will be able to answer each question more fully during an actual interview. Your Q & A sheet is intended not to supply complete and exhaustive information, but to serve as a marketing tool and an easy-to-use guide.

GET INTO THE *DANGER ZONE*

A CONVERSATION WITH BESTSELLING AUTHOR SHIRLEY PALMER

Q. Why did you write *Danger Zone?*

A. I am attracted to writing about women who become warriors, fighting for what they believe to be right, willing to put their lives on the line in the process. In *Danger Zone*, Maggie Cady draws upon a deep internal strength. She is fearless in facing the villains of her past, and in confronting her father, a powerful crime figure. In *A Veiled Journey*, Liz Ryan, a surgeon, goes to Saudi Arabia to find the woman who gave birth to her. She becomes enmeshed in the lives of the women behind the veils and the shutters and risks her own life to prevent the death of a young girl at the hands of her father. In doing so she faces down the man who fathered them both, the powerful Saudi prince who ordered the death of his daughter. Cat Stanton, in *Lioness*, goes to Africa to find out how her twin brother died. She finds his murderer, takes the law into her own hands, and in doing so, finds freedom from a terrible past.

Q. Do you base your characters on people you've known?

A. They are composites of people I know and parts of me as well. My grandmother was widowed at an early age when her husband was killed in WWI, leaving her with five children under the age of ten. My mother raised me alone after my father left us when I was three. I was born in England, and was brought up on the stories of the women in my family during WWII. They endured endless bombing, and fought fires all night; they emerged from bomb shelters to queue for food the next day; they knitted for their men away in the armed forces; they brought up their children alone; they worked in factories and on the land. In short, they were warriors. The characters in my books also struggle to make peace with the past—and to free themselves from the shadows thrown by their fathers.

Q. You've been quoted as saying that, for the first time in your career, you were able to devote yourself entirely to your writing while living in Saudi Arabia. However, when did you know you wanted to write novels?

A. I always enjoyed writing—growing up and also working as a publicist for my husband's architectural firm. However, I never knew I could or would write novels. It wasn't until I was living in Saudi Arabia and with the dilemma of not being able to work, that for the first time in my life, I found myself with the *time* to write. That was a thrilling discovery. Now, because I enjoy the process so, and have so many ideas, I wish I had found the time to start writing sooner.

Page Two/Q&A Shirley Palmer

Q. Are the strong female protagonists you write about a socially conscious decision on your part?

A. It's more that I feel I have something to say about what I see and experience that I wish to convey through my writing. I feel strongly about animal rights, and so I wrote *Lioness*. I feel passionate about women's rights and being true to oneself, and thus *A Veiled Journey* and *Danger Zone* were born.

Q. What familiarity do you have with the places and circumstances you write about?

A. I have lived in other countries and have firsthand experiences that I incorporate into my novels. For *Danger Zone*, although I never experienced the mob firsthand, I read extensively on the subject and interviewed agents for the FBI, BATF, and Coast Guard. I also talked to movie industry experts who are specialists in explosions, boats, helicopters, armaments. I read Peter Maas' *Underboss, Life in the Mafia, Story of Sammy the Bull Gravano* (John Gotti's second in command); *Black Mass,* the story of the Irish Mob and the FBI in Boston by Dick Lehr and Gerard O'Neill. Reading weapons manuals, magazine articles and doing my own internet research on the mob—both Italian and Irish, was part of my education process.

Q. Your novels have dealt with "Headline news"—women's rights and the frightening plight of women in the Islamic culture. Is this intentional?
A. Not really. Although they can be in the news. The injustice to women that takes place in *A Veiled Journey* is something that I experienced firsthand when I lived in Saudi Arabia. I felt compelled to write about it. The poaching and political corruption in East Africa that I wrote about in *Lioness* is also something that I knew about and saw firsthand. What I write about is people, places and things that strike a chord in me!

Q. What are some upcoming topics or places you'd like to write about?

A. My next novel, *The Trade,* which is scheduled to be in bookstores in 2003, deals with the enslavement of women and children—which, very sadly, is the fastest growing criminal enterprise in the world. It is estimated by the United Nations to be worth upwards of twelve billion dollars a year. I would also like to use the backdrop of World War II for one of my stories.

###

For more information, please contact:
Marybeth Adams
Adams Entertainment
marybeth@adamsentertainment.com
818/555–0101

Points for Q & A Sheet

- [ ] Choose questions that underscore important points about you and your novel.

- [ ] Include a brief but informative answer to each question.

- [ ] Use white bond 8½ x 11-inch paper.

- [ ] Use 1-inch margins on top, bottom, left, and right.

- [ ] Set in 12-point Courier New or Times New Roman typeface.

- [ ] Single-space your text.

- [ ] Justify the text on both the left and right sides.

- [ ] On the first page, place a heading that includes the title of your book and your name. (See sample copy on page 262.)

- [ ] Set each question in bold type, and precede it with the letter Q followed by a period.

- [ ] Double-space between your question and your answer, and precede each answer with the letter A followed by a period.

Points for Author's Biography

- ☐ Include basic background information—education, work experience, and travels—in your biography, as well as basic personal information, such as place of residence. Emphasize information that's particularly relevant to your novel.

- ☐ Use white bond 8½ x 11-inch paper.

- ☐ Use 1-inch margins on top, bottom, left, and right.

- ☐ Set in 12-point Courier New or Times New Roman typeface.

- ☐ Single-space your text.

- ☐ Justify the text on both the left and right sides.

- ☐ On the first page, place a heading that includes your name, the title of your book, and the word "Biography." (See sample copy at right.)

- ☐ Double-space between paragraphs.

- ☐ At the bottom of the page, include your contact information.

Shirley Palmer
Author of *Danger Zone*

Biography

In Shirley Palmer's third thriller, *Danger Zone,* which hits book stores this coming October, Maggie Cady is living the perfect life with her loving husband Sam and their four-year-old son Jimmy. However, their idyllic world is shattered one peaceful Sunday morning, when, after a storm of bullets tears across the front of their house in suburban New Orleans, Sam and Maggie discover that Jimmy has been kidnapped. To save her son, Maggie plunges without hesitation back into a perilous and violent world, a world she thought she had left forever. Sam follows her trail and discovers a Maggie he did not know existed.

With her first two novels, *A Veiled Journey* and *Lioness,* Shirley has had the distinction of twice being on the *Los Angeles Times* Bestsellers list. Both books were originally published under Shirley's pseudonym, Nell Brien, her mother's maiden name. *Danger Zone* will mark Shirley's hardcover debut using her given name.

Shirley Palmer was born in London and educated at Sir William Perkins High School for Girls in Chertsey in Surrey, and at Barking Abbey in the county of Essex. Her early career took her to Manhattan, where she worked for the British Delegation to the United Nations, and then, after marriage to an American architect, for the British Consulate General. Later, she and her husband Dan moved to Los Angeles, and Shirley became an American citizen. Several years of rewarding work followed, managing the public relations for her husband's architectural practice. Upon the birth of their son, Shirley retired from the work force for fifteen years to become a full-time mother.

In the early eighties, Dan had the opportunity to participate in the building of a new town on the Red Sea in Saudi Arabia. Shirley and Dan spent five years in the Kingdom.

Next year will see Shirley's fourth book, *The Trade.* In this novel, Shirley shows that the enslavement of women and children is the fastest growing criminal enterprise in the world, estimated by the United Nations to be worth upward of twelve billion dollars a year.

Shirley and her husband share their home in Woodland Hills, California, with a bulldog and three cats.

For more information, please contact:
Marybeth Adams
Adams Entertainment
marybeth@adamsentertainment.com 818/555–0101

The dramatic rights to *Danger Zone* are represented by Ken Atchity, AEI, 323/555–0407.

able to order your book without leaving home. But your website can provide far more than another point of sale for your book. It can help you develop a relationship with your readers by giving them even more reasons to be crazy about you. On your website, you can post a newsletter on all your doings, progress reports on your next novel, press releases, and notices of public appearances. You can create links to articles and interviews, maintain a gallery of favorable reviews, and even offer a sneak peek at a page or two from your next novel. You can also provide an e-mail address that enables fans to contact you directly.

Make sure that your website gives visitors the chance to get on your mailing list so that you can notify them of upcoming events. Unlike spam, which is unsolicited, unwelcome, and a fabulous way to turn the public against you, *requested* e-mail updates give readers the opportunity to stay involved in your work. It's an excellent, low-cost tool that will keep your career focused and on track even when *you're* not feeling that way.

Get your website up and running as early in the marketing process as you can. If you're not fluent in website construction, have a computer-savvy friend design it, pay a service to do it for you (you'll find them online through an Internet search), or refer to the many available books on the subject. Try to get an easy-to-remember web address, preferably based on your name—www.johnsmith.com, for instance. Do *not* use the title of your book as your web address. If you do, how will you use it to promote your future works? Be aware that you'll probably have to invest some money to register your domain name and to have your website built and uploaded. But as long as you don't get too extravagant, it's money well spent.

Once your website is up, make sure that your web address appears prominently on every piece of promotional material that you and your publisher produce—including your novel. Do your best, too, to get it mentioned on all forms of advertising and in every interview that you arrange.

HIRING A PUBLICIST

If you're reading this chapter, you've probably already decided to take care of your own publicity and marketing—or at least to assume those tasks that your publisher is not taking on. Why, then, consider

A website is a highly effective form of advertising. Once you've established your own site, you'll be able to post a newsletter on your activities, offer links to articles and interviews, and enable fans to contact you through an e-mail address. Perhaps most important, you'll provide another point of sale for your novel so that interested readers can buy it even when no copies remain in the bookstores.

hiring a publicist? A publicist can schedule your book tours; get you interviews and reviews; finagle radio, television, and Internet forum appearances; and help you manage your public image. In other words, she can do everything that you can do for yourself. *But*, in addition, a good experienced publicist can give you two things of immeasurable value: time and connections.

If you do choose to hire a publicist, recognize that the best publicists are those that come to you through referral. Ask your agent, if any, your writer friends, and other people you trust to give you the name of a good public relations firm. Ask for specific examples of the firm's successes: Did they open up new markets that the client had not thought of? Did they pull strings to get a particularly coveted interview? When you get on the phone with the publicist, ask the same sorts of questions—and don't hesitate to request references. You'll learn a lot from their other clients. If all else fails, ask your publisher to recommend publicists with whom they've had good experiences—and then screen them, as you would any other candidate. Never be afraid to ask for references.

> Even when you find a publicist through a referral, you'll want to make sure that she's right for the job. Ask the publicist what she's done for other novelists, and never be afraid to request references. You can learn a lot from other clients.

Perhaps you're still thinking "Why should I hire my own publicist? Isn't that what my publisher's in-house publicist is there for?" Again, remember that you have to prove yourself before the publisher spends the PR bucks on you. If you do hire your own publicist, you may be able to awaken signs of life in the publicity and marketing department.

Remember that as you build your career, you're going to want to perform fewer of the tasks that that can be taken care of by someone else, and focus your energy on the one thing that only you can do: write. That's where a good publicist can help. It comes down to a contest between time and money. If time is more abundant than money, you may choose to do your own PR work. If you have the money to spend, though, an experienced publicist who knows the ropes may be a good investment. But always keep in mind that the publicist is there to assist you. You should still assume the full responsibility of promoting your career.

SENDING OUT BOOKS AND PUBLICITY PACKETS

As already discussed, you must send out advance reading copies (ARCs) to the trade journals at least four months before the publication of your book. The ARCs should not be accompanied by a publicity packet. But do enclose a cover letter that includes a pitch of the book and offers all of your contact information. (See the sample letter on page 268.) Then pack the ARC and cover letter in a padded envelope—preferably padded with bubble wrap—and send it by regular mail.

Once your book is in print and has made its way into the bookstores, you'll be able to send off a *final* copy of the book and a cover letter to other target reviewers, or to reviewers who've expressed an interest but haven't yet made a decision. Again, pack everything into a padded envelope and send it by regular mail.

When you've sent out packages to all potential reviewers, you'll be able to turn your attention to any print venues that might be willing to conduct an interview or write a feature article, and to TV and radio stations that might be interested in interviews. This time, you'll be including your prepared publicity packet, a copy of the printed book, and a cover letter. (See the sample letter on page 270.) As usual, you'll want to use the padded envelope and regular mail.

Two to three weeks after each mailing, start making your follow-up calls. Be aware that most of the time, you'll get the individual's voice mail, but sometimes, you'll actually speak to the person to whom you sent the package. Whether you encounter voice mail or a human being, briefly explain that several weeks ago you sent them a copy of your book for review—or for whatever—and that you're just following up. Then make a short pitch for your book. (See page 72 of Chapter 4 for information about the pitch.) This will serve two purposes. If the individual has actually looked at the package you sent, it might serve to jog her memory. If she *hasn't* yet made her way through the tottering pile of review copies on her desk, your call might trigger some interest and impel her to sift through the pile. Whatever you do, don't go on and on with an overly long description of your novel. Be upbeat and enthusiastic, but know when it's time to end the call.

Throughout this process of mailing out packets and making phone calls, try to be realistic. It certainly would be great to see your book reviewed in *Booklist, Kirkus*, or one of the other trade publications. But with over 50,000 new titles published each year in the United States, only a tiny percentage get reviewed. Moreover, it's especially difficult to get a review published in a trade journal. You have a better chance of landing a review in another type of publication, and an even better chance of securing a feature article or interview—especially if you tar-

If you do manage to secure a review, don't be too concerned if it is less than glowing. Many reviewers, determined to offer a "balanced" critique of each book, find one or two negative things to say about *every* book. Keep in mind that even bad publicity is publicity.

417 E. Littleton Avenue
Kansas City, MO 64114
Phone: (816) 555–7887
Email: JerAd@hotmail.com

(Current Date)

Marvin Fishman, Book Editor
The Kansas City Star
1729 Grand Boulevard
Kansas City, MO 64114

Dear Mr. Fishman:

As a long-time, avid fan of your weekly book reviews, I thought you might find my new book especially interesting, since it's set in Kansas City and its plot involves our local history. (I was born here and attended Rockhurst High School and UMKC.) Please find enclosed an advance reading copy of my mystery novel *Stealing Back Shiraz.* The book won Burdette College's Mystery Writer's Award last year and an excerpt was recently featured in my hometown paper, *The Boonsboro Messenger.*

The day he was foaled, Shiraz was already worth two million, and he has never lost a race. He's the pride and joy—and sole companion—of his reclusive billionaire owner Percy Gentry. But now he has vanished. *Stealing Back Shiraz,* a mystery set in such exotic locales as Casablanca, Mombasa, Bombay, Kyoto, and Perth, traces Percy Gentry's desperate struggle to track down the thieves who have stolen this remarkable stallion. As Percy emerges from seclusion to search for his beloved companion's abductors, Shiraz reappears at the last second to run the most prestigious races across the globe before being whisked away again. The thieves taunt Percy by mailing him strands of the animal's cherry-colored mane, along with clues to the date of Shiraz's next race. Percy, who hasn't left the confines of his mansion in more than eight years, finds himself drawn farther and farther away from everything safe and familiar.

I'm an avid mystery reader and charter member of the Mid-Western Mystery Writers' Guild. To create *Stealing Back Shiraz,* I combined my master's degree in creative writing from UMKC with my lifelong love of horses. I was raised on a farm in Blue Springs that bred Standardbreds for the racetrack. During my first career as a sports journalist, I traveled to each of the locales featured in the book.

Please feel free to contact me by phone or email with any questions. Thank you for taking the time to consider my novel for review.

Cordially,

Jerome Adashek

Jerome Adashek

get small local newspapers, which are always hungry for arts and entertainment features that will fill their columns.

USING INTERNET MARKETING

Tired of driving to the post office with a car full of publicity packets? These days, many authors are finding that the Internet is a powerful marketing tool that can focus attention on their book and effectively connect them to their readers. And the only media packet needed can be sent with the push of a button.

The Internet can be used in a variety of ways. Now, an increasing number of authors opt to do live interviews and audience chats via the Internet. An online forum is a terrific selling tool, as well as an opportunity for you to interact directly with your public. If you've ever been in an online chat room, you know the basic setup. Via your computer, you'll enter the "room" with the host, who will introduce you and conduct a formal interview. All of the dialogue will appear as typed lines on your screen, and you'll answer by typing your response into a box and "sending" it into the room. The host will then turn the floor over to you and give you the opportunity to field questions from the audience.

Also consider joining chat groups in subject areas related to your book—science fiction, fantasy, romance, etc. Log on and start talking about your novel. Because people who visit these sites already have an interest in books within your genre, you may be able to start building an audience.

The Internet can also be used for feature interviews. Scour the web for sites dedicated to new books, and write to ask if they'd consider an interview, sending along an electronic version of your press kit that includes a photo. You may be surprised by the number of sites that express an interest—especially if your press kit contains blurbs, favorable reviews, and good interviews.

Another way to employ the Internet is to use a search engine to locate online newsletters and sites that pertain to your book's genre and/or topic. Contact the sites and offer an excerpt from your book or a free column. In exchange, ask if the site would be willing to provide a link to your website.

Some reading groups use the Internet to post their book selections, while others actually hold their "meetings" online. Search the

Look for websites designed to keep subscribers informed of new books. DearReader.com, for instance, enables readers to join the book club of their choice—one that focuses on horror, mystery, romance, or sci-fi, for instance—and then e-mails them bits of new novels every day. Subscribers can then buy any books that pique their interest.

Begin your search for both in-person and online reading groups by visiting www.book-clubs-resource. com. There you'll find links to a range of reading groups and book clubs.

417 E. Calhoun Street
Kansas City, MO 64114
Phone: (816) 555–7887
Email: JK323@hotmail.com

(Current Date)

Kevin N. Ryan, Programming Director
KCPT Channel 4
1012 West 55th Street
Fairhill, KS 66040

Dear Mr. Ryan:

As a native Kansas Citian and avid fan of your station's weekly TV program *Local Treasures,* I thought you might be interested in taking a look at my new novel, *The Trinity,* and consider interviewing me for an upcoming segment of the show.

I'm convinced that your viewers will find *The Trinity* riveting, since it has deep roots in Kansas City and is based on our legendary local mystery surrounding the three identical homes that stand side by side on Dressman Road. Was it truly a mobster family that built them that way back in the '30s? Are the legendary tunnels beneath them mere passageways between the three homes, designed for late-night meetings, or was their purpose far darker than that?

The Trinity offers a fictional but fact-based answer to both questions. It's a fast-paced story rich in local history, and it's troubling food for thought.

As a lifelong resident of Kansas City, a history buff, and a graduate of UMKC with a masters in creative writing, I believe I'm a perfect fit for *Local Treasures,* and I hope you'll give *The Trinity* serious consideration. I've enclosed my publicity packet and a signed copy of the novel. Please feel free to contact me by phone or email if you'd like to discuss it further.

Thank you for your time.

Cordially,

John Kenny

John Kenny

web for groups that may be interested in your book, and e-mail the group's host or website manager to see if you can send a complimentary copy for consideration. It may help to let the host know that should the group select your book, you will be more than glad to make yourself available by phone, online, or in person for an upcoming meeting.

If you're interested in participating in an Internet book tour, contact The Virtual Book Tour. (See the Resource List.) This service allows authors to connect with interested readers by providing an Internet tour in which the author "stops" at a given number of websites in a given amount of time, just as she might stop at bookstores during a real tour. At each of these stops, the author may be interviewed, take over the site for the day, answer questions from readers, or get her book reviewed—or, possibly, all four. Typical tours last one week, with one stop a day. Note that The Virtual Book Tour does *not* accept self-published authors.

Every year, new websites appear, along with new marketing possibilities. Use your favorite search engine to remain current on what the Internet is offering and on how you can use it to promote this and future titles.

Virtual tours are free to the author only when The Virtual Book Tour service approaches the author first. When the author approaches The VBT she is charged an initial fee as well as per-hour fees.

MAKING PERSONAL APPEARANCES— BOOK SIGNINGS, READINGS, LECTURES, AND CONVENTIONS

Most novelists dream of book signings, imagining long lines of eager readers waiting for them to sign their latest masterpiece. Some publishers, in fact, require all authors to do book signings via their contracts. And despite the growing popularity of the Internet, nothing has replaced the allure of the good old-fashioned in-person book signing.

Be aware, though, that the typical bookstore author signing isn't the glamorous event you're probably imagining—not for first-time authors, at least. To start, the staff might give you a warm introduction and offer you a cup of coffee, or it might dismissively point to a mangled card table and leave you on your own with a half dozen shop-worn copies of your book. Then, instead of a long line of adoring fans, you may have a very small showing—or nobody at all. This can be humiliating if you're not prepared for it.

Are book signings even worth the trouble, then? If you're counting on selling lots and lots of books at the signing, you may be disappointed. But if you can view the signing as more of a publicity event, it may be worthwhile—especially if you coordinate it with the store's community relations manager. The store will very likely put up posters announcing the event, and may advertise it in a monthly newsletter or events flier. It will probably also notify local newspapers about the signing, and it may create a special in-store display to highlight the book. Sometimes, these activities start selling books *before* the actual event.

Is there anything you can do to make a book signing more successful? Absolutely! First of all, tell everyone you know about the book signing. Sometimes, writers are asked to give lists of names and addresses to the bookstore, which takes care of mailing out promotional fliers. If not, ask the bookstore for copies of the flier and do the actual mailing yourself. Also use any other means, from phone calls to e-mail, to let family members, friends, acquaintances, and business contacts know about the signing. Do everything you can to fill the store with people—even if they won't all make purchases. Also think of ways to make the signing an "event." For instance, as long as the bookstore agrees, you may want to hold a drawing for a free copy of your novel. Or consider presenting a "How to Get Published" lecture at which, aside from giving advice, you work in appropriate mentions of your book. And just in case you actually run short of copies, be sure to put a carton or two in your car. You never know.

If you don't choose to appear at bookstores—or if you simply have no luck in arranging book signings—consider other types of public appearances. Contact your local library to see if they would like you to give a short lecture or reading. If you've written a mystery, set up a talk with a local mystery club. If you've written a science fiction novel, try arranging an appearance at a sci-fi convention. Ask your local bookstore for the names of people who organize reading groups in your area, and offer to speak to the group after they've read your novel. Finally, consider writers' conventions and workshops, where, as you know, published authors often give lectures or hold workshops. Now that you're a published author, you can do the same! Wherever you plan to speak, ask if it would be okay to sell your book. If it is, be sure to bring along a carton or two.

Some bookstores arrange signings only for well-known authors, but are willing to bend the rules for "locals." Take advantage of this, and contact the bookstores in your area before looking farther afield.

ARRANGING BOOK TOURS

A book tour, also known as a publicity tour, involves visiting from three to ten cities over a one- to three-week period. In each city, you may be interviewed at local radio and TV stations, meet newspaper reporters, give lectures and readings at bookstores, and do book signings. If you have the budget, you can hire a publicist to arrange all of the events and to also arrange transportation to and from the airport, the hotel, and the various appointments. If you don't have a big budget, though, you can arrange a media tour on your own and use less-expensive transportation—a rental car, for instance—to get from event to event.

If this sounds like a lot of work, it is. Even if you are able to afford a publicist to make the arrangements for you, book tours can be exhausting. If you go the route of booking the tour yourself, you have a mighty task ahead of you. And there's no guarantee that the tour will elicit the sales you're after. Just like a book signing, a publicity tour is a gamble.

Only you can decide if a book tour is worthwhile. If you enjoy doing interviews and making personal appearances; if you have contacts that can help create successful media events in various cities; and if you have the budget for even a pared-down tour, this can be an effective way to increase your book's visibility and create a local buzz about your title.

USING OFFBEAT ADVERTISING AND PROMOTION

You now know more about the various traditional means of promoting a new book. But there's no need to confine yourself to the standard book signings, reviews, and interviews. Creative marketers often use nontraditional means of advertising and promoting their products. Sometimes referred to as *guerilla marketing* because it is as different from conventional marketing as guerilla warfare is from conventional warfare, this type of promotion seeks to get maximum results from minimal resources. As such, it is

---

WORDS FROM A PRO

Kathryn Falk

CEO/Founder *Romantic Times Book Club Magazine*

Women seem to have the edge on book publicity. They're not afraid to get out and meet and greet, as well as think up original promotional ideas. It isn't easy, but if you understand the process (from publisher to distributor, bookseller to book buyer, hands-on selling through the power of web pages) you can gain some control over the sales and publicity of your book. But start planning the promotion the minute you know the pub date.

Guerilla marketing can help you get great results even when working with limited resources. Don't be afraid to use your imagination and find creative ways to let people know about your novel.

especially helpful for the author who is short on funds but long on creativity.

Guerilla marketing can take almost any form imaginable; the sky's the limit. These are just a few ideas that fall into this category:

- Print a flier advertising your book and have it distributed in your area, either by neighborhood kids or by a professional distribution service. If the fliers work, move on to other areas.

- Print up clever T-shirts that advertise your book, and ask friends and family to wear them. If possible, arrange for the staff at your local bookstore to wear them, too.

- Have business cards printed with the cover of your book on the front of the card, and a short summary of your book plus your name and website on the back. Then hand them out wherever you go.

- Provide free waiting-room copies of your book for doctors' offices, dentists' offices, airport and train stations, and other places where people spend time waiting. Make sure to attach a clear sales promotion that tells the reader how she can get a copy of the book.

- Have brightly colored balloons printed with the title of your book and, perhaps, a few intriguing words. Then fill them with helium and hand them out at a local park or shopping district—any place where people gather.

- Set up a booth at a local flea market and bring along a few cartons of books to sell.

- Send autographed copies of your novel to people who can bring it to the attention of the public through print or electronic media. Don't ask for anything in return; just enclose a personal note telling the recipient how much you've enjoyed her column, articles, or interviews over the years. (Do *not* send a publicity packet with the book.) The result might be a blurb or even an interview.

- Call local bookstores and, without giving your name, ask them if they carry your novel. You don't have to order the book. If the bookstore receives enough calls of this type, though, it might start stocking it. This, at least, will get your novel onto the bookstore shelves and in front of the consumer.

As you consider various ways to promote your book, you'll see that you don't have to have a lot of money—or a friend at *Publishers Weekly*—to let your potential readers know about your novel. Be aware, though, that guerilla marketing is not meant to work alone, but to be part of a well-planned advertising strategy.

IN CONCLUSION

If all this marketing, schmoozing, and selling seems like a Herculean effort, it is. And it won't end with your first novel. You'll have to go through the same process with every book you publish. The good news is that with each new book, you'll be able to capitalize on the experience and contacts you gained during previous promotions. And as your success builds, so will your marketing allies—and the funds you have available to spend on your efforts. The more successful you become, the harder your publisher will work to promote you because you've demonstrated that your work can sell. And nothing succeeds like success.

But I can't stress enough the importance of starting your promotion several months before your book becomes available. If you wait until your novel's on the bookstore shelves, you've waited too long. Your book may be in the stores for only a couple of weeks before it's swept aside to make room for the next crop of newcomers. Begin building the excitement well in advance of your novel's release; whet the public's appetite just in time for its arrival; and sell, sell, sell for as long as you can.

Finally, you may have gathered through the reading of this chapter that there's a lot to learn about marketing and publicity—more than I have space to address in this book. Fortunately, a number of good books focus on ways to promote your novel. They include *1001 Ways to Market Your Books* by John Kremer; *Publicize Your Book* by Jacqueline Deval; and *Guerilla Marketing for Writers: 100 Weapons to Help You Sell Your Work* by Jay Conrad Levinson, Rick Frishman, and Michael Larsen. Gather all the tools that are available to the new writer, add enthusiasm and commitment, and begin your work. You can do it. Now's the time to start.

CONCLUSION

"If I live, I should speak my mind."
—EDMUND BURKE, PARLIAMENTARY ORATOR (1729–1797)

Conventional wisdom has it that only one out of ten writers ever attempts a novel; that one out of ten who attempt a novel actually finish it; that one out of fifty who submit it for publication see it published. The only way to get all the way from the first of these groups to the last is to *make the attempt*. I hope I've armed you with enough information to not only make that attempt, but to succeed.

The fact that you've come to the end of this book indicates that you have the drive you need to reach your goal. By now, you've probably learned enough about the book business to deal with it intelligently. But there's also a very good chance that you're now somewhat intimidated by the steps involved in getting a book into publication. If so, I'm not surprised. But here are two thoughts to help you move forward. First, reading all this information in a relatively short period of time is bound to be a little overwhelming; after all, it took me a lifetime to collect it, and I still feel I'm learning about the business. In real life, you'll only need a little bit of it at a time. This book can sit on your shelf, awaiting consultation. The second thought is that motivational banner known to all intrepid gamblers: "The odds don't apply to me." Winners in publishing are like winners in every other field of endeavor. They are absolutely convinced that they're going to achieve their goals, and they'll let nothing stand in their way.

After being involved in the publication of hundreds of novels over the years, I have to admit that the moment a newly printed volume arrives on my desk, a reverential feeling comes over me. Something important has been born into the world. All the difficulties that went into its birth seem irrelevant all of a sudden, and I look forward to watching it make its way to its audience.

If you've finished your novel but are still waiting for it to be "born" into the world of published books, I wish you the best of luck, and hope that very soon you'll reach your goal.

Your audience is waiting.

$\mathcal{G}$LOSSARY

All words that appear in *italic type* are defined within the glossary.

acceptance. The legal term for the *publisher's* act of agreeing to produce your *novel.*

accounting. The section of a publishing contract that establishes who will be responsible for maintaining records of a book's sales. In general, publishing contracts bestow this responsibility on the *publisher,* specify the interval at which the publisher will give the *author* a statement of the book's earnings, and state the means by which the author can examine the publisher's records.

acquisitions editor. The individual at a publishing house who is responsible for acquiring new books. This person may not have the actual title of acquisitions editor, but instead be called the editor, senior editor, *executive editor,* submissions editor, or *publisher.*

act. A collection of *scenes* that move the story from one phase to another. All good *fiction* contains three acts: a beginning, or setup; a middle, or development; and an end, or resolution.

action. The incidents that occur in a *story* to bring it to its dramatic conclusion.

action line. The direction in which the *story* moves. The action line consists of both *action* and *dialogue.*

action tag. Text added before or after a line of *dialogue* to describe any physical motion that accompanies the character's words.

adaptation. The process of recasting a story in a new form, as from a *novel* to a movie.

advance. The amount of money a *publisher* pays to an *author* in advance of publication, once the book is under contract. Sometimes called "advance against royalties," the advance is usually a prepaid portion of the money that will be paid for future *royalties* and *subsidiary rights* sales. Authors don't receive any additional payments until the royalty earnings have surpassed the amount of the advance.

advance reading copies (ARCs). Bound versions of page *proofs* with plain paper or cardboard covers, usually not in color, distributed to booksellers, book reviewers, and various media outlets for the purpose of publicity.

adventure novels. The category of *novels* in which action is the key ingredient. In most adventure novels, the main *character,* who is always in tremendous jeopardy, must resort to action—and, usually, to some degree of violence—in order to triumph over the foe.

agent. See *literary agent.*

ancient evil. A subcategory of *horror novels* that tells the story of evil, often hidden for centuries, that is awakened and threatens civilization.

antagonist. The main *character* of a story who works against the *protagonist,* but is not necessarily a villain.

apocalyptic fiction. A subcategory of *religious novels* that deals with the end of life as we know it, and often involves elements such as the rise of the Antichrist.

ARCs. See *advance reading copies*.

author. The original creator of a written work, and the original owner of all rights to that work.

author-investment publisher. See *vanity press*.

author's copies. Copies of the *author's* work given to him or her free of charge directly after publication. The number of author's copies is generally stated in the publishing contract.

author-subsidized publisher. See *vanity press*.

backlist. *Titles* that were produced by a *publisher* in previous seasons, but that are still in print and available from the company. If a book is newer than nine months old, it's generally on the publisher's *frontlist*. See also *complete list*; *frontlist*; *seasonal list*.

back-story. The history behind the situation at the start of the *novel*.

bestseller. Normally, a novel that has sold more than 25,000 hardback copies. Several publications maintain bestseller lists; of these, *The New York Times* is the most famous and influential.

biblical fiction. A subcategory of *religious novels* that involves stories of characters, both real and imagined, who lived or might have lived in the times of the Old and New Testaments.

black magic. A subcategory of *horror novels* that involves magic which is used for evil purposes.

bluelines. Proofs of a book provided by a printer for the purpose of finding and correcting any technical errors before the book goes to press. Commonly referred to as blues, bluelines got their name because they were originally printed in blue on yellow photosensitive paper. These days, most proofs are printed in black ink on white paper.

blues. See *bluelines*.

blurb. A celebrity endorsement of a book that's printed on the book's cover.

caper mysteries. A subcategory of *mysteries* that involves a light story and generally some bumbling on the part of the good or bad guys.

category fiction. Also known as formula fiction, category fiction tells its story according to an expected formula, and targets a niche market rather than a general readership. Popular forms of category fiction include *romance novels*, *science fiction*, *mysteries*, and *Westerns*. These various types of category novels are often referred to as genres.

category romances. A subcategory of *romance novels* in which books are published in monthly "lines," and for the most part take place in the present, but are shorter than the typical *contemporary romance*. This category of books is sometimes referred to as series romances.

chapterization. A means of breaking up a written work into segments, borrowed from *nonfiction*. Novelists conventionally break their *novels* into chapters, but there's no hard and fast rule as to length, number, or content, and some authors dispense with chapters completely.

character. A representation of a person in a work of *fiction* such as a *novel*. See also *antagonist*; *function character*; *minor character*; *protagonist*; *supporting character*.

chick-lit. A type of *romantic humor novel* written for young women—especially single women in their twenties who work in the business world.

classic whodunits. A subcategory of *mysteries* that features strong puzzle elements, quirky but bright detectives, and little sex or explicit violence.

clever crook mysteries. A subcategory of *mysteries* that involves elegant criminals, sometimes known as rogues, who steal from the rich.

cliffhanger. A suspenseful situation that occurs at the end of a chapter or act, leaving the reader desperate to know what happens next, as when the hero is left literally dangling from a cliff. This is a time-honored way of carrying readers from one chapter to the next, or from one act to another.

climax. The dramatic pinnacle of the story at which the *protagonist* faces the ultimate *obstacle*—the one which, if overcome, will allow the character to achieve his or her *mission.*

comic fantasy. A subcategory of *fantasy novels* that is set in imaginary worlds and is primarily humorous in intent and tone.

comic mysteries. A subcategory of *mysteries* that involves a humorous approach.

commercial fiction. *Fiction* written primarily for a broad readership, focusing on subjects that interest large numbers of people. Commercial fiction, which may be either *category* or *mainstream,* focuses more on *story* than on style.

complete list. All of a publisher's *titles,* old and new, that are still in print and available from the company. See also *backlist; frontlist; seasonal list.*

conflict. Opposition that occurs in a *novel* when a *protagonist* encounters *obstacles* to his *mission.* The shape of a novel is created by one conflict after another, with each conflict altering the protagonist's future.

contemporary fantasy. A subcategory of *fantasy novels* that is set in the real world in contemporary times, where, it is revealed, supernatural creatures exist.

contemporary horror. A subcategory of *fantasy novels* that is set in contemporary times and includes familiar settings.

contemporary religious fiction. A subcategory of *religious novels* that deals with one or more religious *themes* through stories set after World War II.

contemporary romances. A subcategory of *romance novels* that takes place in the present, and sometimes touches upon serious real-life issues such as alcoholism and spousal abuse.

cooperative publisher. See *vanity press.*

copyeditor. The individual in a publishing company who is responsible for making *manuscript* changes necessary for stylistic consistency; for correcting spelling, grammar, and typographical errors; and for fact checking.

copyright. The legal overall right granted to an *author* or *publisher* for ownership of a written work. Under this ownership comes a number of specific rights, including the exclusive rights to print, sell, distribute, and translate the literary work.

cover letter. A brief letter accompanying a *manuscript* or a portion of a manuscript written to an *acquisitions editor* in order to spark his or her interest in a project. See also *query letter.*

cozy mysteries. A subcategory of *mysteries* containing gentle reads that feature amateur detectives, a small town, and detailed character relationships.

crime mysteries. A subcategory of *mysteries* that involves illegal activities such as drug trafficking.

crossover novel. *Category* or *literary fiction* that also appeals to a *mainstream* readership.

dark suspense. A subcategory of *horror novels* that relies on psychological terror.

delivery and acceptance (D&A). The process of handing the completed, edited *manuscript* over to the *publisher.* If the publisher agrees that the manuscript is ready for publication, it's formally accepted.

detective mysteries. A subcategory of *mysteries* that features amateur or professional detectives who rely on personal skills and experience to solve the crime.

dialogue. A conversation between two or more *characters* in a *novel* or other dramatic work.

dialogue tag. Text added before or after a line of *dialogue* to identify the speaker and/or indicate how the words were said.

disaster adventure. A subcategory of *adventure novels* that involves some sort of dramatic natural or man-made disaster, such as a tornado or fire.

distributor. A company that inventories and sells the books of one or more *publishers* to bookstores, libraries, and nontraditional outlets on an exclusive or nonexclusive basis. Although the terms formerly meant different things, the words distributor, jobber, and wholesaler are now used interchangeably. See also *independent distributor.*

dramatic rights. The rights to adaptations of a literary work for dramatic productions, including motion pictures, stage plays, and television and radio presentations. This is sometimes referred to as performance rights.

dust jacket. A removable paper cover used to protect the binding of a book, especially a *hardcover* book.

e-book. A book in electronic form that can be read on a personal computer or hand-held reader, or downloaded to a printer.

editor. The individual in a publishing house who actually shapes a *manuscript*. See also *acquisitions editor; copyeditor; editorial assistant; managing editor.*

editorial assistant. The individual in a publishing house who helps the *editor* by making photocopies, filing, proofreading, and performing similar tasks. The editorial assistant may also review manuscripts in the *slush pile* to see if they may be appropriate for that particular publishing house.

electronic format. Available on a computer disk, CD, or CD-ROM, or via the Internet.

electronic publishing. The production and distribution of electronic versions of books—commonly known as *e-books*—to customers via the Internet. This is also called e-publishing.

electronic rights. The rights to reproduce a literary work through an electronic medium. The term refers to CD-ROMs, computer games, and online publications and databases.

e-mail submission. The sending of a *submission package* to an *editor* via e-mail. This is also called an electronic submission.

e-publishing. See *electronic publishing.*

erotic adventure. A subcategory of *erotica* that fuses elements of an adventure tale with sexual *themes.*

erotic contemporary. A subcategory of *erotica* that sets an erotic *novel* in a contemporary setting.

erotic fantasy. A subcategory of both *erotica* and *fantasy novels* that blends elements of a fantasy novel with sexual *themes.*

erotic Gothic and Victorian. A subcategory of *erotica* that tends to deal with fetishes, such as bondage.

erotic horror. A subcategory of both *erotica* and *horror novels* that blends elements of the horror novel with sexual *themes.*

erotic science fiction. A subcategory of *erotica* that blends elements of *science fiction* with sexual *themes.*

erotica. The category of *novels* in which sex pervades the *theme*, the tone, and the *action.*

espionage adventure. A subcategory of *adventure novels* that involves spies and secret agents.

espionage mysteries. A subcategory of *mysteries* that includes all activities related to finding and sharing secret information. This subcategory is sometimes referred to as spy mysteries.

ethnic novels. The category of *novels* that features *characters* from a group of people who share a common and distinctive racial, national, religious, linguistic, or cultural heritage, and who are living outside their country or area of origin.

exclusive rights. Rights that grant sole usage to a single party. Exclusive rights can be sold only once, to one buyer.

executive editor. The head of the editorial department who assigns projects and oversees the work of the *editors,* who are responsible for the actual shaping of *manuscripts.* In some companies, the executive editor works as an *acquisitions editor.*

fantasy, futuristic, and paranormal romances. A subcategory of *romance novels* that leaves the real world behind and may include *characters* such as aliens or werewolves.

fantasy novels. The category of *novels* in which the story takes place in a world that is different in some way from the world we know, and this difference is the result of magic or some anomalous phenomenon, rather than science or technology.

feminist novels. The category of *novels* that uses the story line to explore *themes* of interest to feminists.

fiction. A work derived primarily from the writer's

imagination—a *story*. Although not all works of fiction are *novels*, all novels are fiction, even those based upon true events, because they are a dramatization of those events. See also *nonfiction*.

film treatment. A short written description of a *story* that is intended to be turned into a *screenplay*. The treatment plots the narrative as it will appear on the screen in a straightforward prose style in the present tense. It offers a *hook* into the story, sketches the main *characters* and *setting*, and describes the *action line* by acts.

first serial rights. See *serial rights*.

first-person narrative. Any narration in which the *story* is told by one of the *characters* of the *novel*. This person, who is often the *protagonist*, can report only what he or she knows.

force majeure. An unexpected event that can't be controlled, such as a restriction imposed by governmental agencies, a labor dispute, or an unavailability of materials necessary for a book's manufacture. According to the standard publishing contract, the failure of the *publisher* to publish or reissue a work wouldn't be considered a breech of the agreement or give rise to termination if it were caused by events such as these because they're beyond the publisher's control.

foreign rights. The *subsidiary rights* that allow an *author*, *agent*, and/or *publisher* to sell the translation rights of a work to another publisher located in a foreign country. The right to sell the foreign language edition may apply to a specific country, a group of countries, or any country in which the foreign language is spoken, as specified in a foreign rights agreement. Authors' *royalties* on the sale of foreign rights are usually calculated according to a separate royalty scale.

forensic mysteries. A subcategory of *mysteries* that emphasizes scientific crime solving.

formula fiction. See *category fiction*.

freelance editor. An *editor* who sells his or her services to an employer—a publishing house or writer, for instance—without making a long-term commitment to that employer.

frontlist. *Titles* produced by a *publisher* within the last nine months. See also *backlist*.

function character. A non-major *character* who, unlike a *supporting character* or *minor character*, has no defining feature, but is included only to perform a single function, such as serving a drink or delivering a telegram.

galleys. Originally, long strips of typeset copy created from an edited *manuscript*. Today, this term is sometimes used to refer to the first set of typeset pages. See also *proofs*.

genre. A category or type of *novel*.

gentle reads. A subcategory of *religious novels* that includes generally cheerful, positive stories set in a comfortable setting, such as a small town, and offers ordinary *characters* dealing with ordinary situations.

ghost stories. A subcategory of *horror novels* in which spirits of the dead intervene in some way.

ghostwriter. A type of *writer-for-hire*, so called because he or she writes the work for a fee, then "disappears." Ghostwriters retain no rights to the written material, and are not credited on the cover of the book or within its pages.

GLBT. The category of *novels* that focuses on *themes* important to gay, lesbian, bisexual, and transgender readers.

Gothic horror. A subcategory of *horror novels* that includes elements of the *Gothic novel*, such as ruined castles and wild landscapes.

Gothic novels. The category of *novels* whose distinctive features include a castle *setting*; an atmosphere of brooding, gloom, mystery, and suspense; omens, portents, secrets, and visions; supernatural and otherwise inexplicable events; high, even overwrought emotions; and women in distress—especially a lonely and oppressed heroine who is threatened by a tyrannical passion-driven male.

Gothic romances. A subcategory of *romance novels* that involves dark emotions, brooding heroes, and other elements of the *Gothic novel*.

guerilla marketing. A nontraditional means of advertising and promoting a product, so-called because it is as different from conventional marketing as guerilla warfare is from conventional warfare. The goal of guerilla marketing is to get maximum results from minimal resources.

hard science fiction. A subcategory of *science fiction* that is characterized by a pronounced focus on natural science and technological developments. See also *soft science fiction.*

hardback. See *hardcover.*

hard-boiled mysteries. A subcategory of *mysteries* that features detectives who are rough and physical in their approach.

hardcover. A book bound between rigid board covers over which is stretched a material such as cloth. Typically, a hardcover edition is of high quality, and is covered in a full-color paper *dust jacket.*

high fantasy. A subcategory of *fantasy novels* that is serious in tone, epic in scope, and includes fantastical races such as elves and dwarves.

high society humor novel. A subcategory of *humor novels* in which the writer pokes fun at the eccentricities and excesses of the upper class.

historical fantasy. A subcategory of *fantasy novels* that is set in a specific historical period, but includes fantasy elements.

historical horror. A subcategory of *horror novels* that is set in the past, using realistic settings.

historical novels. The category of *novels* set in a time period that occurred at least fifty years before the writing of the book, and written by an author who was not alive at the time of those events.

historical romances. A subcategory of *romance novels* in which the action is set in the past, usually before World War II.

holdbacks. Also called reserves, a percentage of earned *royalties* the *publisher* retains for a specified length of time—typically three months—until the company is certain that the booksellers have actually sold that number of books to the public, and won't be returning them for credit.

hook. An intriguing detail or incident that grabs the reader's attention and compels him or her to read more. A good *query letter* opens with a hook.

horror humor novels. A subcategory of *humor novels* that includes elements of the *horror novel,* and may involve a monster who is funny rather than frightening.

horror mysteries. A subcategory of *horror novels* that includes a detective and other elements of *mysteries.*

horror novels. The category of *novels* designed to elicit fear and dread on the part of the reader.

horror sagas. A subcategory of *horror novels* that follows several generations of doomed or evil families.

HTML. HyperText Markup Language—the markup language designed for the creation of web pages.

humor novels. The category of *novels* that generally features comical *characters* embroiled in outrageous situations.

hyperlink. A reference in a web document to another web document or resource. When clicked upon, a hyperlink takes you immediately to the second document or resource.

ID. See *independent distributor.*

imprint. In a publishing house, a brand name under which a work is published. A single company may have multiple imprints, each of which specializes in a particular category of *novels.*

inciting incident. See *turning point.*

independent distributor. Commonly referred to as an ID, a company that inventories and sells *mass market paperbacks* to high-traffic retails outlets like drugstore chains, supermarkets, discount chain stores, and airport bookshops.

independent publisher. Any publishing house that is managed by its owners as opposed to being publicly held or part of a large publishing house or business entity.

industrial financial adventure. A subcategory of *adventure novels* that involves intrigue and spying by large industrial and financial organizations.

in-house. Within a specific publishing company. Editors often refer to the "in-house style"—styles of punctuation, spelling, capitalization, hyphenation, etc.—followed within that particular publishing company.

inspirational romances. A subcategory of *romance novels* in which religious faith is a significant element of the story.

intellectual property. A work—*a novel*, for instance—that is the product of the mind or intellect, but that nevertheless is considered and protected as property.

intellectual property lawyer. A lawyer who specializes in literary works and their inherent rights.

International Standard Book Number (ISBN). The unique multi-digit number that *publishers* assign to each edition they print for means of identification.

ISBN. See *International Standard Book Number.*

kill. To reject a *manuscript* proposal.

legs. Staying power. A *novel* that is said to have "legs" will see snowballing sales.

libel. A false written or printed statement that maliciously damages a person's reputation.

line edit. An intensive line-by-line edit of a *manuscript*, generally performed by the *editor*.

literary agent. A legal representative of an *author* who sells the author's work to a third party, such as a *publisher*, and receives a commission on all monies derived from the work. As part of their work, literary agents create *submission packages*, target appropriate publishers, contact publishers, negotiate contracts, and work with the author throughout the publication process and beyond. See also *literary manager.*

literary fiction. *Fiction* written primarily to follow the author's personal vision, conform to his or her esthetics, or deliver a specific message, rather than conform to a commercial readership. Literary fiction is sometimes viewed as a subcategory of *mainstream fiction.*

literary manager. A legal representative of an *author* who, just like a *literary agent*, sells the author's work to a third party, such as a *publisher*, and receives a commission on all monies derived from the work. In addition to maintaining contacts in the publishing world, though, a manager is also involved in the film production industry, and can serve as producer if the *novel* is turned into a film.

logline. A one-sentence description of a *novel* that can serve as an advertisement when approaching potential *literary agents* or *publishers.*

mainstream fiction. The category of *novels* intended for general readership. Sometimes called mainstream/contemporary, the books in this category do not follow a formula, such as that used in a *romance novel*, although they may borrow elements from *category fiction.*

male action adventure. A subcategory of *adventure novels* that involves relatively stereotypical *characters* and considerable action and violence.

managing editor. The individual in a publishing company who oversees the timely coordination of different departments to maintain a smooth production process and meet deadlines. The managing editor is sometimes called a production editor.

manuscript. The unpublished, unbound draft of a literary work.

market. The segment of the population considered buyers for a particular book. Markets are typically defined by demographics: age, gender, ethnicity, socioeconomic level, geographic location, and interests.

marketplace. A place or system through which books are sold to consumers, such as a bookstore, library, or other book outlet.

mass market outlet. A book outlet found in high-traffic areas such as airport stores, newsstands, drugstores, discount retailers, and supermarket chains. These outlets can reach the "mass" audience rather than the general bookstore's trade audience.

mass market paperback. A $4\frac{1}{2}$-by-7-inch paperback, originally designed to fit small book racks, such as those found in grocery stories and newsstands. Mass market *novels* may be first editions or reprints of hardbound editions. Mass markets differ from *trade paperbacks* in that they are smaller, and typically of lesser quality. Although occasionally sold in bookstores, they are primarily designed for sale in high-traffic areas such as newsstands, drugstores, and supermarket chains.

military adventure. A subcategory of *military/war novels* that involves life-threatening situations, details of military operations, and action-packed endings.

military historical. A subcategory of *military/war novels* that revisits a war or battle which occurred in the past and incorporates real-life people.

military lifestyle. A subcategory of *military/war novels* that explores the day-to-day life of a soldier.

military mystery. A subcategory of *military/war novels* that often involves spies or espionage, as well as a war crime or unexplained event that must be investigated.

military saga. A subcategory of *military/war novels* that follows either one *character* or a group of characters through a long conflict or a series of conflicts.

military science fiction. A subcategory of *military/war novels* that generally takes place in the not-too-distant future, and usually includes an enemy who is from another planet or star system and is a threat to mankind.

military thrillers. A subcategory of *military/war novels* that is often contemporary, and includes a high degree of technology and unusually high stakes, as well as an enemy who is often a terrorist.

military/naval adventure. A subcategory of *adventure novels* in which members of the armed forces are placed in some sort of war or military conflict.

military/war novels. The category of *novels* that features *characters* and situations which have military *themes* as their defining feature. The action generally takes place in the center of a conflict, and sometimes incorporates real historical events and people.

minor character. A non-major *character* who has a single defining attribute, such as greed, ambition, lechery, or vanity, and who does not change during the course of the *novel*. See also *function character; supporting character*.

mission. The *protagonist's* main job or goal, which is fueled by his *motivation*. This mission may be chosen by the protagonist or thrust upon him or her, but must be involved enough to sustain the story for the duration of the *novel*, and must lend itself to challenges.

motivation. A *character's* major motivating drive, such as love, hate, fear, anxiety, revenge, rage, jealousy, or greed. This is the drive that makes the character "tick."

multiple submission. See *simultaneous submission*.

mysteries. The category of *novels* that involves an unresolved or unexplained event—usually a murder—that the reader is challenged to solve before it is solved by a professional or amateur detective.

mystery humor novels. A subcategory of *humor novels* that includes elements of the *mystery*, and features absurd cases, quirky plot twists, and unlikely detectives and suspects.

narrator. The teller of the *story*. It's a convention of contemporary *novels* that the narrator be somebody other than the *author*. See also *first-person narrative; second-person narrative; third-person narrative*.

net price. The price actually charged by the *publisher* to any of the customers to whom it sells directly. This can include any book resaler or direct-to-consumer sale. The prices charged by the publisher may be the same as the retail price, or may be lower, based on an established discount schedule. The cost of shipping the book isn't calculated as part of the net price. See also *retail price*.

net sales. The actual number of books a bookstore has sold to customers, in contrast to the number it originally bought from the *publisher* or *distributor*. Publishers pay *royalties* on the number of net sales, not on the full number they originally sell to bookstores, because bookstores may return for full credit any books they don't sell within a specific period of time.

nonfiction. A book that offers facts and information, as opposed to *fiction*, which is a product of imagination.

North American rights. The right to sell a book in the United States and Canada, as granted by the author to a *publisher*.

novel. A written work of *fiction* of considerable length, usually having a *plot* that is unfolded through the actions, speech, and thoughts of the *characters*. Although not all fictional works are novels, all novels are fiction—even those based on true events—because, as *stories*, they are dramatizations of the events rather than factual accounts. Today's novels typically range from 70,000 to 100,000 words and 200 to 450 pages in length.

obstacle. Any force, situation, or individual that gets in the way of the *protagonist* achieving his or her dramatic *mission*. In a typical *novel*, a hero faces many obstacles. Ideally, the obstacles escalate in difficulty as the novel progresses.

occult novels. The category of *novels* that features some aspect of the supernatural as a major element of the story line. Specifically, *titles* in this category deal with pagan beliefs and practices, such as witchcraft, voodoo, sorcery, demonism, shamanism, ceremonial magic, the evocation of spirits, and clairvoyance, as well as the more mystical elements of various religions.

option clause. A clause in a contract that gives the *publisher* an option to acquire the *author's* next book before the project is offered to another publisher.

out of print. A term describing a *title* that is no longer available from the *publisher*. Typically, a contract states that a publisher will take the book or edition out of print when "it shall cease to be profitable."

page proofs. See *proofs*.

payout schedule. The time frame in which an *advance* will be paid, as specified in the publishing contract. This schedule varies from *publisher* to publisher.

performance rights. See *dramatic rights*.

pitch. An oral description and summary of a *story*, told for the purpose of selling it.

plagiarism. The act of using the writing of another person without proper acknowledgment of the original source.

plot. The unified structure of incidents in a *novel*, including all of the motivations behind the actions.

plot twist. An unexpected turn of events or revelation that accelerates the action in a *novel*. Not all novels have twists.

POD. See *print-on-demand publisher*.

police procedurals. A subcategory of *mysteries* that details the day-to-day realities of police work.

political intrigue adventure. A subcategory of *adventure novels* that involves a government *setting* along with political *characters* and situations.

print run. The number of copies a printer makes when a book goes to press.

print-on-demand (POD) publisher. An online *publisher* that keeps an electronic version of a book on file, and prints and binds copies of the book only when a customer orders it.

private eye mysteries. A subcategory of *mysteries* that involves paid professionals working alone.

proceed to contract. The step in the closing of a publishing deal in which the *publisher* and *author* (sometimes via a *representative*) reach an oral or "handshake" agreement, which the publisher then transfers to the written contract.

production company. A company that oversees the creation of a film, from its inception to the distribution of the finished product. Novelists who wish to sell motion picture rights to their *novels* most often approach production companies with a *film treatment*, or do so through their representatives.

production editor. See *managing editor*.

proofread. To read typeset copy for the purpose of finding and correcting typographical errors and other problems before the book goes to press.

proofs. The typeset version of a *novel* that is produced after the *manuscript* has been edited. Also called page proofs, and years ago referred to as galleys, proofs are given to the *author* and *editor* to be *proofread*.

protagonist. The hero or main character of a *story* who serves as a focus for the story's *themes* and incidents.

publicist. A publicity professional who handles the press releases for a new book and arranges promotional events such as publicity tours, interviews, speaking engagements, and book signings.

publicity packet. A packet of materials sent to media outlets such as magazines, newspapers, television shows, and radio shows as a means of informing them about an upcoming book so that they might arrange an interview with the *author* or write an article about the book or author. In the case of a *novel*, a publicity packet usually includes a full-cover copy of the book cover; a photo of the author; a two- to three-page teaser, or overview, of the book; a brief biography of the author; and a question-and-answer page.

publisher. A business entity that invests in the publication of a work, editing, producing, distributing, marketing, and otherwise making it available to the public. Also the person at a publishing house who oversees every aspect of operation of all of the company's departments, including editorial, art, marketing, sales, etc.

quality paperback. See *trade paperback*.

query. A request, traditionally made via a mailed business letter, but also via e-mail, for permission to submit a literary work. *Authors* may also deliver oral queries—sometimes referred to as *pitches*—when meeting with prospective *publishers* or *representatives*. A query typically includes a statement of the intended readership plus a brief *synopsis* of the story, along with a request for a response from the query recipient and the author's contact information. When delivered on paper or via e-mail, a *query letter* follows standard business letter format.

query letter. A *query* submitted in the form of a letter.

radio drive time. The period between 6:00 or 7:00 AM Eastern Time and 8:00 or 9:00 AM Pacific Time, when people are typically driving to work and listening to

their radios. This is the best time to address a radio audience

Regency romances. A subcategory of *romance novels* in which the action is set in Regency England. Regency romances, however, are noticeably different from *historical romances* set in the Regency period, as they are shorter and tend to emphasize *dialogue* over action and sex.

rejection. The act, on the part of a *publisher* or *representative*, of declining to publish or represent a literary work. Rejections are typically delivered via mail, telephone, or e-mail.

religious fantasy and science fiction. A subcategory of *religious novels* that combines religious *themes* with those of *fantasy novels* or *science fiction*.

religious historical fiction. A subcategory of *religious novels* that presents historical themes in stories set before World War II.

religious mystery/suspense. A subcategory of *religious novels* that presents suspenseful stories using religious *themes* and perspectives, and often involves clergy who are sleuths.

religious novels. The category of *novels* that deals with a particular religious tradition, such as that of Christianity or of a specific denomination of Christianity.

religious romance. A subcategory of *religious novels* that involves romantic stories which use religious *themes*.

remaindered books. Books sold by the *publisher* to a discounter for a price that is slightly above or below the manufacturing cost. Books are often remaindered after their sales fall off.

representative. A *literary agent, literary manager,* or attorney who negotiates with a *publisher* on behalf of the *author*.

reserved rights. A contractual clause stating that the *author* retains any rights not otherwise mentioned. This statement also covers rights to media not yet invented.

reserves. See *holdbacks*.

retail price. The full price of a book as marked on the book itself and/or as listed in a consumer catalogue and/or other consumer-oriented promotional literature. This is usually different from the *net price.*

reversion. A contractual term defining the circumstances—bankruptcy, out of print, etc.—under which the rights an *author* has granted to a *publisher* will be returned to the author.

right of first refusal. The right of a *publisher* to acquire or reject a previously contracted *author's* next work before it is offered to another publisher. See also *option clause.*

rights of termination. A contractual clause stating the circumstances under which an *author* or *publisher* can terminate the agreement. The contract may become void, for example, if the publisher doesn't publish within a certain time frame, if the author doesn't deliver the *manuscript* on time, or if the author's revisions aren't acceptable.

romance novels. The category of *novels* that focuses on the romantic love between a man and a woman, and has a positive, emotionally satisfying ending that leads one to believe that the couple's love will endure forever. The romance novel story line follows a well-known formula in which the heroine is in some kind of need and the hero can fill that need, but some type of barrier prevents them from getting together until the conclusion of the novel, when the obstacle is overcome.

romantic fantasy. A subcategory of *fantasy novels* that deals with the development of a romantic relationship but includes fantasy elements.

romantic humor novel. A subcategory of *humor novels* that includes humorous versions of the *romance novel.*

romantic suspense. A subcategory of *romance novels* that blends romance with danger, and often involves drug dealers, smugglers, serial killers, and the like.

romantica. A subcategory of *erotica*, designed specifically for women, that combines erotica with elements of *romance novels.*

royalties. The money received by an *author* based upon the sales of his or her book. The publishing contract specifies the royalty percentage for each form of the book being produced, and shows whether it's being based on the *retail price* or *net price.*

sales sheet. A one-page handout that offers promotional copy on a forthcoming *title*, including a description of the book, information on the *author*, and book specifications such as *trim size* and page length. This promotional tool is used by the *publisher's* sales representatives in meetings with booksellers.

SASE. A self-addressed, stamped envelope. Every *submission package* should include an SASE.

scene. A unit of drama that centers on a *conflict* which, when resolved, moves the story forward.

science fiction. The category of *novels* that depends fundamentally upon a scientific premise, without which the story could not be told. Almost all science fiction tends to predict or define the future, and the best sci-fi uses the genre to explore some aspect of human society.

science fiction humor novel. A subcategory of *humor novels* that includes science that is questionable, outlandish, or utterly nonsensical.

screenplay. The script for a motion picture that includes all of the *dialogue*, locations, and descriptions of actions, and includes a minimum of *character* and camera directions.

season. A specified time of the year in which a *publisher* presents a new group of *titles* for sale. *Fiction* publishers usually have two to four seasons: either spring and fall; or winter, spring, summer, and fall.

seasonal list. A *publisher's* new winter, spring, summer, or fall titles. See also *backlist; frontlist; complete list.*

second serial rights. See *serial rights.*

second-person narrative. Any narration in which an omniscient *narrator*, who knows everything that is going to happen in a godlike way, addresses the *protagonist* as "you." This type of narrative is very rare.

self-publishing. A publishing option in which the

author arranges and pays for every stage of the publishing process, from editing to typesetting to printing and binding, and often sets up a business to take care of the promotion, distribution, and sales of his or her book. Self-publishing can be a viable springboard to traditional publishing.

serial rights. The right to publish an excerpt of a book in a periodical or newspaper. The term "first serial rights" refers to the exclusive right to print an excerpt prior to publication of the book. "Second serial rights" refers to the nonexclusive right to print an excerpt after the book's publication.

series romances. See *category romances.*

setting. The time, place, and circumstances in which the action of a *novel* takes place.

simultaneous submission. The practice of sending a *submission package* to several different *publishers* at one time. This practice is also called multiple submission.

slush pile. The stack of *unsolicited manuscripts* sitting in a *representative's* or *editor's* office, waiting to be read. These are usually the last to get attention, and in the case of many large publishing companies, are generally returned to the author unread.

social satire humor novel. A subcategory of *humor novels* in which everyday life is presented comically to highlight the absurdities of modern life.

soft science fiction. A subcategory of *science fiction* that focuses less on physical laws and technological hardware, and more on philosophy, politics, and sociology—the soft sciences. See also *hard science fiction.*

speculative fiction. A term sometimes used to embrace both the category of *science fiction* and that of *fantasy novels.*

spiritual afterlife fiction. A subcategory of *spiritual/New Age novels* that explores *themes* of life after death.

spiritual fables. A subcategory of *spiritual/New Age novels* in which the spiritual message is wrapped in metaphor and folk elements.

spiritual journey fiction. See *spiritual quest fiction.*

spiritual mystery/suspense. A subcategory of *spiritual/New Age novels* that includes mysteries driven by spiritual *themes* and perspectives.

spiritual quest fiction. A subcategory of *spiritual/New Age novels* that deals with the search for spiritual knowledge, including the knowledge of good and evil, of the self, and of the mysteries of life. This category is also referred to as spiritual journey fiction.

spiritual science fiction. A subcategory of *spiritual/New Age novels* in which *science fiction* elements are used to explore spiritual *themes.*

spiritual/New Age novels. The category of *novels* that explores the nonmaterial world without association to a particular religion. *Themes* include man's ability to more fully realize and develop his spiritual potential; man's relationship to others, to a higher power, and to the universe; and the existence of spiritual beings; as well as New Age themes such as reincarnation.

sports novels. The category of *novels* that focuses on a given sport and its participants.

spy mysteries. See *espionage mysteries.*

story. A structured, dramatic telling of events.

submission. The act of sending a *manuscript* for consideration, typically to a *publisher* or *representative*; or the submitted manuscript itself.

submission package. A book proposal that is designed to summarize a book and pique an *editor's* or *representative's* interest in the project. For *novels*, the typical submission package includes a *cover letter*, a *synopsis*, and a portion of the *manuscript*—usually, the first three chapters.

subsidiary rights. Those rights derived from the literary work other than the primary right to publish the work. These are the rights that the *publisher* intends to license to a third party, such as a motion picture or software company. Subsidiary rights may include such items as periodical or newspaper publications; condensations or abridgements; book club publications; foreign-language publications; English-language publications not covered in the "Rights" section of the contract; reprint editions; motion picture, television, radio, and stage interpretations; audio recordings; electronic recordings; public reading rights; Braille, large-type, and other editions for the handicapped; and calendars, greeting cards, posters and other "merchandising/commercial" applications of the work.

subsidy publisher. See *vanity press.*

supporting character. A non-major *character* who has a single identifying characteristic such as greed, lechery, or vanity, and who changes in some way during the course of the *novel.*

survival adventure. A subcategory of *adventure novels* that tells the story of one or several persons' survival in the wilderness or another threatening or isolated area.

suspense novels. The category of *novels* in which the story centers on a largely external *conflict,* usually takes place in the present time, and has an exciting *plot* that features *characters* in high jeopardy—usually with life or death stakes. An atmosphere of menace is key so that readers are kept on the edge of their seat.

sword and sorcery. A subcategory of *fantasy novels* that features muscular heroes in violent conflict with villains who, unlike the heroes, have supernatural powers.

synopsis. A part of the *submission package* in which the author summarizes his *novel's* story line. A synopsis is usually written as a narrative in third person, present tense, using brief, attention-grabbing paragraphs.

territory. The geographic area in which the *publisher* is granted rights to sell the book in accordance with the contract.

theme. A unifying idea or message that serves as a recurrent element in a *novel* or other dramatic work.

third-person narrative. Any narration in which the *narrator* is not a *character* in the story, but an outside observer who knows everything and is able to explore all of the characters and events in the *novel.*

thriller adventure. A subcategory of *adventure novels* that takes the thriller to maximum intensity by focusing on the hero's survival in an action-filled plot involving narrow escapes, chases, and rescues.

thrillers. A subcategory of *mysteries* that involves a high degree of action and adventure.

time travel romances. A subcategory of *romance novels* that generally features a heroine who travels backwards in time and meets her true love.

title. The formal name of a book; or a written work that will be or has already been published.

trade book. A book designed for the general reader, and primarily sold in bookstores. Trade books include hardcover books and full-sized ($5\frac{1}{2}$-by-$8\frac{1}{2}$-inch or larger) paperbacks known as *trade paperbacks.*

trade paperback. A $5\frac{1}{2}$-by-$8\frac{1}{2}$-inch or larger softcover book, also called a quality paperback. Unlike *mass market paperbacks,* which are often sold in drugstores and other nontraditional outlets, trade paperbacks are usually sold in bookstores, and typically are of higher quality than mass market paperbacks. Trade paperbacks may be first editions or reprints of hardbound editions.

trade show. An event designed to enable *publishers,* booksellers, writers, and other people in the book industry to network, sell rights, and conduct business. Good trade shows for novelists include BookExpo America (BEA) and BookExpo Canada.

treatment. See *film treatment.*

trim size. The outer dimensions of a finished book.

turning point. A dramatic event in a *story* that fundamentally alters the action. Good drama has at least two major turning points. The first—sometimes called the "inciting incident"—occurs early in the story, and launches the *protagonist* on his or her *mission.* The second occurs toward the end of the story, and is often called the *climax.*

twist. See *plot twist.*

unagented manuscript. A *manuscript* that isn't represented by a *literary agent.*

unsolicited manuscript. A *manuscript* that an *editor* or *representative* hasn't specifically asked to see.

urban erotic fiction. A subcategory of *erotica* that uses a city *setting* and often features African-American *characters*.

URL. Uniform Resource Locator—the address of a website.

vanity press. A company that requires the author to pay a fee for the cost of production and distribution, rather than paying the author for the rights to his or her work. Also called a "subsidy publisher," "author-subsidized publisher," "author-investment publisher," and "cooperative publisher," a vanity press is not an actual publisher because a *publisher* is an entity that invests in the publication of a work.

warranty. A legal assurance by the *author*—stipulated in the publishing agreement—that he or she is the sole proprietor of the work, and that the work doesn't contain any material that is libelous or that violates any right of privacy.

Westerns. The category of *novels* set in the American West, usually from 1850 to 1900. The usual formula involves a "good guy" who must defeat a "bad guy," who has threatened the peace of the community.

wholesale price. The price of a book that has been discounted based upon the *publisher's* established discount schedule, and is sold to only a recognized reseller of the *title*. See also *net price; retail price*.

world English rights. The right to sell a book in any country, in English only, as granted by the *author* to a *publisher*.

world rights. The right to sell a book in any country and any language, as granted by the *author* to a *publisher*.

writer-for-hire. A person who writes a work in exchange for a flat fee, a percentage of royalties, or a combination of a fee and royalties, but waives all legal rights to the work and is not credited as the *author* anywhere on the book.

writer's guidelines. The specific submission requirements of an individual publishing house. The writer's guidelines specify the categories and/or *genres* that the *publisher* will or won't accept, as well as the means by which the company wants to be contacted and the materials it wishes to receive.

RESOURCE LIST

Many fine books and periodicals offer insights into the world of publishing, and provide helpful guidelines for producing effective submission packages, improving your manuscript, developing your writing skills, negotiating contract terms, self-publishing your work, effectively marketing your book, and other subjects that may be of interest to you. In addition, a number of groups and organizations—including many that are accessible through the Internet—can offer helpful information and support. Keep in mind that this list is intended only to get you started. Your library and local bookstore may provide other helpful readings, and, of course, new online groups and resources are cropping up all the time.

BOOKS

RESOURCE DIRECTORIES

Bowling, Ann, editor. *Novel & Short Story Writer's Market.* Cincinnati: Writer's Digest Books, updated annually.

One of the best places to start your hunt for a publisher, this book lists hundreds of book publishers—including United States companies and publishers in Canada and other English-speaking foreign countries—and helpfully focuses on the fiction market only. Also included are articles and interviews featuring editors and writers, as well as information on literary agents, contests and awards, and conferences and workshops. This resource is quite affordable so that you can add it to your home collection rather than relying on the library's reference copy.

Dickerson, Donya, editor. *Guide to Literary Agents.* Cincinnati: Writers' Digest Books, updated annually.

This book lists hundreds of literary agencies, as well as script agents, freelance publicists, and writers' conferences. Information on working with reps is included, as are lists of professional organizations and books and websites of interest. Although this resource doesn't provide the personal insights offered in *Jeff Herman's Guide,* it does list additional agencies and also allows you to double-check the information you find in other books.

Herman, Jeff. *Jeff Herman's Guide to Book Publishers, Editors, and Literary Agents.* **Waukesha, WI: Kalmbach Publishing Co, updated annually.**

In this wonderful resource, Herman lists publishers, editors, and agents, and provides insightful articles on various aspects of the business. He also offers a lot of information the other guides don't—background information on the various reps and publishing companies, for instance. Written in a conversational tone and designed for people outside the industry, *Jeff Herman's Guide* is very easy to use, is affordably priced, and is also offered on CD-ROM.

Herman, Jeff. *Writer's International Guide to Book Editors, Publishers, and Literary Agents.* **Rosedale, CA: Prima Lifestyles, 1999.**

This guide to the English-speaking publishing world lists both publishers and literary agents in the United Kingdom, Canada, Australia, Hong Kong, Singapore, South Africa, and more. Herman also provides marketing suggestions and insightful essays from top literary professionals.

ILMP. **New Providence, NJ: R.R. Bowker, updated annually.**

The international version of the *Literary Market Place,* the *ILMP (International Literary Market Place)* provides the same information offered in the *LMP*—listings of publishers, literary agents, etc.—for foreign markets. The directory covers over 180 countries, both English-speaking and non-English-speaking.

The International Directory of Little Magazines & Small Presses. **Paradise, CA: Dustbooks, updated annually.**

This unique directory lists over 5,000 small publishers and magazines. In addition to basic contact information, most entries offer payment rates, proposal requirements, and recent publications. Subject and regional indexes are included. If you're focusing on small presses, this is an invaluable reference.

Literary Market Place. **New Providence, NJ: R.R. Bowker, updated annually.**

Considered the bible of the publishing industry, the *Literary Market Place* is a comprehensive listing of American and Canadian publishers; literary agents; editorial services; trade associations and foundations; book trade courses; writer's conferences and workshops; trade shows; awards and contests; book reviewers; book clubs; manufacturers; and more. The *LMP's* high price makes it impractical for individual purchase, but it can be found in the reference section of any library. Although the format makes it a bit unwieldy for novelists, it not only includes publishers not listed in other guides, but also offers business-related information not found elsewhere.

Publishers' International ISBN Directory. **Berlin, Germany: International ISBN Agency, updated annually.**

Here is the most comprehensive listing of worldwide publishers—including, of course, publishers in English-speaking foreign countries. All in all, over 200 countries and more than 600,000 publishers are included in a format that allows you to find a publishing house by either country or name. Like the *Literary Market Place,* though, this book has a prohibitively high price, so look for a copy in the reference section of a large public library rather than your local bookstore.

Writers' & Artists' Yearbook: A Directory for Writers, Artists, Playwrights, Writers for Film, Radio and Television, Designers, Illustrators, and Photographers. **London, England: A & C Black, updated annually.**

This best-selling guide to all areas of the media presents listings of publishers in the United States, the United Kingdom, Ireland, Australia, and New Zealand, including all contact information. Also included is advice on proofreading, marketing your book, acquiring an agent, and other topics of interest. As a plus, *Writers' & Artists' Yearbook* is affordably priced so that you can easily add it to your home reference library.

BOOKS ON THE CRAFT OF WRITING

Atchity, Kenneth. *A Writer's Time: Making the Time to Write.* **New York: W.W. Norton, 1995.**

This guide applies commonsense time-management principles to your writing. You'll learn how the creative mind works, and how to master your schedule, combat writer's block, and maximize your creative output.

Bickham, Jack M. *Writing and Selling Your Novel.* **Cincinnati: Writer's Digest Books, 1996.**

Bickman offers practical advice on writing professionally, from attitude to technique. Here are invaluable tips on the craft geared toward the goal of a sale.

Burack, Sylvia K. *Writing and Selling the Romance Novel.* **Boston: Writer, Inc., 1983.**

Here is a complete guide to writing and selling romance category fiction. Each subcategory is discussed in detail, and practical information is provided on understanding the market and writing effective queries.

Card, Orson Scott. *Characters and Viewpoint: Elements of Fiction Writing.* **Cincinnati: Writer's Digest Books, 1999.**

Written by a successful sci-fi writer, this book shows you how to breathe life and believability into your characters and mold them to fit your story. Topics include factors that make good characters, transformations in the lives of characters, point of view, and much more.

The Chicago Manual of Style. **Fifteenth Edition. Chicago: University of Chicago Press, 2003.**

Since 1906, this well-known resource has helped set editorial standards, providing systematic guidelines for editors, proofreaders, indexers, publishers—and writers. It's an important reference tool when you're unsure of where to place a comma, or whether or not you should spell out the number or use a numeral.

The most recent edition reflects changes made in style, usage, procedure, and technology, with substantial sections on preparing manuscripts for electronic publishing. Be aware, however, that publishers often have their own in-house style, which may conflict with this manual.

Collier, Oscar, and Frances Spatz Leighton. *How to Write and Sell Your First Novel.* **Third Revised Edition. Cincinnati: Writer's Digest Books, 1997.**

This reader-friendly guide offers the do's and don'ts of writing, querying, and submitting a novel to publishers. Here is an inspirational shot in the arm to aspiring writers, plus proven strategies for getting your novel into print.

Vogler, Christopher. *The Writer's Journey: Mythic Structure for Writers.* **Second Edition. Michael Wiese Productions, 1998.**

This is an excellent, user-friendly guide to myth and the way it informs your story's structure, including a comprehensive discussion of the twelve steps of the Hero's Journey. Vogler draws heavily on Joseph Campbell's exploration of myth, but adapts it for contemporary storytellers, explaining that all stories consist of a few common structural elements that are found universally in myths and fairy tales. This book will revolutionize the way you structure your stories.

BOOKS ON GETTING PUBLISHED

Appelbaum, Judith. *How to Get Happily Published: A Complete and Candid Guide.* **Fifth Edition. New York: Harper Resource, 1998.**

This book provides insight into the world of publishing and offers tips on improving your material, successfully submitting your manuscript, acting as your own sales force, and more. The self-publishing option is explored in depth, and a truly staggering resource section of over a hundred pages guides you to helpful books, journals, websites, and organizations.

Boswell, John. *The Insider's Guide to Getting Published: Why They Always Reject Your Manuscript—and What You Can Do About It.* **New York: Main Street Books, 1997.**

Boswell presents a starkly realistic view of the modern publishing industry, including a comprehensive explanation of its shortcomings. Most important, the author explains how industrious writers can succeed in spite of the industry.

Henderson, Bill, and Andre Bernard, editors. *Pushcart's Complete Rotten Reviews and Rejections: A History of Insult, a Solace to Writers.* **Wainscott, NY: Pushcart Press, 1998.**

This book is a great pick-me-up if you've ever received a rejection letter of your own, or if you just want a good laugh. The editors have compiled some of the nastiest comments received by well-known published authors, including Shakespeare, Melville, Twain, Updike, and Dickens. You'll probably be most interested in the comments about novelists, but all are fun to read.

Levin, Martin. *Be Your Own Literary Agent: The Ultimate Insider's Guide to Getting Published.* **Berkeley, CA: Ten Speed Press, 2002.**

Levin provides clear step-by-step instructions for writing a successful book proposal, negotiating a contract, and otherwise acting as your own literary agent. Included is a wealth of model proposals, as well as a helpful glossary and a list of small publishers who, according to the author, are most likely to read and accept your book. But perhaps the most valuable feature is a section-by-section review of a sample literary contract.

Lyon, Elizabeth. *The Sell Your Novel Toolkit: Everything You Need to Know About Queries, Synopses, Marketing, & Breaking In.* **Portland, OR: Blue Heron Publishing Company, 1997.**

This is a great resource, particularly for the query and submission phase. Extensive examples of query letters, good and bad, are included.

Masello, Robert. *Writer Tells All: Insider Secrets to Getting Your Book Published.* **New York: Owl Books, 2001.**

Masello's humorous, lighthearted, candid view of the writing business includes charming anecdotes from the "trenches." Learn the pitfalls, heartbreaks, and challenges of promoting your writing, and then find time-tested ways to succeed anyway.

BOOKS ON THE BUSINESS OF WRITING

Bunnin, Brad, and Peter Beren. *The Writer's Legal Companion: The Complete Handbook for the Working Writer.* **Third Edition. New York: Perseus Books, 1998.**

Here is a complete guide to the many legal concerns writers face. The book covers agents, contracts, copyright law, and more, and everything's written for the average person—not the attorney.

Jassin, Lloyd J., and Steven Schechter. *The Copyright Permission and Libel Handbook: A Step-by-Step Guide for Writers, Editors and Publishers.* **New York: John Wily & Sons, 1997.**

Here is a thorough guide to legal issues of concern to writers—libel, copyright, permissions, etc.—including practical, accessible advice on how to protect yourself against lawsuits.

Kirsch, Jonathan. *Kirsch's Guide to the Book Contract.* **Los Angeles: Acrobat Books, 1999.**

Written by an intellectual property attorney and designed for use by authors, publishers, editors, and literary agents, this book begins with a model book contract, and then takes you through the contract on a clause-by-clause basis. Presented in reference-guide format, *Kirsch's Guide* allows you to turn to the portion of the contract you need to know about in a given situation. The author also provides a wealth of tips for negotiating the deal, as well as cautions about contract elements that may prove problematic.

Kozak, Ellen M. *Every Writer's Guide to Copyright and Publishing Law*. Third Edition. New York: Owl Books, 2004.

This straightforward text doesn't overwhelm you with legal terminology, but simplifies confusing terms and issues that arise for new authors. Some subjects that will be of interest are U.S. copyright law, including e-copyrights; fair use; libel; work for hire; collaboration agreements; and contract information.

BOOKS ON MARKETING AND PROMOTION

Deval, Jacqueline. *Publicize Your Book!: An Insider's Guide to Getting Your Book the Attention It Deserves*. New York: Perigee, 2003.

Here is a realistic guide to gaining publicity—ranging from hiring a publicist to personally arranging events, and covering everything from local weekly papers to *Oprah*. Included is clear and necessary information on how the publishing industry works.

Jenkins, Jerrold R., and Anne M. Stanton. *Publish to Win: Smart Strategies to Sell More Books*. Rhodes and Easton, 1997.

A must-read for anyone considering self-publishing, *Publish to Win* guides you in evaluating the marketability of your book idea, defining your target audience, finding a distributor, creating publicity, and more, including—and, perhaps, most important—selling your book to nontraditional markets.

Kremer, John. *1001 Ways to Market Your Books*. Fifth Edition. Fairfield, IA: Open Horizons, 1998.

This book provides literally hundreds of marketing tips and suggestions for writers in any stage of their careers, including information on the basics of publishing, researching your market, getting book reviews, obtaining print and radio interviews, ar-

ranging talk show appearances, organizing author tours, using direct mail, marketing via telephone, selling books via the computer, working with bookstores, arranging offbeat advertising and promotions, and much more.

Levinson, Jay Conrad, Rick Frishman, and Michael Larsen. *Guerilla Marketing for Writers: 100 Weapons for Selling Your Work*. Cincinnati: Writer's Digest Books, 2000.

Written by expert publicists, this book helps you assess your strengths, arms you with the tools you need, and then provides a wide range of ways to promote your book—from pricey to free, from difficult to easy.

Ross, Marilyn, and Tom Ross. *Jump-Start Your Book Sales: A Money-Making Guide for Authors, Independent Publishers and Small Presses*. Communication Creativity, 1999.

Here is a treasure-trove of information on marketing techniques for the entrepreneurial author. Both traditional and nontraditional techniques are explored, and a wealth of real-life examples is included.

Smith, Bud and Arthur Bebak. *Creating Web Pages for Dummies*. New York: Wiley Publishing, 2002.

Here is everything you need to know to create your own web page. Emphasis is placed on the basics so that you can create a personal website quickly, without getting overwhelmed. Included are the fundamentals of HTML.

Warren, Lissa. *The Savvy Author's Guide to Book Publicity*. New York: Caroll & Graf, 2003.

Written by an experienced promoter of both fiction and nonfiction, this book is filled with immediately useful tips on promoting your book. The author also provides a crash course in publishing industry jargon.

BOOKS ON SELF-PUBLISHING

Poynter, Dan. *The Self-Publishing Manual: How to Write, Print & Sell Your Own Book.* Fourteenth Edition. Santa Barbara, CA: Para Publishing, 2003.

A how-to book by the leader in the field of self-publishing, this is a complete guide to writing, publishing, and selling your own book. It helps you get your book up to commercial standards, provides tools for marketing and promoting, and presents clear information on getting your self-published book distributed through the channels used by traditional publishers. Here is an indispensable work for anyone considering self-publishing.

Ross, Tom, and Marilyn J. Ross. *The Complete Guide to Self-Publishing: Everything You Need to Know to Write, Publish, Promote and Sell Your Own Book.* Fourth Edition. Cincinnati: Writer's Digest Books, 2002.

Tom and Marilyn Ross provide a comprehensive discussion of self-publishing, from setting up your own business to finding a printer to distributing and marketing your book. The book is packed with helpful information, particularly if you're self-publishing on a tight budget.

BOOKS ON ELECTRONIC PUBLISHING

Curtis, Richard. *How to Get Your E-Book Published: An Insider's Guide to the World of Electronic Publishing.* Cincinnati: Writer's Digest Books, 2002.

This is the most comprehensive guide I've seen on e-publishing by one of the industry's leaders. Curtis discusses the current state of the industry, including its substantial drawbacks; hints at where e-publishing might be taking us in the future; and offers guidelines for writers who are ready to take the plunge into electronic waters. He also discusses the different

types of e-publishers, e-self-publishers, vanity e-publishers, and more.

Fischer, Rusty. *Ebook Marketing Made Easy: 101 Great Ways to Promote and Sell Your eBook.* Bookbooters.com, 2002.

In this book, marketing expert Rusty Fischer guides you in promoting your e-book to the widest possible audience. Included are many free, easy, and effective ways to sell your electronic book.

Henke, Harold. *Electronic Books and ePublishing: A Practical Guide for Authors.* New York: Springer Publishing, 2001.

This complete guide to e-publishing includes a handy CD—which contains the whole book in pdf format—as well as an interesting history of electronic publishing.

Rosenborg, Victoria. *ePublishing for Dummies.* New York: Wiley Publishing, 2000.

Rosenborg takes confusing technical information and makes it easy-to-understand—even fun—in this complete course in electronic publishing. You'll learn everything from how to design and format your e-book to how to make e-publishing pay.

BOOKS ON SELLING STORIES TO HOLLYWOOD

Atchity, Kenneth, and Chi-Li Wong. *Writing Treatments That Sell: How to Create and Market Your Story Ideas to the Motion Picture and TV Industry.* Second Edition. New York: Henry Holt & Co., 2003.

Here is an insiders' guide to crafting the motion picture industry's primary selling document: the treatment. The authors explain the nature and structure of both film and television treatments, guide you in writing an adaptation treatment from your novel or other work, and explain how to use your treatment to sell your story to Hollywood.

Field, Syd. *Screenplay: The Foundations of Screenwriting.* **New York: Dell Publishing, 1984.**

One of the bibles of the film trade, Field's book makes filmwriting accessible to novices while helping practiced writers improve their work. Included is a step-by-step technique for writing a script that sells.

Goldman, William. *Adventures in the Screen Trade.* **New York: Warner Books, 1989.**

Written by a highly successful screenwriter, this is a humorous, hard-hitting, anecdotal view of Hollywood—what makes it tick, how to get inside, and how to survive once you're there.

Seger, Linda. *The Art of Adaptation: Turning Fact and Fiction Into Film.* **New York: Henry Holt & Co., 1992.**

Seger explains how to transform novels, plays, and true-life stories into screenplays. Included are discussions of character, story, setting, mood, and more.

Wilen, Lydia, and Joan Wilen. *How to Sell Your Screenplay: A Realistic Guide to Getting a Television or Film Deal.* **Garden City Park, NY: Square One Publishers, 2001.**

Written by two veteran screenwriters, this book gives you an insider's understanding of the film business, guides you in putting your script into the proper format, provides a proven system for query submission, and aids you in making the best deal possible.

PERIODICALS

Booklist
American Library Association
50 E. Huron
Chicago, IL 60611
Phone: 800-545-2433
Website: www.ala.org

For more than ninety years, this publication of the American Library Association has been the librarian's leading choice for reviews of the latest books and electronic media. Each year it reviews more than 4,000 books for adults. *Booklist* also offers author interviews, bibliographies, book-related essays by well-known writers, and a selection of columns, including a wealth of information on industry trends.

Publishers Weekly
360 Park Avenue South
New York, NY 10010
Phone: 800-278-2991
Website: www.publishersweekly.com

The most important journal within the book trade, *PW* is read by publishers, bookstore buyers, librarians, and other people in the industry. A window on the publishing world, it provides book reviews, profiles of best-selling authors, and an insider's look at book and marketing trends, as well as lists of best-sellers.

The Writer
Kalmbach Publishing Co.
21027 Crossroads Circle
P.O. Box 1612
Waukesha, WI 53187-1612
Phone: 800-533-6644
Website: www.writermag.com

Designed for the professional writer, this journal presents interviews with successful writers; lists of helpful books and other writing tools; notices of literary contests, workshops, and conferences; writing tips; and more.

Writer's Digest
F & W Publications, Inc.
4700 E. Galbraith Road
Cincinnati, OH 45236
Phone: 513-531-2222
Website: www.writersdigest.com

This easy-to-read magazine is filled with interviews of authors and with articles about improving your writing, working with editors, writing better proposals, and more. Included is a special section that guides you to writers' workshops, conferences, and classes; literary contests; professional editorial services and ghostwriters; and literary agents.

GROUPS & ORGANIZATIONS

The Association of Author's Representatives

P.O. Box 237201
Ansonia Station, NY 10003
Website: www.aar-online.org

Through its website, this nonprofit association of literary representatives offers a searchable database of agents as well as helpful guidelines for choosing an agent.

The Author's Guild

31 East 28th Street, 10th Floor
New York, NY 10016-7923
Phone: 212-563-5904
Website: www.authorsguild.org

A professional organization for published writers, the Guild represents more than 8,000 authors. The Guild's legal staff reviews members' publishing and agency contracts, intervenes in publishing disputes, and holds seminars and symposia on issues of importance to writers. The Guild also lobbies at the national and local levels on behalf of all authors on issues such as copyright, taxation, and freedom of expression. Reports bring members up-to-date on professional issues.

Poets & Writers, Inc.

72 Spring Street, Suite 301
New York, NY 10012
Phone: 212-226-3586
Website: www.pw.org

The nation's largest nonprofit literary organization, Poets & Writers provides information, support, and guidance for creative writers. The group produces *Poets & Writers Magazine*; sponsors literary events; and, through its website, offers listings of conferences, contests, and services for writers; a message forum that enables writers to discuss topics of interest; as well as a wealth of valuable advice.

Publisher's Marketing Association (PMA)

627 Aviation Way
Manhattan Beach, CA 90266
Phone: 310-372-2732
Website: www.pma-online.org

Founded in 1983, this trade association of independent publishers has a membership of over 3,000 United States and international publishers—including self-publishers. Through its newsletter, online chat group, and other publications and services, the PMA can guide you to reputable typesetters, printers, editors, and more; inform you of worthwhile publishing fairs, seminars, workshops, exhibits, and awards; and otherwise provide you with the information you need to succeed as a self-publisher. Services are provided for members only.

Small Publishers Association of North American (SPAN)

1618 W. Colorado Avenue
Colorado Springs, CO 80904
Phone: 719-632-8226
Website: www.spannet.org

Founded in 1996, SPAN's stated mission is "to advance the image and profits of independent publishers through education and marketing opportunities." SPAN offers its members—over 1,000 small presses and self-publishers—a range of resources and services, including an information-packed monthly newsletter; a variety of conferences and seminars on publicity and marketing; discounts on health insurance, shipping, office supplies, and industry publications; and a membership resource directory that will allow you to network with other SPAN members. Like the PMA, SPAN provides these services for members only.

U.S. Copyright Office

Library of Congress.
101 Independence Ave. SE
Washington, DC 20559–6000
Phone: 202-707-3000
Website: www.copyright.gov

If you're worried that a publishing company might steal your work, the U.S. Copyright Office can provide legal protection by copyrighting your manuscript. You can either order the necessary forms over the phone or download them from the website. Be sure to observe the fee information. The website also explains how to register your work, and provides information about licensing, patents, and trademarks.

Writers Guild of America, East

555 West 5th Street, Suite 1230
New York, NY 10019
Phone: 212-767-7800
Website: wgaeast.org

Contact the Writers Guild branch nearest you when you're ready to register the film treatment of your novel before sending it to anyone in Hollywood. The Guild's registration services, which are open to non-members, will protect your claim of ownership.

Writers Guild of America, West

7000 West Third Street
Los Angeles, CA 90048
Phone: 213-782-4540
Website: www.wga.org

Like Writers Guild East, this branch of the Writers Guild can register your screenplay, protecting your claim of ownership. Registration can be accomplished easily on the Guild's website.

INTERNET SITES

AEI

Website: www.aeionline.com

The website of Atchity Entertainment International, Inc. (AEI)—a literary management and motion picture production company—offers a what's hot and what's not list of topics, as well as articles on various subjects of interest to aspiring writers.

American Booksellers Association (ABA)

Website: www.bookweb.org

A nonprofit trade association that represents independent bookstores in the United States, the ABA also hosts the annual ABA Convention in conjunction with BookExpo America each spring. Visit the association's website to find book industry research and statistics, and to learn about related organizations and events.

Author Network

Website: www.author-network.com

This site provides an extensive range of resources for writers, including a directory of literary agents, a Website Creation and Design Service, articles on topics of importance to writers, and much more.

Authorlink

Website: www.authorlink.com.

A great place to start your search for a rep, Authorlink offers a large database of literary representatives, along with their e-mail addresses and query guidelines. And through the Author Showcase, Authorlink provides an opportunity for authors to present their manuscripts to editors. A reasonable annual subscription fee will give you access to the site.

Book-Clubs-Resource.com

Website: www.book-clubs-resource.com

This is a wonderful place to start your search for an

in-person or online reading group or book club that might be interested in your new novel.

BookExpo America (BEA)

Website: www.bookexpoamerica.com

Visit this website to learn about BookExpo America—an important annual event that can put you in touch with publishers, editors, agents, and other people in the world of book publishing. BookExpo is also a great place to learn about industry trends.

DearReader.com

Website: www.dearreader.com

This site enables readers to join the book club of their choice—one that focuses on horror, mystery, romance, or sci-fi, for instance—and then e-mails them bits of new novels every day. Here is a great marketing opportunity for new writers who want to advise potential readers of their novels.

Forwriters.com

Website: www.forwriters.com

This site provides links to numerous writers groups, dividing them into three categories: professional, local, and online. Other services of interest are also offered.

Manuscript Editing

Website: http://manuscriptediting.com

Visit this site and click on "Writers' Groups." There, you'll find links to a wide range of groups, both online and in-person.

PayPal

Website: www.paypal.com

Should you choose to sell your own books, this com-pany will enable you to quickly and easily receive payments online.

Submit Express

Website: www.submitexpress.com

When you create your own website, this free service will get the site listed on forty or more of the most commonly used search engines, allowing potential readers to easily find you.

The Virtual Book Tour

Website: www.virtualbooktour.org

This online service allows writers to connect with interested readers by arranging an Internet tour in which the author "stops" at a given number of websites in a given amount of time. At each of these stops, authors may be interviewed, take over the site for the day, answer questions from readers, or get their book reviewed. Unless you are approached by the service, you will be charged both initial and per-hour fees.

The Writer's Lifeline, Inc.

Website: www.thewriterslifeline.com

The Writer's Lifeline can provide a written assessment of your project's strengths and weaknesses, focusing on action line, character, dialogue, setting, and tone. Editorial and ghostwriting services are available. A section on market trends guides you to hot categories and topics.

Writers Net

Website: www.writers.net/agents.html

Designed for writers, agents, editors, and publishers, this site offers a free directory to literary agents, which you can search by location or topic. This site also provides access to various discussion forums.

About the Authors

Ken Atchity is the author of 14 books, including *A Writer's Time: A Guide to the Creative Process, from Vision through Revision* (W. W. Norton), which *The New York Times* called "the best recent book on writing"; (with Chi-Li Wong) *Writing Treatments That Sell: How to Create and Market Your Story Ideas to the Motion Picture and TV Industry* (Holt), #4 on *The Los Angeles Times Book Review's* Hollywood Bestseller List; and *How to Escape Lifetime Security and Pursue Your Impossible Dream: A Guide to Transforming Your Career* (Helios). Ken has produced 23 films, including "Joe Somebody" (Tim Allen and Jim Belushi), "Life, or Something Like It" (Angelina Jolie and Ed Burns), and is producing, with his partner Chi-Li Wong, Larry Gordon Productions ("Die Hard," "Lara Croft"), Nick Nunziata, and Guillermo del Toro ("Hellboy") *Meg*, based on the novel by Steve Alten, at New Line with Jan de Bont ("Twister," "Speed") directing; as well as a series of Ripley's Believe-It-Or-Not™ films in co-production with Alphaville ("The Mummy," "Day of the Jackal") at Paramount.

As professor of comparative literature and creative writing at Occidental College and Distinguished Instructor at UCLA Writers Program, Ken has given courses entitled "Writing Your Novel in Ten Weeks," "Writing Your Novel for Hollywood," and "Turning Truth into Fiction," as well as numerous courses in literary criticism and analysis. During his year as Fulbright Professor of American Literature at the University of Bologna, Italy, he lectured on classical and speculative novels in Trieste, Milan, Turin, Florence, Palermo, and Rome. As a reviewer for *The Los Angeles Times Book Review*, he has reviewed hundreds of novels, including Umberto Eco's *The Name of the Rose*, Hubert Selby, Jr.'s *Requiem for a Dream*, Peter Feibleman's *Charley Boy;* and published academic articles on novels from Cervantes to Saul Bellow.

During his academic years, Ken also co-founded (with Marsha Kinder), the journal *Dreamworks*, dedicated to the relationship between dreams and the arts. *Dreamworks'* advisory board and contributors included novelists Ursula LeGuin, Joyce Carole Oates, Carlos Fuentes, John Fowles, Paul Bowles, Georges Simenon, and John Rechy.

As chairman of Atchity Entertainment International, Inc. ("AEI"), a literary management and motion picture production company, and of The Writer's Lifeline, Inc., a consulting company dedicated to helping writers perfect their craft to the commercial and professional level, Ken divides his time between Los Angeles and New York, where he introduces his storytellers' works to publishers and motion picture studios, then produces their films. AEI's sold novels include Steve Alten (*Meg, The Trench, Domain, Goliath, The Loch*), April Christofferson (*Clinical Trial, Patent to Kill, Buffalo Medicine*), Jamise Dames (*Momma's Baby, Daddy's Maybe; Pushin' Up Daisies*), Patricia Davis (*Midnight Carol*), Nancy Freedman (*Sappho: The Tenth Muse*), Lois Gilbert (*River of Summer, Without Mercy*), John Robert Marlow (*Nano*), Noire (*G-Spot, Candy Licker*), Shirley Palmer (*Lioness, Veiled*

Journey, Danger Zone, The Trade), James Michael Pratt (*The Last Valentine, The Lighthouse Keeper, Ticket Home, Paradise Bay*), Mitchell Rossi (*The Hong Kong Sanction*), Alvin Schwartz (*An Unlikely Prophet, The Blowtop*), John Scott Shepherd (*Henry's List of Wrongs, The Dead Father's Guide to Sex and Marriage*), and Tracy Price-Thompson (*Chocolate Sangria, A Woman's Worth*). Dr. Atchity's company has sold client novels to New Line Cinema, Walt Disney Productions, NBC, Saban Entertainment, Peak Productions, Propaganda Films, and HBO Pictures, among others.

Julie Ann Mooney has worked as a freelance writer and editor in association with AEI since 1996, and with Writer's Lifeline since 1998. She worked with Minnesota Governor Jesse Ventura on his autobiography, *I Ain't Got Time to Bleed* (Villard), and his treatise on populist government, *Do I Stand Alone?* (Pocket Books). She co-wrote with the editors of Ripley's Believe-It-or-Not!™ *The World of Ripley's Believe It Or Not!* and *Ripley's Believe It or Not! Book of the Bizarre* (Black Dog & Leventhal); as well as the Learning Annex series of books. Julie writes nonfiction book proposals for the Writer's Lifeline program and coaches writers in developing their novels and screenplays.

Andrea McKeown, Chief Operating Officer of Writer's Lifeline, was born in Kansas City, where she studied writing and literature at UMKC. She joined AEI, Writer's Lifeline's management and production affiliate, working as a story and script analyst on "Shadow of Obsession" (NBC-Saban Entertainment, starring Veronica Hammel and based on the novel *Unwanted Attentions* by K. K. Beck).

When AEI expanded into literary management in 1996, Andrea moved into an editorial capacity for the Writer's Lifeline in addition to her duties with AEI Production-Management. As a senior editor, she discovered and was associated with Rick Lynch's *180 Seconds at Willow Park*, which was sold to New Line Cinema and to Dove Books. She was instrumental in editing James Michael Pratt's *The Last Valentine*, which sold to St. Martin's Press and to the Literary Guild and Doubleday Book Club at auction; Shirley Palmer's *The Trade* (Mira); and Jamise Dames' *Pushin' Up Daisies.*

Margaret O'Connor is a graduate of State University of New York College at Purchase (B.A., Literature 1999), and worked with AEI as Assistant Manager for Books, 2003—2005. Before that she was a Marketing Associate for Cambridge University Press in NY. At AEI she was responsible for maintaining the in-office operations of the book division, including but not limited to: reading, editing and providing notes on manuscripts and proposals from prospective and existing clients; submitting and following up on submissions to publishers; creating marketing strategies for each individual book project; maintaining contacts with clients in regards to all stages of their writing career, from manuscript to published book, PR, marketing, and all other media opportunities, including teaching classes at The Learning Annex, submitting articles for publication in magazines and newspapers, speaking engagements, and seeking out and exploring dramatic rights for film.

Author Contact Information

Ken Atchity welcomes updates and corrections—and especially comments and suggestions—that might improve future editions of this work. His companies welcome representation or consulting queries from writers. If your novel is ready, and you're seeking representation, contact: Jennifer Pope, Atchity Entertainment International, Inc., 9601 Wilshire Boulevard #1202, Beverly Hills CA 90210; Email: jp@aeionline.com.

INDEX

A

Accounting, in contracts, 170
Acknowledgments, writing, 217
Acquisitions editor, 214
Action line, 232
Action tags, 235
Acts, use of, in novel structure, 237
Adams, Charles, 31
Advance reading copies (ARCs)
    purpose of, 221
    using, to obtain blurbs, 253, 256
    using, to obtain reviews, 254, 266–267
Advances
    in contracts, 169
    in large publishing houses, 51
    in mid-sized houses, 54
    negotiating, 177
    in small publishing houses, 57
Adventure novels, 14–15
Agents. *See* Literary agents.
Alice in Wonderland, 237
All Around the Town (Clark), 36
All That Remains (Cornwell), 218
Alten, Steve, 227, 241, 244
Ancient evil novels, 24
Andersen, Susan, 32
Angels & Demons (Brown), 240
Antagonists, 226–230

Anthony, Piers, 18
Apocalyptic fiction, 29–30
Approach, as potential roadblock to publication, 184–185
ARCs. *See* Advance reading copies.
Armstrong, Kelley, 29
Art of Adaptation (Seger), 208
As I Lay Dying (Faulkner), 239
Asimov, Isaac, 33
Associate editor, 214
At Home in Mitford (Karon), 30
Atwood, Margaret, 19
Audience, understanding your, 38–39, 253
Aury, Dominique, 16
Author's biography. *See* Biography, author.
Author's copies, in contract, 164–165
Author's credibility, establishing, in cover or query letter, 115–116
Author's discounts, in contract, 165, 179
Author's promotional responsibilities, in contract, 165–166
Author's self-promotion of novel. *See* Promotion of novel by author.

B

Bach, Richard, 34
Back-story, revealing, 230
Bankruptcy clause, in contract, 175
Barnett, Jill, 32
BEA. *See* BookExpo America.
Benchley, Peter, 233
Benefit section, in contracts, 173–174
Bestseller status, 252
Beverley, Jo, 32
Biblical fiction, 31
Big Bad Wolf, The (Patterson), 36
Binding of novel, 222
Biography, author, 258
    sample, 264
Birdy (Wharton), 226
Bitten (Armstrong), 29
Black magic novels, 24
Black Narcissus (Godden), 239
Bleachers (Grisham), 35
Bluelines, 222
Blues, 222
Blurbs, obtaining, 255–256
Bonfire of the Vanities, The (Wolfe), 12
Book clubs, 44
Book cover design, 219–220
Book reviewer, sample letter to, 268

Book reviews, obtaining. *See*
    Advance reading copies.
Book signings, 271–272
Book tours, 273
BookExpo America (BEA), 105
BookExpo Canada, 105
Booklist, 254
Bookstores
    online retail, 42
    specialized retail, 41–42
    traditional retail, 41
Bradley, Marion Zimmer, 19
Braun, Lillian Jackson, 27
Bride Stripped Bare, The
    (Gemmell), 16
Bridges of Madison County, The
    (Waller), 12
Bridget Jones's Diary (Fielding), 25
Bronte, Charlotte, 226
Bronte, Emily, 21
Brown, Dale, 26
Brown, Dan, 240

C

Camus, Albert, 14
Caper mysteries, 27
Card, Orson Scott, 234, 242
Castle of Otranto, The (Walpole),
    22
Catalogue, publisher's book
    frontlist, 144
    full, 144
    lessons to be learned from, 81,
        144–145
    requesting, 142–143
    specialty, 144
Catch-22 (Heller), 238
Categories, novel
    adventure novels, 14–15
    erotica, 15–17
    ethnic novels, 17–18
    and expectations of readers,
        38–39
    fantasy novels, 18–19
    feminist novels, 19–20

gay, lesbian, bisexual, and
    transgender (GLBT) novels,
    20–21
Gothic novels, 21–22
historical novels, 22–23
horror novels, 23–24
humor novels, 25
importance of defining, 8–9
learning about your, 190–191
literary novels, 11, 13–14
mainstream novels, 9, 10–12
military/war novels, 26–27
mysteries, 27–28
occult novels, 28–29
religious novels, 29–30
romance novels, 31–33
science fiction, 33–34
spiritual/New Age novels,
    34–35
sports novels, 35–36
suspense novels, 36–37
Westerns, 37–38
Categorizing your book. *See*
    Categories, novel.
Category fiction, 9, 11. *See also*
    Categories, novel.
Category romances, 32
CBA. *See* Christian Booksellers
    Association.
Celestine Prophecy, The (Redfield),
    34
Change within characters,
    229–230
Chapters
    sample, 127–131
    writing, 245–246
Characters, creating, 225–232
    basing on real people, 247
    function, 231
    main, 226–230
    minor, 231
    supporting, 230–231
Characters and Viewpoint (Card),
    242
Charlie Boy (Feibleman), 232

Chat groups, online, 269
Checklist, submission package,
    149
Chick-lit, 25
Christian Booksellers Association
    (CBA), 105–106
Christie, Agatha, 11, 28
Christofferson, April, 40
Church of Latter-Day Saints, 253
Clancy, Tom, 12, 26, 59
Clark, Mary Higgins, 36
Classic whodunits, 27
Clear and Present Danger (Clancy),
    26
Clever crook mysteries, 27
Clichés, use of, 236
Climax as component of action
    line, 234
Clinical Trial (Christofferson), 40
Cockpit (Kosinski), 228, 239
Codex, The (Preston), 15
Cold Mountain (Frazier), 23
Comic fantasy novels, 19
Comic mysteries, 27
Commercial publishing houses,
    47–59
    definition of, 47
    large, 48–51
    moderate-sized, 51–55
    small, 55–58
Condon, Richard, 15
Confederacy of Dunces, A (Toole),
    25, 59, 228
Conflict as component of action
    line, 232–233
Conroy, Pat, 239
Contact information
    importance of including
        author's, 117
    importance of verifying
        publisher's, 141–143
Contemporary fantasy novels, 19
Contemporary horror novels, 24
Contemporary religious fiction,
    30

Contemporary romances, 32
Contractions, use of, 236
Contracts, 157–182
    accounting section, 170
    advance section, 169
    agent, identification of, 175
    author's copies section,
        164–165
    author's discounts, 165, 179
    author's promotional
        responsibilities section,
        165–166
    bankruptcy section, 174
    benefit section, 173–174
    copyright section, 171–172
    editing, proofs, and
        publication section, 163–164
    force majeure section, 174–175
    hiring a lawyer for, 158
    hiring a literary agent for,
        158–159
    identifying the parties in, 160
    manuscript section, 162–163
    negotiations, 175–181
    option clause, 172
    out-of-print provision section,
        166
    proceedings section, 173
    reserved rights section, 171
    reviewing multiple, 181
    rights of termination section,
        172–173
    rights section, 161–162
    royalties section, 166–169
    royalty-free copies, 168–169
    subsidiary rights section, 162
    warranty and indemnification
        section, 170–171
Copyediting, process of, 217–218
Copyeditor, 214
Copyright, obtaining, 135–136
Copyright section, in contracts,
    171–172
Corey, John, 229
Cornwell, Patricia, 218, 246

Corps, The (Griffith), 26
Cover letters
    definition of, 109
    sample, 111–112
    writing, 109–110, 113, 115–117
Cozy mysteries, 27
Craft of Fiction, The (Lubbock), 242
Creating Web Pages for Dummies
    (Smith), 207
Crime and Punishment
    (Dostoevski), 229
Crime mysteries, 27
Cunningham, Michael, 19

D

Danger Zone (Palmer), 229
    publicity packet for, 260–264
Dark suspense novels, 24
Daughter of Time (Tey), 28
De Cervantes, Miguel, 226
De Sade, Marquis, 16
DearReader.com, 269
Defoe, Daniel, 15
DeMille, Nelson, 36, 217, 228–229,
    233, 239–240, 246
Design and typesetting, 218–220
Detective mysteries, 27
Deval, Jacqueline, 275
Devil's Heiress, The (Beverley), 32
Dialogue, writing, 234–236
Dialogue tags, 235
Dickens, Charles, 232
Disaster adventure novels, 14
Dolby, Tom, 20
Domain (Alten), 227, 241
Don Quixote (de Cervantes), 226,
    243
Dostoevski, Fyodor, 229
Drive time, 257
Du Maurier, Daphne, 21, 234
Dune (Herbert), 33

E

Eagle, Kathleen, 32

Ebook Marketing Made Easy
    (Fischer), 207
Eco, Umberto, 13, 29
Editing, proofs, and publication,
    in contracts, 163–164
Editorial assistant, 214
Editorial director, 214
Editorial services, 199
Editors, 214
Electronic Books and ePublishing
    (Henke), 206
Electronic publishing, 204–207
E-mailing submission packages,
    153
Ender's Game (Card), 234
Envelopes, for mailing
    submission packages, 148,
    149
Envelopes, self-addressed,
    stamped, 131–133
E-publishing. See Electronic
    publishing.
ePublishing for Dummies
    (Rosenborg), 206
Erotic adventure novels, 16
Erotic contemporary novels, 16
Erotic fantasy novels, 16, 19
Erotic Gothic and Victorian
    novels, 16
Erotic horror novels, 16, 24
Erotic science fiction novels, 16
Erotica, 15–17
Escape From Five Shadows
    (Leonard), 38
Espionage adventure novels, 14
Espionage mysteries, 27
Esquivel, Laura, 13
Ethan Frome (Wharton), 239
Ethnic novels, 17–18
Ewell, Bob, 227
Executive editor, 214
Expectations of readers of
    different categories, 38–39

F

Falk, Kathryn, 248, 273
Fantasy, futuristic, and paranormal romances, 32
Fantasy novels, 18–19
Farewell to Arms, A (Hemingway), 246
Farnham's Freehold (Heinlein), 33
Faulkner, William, 237, 239
Faxing submission packages, 148
Feibleman, Peter, 232
Feminist novels, 19–20
Field, Syd, 208
Fielding, Helen, 25
Film treatment, adapting novel to, 207–208
Final Prophet (Nottingham), 34
Finch, Atticus, 226, 227
First-person narrative, 240
Fischer, Rusty, 207
Fisher, Carrie, 25
Flight of the Old Dog (Brown), 26
Force majeure, in contracts, 174–175
Forensic mysteries, 27
ForeWord, 254
Formula novels, 9, 11
Foucault's Pendulum (Eco), 29
Fountainhead, The (Rand), 14
Frankenstein (Shelley), 21
Frazier, Charles, 23
French Lieutenant's Woman, The (Fowles), 238
Fried Green Tomatoes (Flagg), 12
Frishman, Rick, 79, 275
Frontlist catalogue, 144
Full catalogue, 144
Full Court Press (Lupica), 35
Function characters, creating, 231

G

Gabaldon, Diana, 32
Galleys, 220
Gay, lesbian, bisexual, and transgender (GLBT) novels, 20–21
Gemmell, Nikki, 16
Genres. *See* Categories, novel.
Gentle reads, 30
Getting Lucky (Andersen), 32
Ghost stories, 24
Ghost Story (Straub), 24
Ghostwriters, working with, 198–199
GLBT novels. *See* Gay, lesbian, bisexual, and transgender novels.
Goals, personal publishing, 78–80
Godden, Rumer, 239
Goethe, Johann Wolfgang, 215
Goldman, William, 238
Gone With the Wind (Mitchell), 23
Gothic horror novels, 24
Gothic novels, 21–22
Gothic romances, 32
Grafton, Sue, 27, 28
Grey, Zane, 38
Griffith, W.E.B., 26
Grisham, John, 35, 78
G-Spot: An Urban Erotic Tale (Noire), 16
Guerilla marketing, 273–275
Guerrilla Marketing for Writers (Levinson), 79, 275
Guide to Literary Agents, 69
Gutenberg, Johann, 46

H

Hall, Radclyffe, 20
Handmaid's Tale, The (Atwood), 19
Hard science fiction, 33
Hard-boiled mysteries, 28
Harris, Thomas, 24
Heinlein, Robert, 33
Heller, Joseph, 238
Hellman, Lillian, 232
Hemingway, Ernest, 246
Henke, Harold, 206
Henry's List of Wrongs (Shepherd), 238
Herbert, Frank, 33
Herman, Jeff, 104. See also *Jeff Herman's Guide to Book Publishers, Editors, & Literary Agents.*
High fantasy novels, 18
High society humor novels, 25
Historical fantasy novels, 19
Historical horror novels, 24
Historical novels, 22–23
Historical romances, 32
Hobbit, The (Tolkien), 12
Hollywood, selling novel to, 207–209
Horror humor novels, 25
Horror mysteries, 24
Horror novels, 23–24
Horror sagas, 24
Horror Writers Association, 23
Hours, The (Cunningham), 19
How to Sell Your Screenplay (Wilen), 208
Humor novels, 25
Hunt for Red October, The (Clancy), 12, 59

I

Index cards, use of, in plotting novel, 237, 238
Independent publishers, 55
Independent Publishers Resource Directory (PMA), 103
Industrial/financial adventure novels, 14
Inspirational romances, 32
Intellectual property lawyers, 66, 158
International Directory of Little Magazines & Small Presses, 98
sample entry of, 102
using, to create list of potential publishers, 99–102

International Literary Market Place,
    104
International publishers, finding,
    103–104
Internet, use of
    to find publishers, 104–105
    to find representatives, 71
    to market book, 269, 271
Interviews
    online, 269
    and question-and-answer
        sheet, 259, 262–263
    setting up, 257–258, 266, 273
Irving, John, 12, 239

J

Jane Eyre (Bronte), 226
Jaws (Benchley), 233
*Jeff Herman's Guide to Book
    Publishers, Editors, & Literary
    Agents* (Herman)
    as means of finding
        representatives, 68–69
    sample entry of, 92
    setup of, 90–91
    using, to create list of potential
        publishers, 92–93
Jenkins, Jerrold R., 79
Jenkins, Jerry B., 30
Jonathan Livingston Seagull (Bach),
    34
Journey to the Center of the Earth, A
    (Verne), 33
Joy Luck Club, The (Tan), 17
Jubal Sackett (L'Amour), 38
Junger, Sebastian, 227
Junior editor, 214
Just Before Sunrise (Neggers), 72

K

Kallmaker, Karin, 20
Karon, Jan, 30
Karp, Jonathan, 151
King, Stephen, 24, 78
Kirkus Reviews, 254

Koontz, Dean, 24
Kosinski, Jerzy, 193, 228, 239
Kremer, John, 79, 204, 275

L

LaHaye, Tim, 30
Lahiri, Jhumpa, 17
L'Amour, Louis, 38
Large commercial publishing
    houses, 48–51
Larsen, Michael, 79, 275
Last Valentine, The (Pratt), 200
Lawyers. *See* Intellectual property
    lawyers.
Lectures as means of promotion,
    272
Lee, Harper, 226, 246
*Left Behind: A Novel of the Earth's
    Last Days* (LaHaye and
    Jenkins), 30
Leonard, Elmore, 38
Letters. *See* Cover letters; Media,
    sample letter to; Query
    letters; Trade journals,
    sample letter to.
Levinson, Jay Conrad, 79, 275
Libraries, 43
Library Journal, 254
Like Water for Chocolate (Esquivel),
    13
Literary agents, function of, 66,
    67, 158–159. *See also*
    Representatives.
Literary managers, function of,
    66, 67. *See also*
    Representatives.
Literary Market Place (LMP)
    as means of finding book
        manufacturers, 203
    as means of finding
        ghostwriters, 198
    as means of finding
        representatives, 69–71
    sample entries of, 96, 97, 99
    setup of, 93–94

using, to create list of potential
    publishers, 95–98
Literary novels, 11, 13–14
Literary representatives. *See*
    Representatives.
LMP. See Literary Market Place.
Loglines, creating, 72
Lonesome Dove (McMurtry), 12
Lord of the Rings (Tolkien), 18
Love in the Time of Cholera
    (Márquez), 13, 239
Lubbock, Percy, 242
Lupica, Mike, 35

M

M is for Malice (Grafton), 28
Magazine publicity. *See*
    Newspaper and magazine
    publicity.
Mailing out submission packages,
    146–148, 152–153
Main characters, creating,
    226–230
Mainstream novels, 9, 10–12
Malamud, Bernard, 35
Male action adventure novels, 14
Mama (McMillan), 17
Managers. *See* Literary managers.
Managing editor, 214
Manchurian Candidate, The
    (Condon), 15
Manuscript, in contracts, 162–163
Manuscript, revising, process of,
    213, 215–217
Marcinko, Richard, 26
Marketing, guerilla, 273–275
Marketing and promotion
    opportunities for the author,
        79. *See also* Promotion of
        novel by author.
    publisher's plans regarding,
        222–224
Marketplaces
    book clubs, 44
    bookstores, online retail, 42

bookstores, specialized retail,
    41–42
bookstores, traditional retail,
    41
importance of understanding,
    39–40
libraries, 43
mass market outlets, 42–43
Márquez, Gabriel García, 13, 239
Mass market outlets, 42–43
Mass market paperbacks, 43
Master and Commander (O'Brien),
    23
McHugh, Elisabet, 70
McMillan, Terry, 17
McMurtry, Larry, 12
Media
    sample letter to, 270
    targeting, for publicity, 256–
    258. *See also* Promotion of
    novel by author.
Meg: A Novel of Deep Terror
    (Alten), 244
Melville, Herman, 238
Middle, beating the, 248–249
Military adventure novels, 26
Military historical novels, 27
Military lifestyle novels, 27
Military mystery novels, 27
Military saga novels, 27
Military science fiction, 27
Military thrillers, 26
Military/naval adventure novels,
    14
Military/war novels, 26–27
Minor characters, creating, 231
Mirror Crack'd, The (Christie), 28
Mission of characters, 227
Mists of Avalon, The (Bradley), 18
Mitchell, Margaret, 23
Moby Dick (Melville), 238, 243
Moderate-sized commercial
    publishing houses, 51–55
Motivational conflict of
    characters, 226

Mysteries, 27–28
Mystery humor novels, 25

N

Name of the Rose, The (Eco), 13
Namesake, The (Lahiri), 17
Narrative voice, 240, 242–243
Natural, The (Malamud), 35
Naval Institute Press, 59
Neggers, Carla, 72
Negotiations, contract, 175–181
New Age novels. *See* Spiritual/
    New Age novels.
Newspaper and magazine
    publicity, 256, 257, 258. *See
    also Media.*
Nielsen's BookScan, 51
Night Fall (DeMille), 217, 229–
    230, 233, 246
Night Life of the Gods (Smith), 25
Nine Coaches Waiting (Stewart), 32
Notary public stamp, obtaining,
    136
Notebook, The (Sparks), 12
Nottingham, Theodore J., 34
Novel, promotion of. *See*
    Promotion of novel by
    author.
*Novel & Short Story Writer's
    Market*, 85
    sample entries of, 88, 89, 90
    setup of, 86
    using, to create list of potential
    publishers, 87–90
Novel categories. *See* Catgories,
    novel.
Novel structure, 237–238

O

Oates, Joyce Carol, 238
O'Brien, Patrick, 23
Obstacles of characters, 228
Occult novels, 28–29
On a Pale Horse (Anthony), 18
1001 Ways to Market Your Books
    (Kremer), 79, 204, 275

Online retail bookstores, 42
Online resources
    for finding publishers,
        104– 105
    for finding representatives, 71
    See also Internet, use of.
Option clause, in contracts, 172
O'Reilly, Ignatius, 228
Outlander (Gabaldon), 32
Out-of-print provision, in
    contract, 166

P

Page proofs, 220
Palmer, Shirley, 229, 260–264
Panza, Sancho, 226, 227
Paragraph breaks, 245–246
Patterson, James, 36
Percy, Walker, 59
Perfect Storm, The (Junger), 227
Personal appearances, 271–273
Phillabaum, L.E., 59
Pitching your story, 72, 73
Plot, 232
Plot twists, 234
PMA. *See* Publishers Marketing
    Association.
Police procedurals, 28
Political intrigue adventure
    novels, 14–15
Positronic Man (Asimov), 33
Postcards From the Edge (Fisher),
    25
Poynter, Dan, 203
Pratt, James Michael, 200
Preston, Douglas J., 15
Price, Nancy, 19
Printing of novel, 221–222
Print-on-demand (POD)
    publishers, 202–203
Private eye mysteries, 28
Proceedings section, in contract,
    173
Production editor, 214
Profit-and-loss statements, 49

Promotion of novel by author,
    251–275
    book signings, 271–272
    book tours, 273
    choosing goals and objectives,
        252
    creating marketing plan,
        252–255
    creating publicity packet,
        258–259, 260–264
    hiring publicist, 265–266
    Internet marketing, 269, 271
    involving publishing company
        in, 254–255
    lectures, 272
    need for, 251
    obtaining blurbs, 255–256
    offbeat, 273–275
    sending out publicity packets,
        266–267, 269
    targeting media, 256–258
Proofs, 220
Protagonists, 226–230
Protecting your work, 135–136
Proust, Marcel, 14
Publicist, hiring, 265–266
Publicist, publisher's in-house,
    223
Publicity by author. *See*
    Promotion of novel by
    author.
Publicity packet
    creating, 258–258
    sample, 260–264
    using, 266–267, 269
Publicize Your Book (Deval), 275
Publish to Win (Jenkins), 79
Publishers
    age of, 81
    assessing a, 180
    big-name, 79–80
    choice of, as potential
        roadblock to publication,
        186–197, 194–195
    choosing the right, 77–106

    creating list of potential,
        84–106
    definition of, 214
    location of, 84
    marketing and sales of, 82–83.
        See also Marketing and
        promotion.
    offer of, 84. *See also* Contracts.
    publicity of, 83
    quality of work of, 82
    size of, 81–82
    specialty of, 81
    See also Publishing houses.
*Publishers' International ISBN
    Directory*, 104
Publishers Marketing Association
    (PMA)
    as means of finding small
        publishers, 103
    as means of learning about
        self-publishing, 204
Publishers Weekly, 106, 254
Publishing, history of, 45–47
Publishing agreements. *See*
    Contracts.
Publishing houses
    commercial, definition of, 47
    large commercial, 48–51
    moderate-sized commercial,
        51–55
    small commercial, 55–58
    university, 59
    See also Publishers.
Purity in Death (Robb), 32
*Pushcart's Complete Rotten Reviews
    and Rejections*, 185

Q

Query letters
    definition of, 109
    sample, 114
    writing, 109–110, 113, 115–117
Question-and-answer sheet, 258,
    259
    sample, 262–263

Quixote, Don, 226, 227, 228

R

Radio interviews, 256, 257–258,
    267. *See also* Media.
Rand, Ayn, 14
Raskolnikov, 229
Reading audience, understanding
    your. *See* Audience, reading.
Reading groups, contacting, 269,
    271
Rebecca (Du Maurier), 21, 234
Red Dragon (Harris), 24
Redfield, James, 34
Regency romances, 32
Rejection of submissions
    dealing with, 183–210
    identifying the problem,
        184–192
    other options, 199–210
    profiting from, 189
    solving the problem, 192–199
Relatability of characters, 228–
    229
Religious fantasy and science
    fiction, 30
Religious historical fiction, 30
Religious mystery/suspense, 30
Religious novels, 29–30
Religious romance, 30
Remembrance of Things Past
    (Proust), 14
Representatives
    determining need for, 64–65
    finding, 67–75
    function of, 63–64
    types of, 65–67
    See also Literary agents.
Research, role of, in writing
    process, 241
Reserved rights, in contracts, 171
Resource books
    for locating agents, 68–71
    for locating publishers, 85–104
Resource Directory of Independent

Publishers and Publishing Industry Vendors (SPAN), 102–103

Responses to submission packages, 150–152, 153, 154. *See also* Rejection of submissions.

Reversals. *See* Plot twists.

Revising manuscript, process of, 213, 215–217

Rice, Anne, 24, 29, 239

Riders of the Purple Sage (Grey), 38

Rights
in contract, 161–162
of first refusal, 172
of termination, 172–173

Robb, J.D., 32

Robinson, Tom, 227

Robinson Crusoe (Defoe), 15

Rogue Warrior series (Marcinko), 26

Romance novels, 31–33

Romantic fantasy novels, 19

Romantic humor novels, 25

Romantic suspense novels, 32

Romantic Times Book Club Magazine, The, 11, 248, 273

Rome, copying of manuscripts in ancient, 45

Rosenborg, Victoria, 206

Ross, Chuck, 193

Royalties
being realistic about, 78–79
in contract, 166–169
negotiating, 177–178

Royalty-free copies, 168–169

Rushdie, Salman, 30

S

Sacher-Masoch, Leopold Von, 16

Sales sheets, 223

Salutations, appropriate, 110, 146

Sample chapters, 127–131

Sample cover and query letters, 111, 112,114

Satanic Verses (Rushdie), 30

Scenes, use of, in novel structure, 237

Science fiction, 33–34

Science fiction humor novels, 25

Screenplay (Field), 208

Screenplays, adapting novel to, 208–209

Second-person narrative, 240, 242

Seger, Linda, 208

Self-addressed, stamped envelopes, 131–133

Self-promotion. *See* Promotion of novel by author.

Self-publishing, 199–204

Self-Publishing Manual, The (Poynter), 203

Senior editor, 214

Sentimental Journey (Barnett), 32

Series romances, 32

Setting of novel, 239–240

Shelley, Mary Wollstonecraft, 21

Shepherd, John Scott, 238

Sisters of the APF (Zane), 16

Slang, use of, 236

Slaughterhouse Five (Vonnegut), 12

Sleeping With the Enemy (Price), 19

Small commercial publishing houses, 55–58

Small Publishers Association of North America (SPAN)
as means of finding small publishers, 102–103
as means of learning about self-publishing, 204

Smith, Bud E., 207

Smith, Thorne, 25

Social satire humor novels, 25

Soft science fiction, 34

SPAN. *See* Small Publishers Association of North America.

Sparks, Nicholas, 12

Specialty catalogue, 144

Speculative fiction, 18

Spiritual afterlife fiction, 35

Spiritual fables, 35

Spiritual journey fiction, 35

Spiritual mystery/suspense, 35

Spiritual quest fiction, 35

Spiritual science fiction, 35

Spiritual/New Age novels, 34–35

Sports novels, 35–36

Spy mysteries, 27

Square One Book Classification System, 9–38

Square One System for proposal submission, 139–156

Stand, The (King), 24

Stanfill, Francesca, 21

Stanton, Anne, 79

Stationery, choosing, 137–138

Steps (Kosinski), 193

Story of O, The (Aury), 16

Stranger, The (Camus), 14

Straub, Peter, 24

Subject of novel
choosing familiar, 246–247
as potential roadblock to publication, 184, 192–193

Submission package(s)
book synopses, 117–127
checklist, 149
common errors in, 132–133
components of, 108–133
cover and query letters, 109–117
electronic, 153
envelopes for, 148, 149. *See also* Self-addressed, stamped envelope.
faxing, 148
goal of, 107–108
mailing out. *See* Mailing out submission packages.
polishing, 133–134, 136–138
as potential roadblock to publication, 187–188
responses to. *See* Responses to submission packages.

sample chapters, 127–131
sample letters, 111, 112, 114
sample synopsis, 119–126
self-addressed, stamped
    envelope, 131–133
Square One System for
    sending, 139–156
synopsis, 117–127
Tracking Chart for, 143–146
Subsidiary rights
    in contract, 162
    negotiating, 178–179
Substitute for Love (Kallmaker), 20
Supporting characters, creating,
    230–231
Survival adventure novels, 15
Suspense novels, 36–37
Sword and sorcery novels, 19
Sympathetic aspect of characters,
    228–229
Synopsis, book
    definition of, 117
    sample, 119–126
    writing, 117–118, 127

T

Tag of characters, 230–231
Tale of Two Cities, A (Dickens), 232
Tan, Amy, 17
Teaser, 258
    sample, 260–261
Television publicity, 256, 257, 258,
    267. *See also Media.*
Theme of novel, 238–239
Third-person narrative, 242
Thriller adventure novels, 15
Thrillers, 28
Time Machine, The (Wells), 33
Time management in writing, 248
Time travel romances, 32
Timing, as potential roadblock to
    publication, 155, 186
To Kill a Mockingbird (Lee), 226,
    227, 246
Tolkien, J.R.R., 12, 18

Tone of narrative, 242–243
Toole, John Kennedy, 25, 59, 228
Tracking Chart, submission
    importance of, 143–145
    sample, 146–147
Trade journals
    getting reviews from, 254,
        266–267, 269
    sample letter to, 268
Trade Show News Network, 106
Trade shows, as means of
    learning about publishers,
        105–106
Trouble Boy (Dolby), 20
Turning points, as component of
    action line, 233
Tyne, Billy, 227
Typeface, suggested submission
    package, 138
Typesetting of novel, 218–220

U

Unity of novel, 243–244
University publishing houses, 59
Unsolicited manuscripts, 50
Up Country (DeMille), 36
Urban erotic fiction, 16

V

Vanity presses, 208–209
Verne, Jules, 33
Virtual Book Tour, The, 271
Vonnegut, Kurt, 12, 237

W

Wakefield Hall (Stanfill), 21
Waller, Robert James, 12
Walpole, Horace, 22
Warranty and indemnification
    section, in contract, 170–171
Website, creating, for promotion
    of novel, 254, 259, 265
Well of Loneliness, The (Hall), 20
Wells, H.G., 33
Westerns, 37–38
Wharton, Edith, 239

Wharton, William, 226
Wilen, Joan, 208
Wilen, Lydia, 208
Witching Hour, The (Rice), 29
Wodehouse, P.G., 25
Wolfe, Tom, 12
Wong, Chi-Li, 208
Words, choosing carefully,
    249– 250
World According to Garp, The
    (Irving), 12
Writers' and Artists' Yearbook, 104
Writers' conferences and
    workshops
    as means of finding
        representatives, 71–72, 73
    as means of improving writing
        skills, 197–198
    as means of promoting book,
        272
Writers' groups, 197
Writer's guidelines
    importance of, 100–101
    obtaining, 101
    sample, 100–101
*Writer's International Guide to Book
    Editors, Publishers, and
    Literary Agents* (Herman), 104
Writer's Lifeline, The, 190
Writing, making place and time
    for, 247
Writing classes, 196–197
Writing skills, improving, 225–
    250. *See also* Writing classes.
Writing techniques and tips,
    244–250
Writing Treatments That Sell
    (Atchity), 208
Wuthering Heights (Bronte), 21

 Y

You Never Can Tell (Eagle), 32

OTHER SQUAREONE WRITERS GUIDES

HOW TO PUBLISH YOUR CHILDREN'S BOOK

A Complete Guide to Making the Right Publisher Say Yes

Liza N. Burby

A successful children's writer explains the world of children's books and offers a proven system for approaching the right publishers.

$17.95 • 288 pages • 7.5 x 9-inch quality paperback • ISBN-7570-0036-3

HOW TO PUBLISH YOUR ARTICLES

A Complete Guide to Making the Right Publication Say Yes

Shirley Kawa-Jump

Here is complete information on getting articles into magazines, journals, newspapers, and newsletters. Tips are included for building a freelance career.

$17.95 • 352 pages • 7.5 x 9-inch quality paperback • ISBN-7570-0016-9

HOW TO SELL YOUR SCREENPLAY

A Realistic Guide to Getting a Television or Film Deal

Lydia Wilen & Joan Wilen

Veteran screenwriters tell you how to properly format your script, work with industry "players," prepare a perfect pitch, and make the best possible deal.

$17.95 • 320 pages • 7.5 x 9-inch quality paperback • ISBN-7570-0002-9

HOW TO PUBLISH YOUR POETRY

A Complete Guide to Finding the Right Publishers for Your Work

Helene Ciaravino

This guide to print poetry helps you focus on appropriate publications, write a persuasive submissions package, and submit it in the best way possible.

$15.95 • 192 pages • 7.5 x 9-inch quality paperback • ISBN-7570-0001-0

HOW TO PUBLISH YOUR NONFICTION BOOK

A Complete Guide to Making the Right Publisher Say Yes

Rudy Shur

Designed to maximize success, this book guides you in choosing the best publishers, crafting a winning proposal, and effectively submitting your package.

$16.95 • 252 pages • 7.5 x 9-inch quality paperback • ISBN-7570-0000-2

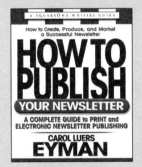

HOW TO PUBLISH YOUR NEWSLETTER

A Complete Guide to Print and Electronic Newsletter Publishing

Carol Luers Eyman

This guide to creating, maintaining, and marketing an effective and cost-efficient newsletter details every aspect of the process, from planning to distribution.

$19.95 • 268 pages • 7.5 x 9-inch quality paperback • ISBN-7570-0045-2